Misl, Sikh State and the Institution of Khalsa

Dr. J.C. Dua

Foreword by

Dr. Jaspal Singh

Originals

Delhi-110052

Distributed by
D.K. Publishers Distributors (P.) Ltd.
4834/24, Ansari Road, Darya Ganj,
New Delhi-110002
Phones: 51562573-77, 51562578
e-mail: dkpd@del3.vsnl.net.in
visit us at: www.dkpd.com

First Published 2006

ISBN 81-88629-56-1

Published by
Originals

A-6, Nimri Commercial Centre,
Near Ashok Vihar Phase-IV, Delhi-110052
Phones: 27302453
e-mail: lpp@nde.vsnl.net.in
visit us at: www.lppindia.com

Printed at
D K Fine Art Press P Ltd.
Delhi-110052

PRINTED IN INDIA

Dedicated to the Memory of

My teacher and mentor

Late Professor B.R. Grover

Former Chairman

Indian Council of Historical Research,

New Delhi

Foreword

Dr. J.C. Dua's book entitled *Mist, Sikh State and Institution of Khalsa* is a collection of articles on 18th-19th century Punjab history presented at various seminars. The subjects of these articles range from the working of the misls during the second half of the 18th century, British historiography, Maharaja Ranjit Singh, the village system and above all, the position of the institution of Khalsa during the 19th century.

In fact, the Creation of the Khalsa on the Baisakhi Day of 1699 A.D. has been a great event in the history of Sikhism. A new social order of Saint-Soldiers infused with the spirit of unique devotion and rare bravery was borne with a strong urge to defend the weak and downtrodden and to destroy the armies of the wicked.

History is a witness that many a poor class people who had long been deprived and considered the dreg of the society became leaders of people and suddenly found power in their hands and a respectability to their names that they could never dream of. A lowly man, say even a common scavenger, had only to join to ranks of Khalsa Panth and return to his village some times later to a grand reception from the wealthy and high born, the same people who had earlier abused and kicked him about.

This transformation of a lowly man, otherwise an insignificant creature of poor and oppressed society into a high dignitary, was nothing short of a miracle but this had been exactly what the Sikh Gurus had predicted and diligently worked for. For Guru Gobind Singh it was the sacred mission to raise the status of the teeming millions of the poor classes, the downtrodden, to a point where they were masters of their own destiny and not the helpless vassals of tyrannical social and political system, as had been the case till then. In fact, the Guru made commitment to the downtrodden to establish new society based on social justice and commitment to bring about a social change by which the people who had been exploited socially, economically and politically for centuries get their share in decision making and a decisive role in political process.

However, one fact of history must be remembered here. If we go back to historical developments preceding to the great event of the birth of Khalsa there is no denying of the fact that the task of highlighting the basic qualities of the Sikh Panth and giving it an organized status was performed by the Tenth master Guru Gobind Singh, but the process of creating the Panth was begun by the first Guru and subsequently other Gurus made significant contributions in evolving the Sikh organization. Undoubtedly, it was the culmination of the Sikh movement initiated by the first Guru. The process of organization which started from the days of Guru Nanak and which was step by step consolidated by the succeeding Gurus, attained its logical conclusion and completion on the Baisakhi day of 1699 at Anandpur Sahib. The Gurus had imbued their disciples with saintly and soldierly features and both these traditions complemented each other in the Sikh traditions. The Khalsa Panth grew out of this great Sikh tradition. It was a manifestation of conscious and consistent efforts of the Gurus who had a definite plan to give their disciples a distinct and organized identity. The Guru completely repudiated the doctrine which divides the society on the basis of caste and spearheaded the revolution in the social field with the aim to make it possible for the people to become equal partners of an egalitarian set up.

In the articles included in the book Dr. Dua has very scholarly given a detailed account of social, economic, political aspects of Sikh history in the backdrop of 18th century, when Khalsa emerged as a formidable force to reckon with. He recounted that the Creation of the order of the Khalsa had been making a stimulating appeal and infusing a rigorous spirit into the Sikhs since its inception. The Khalsa had been fighting for all accomplished mission which converted into a political reality with the carving out of an extensive 'Khalsa Raj' under Maharaja Ranjit Singh.

Dr. Dua is a prolific writer and has published a number of books and research papers in History. He has time and again enriched the listeners in several national and international seminars. When history is analysed and interpreted, opinions may differ. It is not possible to reach an agreement on all accounts of historical events. What matters is objectivity and rationality while we interpret history. In this context, it is my considered view that Dua's writings can be meritoriously used for research purposes. I firmly believe that this book by him will captivate the attention of a large number of readers.

Dr. Jaspal Singh
Principal
Sri Gobind Singh College of Commerce
University of Delhi
And Former High Commissioner

Preface

The present publication brings together a series of articles written during the various phases of the career and presented at various seminars and also published from time to time except the article on the Khalsa. The articles have been chosen in order to highlight some of the aspects of the history of Punjab and the Khalsa during the eighteenth and the nineteenth centuries. It is primarily due to the interest shown by some of my colleagues and friends, that these essays are being put together in the form of a book.

These papers fall neatly into three parts: the first consists of the papers on the activities of the Sikh sardars/*misls* during the eighteenth century and the appraisal of the British historiography and their understanding of the events; the second part consists of the events related to the period of Maharaja Ranjit Singh and aspects of polity during the early British rule; the third consists of the Khalsa during the nineteenth century.

The articles presented here aimed at creating better understanding of the *misls*, the Sikh state and above all, the Khalsa during the period under study. I shall feel gratified if these articles help in arriving at a more balanced appraisal of the British historiography on the Sikh struggle for supremacy during the 18th century, as well as the role of the Sikh sardars, Maharaja Ranjit Singh and other social and religious institutions to further the cause of the Khalsa without rationalizing their blemishes, or overlooking their achievements.

Several friends encouraged and helped me in preparing the volume for press. I am grateful to all of them. Notable among them is Dr. Jaspal Singh, Princial, Sri Guru Gobind Singh College of Commerce, University of Delhi and former High Commissioner for not only inviting me to deliver the lecture on 'The Khalsa in 19th century' in the Seminar on "Three Centuries of the Khalsa" organized on the occasion of the Founder's Day celebrations but also writing a Foreword for this book. The contributions of Dr. Mohinder Kaur Gill, former Principal, Mata Sundri College for Women (University of Delhi) and Dr. Harbans Kaur Sagoo, Reader in History, SGTB Khalsa Evening College (University of Delhi) are indispensable as some of the papers being published in this volume are the lectures invited to deliver in their respective institutions commemorating various occasions relating to the Sikh *Itihas*.

No less important was the support from Principal Deepak Malhotra, Professor Dilbag Singh (JNU), Lala Bhagwan Dass Goel, former Director Prosecution, Mr. Mohinder Singh, Advocate Supreme Court, and Mr. Ashok Kumar Singh, Reader in History, Dyal Singh Evening College (University of Delhi) who had been eagerly waiting for this volume.

I express my sincere thanks to Shri Pradeep Mittal, Publisher, Originals (an imprint of Low Price Publications), for his keen interest in this volume. I would like to express my gratitude towards Mrs. Anita Dua, Silky and above all dear Jimmy.

This volume is dedicated to my teacher and mentor late Professor B. R. Grover, former Chairman, I.C.H.R., New Delhi.

27th November 2005

Dr. J.C. Dua
New Delhi

Introduction

The book entitled *Misl, Sikh State and Institution of Khalsa* is a collection of articles on 18th-19th century Punjab history presented at various seminars. The subjects of these articles range from the working of the misls during the second half of the 18th century, British historiography, Maharaja Ranjit Singh, the village system, and above all the position of the institution of Khalsa during the 19th century.

I

The Khalsa that had been fighting for a cause right since its inception found its job partially accomplished in the 19th century. The sacrifices of the Sikh Gurus, the longstanding tradition of the Khalsa created by Guru Gobind Singh, and the 'heroic' 18th century 'of the Khalsa' were all precursor to the ultimate establishment of the Khalsa Raj under Maharaja Ranjit Singh. Though the Maharaja never allowed the religion to intervene in his polity, the Khalsa 'prefix' determined the nomenclature of the state as Sarkar Khalsa, its court as Khalsa Darbar and the war cry of the Khalsa Fauj as '*Wah! Guruji Ka Khalsa! Wah! Guruji Ki Fateh!*

Since all the Sikhs had not become the Khalsa, the ideological differences could be marked especially during the early 19th century. The Mazhabi Sikhs, Sehajdaari Sikhs, and the Udasi version of Sikhism all flourished during the 19th century. Moreover, some sort of tension continued to exist between the Akali and the Nihang ideologues of the Khalsa and Maharaja Ranjit Singh.

After the death of the Maharaja there was not only the gradual decline of the 'pillars' of the Khalsa empire, the Christian missionaries, the Brahmo Samaj, the Arya Samaj, the Dev Samaj, the Shuddhi movement, the 'Hindu Nationalism', the Wahhabis, and the Ahmadiyah had deep-rooted impact on the Khalsa ideology. The Khalsa in the 19th century also witnessed the Nirankari, Namdhari (Kuka), and the Singh Sabha Movements.

The Khalsa of the days of Guru Gobind Singh and Banda Bahadur was a purely religious community, suffering from great persecution, and in taking up arms, their object had been the defence of their religion and individual existence. Later on, however, the case was different. The Khalsa was then fighting principally for a dominion.

During the second half of the 18th century, the emergence of the Khalsa misls based on the traditional territorial *zamindari* pattern with landed hierarchy, the suppression of other landed castes into *khud, kasht, riaya* and *muzarian* for the realization of the revenues and the extraction of the surplus produce, the inter-*misl* rivalry and mutual warfare, the attempt on the part of powerful misl for the establishment of its suzerainty in the name of the Panth, the realization of *malia* (*muamla*), *nazrana*, etc. from the suppressed *misls* and chiefs was a continuous feature till the emergence of Lahore kingdom under Ranjit Singh by the end of the 18th and early 19th century.

There was certainly a tension between the Khalsa 'State' and the Akalis, the whole time defenders and ideologues of the Khalsa. Ranjit Singh tried to maneuver with them by responding to their semi-theocratic influence and at the same time keeping under his monarchical hegemony.

The Khalsa and the Punjab in the 19th century underwent a revolutionary change after the death of Maharaja Ranjit Singh. The Punjab as a province became larger as the districts comprising Thanesar, Ambala, Ludhiana and Ferozepur were merged with the Punjab in 1849. In 1858, the Delhi division of the North Western Provinces comprising the six districts of Delhi, Gurgaon, Panipat, Rohtak, Hissar and Sirsa was also merged with the Punjab. As such, with the annexation of the Khalsa kingdom, Punjab as it stood under British rule became a land of seven rivers adding Indus and Jamuna to the traditional five.

The period after the annexation found attempts towards the regeneration of the Khalsa. Concrete steps were taken towards the introduction of modern education and education in English literature, western sciences and social studies. The Khalsa was subjected to social and economic transformation, which resulted in the growth of professional middle class. It was also a crucial period for the Khalsa. Certain movements especially like the Arya Samaj, Dev Samaj, Ahmadiyah, Nirankari, Namdhari, etc. partially threatened the very existence of the Khalsa. It is also believed that if *Guru-gaddi* had not been accepted and propogated by the Namdharis as a part of their creed, the movement would have been a marvelous success and would have found favour with a much larger population of the Sikhs.

However, Singh Sabha was the first movement among the Sikhs, which possessed a definite constitution to regulate its affairs and carry out its programmes and policies. It was felt that attempt at reform in the Khalsa made in the shape of Namdhari had not been successful owing to the want of common feeling among the Sikhs, which could be engendered only by education.

As such, Khalsa during the 19th century had to see a number of ups and downs. It saw the partial fulfillment of the aims of the Khalsa in the form of the establishment of Ranjit Singh's empire but everything seemed to have got nullified immediately after the death of the Maharaja. It certainly goes to the credit of determination of the Khalsa that, unlike the Mughals after their political downfall, it did not remain in depression for a long time and soon recovered. Moreover, different social and religious reform movements could have brought the dismemberment of the Khalsa but the good sense prevailed and it took the refuge of all round education and social reforms, which once again brought them into the forefront.

II

The paper on Sardar Ala Singh is based on the original documents preserved in the Punjab State Archives, Patiala, and those published by P. Saran, G.S. Sardeasi, and J.N. Sarkar and other contemporary and near contemporary writings, e.g., *Tarikh-i-Patiala, Jang Namah, Kitab-i-Qissia-i-Tahmas Miskin, Ebratnamah, Tarikh-i-Kunjpura,* etc.

During this period a large number of zamindars of different denomination besides the well-known categories of so-called *mufsids* (disturbers) — Sikhs, Jats, Marathas, and Afghans, struggled for greater share in the revenues and in power over the region, ultimately aiming to establish sovereignty in different parts of *subahs* of Punjab and Delhi.

The Mughal Emperor Muhmmad Shah in his *Farman* dated 3rd June 1725 A.D. recognized Ala Singh as a *chaudhuri* and as a landed intermediary. As a result of the support provided by Ala Singh to the Mughals against Afghan army under Ahmad Shah Abdali during the battle of Manupur in 1748, the Crown Prince Ahmad rewarded him with a robe of honour along with a caparisoned horse. With occupation of the cis-Sutlej territories by Durranis in 1757, Ala Singh shifted his loyalties to them and accepted their sovereignty. The records pertaining to the years 1761 and 1763 specially mention about an enhanced status of Ala Singh Jat. He was recognized as zamindar that had the jagirs in the category of *wukala-i-ali* (*Jagir-i-wukala-i-ali*). In other words the Durrani state appointed him as *wakil-i-ali* (chief representative). In 1762, he was bestowed with the *khillat* and the title of *Rajgi* and undertook to pay Rupees three and a half lakhs as annual *malguzar*. The institutional relationship for the payment of *muamla/peshkash* on the part of the Patiala chiefs (as zamindars) to the Durrani state continued during the periods of Maharaja Amar Singh and to a lesser degree even of Raja Sahib Singh all through eighteenth century.

One of the symbols of extension of Ala Singh's power was the system of *rakhi* adopted by him. The term *rakhi* has been described by the English writers as 'blackmail' and have described the Sikh Sardars as robbers', 'committing depredation' and 'highway robbery'. It is right when they club the collection of *rakhi* with the Maratha system of the collection of *chauth*, but it is wrong on their part to describe both of them as 'blackmail'. In this regard it can safely be pointed out that this is a concept usually used from the imperialist view point. Whenever, the revolting zamindars or Sardars realized the revenue of a particular area after occupation, from the imperialist angle it was described as plunder, loot, pillage etc.

Ala Singh was seldom guided by any religious considerations and political expediency was the guiding principle of relations with the contemporary political powers.

The term 'Sikh' or a group of Sikhs did not essentially connote belonging to a particular religious faith. It seems the Sikhs and the *Singhan* denoted those militant followers of the *Nanak Panth* and Guru Gobind Singh who had taken to arms against the Mughals or the Durranis for the vindication of their religious rights and temporal power.

It is extremely doubtful that Ala Singh ever took his vassalage seriously. The *de jure* appearances were immaterial so long as he could possess the *de facto* power in his own hands.

III

In the three Papers on Historiography an attempt has been made to analyse the historiographical trends of some of the important English writings, including the correspondence contained in the *Calendar of Persian Correspondence* and *Foreign Department/Secret Proceedings*, pertaining to the role played by one of the most important chiefs of the 18th century Punjab, Sardar Jassa Singh Ahluwalia in the struggle for power in the Punjab. The analysis has been made with help of English, Punjabi, Persian, and Marathi records.

A critical examination has also been made of the aims, objectives, and insight of the English writers and government and, above all, their understanding of the Sikh struggle for power in the Punjab during the 18th century. Moreover, the eighteenth century background is indispensable for the critical appraisal of study of British historical writings on India. This paper makes it clear that these writings were inspired by efforts at self-understanding as well as by self-interest.

Apart from analyzing the approach of the British writers, an attempt has also been made to understand the motivation and the purpose of these writers and pin point significant changes in their motives and outlook that occurred during the intermittent periods and also how far the English writers were correct in their analysis in contrast to other contemporary Persian, Punjabi, and Marathi source material.

IV

Sardar Jassa Singh Ahluwalia was one of the most important chiefs of Punjab who during the eighteenth century struggled for greater share in the revenues and power over the region ultimately aiming to establish sovereignty in different parts of the *subahs* of Punjab and Delhi.

Knowing the Sikh strong instinct for individuality and independence, it was by no means an easy task for Sardar Jassa Singh Ahluwalia to keep them welded together.

The routes of future Khalsa rule in the Punjab were firmly laid by the creative genius and leadership of Jassa Singh.

The struggle of Sikhs under Saradar Jassa Singh Ahluwalia was not for any narrow objectives or for capturing personal power but it was for the defence of India and its culture.

V

Papers on Maharaja Ranjit Singh show that he was the man who liquidated the warring *misls*, nurtured the consciousness of regional nationalism to forge a united kingdom.

A noteworthy change in the character of the Sikh community during the 17th and 18th centuries was that they were not only drawn only from the regions of Punjab alone but also from cis-Satluj territories, the regions around Delhi and other places in India.

The terms like — *Sarbat Khalsa, Gurmata, Dal Khalsa, rakhi*, *misl* etc. have been critically examined with the help of contemporary Punjabi, Persian, and English records. It is maintained that the policy of conciliation that Maharaja Ranjit Singh maintained towards the English was perhaps inspired by the dread of their power and his own limitations. It was not the result of any genuine feeling of trust or good-will, as has been supposed by several writers. He repeatedly professed friendship and regard, and often sought similar assurances from the Company's representative.

Another point highlighted is that the Sikhs and the Sikh Sardars were in no way different from their contemporary Indian political chiefs, e.g. the Nawabs of Carnatic, Awadh, Bengal, etc. The Sikhs had also failed to understand the aggressive and expansionist nature of the British, who wanted to check the growth of Sikhs as political power.

In order to have a dependable and accurate picture of socio-economic and cultural life of people especially of the pre-colonial period one has to have a disciplined and objective approach. Since the gullible mind is always prone to misconceived past historical analysis, more especially on the socio-religious matters, it is imperative that such work should not be influenced by vested political interests.

VI

Papers on comparative position of village *patwari/karnam* and *muqaddam/lambardar/patel* in the Madras Presidency (one of the first to be brought under a regular settlement) and Punjab (the last) during the early British rule.

In these well documented (documents from Punjab and South India Archives) papers, attempt has been to highlight the hypothesis that, whereas in the Madras Presidency, the English administrators could not deviate much from the past practice as far as the basic position and power enjoyed by these village officials were concerned, but made unhesitating deviation in a bigger way as far as Punjab was concerned.

In case of the Madras Presidency it must have been either due to the hesitancy on the part of the English administrators to introduce any drastic changes in the village administration or due to the influence enjoyed by these village officials in the local, political and agrarian matters, or may be due to the influence and policies of the administrators like Thomas Munro. In case of Punjab, the vast administrative experience, political authority and military power that the English had acquired by the time Punjab was conquered, accounted for unhesitating deviation, from the position enjoyed by these village officials and the policy towards them adopted by the earlier rulers, in a very big way.

VII

The article on Dr. Ganda Singh is in the nature of an obituary paid to one of the most respectable historians of Sikh Itihas.

VIII

The idea behind publishing these articles is to focus the attention of the readers on how the events after the institution of Khalsa by Guru Gobind Singh in 1699 were reported, narrated, and interpreted by the contemporary, near contemporary writers and the modern historians on the history of Punjab during the 18th and 19th centuries. The Sikh movement during the period under study evolved with time and varied from period to period due to the differences in the objectives of the main actors on the scene. The reader may become aware of relative and haltingly progressive nature of the Khalsa, which has never remained static.

Contents

1

The *Khalsa* in 19th Century

The *Khalsa* that had been fighting for a cause right since its inception found the job partially accomplished in the 19th century. The sacrifices of the Sikh Gurus and their followers, the longstanding traditions of the *Khalsa* created by Guru Gobind Singh, and the 18th century, a "heroic period of Sikh tradition" and "heroic century of the *Khalsa*"[1], were all precursor to the ultimate establishment of the *Khalsa* Raj under Maharaja Ranjit Singh. The process of identity and self-assertion, which had started in the 18th century, continued even during the 19th century. Though Maharaja Ranjit Singh never allowed the religion to intervene in his polity or prevail upon the natives of the state, the *Khalsa* 'prefix' determined the nomenclature of the state as *Sarkar Khalsa,* its court as *Khalsa Darbar,* and the war cry of the *Khalsa Fauj* as *'Wah! Guruji Ka Khalsa! Wah! Guruji Ki Fateh!* Right in the early 19th century itself, the Maharaja was recognized by the English as the sole sovereign ruler of the Punjab and was allowed the freedom to round of his conquests in the erstwhile Mughal *subah* of Lahore, to oust the Afghans from Multan and Kashmir and finally, to oust the successors of Ahmed Shah Abdali from the former Mughal *subah* of Kabul.[2] The agricultural production, trade, manufacturing, cities and towns expanded during this period. Enormous encourangement was given to the new development of great cultural significance like some important historical and literary works. The *Khalsa* Darbar provided revenue-free grants without any consideration to the religion, caste and creed. Since all the Sikhs had not become the *Khalsa*, the ideological differences could also be marked especially during the early nineteenth century. The *Mazhabi* Sikhs, *Sehajdhaari* Sikhs, and the *Udasi* version of Sikhism all flourished during the 19th century. Some sort of tension continued to exist between the *Akali* and the Nihang ideologues of the *Khalsa* and Maharaja Ranjit Singh. After the death of the Maharaja, there was a gradual decline of the 'pillars' of the *Khalsa*

Seminar on "*Three Centuries of the Khalsa*," Founder's Day Seminar, Sri Guru Gobind Singh College of Commerce, University of Delhi, 24th January, 2002.

Empire and the 'paternal' rule was replaced by the 'machine rule' of laws, codes, and procedures. There was spread of English education. Despite Punjabi being the dominant language of the province, Urdu was introduced as the medium of education in the government schools upto the matriculation level. The Christian missionaries, the Brahmo Samaj, the Arya Samaj, the Dev Samaj, the *Shuddhi* movement, the 'Hindu nationalism', the *Wahhabis,* and the *Ahmadiyah* had deep-rooted impact on the *Khalsa* ideology. The *Khalsa* in the 19th century also witnessed the *Nirankari, Namdhari* (*Kukas*), and the *Singh Sabha* Movements. However, the British government recognized the valour of the Khalsa and their proportion in the Indian army was raised to a very large extent.

Before going into the details of the *Khalsa* in the 19th century, it is imperative to have a peep into the political and institutional backdrop since the inception of the *Khalsa* in 1699. The 18th century is a very crucial period for the history of the Khalsa. During this period the Punjab was passing through an era of political turmoil and turbulation and the Khalsa struggle for power. Eighteenth century Punjab had witnessed the disintegration of the Mughal empire, the foreign campaigns of Nadir Shah and the Durranis, the attempts made by the Rohillas, Rajputs, Jats and the Afghans to establish their respective regional governments and the emergence and rise of the Marathas and the Sikhs.[3]

In the Punjab, the Sikh Sardars, during this period, not only confronted the political powers, especially like the Mughals and the Durranis, but were able to carve out their own independent/semi-independent territories (*zamindaries*) for the purposes for revenue realization and administration. The most significant feature of the Sikh history during the course of the 17th and the 18th centuries is that the Sikh community/*Nanak Panth* which originally was socio-religious in character gradually transformed into socio-religious-cum political force comprising members of various clans and castes.[4] The *Khalsa* of the days of Guru Gobind Singh and Banda Bahadur was a purely religious community, suffering from great persecutions. In taking up arms, their chief object had been the defence of their religion and individual existence. Their predatory practice was merely the means of securing that object. Later on, however, the case was different. The *Khalsa* was then fighting principally for a dominion.[5] Initially, the *Nanak-Panth* mostly comprised the *khatris,* artisans, craftmen, petty traders, low caste Hindus and a section of poor peasantry, more especially from the *Majiha* territories. The various *Hukmnamas* of the Gurus reveal that the *sangat* of Gurus (Sikhs) were equally drawn from the prosperous commercial classes and other sections of the peasantry as well. Another noteworthy change in the character of the *Khalsa* during the 17th and the 18th centuries was that they were not only drawn from the regions of the

Punjab alone but also from *Cis*-Satluj territories, the regions around Delhi and other places in India. The socio-economic phenomenon involving the emergence of the new dominant clans in the landed structure in the Punjab and territories of Delhi, the conversion of these clans more especially the peasantry to Sikhism in the course of the 17th and the 18th centuries added a new dimension to the character of the *Khalsa*.

The initiation of the *Khalsa* by Guru Gobind Singh, the armed struggle by Banda Bahadur in the territories of *subah* Delhi, hilly and plain regions of the Punjab against the Mughal state in the early 18th century, the later division of the *Khalsa* into *Bandais* (after Banda's death) and the *Tat Khalsa,* the ultimate supremacy of the latter further moulded the militant character of the *Singhan* for safeguarding the interest of the *Panth.* But the emergence of *Khalsa* as a political force cannot be studied in isolation, rather the dissolution of the Mughal empire and the rise of the Marathas, Bundelas, Rajputs, the Jats and Afghans in other parts of India have also to be taken into consideration. The Mughal empire which, for its governance and stability during the 16th and 17th centuries, had depended upon its alliance with the Rajputs and its own nobility had been shaken to the point of dismemberment due to its fight with other socio-political forces during the 18th century. Inspite of considerable element of continuity in the traditionally form of regional polity, administration and economic system, the other event had great impact on the social, economic and political developments during the 18th century which transformed the *Khalsa*, not only a mere political force but a force to reckon with.[6]

A critical examination of the Punjab politics during the 18th century shows that there were as many as four main political powers *viz.*, the Mughals, the Marathas, the *Khalsa*, and the Durranis of Kabul who fought for supremacy there. Of course, during the first half of the century the struggle was basically confined between the Mughals and the *Khalsa* whereas during the second half, after the Marathas had been defeated at Panipat and the Mughal sovereign rights over the Punjab territories had practically vanished, the Durranis had claimed political sovereignty and started realizing *peshkash,* it mainly became a tussle between the *Khalsa* and the Durranis. Again, during the last three decades of the 18th century, even though the Durranis continued to claim *de jure* political sovereignty, the *Khalsa* in the form of the Sikh Sardars had started asserting the *de facto* power over the Punjab territories.

The *Khalsa* had 'put forward a claim to the rulership and were not to be contended with less than the total overthrow of Mughal rule and the establishment of their power in the province. The high sounding title of *Sachcha Padshah* and the symbols of *deg, tegh* and *fath'* continued to inspire the *Khalsa* even after the ruthless execution of Banda Bahadur and his seven hundred followers in 1715.[7] The *Nihangs/Akalis* (who would claim their original inspiration to Guru Gobind Singh) organized themselves (in 1734) into *Budha Dal* and *Taruna Dal.* Many members of the former *Dal* were the veterans and 'had seen the days of Guru Gobind Singh and fought under the command of Banda Singh'.[8] The prominent members were Nawab Kapur Singh, Jassa Singh Kalal, *Akali* Phoola Singh and others. While the *Taruna Dal,* the Army of the Young, comprised the young Sikhs.[9]

Apart from the Sikh organization of the informal confederacy (*Sarbat Khalsa*) and execution of the plans through the decisions (*Gurmata*) and their implementation with the help of the armed units (*Dal Khalsa*), the twentieth century writings have equally emphasized on the system and role of *rakhi* and Sikh *misls* in the Punjab.

During the second half of the 18th century, the Mughal sovereignty over the Punjab territories had practically vanished and the Durrani rule of Kabul had stepped in. Apart from the occupation of Kashmir and Multan, the Durranis claimed political sovereignty over the Punjab territories and realized *peshkash* more or less on the Mughal pattern. However, the Durrani rule was rather intermittent and the *Khalsa misls* always tried to assert as *de facto* power. During the last three decades of the 18th century, even though the Durranis continued to claim political sovereignty, their effective administrative control was minimal.[10]

On the sacred day of the *Baisakhi*, 29th March 1748, Nawab Kapur Singh organized the entire *Khalsa* fighting body in to Dal *Khalsa*, and appointed Sardar Jassa Singh Ahluwalia its supreme commander. He was bestowed with the title of *Sultan-ul-Quam* (king of the community).[11] The role of *Khalsa misls,* especially that of Jassa Singh Ahluwalia who was selected as *mukhi sardar* and was also bestowed the title of *Nawab* and *Panth ke Malik* by the *Panth* itself and who got the Hari Mandir of Amritsar reconstructed after demolition by Ahmad Shah Durrani, stands unparalleled for the liberation of *Khalsa* from the Durrani rule.[12] In this regard Jassa Singh Ahluwalia can be considered real precursor to Maharaja Ranjit Singh. The Sikh Sardars, particularly Jassa Singh Ahluwalia, were as much interested in the territorial superior *zamindari* claims and suzerainty over the *cis*-Sutlej territories, Sutlej-Jamuna regions (*subah* Delhi), territories to the north and around Delhi itself and even Rajasthan as other powers of the time *viz.,* the Marathas, the Rohillas, and the Jats. *Jassa Singh Binod* is the testimony to the fact that his military expeditions covered the territories of Bharatpur, Bikaner and Jaipur chieftains for the realization of the revenues viz., *malia* and *nazarana* etc. This gives absolutely new perspective to the *Khalsa* polity during the 18th century.[13]

The emergence of the *Khalsa misls* based on the traditional territorial *zamindari* pattern with landed hierarchy, the suppression of the other landed castes unto *khud kasht riaya* and *muzarian* for the realization of the revenues and extraction of the surplus produce, the inter *misl* rivalry and mutual warfare, the attempt on the part of the powerful *misl* for the establishment of its suzerainty in the name of the *Panth,* the realization of *malia* (*muamla*), *nazrana* etc. from the suppressed *misls* and chiefs was a continuous feature till the emergence of Lahore kingdom under Ranjit Singh by the end of the 18th and early 19th century.[14]

The *Khalsa* Raj under Maharaja Ranjit Singh (1799-1839 AD) covered all the territories of the erstwhile Mughal *subahs* of Punjab[15], Kashmir, Multan, some of the Trans-Indus *ilaqas* of *subah* Kabul viz., Peshawar, Kohat, Bannu and few tribal kingdoms. On the eastern side, the chiefs of *cis*-Sutlej territories viz., the chiefs of Malwa and Sirhind, being under the British protection, remained outside the territorial boundaries of Ranjit Singh.[16] It may also be maintained that, following the practice of the Mughal empire, the *Khalsa* Raj not only considered the revenues of the hill chieftainship—Mandi, Suket, Bilaspur, Kulu and Chamba in the former Mughal *subah* of Lahore—as the revenue of the *Khalsa* state, but even inline with the Mughal tradition, fixed the revenues periodically. On submission the hill chiefs were regarded as the servants of the State and in lieu of the service being rendered by them, they were only entitled to certain categories of *jagirs* and other perquisites (*haquq*).[17] The Sikh chiefs of Punjab, including *cis*-Sutlej areas, paid *nazarana* to Ranjit Singh after his occupation of Lahore and before the annexation of their territories, if it was the case. Before the East India Company declared its protection, the chiefs of Patiala, Nabha, Jind, Faridkot, Shahabad, Thanesar, Kaithal, Malerkotla and Rajkot paid regular *nazarana* to the *Khalsa* Darbar. In line with the Mughal tradition, the *Khalsa* sovereign state not only claimed the revenues of the territories of the princely states as that of the Lahore *Darbar*, it fully exercised its discretion with regard to alienation and even regulation for succession to *gaddi* of chieftainship. The relationship between the Lahore *Darbar* and the princely chiefs can not be characterized as simply between then paramountcy and Indian States as in vogue during the succeeding British period of the India occupation. The limitations imposed upon the *zamindaries* of the princely chiefs was of far more penetrating nature and institutionally speaking, with rare exception, such chieftainship could hardly be termed as State whether semi-independent or subordinate merely, what has been considered to be, a 'tribute' comprising particular amount. Most of them enjoyed only limited 'autonomy' confined to internal administration of the chiefship.[18] Ratan Singh Bhangu in his *Guru-Granth Prakash* (published as *Prachin*

Panth Parkash, Wazir-Hind-Press, Amritsar, 1962, 4th edition) has asserted that right since its inception by Guru Gobind Singh, *Khalsa* was sovereign and had not illegitimately occupied Mughal territorials. Since men hailing from all the four *varnas* had merged into one *varna,* the *Khalsa, 'khatris, tarkhans, kalals, nais* and *jhiwars'* laid down their lives for the establishment of the *Khalsa* rule. The *Khalsa* in reality had wrested from the Durranis those provinces, which the Mughals had lost to them. As such, the *Khalsa* ruled over the Punjab in their own right. It was also justified by the sacrifices they had made and upheld by the sword that they had come to wield against oppression.

The *Khalsa* Raj provided enormous encouragement to trade and number of urban centres, which exceeded one hundred, served as centres of trade. Safe passage for the caravans of traders was ensured and imposed very lenient duties. The trade serves as links between the areas of raw material, production and exchange between the manufacturing centres and the markets. There were several routes which connected Punjab with central Asian countries. Here a mention may be made of the 'trans-Himalaya' network of trade routes which ultimately joined with the so called 'silk routes' or 'silk roads' (a term coined in the 19th century by Baron Ferdinand Von Richtehofen) connecting China with Mediterranean after passing through many a region of Central and West Asian countries. The routes from the Punjab and North-Western India traversed through the Hindu Kush, the Pamirs and the Karakoram.[19] Apart from various other items, it was from this route that the import of goat fleece from Yarkand and Tibetan highlands had led to the development of shawl industy in Kashmir. During the period under study it was once again revived and extended to the places like Nurpur and Amritsar.[20] After a period of political uncertainties, Lahore was once again revived as trade centre as well as centre for manufacturing of cotton, wool and silk textiles and its metal work. In fact, cotton and silk textile industries, craftsmanship of war weapons, leather works, gold work, embroidery, woolen carpets, glazed pottery, enameled silver, tailoring and household utensils representing cohesion of West Asian, Central Asian and Punjab cultures flourished during this period. The Punjab salt was supplied over long distances. The *zamindari* of salt mountains at Kheora and Sind Sagar belonged to the *janjua* tribe. The contemporary sources point towards the availability of banking facilities in the shape of the practice of insurance (*bima*) of the goods being transported on the main routes and the system of *hundis.* The *banjaras*/merchants were fully protected in the plains and the hilly regions.[21]

During the *Khalsa* Raj the administration of canal irrigation formed an integral part of the revenue administration of the local government. The *darogh-i-ab-nahar* (canal *darogha*), the *mir-i-ab* (expert irrigation engineer), the *mehmaran* (masons) in cooperation with local *jagirdars* and *zamindars* managed the administration of irrigation as well as for equitable distribution of water to the cultivators.[22]

The establishment of *Khalsa* State was conducive to the patronage and encouragement provided to music, painting, new style of architecture and an enormous amount of historical literature. Ram Sukh Rao, apart from compiling a separate treatise on music—*Sri Radha-Govind-Sangit-Sar*, has given a comprehensive account of Indian classical music, the *ragas, rababis* of the Gurdwaras, musical concerts at the court and the marriage songs in his *Sri Fateh Singh Pratap Prabhakar*.[23] The important historical literature produced during this period include, Sohan Lal Suri's *Umdat ut-Tawarikh,* Ahmad Yar's *Shahnama-i-Maharaja Ranjit Singh* (Persian), Ram Sukh Rao's monumental works on Jassa Singh Ahluwalia, Bhag Singh and Fateh Singh Ahluwalia, Sawan Yar's *Siharfi Sarkar Ki,* Jafar Beg's *Siharfi,* Hakam Singh's *Siharfi* (Gurumukhi). The literature that was meant for the common Punjabi included Qadir Yar's *Qissa Sohni Mahiwal, Puran Bhagat* and *Raja Rasalu,* etc.[24] This articulation of regional identity may be regarded as the cultural counterpart of the secularization of polity by Ranjit Singh, which ensured participation of all-important sections of society on a significant scale.[25]

Ranjit Singh established a liberal and just state, though of course to some extent, within the limitations imposed by the contemporary social atmosphere. He stopped the practice of cow-slaughter and as a symbol of ascendancy of *Khalsa,* he forbade public calls for prayers (*azan*) at certain significant mosques in some cities. The *Khalsa* administration was quite liberal in the *dharamarth* grants. The *Khalsa* Darbar period, with rare exception, renewed even the grants prevalent in the Afghan rule. A separate department of *Dharamarth* was established to maintain records of *madad-i-maash, aimma, muafi* and *waqf* grants bestowed for philanthropic, charitable and educational purposes. The land grants, assignments of revenues of the villages in kind or cash were made to religious persons-*Imams, khadims* (attendants), *mujawars* (holy persons), *faqirs,* pandits as well as institutional establishments of the mosques, *khankas*, temples, *tiraths* and *dharmsalas.* The beneficiaries included the *Sunni* and the *Shia* Muslims, the Hindus, more especially the *Udasis* of the *Nanak Panth.* Mufti Ali-ud-din in his *Ibrat Nama* (1854) comments that the Sikhs during this period had generally shaken off the rituals that the Brahmins fostered on the other Hindu society. They mostly took to agriculture and invariably joined army. Many Sikhs belonged to the *zamindari* clans. They were highly sensitive for the protection of the honour of their womanfolk. They did not observe the practice of preparing a *chauka* before eating meals. Meat was their staple diet but they would never eat meat of any animal slaughtered by a Muslim. They did not observe any formality in the matter of dress and social intercourse. Instead of saying 'Ram Ram' like the other Hindus, they would utter *Waheguru ji ki fateh.* In the morning hours, they would recite only the Guru's *Bani,* i.e., *Japji* and the *Sukhmani.* A large number of Sikhs who embraced Sikhism called themselves *Singh Guruji Ka* and were engaged in the trade. They were, by and large, very fond of wearing arms. Those who could well afford liked riding horses and elephants. The Sikhs made an extensive use of Gurmukhi and read and wrote in that script. In social life they indulged in wine and sex. The sections known as the *Akalis* and *Nihangs* were extremely fanatics.[26]

The early year of *Khalsa* Raj witnessed enough social differentiation in the Sikh community to infringe the idea of equality, the very foundation, on which the Sikh Panth was based in theory. Despite every Sikh being equal in the *sangat,* the *langar,* and in the presence of the Holy Guru Granth Sahib, social difference were legitimized in their life in general. These differences were espoused by a handful of the *Khalsa,* like the *Akalis* and the *Nihangs*. The historically evolved religious authority in the form *Akali/Nihang*[27] factor could never find itself satisfied with head of the *Sardar Khalsa.* The Maharaja respected the *Khalsa* discourse of which the *Akalis* were the protagonists and their religious authority. His policy was compatible with the concept and practice of *langer, sangat, pangat,* and holistic text and context of Guru Granth Sahib. The *Khalsa* 'prefix' determined the nomenclature of the state as *Sarkar Khalsa,* its court as *Khalsa Darbar,* and the war cry of the *Khalsa Fauj* was '*Wah! Guruji Ka Khalsa! Wah! Guruji Ki Fateh!* He described and proclaimed himself as *Ranjit Nagara* (the war drum) of Guru Gobind Singh, hence "a mere instrument of the *Khalsa* for the assertion and execution of its political supermacy."[28] He was addressed as *Sarkar-i-wala,* i.e., one who belongs to the government, not himself a government. He neither occupied the throne nor adorned himself with an emblem of royalty on his simple turban, and issued *Nanak Shahi* coins. Moreover, he wishfully presented himself as a "cog of the *Khalsa* machinery"[29] and assumed the *Khalsa* symbols to illuminate the fruits of the Sikh struggle and in the process presented the elevated status of the *Khalsa* in its first kingdom. In short, he never attempted to rise above the *Khalsa*. But nineteenth century Punjab had inherited the *Khalsa* legacy and Ranjit Singh had to handle it in statesmanlike fashion. The religious zeal of the *Akalis* was nothing but the by-product of the longstanding traditions created by Guru Gobind Singh on the threshold of the 18th century. The long drawn struggle and sacrifices of the Sikh Gurus, the oppression of the Mughal state and the

Durrani invaders would account for shaping and strengthening the 'fanaticism' of the *Akalis*. The *Akalis* that Ranjit Singh faced, as stated by W.G. Osborne were "...religious fanatics, and acknowledge no ruler and no laws but their own; thinking nothing of robbery, or even murder, should they happen to be in the humour for it. They move about constantly, armed to teeth, and it is not an uncommon thing to see them riding about with a drawn sword in each hand, two or more in their belt, a matchlock on their back, and three or four pairs of quoits fastened round their turbans."[30] Guru Gobind Singh, while creating the *Khalsa*, had also activated soldierly qualities, which had already been embedded by the sixth Guru Hargobind (1595-1644) while introducing the concept of *piri* and *miri.* The tenth Guru taught the members of the *Khalsa* to regard the Sword as God and God as the Sword.[31] Apart from the Holy Guru Granth Sahib, the *Akali*, adored with their blue standards, also accorded a very high place to Dasam Granth of Guru Gobind Singh. For the protection of the Sikh faith, the *Akalis*, in brief—

- were committed to acting upon the instructions of the tenth Guru to sacrifice everything;
- had acquired "the character of priests in which capacity they acted effectively while directing the conduct of the Sikh councils at the *Akal Takhat*";[32]
- constituting "the central league of the Sikh religion." they considered themselves as the self appointed guardians of the Sikh faith;[33]
- "exercised a fierce scrutiny as censors in upholding strict compliance with the militant creed of the Singhs";[34]
- stood for a liberated person, free from the fear of danger of death;[35]
- could readily be recognized by their dark blue loose apparel and their ample peaked turban fastened with quoits, insignia of the *Khalsa*;
- were fond of *sukha*, a portion of Indian hemp and would not object to opium eating;
- stressed upon *shakti,* significant of weapon;
- were a privileged class as they were the grantnees of the *Dharamarth* grants and were patronized by the Sikh rulers;
- Amritsar, the real and true symbol of Sikh history was the hub of their activities;[36]
- had assumed "a dictatorial sway in all the religious ceremonies at Amritsar...".[37]

There was certainly a tension between the *Khalsa* 'State' and the *Akalis*, the whole time defenders and ideologues of the *Khalsa*. Ranjit

Singh tried to maneuver his relationship with them by responding to their semi-theocratic influence and at the same time keeping them under his monarchical hegemony. His Sarkar *Khalsa* "was no less and no more than the state of Maharaja Ranjit Singh."[38] He legitimatized the authority of the state by not accepting the *Akalis*' theocratic influence as an ideology. At the same time, he would not be in a position to ignore the long standing *Khalsa* tradition nor would the effective presence of the *Akalis* let the nascent royal will be an absolute one. Moreover, the *Akalis* were not his political rivals. Ranjit Singh would/could have been in a great soup if he had launched a frontal attack on them as the Sikh struggle of the 18th century, which had been dominated by the *Khalsa*, was very much in the memory. Bound by tradition, he had to respect and recognize the *Khalsa*, but did not "rule as the instrument of the theocracy or in the interest of the comparatively small religious community to which he belonged."[39] Ranjit Singh never allowed the *Akalis* to hegemonies the newly born Kingdom with their *Khalsa* discourse. He employed men of other castes and communities in the service of the Sarkar *Khalsa*, notwithstanding the resentment shown by the *Akalis* "against the Muslims, the *Dogras*, the *Misars* and the Europeans in the employ of the Maharaja."[40] Scholars have argued that despite the tremendous power Ranjit Singh had, he neither tried to crush nor defied their religious susceptibility as well as his own because he was their '*Khalsa* Bhai'.[41] Further, he had inherited the *Khalsa* legacy of Sukerchakya *misl* whose founder S. Charat Singh would enroll in his group only those who were *amritdharis*.[42] However, he kept them committed to the ideal of the *Khalsa* Raj without politicizing their fanaticism or their status as clerics of the Sikh community. It is very interesting to note that the *Khalsa* Raj had practically overshadowed the differences in the Sikh community, as there was a vague feeling that the rulers of the land were their people. Moreover, as *Sarbat Khalsa* was losing the unity of action and the institution of *Gurmata* was on the decline, the *Akalis* "gradually lost their influence primarily because the *Akal Takhat* had little role to play in the affairs of Sikhs during the time of Ranjit Singh..."[43] and "court in Lahore had taken the place of the *Sarbat Khalsa* in the political sphere."[44] According to Baba Prem Singh 'Hoti' (*Jiwan Birtant Baba Phoola Singh Ji Akali* (first published-1914) (in Punjabi), reprint Patiala, 1971, p. 72), Maharaja Ranjit Singh was even reprimanded by the *Akalis* for his moral lapse for which Phoola Singh *Akali* awarded a punishment of flogging him on the back in the public, and re-baptized him. In short, the political ambitions of Ranjit Singh could brook no interference from anyone. However, the *Akali/Nihang* politico-religious struggle continued even after the death of Ranjit Singh though, in the course of time, the term *Akali* did not remain confined only to militant *Nihang Singhs*. Late in the 19th and during 20th century one finds them ever "prepared to sacrifice for the protection of the glory of the places associated with the Sikh Gurus, and for the freedom of the Sikh religion" without caring about the consequences.[45]

As mentioned earlier, during the 18th century all the Sikhs had not become *Khalsa*, and there were a large number of *Sehajdhari* Sikhs and the *Udasi* version of Sikhism. The *Udasis* traced their origin to Guru Nanak but gave more prominence to Sri Chand as the real founder of the path of renunciation (*udas*). Without rejecting the line of succession from Guru Nanak to Guru Gobind Singh, they would attach greater importance to the chain of succession from Guru Nanak, through Sri Chand and *Adi Udasis,* to the reigning Mahant of an *Udasi* establishment.[46] They showed great respect for the Holy Guru Granth Sahib, but interpreted its essential message in vedantic terms, shifting the emphasis from a personal God to an impersonal reality. They did not subscribe to the twin doctrine of Guru-Granth and Guru-Panth. The literature produced by them in the early 19th century narrates an interpretation of Sikhism that made them rather 'unorthodox' from the viewpoint of the Singhs. They wrote expositions of several important compositions in the Guru Granth Sahib; they wrote original *mantras* of their own; they produced new versions of *janamsakhis* and *gurbilases;* and they wrote about their own past.[47] The Sikh rulers patronized the *Udasis* and their centres began to proliferate during the early 19th century. By the end of Ranjit Singh's reign the *Udasis* had nearly 250 centres in the *Khalsa* Empire. Since the *Khalsa* Raj needed a broad base for the willing acceptance of its authority, nearly 10% of the state revenue, amounting to about two lakh rupees, was alienated to the *Udasis* by way of *dharmarth.*[48] "The *Sehajdhari* Sikhs regarded Guru Nanak as the founder of a new faith and paid equal reverence to his nominated successors. They regarded Guru Gobind Sahib as the Guru but not as the exclusive Guru, because the founders of the movements were also regarded as *Gurus.* They advocated adoption of specially Sikh ceremonies by birth, marriage and death. However, they did not insist on the baptism of the double-edged sword."[49] The number of *Sehajdhari* Sikhs appears to have been quite large in the *Khalsa* Raj. They were working outside the core region, addressing themselves to the small number of Hindu traders and shopkeepers in the towns of Sindh Sagar Doab. There were ideological difference between the Singhs and the *Sehajdharis.* However, 'the doctrine of Guru-Granth was coming to the fore in place of the doctrine of Guru-Panth. This is understandable because of the doctrine of Guru-Granth was better suited to the situation of the early nineteenth century when social inequalities had to be reconciled to the ideal norm of equality.'[50]

The *Khalsa* and the Punjab in the 19th century underwent a revolutionary change after the death of Maharaja Ranjit Singh. Once the strong hand that governs the affairs is removed, the emergence of the political intrigues is but natural in a medieval phenomenon and monarchical set-up. The *Khalsa* Raj was very unfortunate in one respect. The very able generals of Ranjit Singh—Mokham Chand, Dewan Chand, Hari Singh Nalwa, Ram Dayal—all died during his lifetime. "Only crafty designing men, either weaklings or traitors, survived to command his forces." The *Khalsa* Raj suffered a mighty blow, as the Punjab had become "a scene of the wildest disorder."[51] Ranjit Singh had created discipline, produced order, and respect for authority in the Punjab. But it seems all his achievements, though remarkable, were personal and consequently ephemeral, as his genius and energy were not inherited by his successors. His death was a signal for scramble for power. The prying British eyes, after the occupation of nearly whole of India, would not spare Punjab unless it was able to withstand the threat effectively. Once the strong hand of Ranjit Singh was removed, finding the weakness of the *Khalsa* Sarkar characterized by intrigues, internal dissension, break down of proper law and order machinery and confusion within, the English would exploit the situation and embark upon in a single stroke or in a phased manner. Moreover, the role of the *Khalsa* chiefs like Lal Singh and Tej Singh and that of Raja Gulab Singh could not be brushed aside easily. The *Khalsa* Raj appeared to the British authorities convenient rationalization of their imperialistic ambitions. Lord Hardinge, the Governor General of India, right from the day of assumption of office in July, 1844 had expressed his conviction that the Sikhs had become incapable of maintaining a stable government and the Punjab could not act as a buffer between the British Empire and the Muslim states beyond Indus. And that the role of the *Khalsa* Chiefs as well as Rani Jindan, who were interested in their lives and jagirs rather than the interests of the *Khalsa Darbar*, was really deplorable. However, despite the defeat in the Anglo-Sikh War of 1845-46, the valour and military skill of the *Khalsa Fauj* was very much appreciated by the British. The British Commander-in Chief wrote to Sir Robert Peel, the British Prime Minister, "Policy precluded me from publicly recording my sentiments on the splendid gallantry of our fallen foe, or to record the acts of heroism displayed, not only individually, but almost collectively by the Sikh *sirdars* and army; and I declare, were not from a deep conviction that my country's good required the sacrifice, I could have wept to have witnessed the fearful slaughter of so devoted a body of men."[52] Though the *Khalsa Fauj* was defeated, the British at that time were not in a position to effect the extension of their empire to the Indus. The annexation of the Punjab would have entailed a serious of sieges and guerilla warfare for which neither money nor men at the Governor-General's disposal were at all adequate.[53] Governed by their political policy and financial resources, the English opted for aggression in a phased manner.

As a result of the Treaty of Lahore (9th March 1846), the Lahore Darbar perpetually ceded to the English East India Company all the territories lying to the south of River Sutlej i.e. Ludhiana and Ferozpur, as well as the territories lying between river Sutlej and Beas inclusive of the hilly regions. A war indemnity of one and a half crores of rupees was imposed, but since only fifty lakhs were forthcoming, the Lahore Darbar perpetually ceded all rights (*haquq*) over the hilly territories stretching from river Beas to Sind Sagar inclusive of Kashmir (*diyar-i-Kashmir*) and Hazara. The army of the *Khalsa* State was limited to 20,000 infantry and 12,000 cavalry, and thirty-six guns in addition to those already captured were given up. The Maharaja was precluded from employing any British, European or American subject without the consent of the British Government, nor was he to change the limits of his territories without the concurrence of the British Government.[54]

The English government concluded a separate Treaty of Amritsar (16 March, 1846) with Raja Gulab Singh and bestowed (*ata named*) on him the territories of Kashmir, Hazara along with the hilly regions lying between the west of river Beas to the east of river Sindh as well as the territories to the west of river Ravi comprising Chamba, excepting Lahul in heredity (*nasalan bad nasal wa batan bad batan*) and in perpetuity (*barai doam*) to his descendants. Due to the vehement opposition and insistence on the part of the Chamba Chief, the territories of Chamba to the west of river Ravi were withdrawn and in exchange the Chamba chief ceded Bhadarwah. Due to his inability to curb the revolt of chief zamindars of Muzaffarabad and Hazara, the Raja requested the English government for exchange of these territories with some portions in the plains near river Jehlum of the of the Lahore Sarkar. Consequently as a result of British mediation a Treaty was signed between Raja Gulab Singh and the Lahore Darbar (25 May 1847), the Raja received the territories of Munawar, Sijanpore and Pathankot in exchange for Hazara and Balkot. But after sometime he was obliged to surrender Sijanpore and Pathankot to the English administration and retained only a part of Munawar and the territories of Kathua and Suchetgarh.[55]

The loss of Kashmir and a few other territories of Punjab was a sever blow to the Lahore Sarkar. Even a cursory glance at the terms of the Treaty will show that complete annexation was the only point from which the English government receded. As a matter of fact, the treaty sought to cripple the *Khalsa* power in various ways: by taking away from it the fertile Jullunder Doab; by slicing off the hilly tracts of Kangra, Kashmir and Hazara; by reducing the strength of the *Khalsa* forces; and by exacting an exorbitant indemnity. It was simply a matter of time when Punjab would be absorbed in the British possessions in India. By the Treaty of Bhyrowal (26 December 1846) the British Resident stationed at Lahore became the virtual ruler of the Punjab. He was to have "full authority to direct and control the duties of every department" and unlimited authority in all matters of internal administration and external relations." Above all, a British force was to remain at Lahore.[56] The *Khalsa* Kingdom was ultimately engulfed as a result of the second Anglo-Sikh War in 1849. On March 29, 1849, the proclamation was read at the grand Darbar, "Wherefore the Governor-General of India had declared, and hereby proclaims that the kingdom of the Punjab is at an end; and that all the territories of Maharaja Dalip Singh are now and henceforth a portion of the British Empire in India."[57] The *Khalsa Fauj*, which had been retrenched after 1845-46, was virtually disbanded after 1848-49. The 'majestic fabric' of the *Khalsa* raised by Maharaja Ranjit Singh was a thing of the past. The *Khalsa* was at its lowest ebb at this point of time.

The Punjab as a province of the British empire had become larger after the second Anglo-Sikh War. All other territories of the *Khalsa* kingdom were annexed to the British empire and were incorporated in the newly formed province of Punjab. The administration of the *cis*-Sutlej states as well as districts comprising Thanesar, Ambala, Ludhiana and Ferozepur were merged with the Punjab in 1849. In 1858, the Delhi division of the North Western Province comprising the six districts of Delhi, Gurgaon, Panipat, Rohtak, Hissar and Sirsa was also merged with the Punjab. As such, with the annexation of the *Khalsa* kingdom, Punjab as it stood under British rule became a land of seven rivers adding Indus and Jamuna to the traditional five. It was bounded in the north by the vasty Himalayan range which divided it from China, Tibet and Kashmir, on the East lay river Jamuna and to the south Sindh. River Sutlej separated it from Bahawalpur and Rajputana. To the west lay the Suleiman range, which divided it from Baluchistan and Afghanistan. In 1901, however, Lord Curzon had separated the Districts of Peshawar, Hazara, Bannu and its Marwat *tehsils* as well as the trans-Indus part of Dehra Ismail Khan excepting the *ilaqa* of Vehoa were separated from the Punjab so as to form North West Frontier Province with its capital at Peshawar. In 1911, when capital of British India was shifted from Calcutta to Delhi, the Delhi *tehsil* along with the Mehrauli *thana* of Ballabgarh was separated from the Punjab and formed into the Delhi province. After these changes, the area of province together with 36 big and small states was 1,44,436 square miles. It consisted of five divisions with twenty-nine districts.

The period after the annexation found attempts towards the rediscovery, revival and regeneraion of the *Khalsa.* The new rulers took concrete steps towards the introduction of modern education and education in English literature, western sciences and social studies. Apart from the British government, the Christian missionaries and other social and religious groups came forward for the cause of spreading modern education in the Punjab. The Punjab University was established at Lahore in 1882 paving the way for the growth of higher education in the Punjab. Before the advent of the British rule, education among the Punjabi womenfolk was confined to their acquiring the principal tenets of their respective religion. The first girls' school was opened at Rawalpindi under the auspices of Mr. Brown, Inspector of Schools, Rawalpindi Division, in December 1856. Despite prejudices of social conservatism and the progress was slow, number of girls schools in various cities along with schools for the training of women teachers came into existence during the second half of the nineteenth century.[58] In 1883, after the death of Swami Dayanand, Arya Samaj decided to establish a college in his memory at Lahore. In the last decade of the 19th century a system of Arya education was set up from primary to graduate level. English literature, western science and social studies were combined with Sanskrit and Hindi. This System, by and large, geared to the needs of the westernized Hindu middle class. A *Khalsa* College was set up in Amritsar in 1892. On 22nd October 1893, the institution began as a Middle School. Three years later High classes were opened, and then it was raised to the status of a college by the opening of Intermediate classes. In 1899, came the B.A. classes and in 1905 the science classes up to the B.Sc. The MA class was added in 1960.[59] It remained a premier Sikh institution for half a century thereafter. In all these activities the British government and the Christian Missionaries had a very significant role to play. It is very interesting to note that some of best-known and respected religious teachers, political leaders and intellectual giants studied at the Christian schools, including the veteran leader, Master Tara Singh, Bhai Jodh Singh, Bhai Vir Singh and Prof. Puran Singh and many others.[60] While English was the medium of education in the mission schools, Urdu was introduced as medium of education in government schools up to the matriculation levels, though Punjabi was the dominant language of the province.

The *Khalsa* under the colonial regime was subjected to social and economic transformation, which resulted in the growth of professional middle class. A number of soldiers of the *Khalsa Fauj*, who had been disbanded after the annexation of the Punjab, had returned to their native villages and adopted their age-old profession of farming. The British goods began flooding the markets, giving a fatal blow to the artisan class, which used to cater to the requirements of the countryside. The peasants were hit by the introduction of British land revenue system, creation of big landlords and a new trader-usurer class fleecing them through rents, high rates of interests and compelling them to part with their lands through sales and mortgages. The British government set up a highly repressive regime to rule the province and suppress the least signs of resistance to oppression and exploitation. By the year 1880 there was the collapse of the peasant propriety due "particularly to the innovations of fixed assessments, freedom of contract, individual property in land, and the series of technical laws which benefited the rich and astute at the expense of the poor and the ignorant."[61] Close alliance was forged with princes and big landlords who faithfully supported the British. The increasing number of the tenants-at-will accounted for the impoverishment of the small landholders. The reason behind this new phenomenon was the influx of new legal system. The new class of trade-usurer would sell British manufactured goods to the peasant and purchase raw materials from them cheap for British industries and advance them loans to pay up government dues and to purchase goods. However, a silver lining was provided in the form of the Punjab National Bank, a purely Indian concern, founded in 1895, followed by Bharat Insurance Company and the People's Banking and Commercial Association[62] which helped in the modernization of the *Khalsa* during the 19th century.

The nineteenth century has been a very crucial period for the *Khalsa*. There was a time when even the very existence of the *Khalsa* was seemed to be at stake. After the death of Maharaja Ranjit Singh in 1839, seven successive governments were installed, mainly through violent methods, in Lahore *Darbar* up to the outbreak of the first Anglo-Sikh War. After the annexation, the British government had disbanded thousands of soldiers of the *Khalsa* army. Flocks of Christian missionaries began roaming about the country and converting thousands of ignorant and poor rural folk to the new faith.[63] The onslaught of Christianity, patronized by the new rulers, was corroding the sources of the moral and spiritual heritage of the *Khalsa*. Maharaja Dalip Singh had been converted so also a wing of the Kapurthala rulers. There was an increased number of *Sehajdharis* during the period of Maharaja Ranjit Singh and they 'were fast merging back into their ancient faith Hinduism' and 'fears were openly being expressed that the future of the Sikhs lay only in the past.'[64] Above all, there were British manufactured goods. There was unprecedented degree of commercialization of agriculture which facilitated the emergence of petty commodity producers first in the central districts and then in the canal colonies. The new changes gave a deathblow to the self-sufficient village economy, destroyed cottage industries, and ruined artisans who were thrown into the ranks of agricultural workers or tenants-at-will. A process of de-industrialization set in and pressure of population on land increased. The autonomous village *panchayats* were uprooted. The new land settlements were carried out and converted the state demand in cash instead of in kind. The land tenures were based on the concept of private property in land on the English pattern. This paved the way for sales and mortgages of land to the moneylenders. The Punjab Land Alienation Act of 1900 accentuated socio-economic differentiation among holders which subsequently resulted into greater prominence to the agricultural moneylenders. This accounted for growing expropriation and indebtedness of peasantry. The commercial leadership was provided by the traditional business communities like the *Khatris*, *Aroras* and *Banias* among the Hindus and the *Shaikhs*, *Khojas* and *Pathans* among the Muslims. The British government introduced a complicated legal system on the English pattern, proliferating litigation which proved highly costly and ruinous. The old moneylender community blossomed into usurer through high interest charges. They started forcing the sale of land at below market price, virtually in collusion with the village *munsifs* and lawyers as a result of several social and religious reform movements that substantially changed the character of the *Khalsa*.

The most important movement, which partially threatened the very existence the *Khalsa*, was the Arya Samaj, founded at Mumbai (then called Bombay) on April 10, 1875 by Swami Dayanand (1824-1883). Amongst all the places where he preached, he found the largest following at Lahore, where he reached in 1877.[65] So great was his success that Lahore became the headquarters of the Movement. In Punjab he got the support mainly amongst the middle class, educated city dwellers Hindus. They wanted a religion, which could meet the attacks of Christianity. The watchwords of Swami Dayanand were *'Back to the Vedas'* and *'India for the Indians'*. In other words, Indian *religion* for the Indians, and Indian *Sovereignty* for the Indians. In order to accomplish the first end, Indian religion was to be reformed and purified by a return to the Vedas, and foreign religions as Islam and Christianity were to be extirpated.[66] Thus the programme included *reform* for indigenous religion and *extirpation* for foreign religion. He propagated, among other things, simpler ceremonies for marriage, birth and death, remarriage of 'virgin widows' founding of orphanages, education for girls, Ved *parchar* for the propagation of new ideas and *shuddhi* for reconversion to Arya *dharma*. His work *Satyarath Parkash* (1874) gives the details about his philosophy. He preached against idolatry and caste. He also emphasized man's commitment to the world outside and illumination within, through meditation, on the one Formless God as enjoined by the Vedas. The views of Swami Dayanand on society and religion created a great stir. In his book all prophets of religion, their philosophy and practices were reviled. Jainism, Sikhism, Islam, and Christianity were mercilessly criticized. Guru Nanak was called an ignorant "dambi"[67] (pretender). This section of the book encouraged Aryas and provided them with very useful ammunition for their controversies, but it also created vehement hatred against the Samaj in many quarters. After the death of Swami Dayanand (1883), though the work was carried on with enthusiasm, there was, soon, a split in the Arya Samaj. It broke into the College 'Cultured' party and the Vegetarian or 'Mahatma' party. The former was progressive, stood for modern education and for freedom in diet, and declared that Arya Samaj was the one true universal religion, which must be taught to the entire world. The latter favoured the ancient Hindu education, stood by vegetarianism and declared that the teaching of the Samaj was pure Hinduism, but not the universal religion. In 1893-94, the 'militant Aryas waged a war in print against Christianity, Muslims, Sikhs and the traditionalist Hindus. Earlier, despite the derogatory views, several eminent Sikhs had joined the Arya Samaj, but the 'thoughtless attack' on the Sikh Gurus by the 'fire-brands' Aryas in 1888 brought a decisive break between the two.[68] The confrontation between the Arya Samaj and the Sikhs sharpened the issue of the very identity of the *Khalsa*. The death of Dyal Singh Majithia in 1898 made the question of *Khalsa* identity a legal issue. His will was contested in the court by his widow on the plea that he was not a Hindu but a Sikh. This gave a new twist to the relation between the two communities. This prompted Bhai Kahan Singh to publish, by now a classic exposition of a distinct *Khalsa* identity, his well-known work *Hum Hindu Nahin.*[69] It was further contended 'the Sikh dispensation was an independent entity and not a subsidiary system, based on Hindu philosophy'.[70] In 1900, the Arya Samaj leaders reconverted some Sikhs through a ceremony involving the shaving of their heads in public. Later in the early 20th century *Hindu Sabhas* sprang up in the Punjab and the Punjab Hindu Conference was held successively for six years from 1909 to 1914. The 'Arya' consciousness was being transformed in to 'Hindu' consciousness. The confrontation between the Arya Samaj and the *Khalsa* continued into the twentieth century as the latter evolved their own programme of purification (*shuddhi*).

An acknowledged reformer of the Hindu society, Dev Atma (Shiv Narayan Agnihotra), established the Dev Samaj on 16th Februray 1887. It sought to create a social atmosphere, which could do away with superstitions and caste system. He put into action all the social reforms for which he had fought. He made it imperative for the members of his society not to get their daughters married before the age of sixteen and their sons before the age of eighteen. He made it a condition for members of his society not to indulge in bigamy. He was of the view that education alone could open for women opportunities for enlightenment and independence, professional and public life. He made women's education as the chief plank of his Society's contribution to social reforms. Dev Samaj's service in women's education came to be publicly appreciated and acknowledged. The Dev Samaj institutions not only provided high standard of education, but also inculcated moral culture of highest quality.[71] Dev Samaj had a deep impact on the *Khalsa* initiative for creating a society devoid of unnecessary rituals and thinking in terms of providing educational facilities, especially for the women folk.

The *Ahmadiyah* Movement arose towards the end of the nineteenth century, amidst the turmoil of the downfall of the old Islamic society and the infiltration of the new culture, with new attitudes, its Christian missionary onslaught and Sir Sayyid Ahmad's rationalization and westernization.[72] Mirza Ghulam Ahmad of Qadian, the founder of the movement, through his *Burahinh-i-Ahmadiyah* (1880-1884), made a contribution to religious controversy. The movement, which was meant to rejuvenate Islam on the basis of the *Quran*, tried to refute the Christian missionaries, the Arya Samajists and Brahmos. He also argued that Guru Nanak was, in fact, a Muslim. Not to speak of the Hindus, Sikhs and Christians, his writings were not at all to the tastes of the Muslims either. All these religious communities reacted sharply that made the last decade of the nineteenth century full of religious controversies.[73]

Even when the *Khalsa* Raj was in its hey days there was some evidence of religious turmoil among the *Khalsa*. One such evidence was the Nirankari movement. There after other movements—the *Namdhari* or the *Kooka* movement, the *Singh Sabha* Movement and *Akali* movement—followed. Incidently all these movements were either inspired or controlled by *Sahjdhari Sikhs* or recent Hindu converts to Sikhism.[74]

Baba Dayal (1783-1855), the founder of the Nirankari movement was a Malhotra Khatri Sahjdhari Sikh of Rawalpindi. He preached against the worship of gods and goddesses and was against useless and meaningless Brahmanical rituals, ceremonies, superstitions and practice of idolatory. He would ask his fellow Sikhs to believe in only the *nirankar* the Formless One and conform their lives to the teachings of Granth Sahib. His slogan was *"Japo piario dhann Nirankar, Jo deh dhari sab khuar"*. The sect was in existence even during Ranjit Singh's reign, but 'fear kept them quiet'.[75] Baba Dayal died on 30th January 1855 and was succeeded Baba 0Darbara Singh. He established a number of centres in towns and villages outside Rawalpindi. He appointed *biradar,* i.e. representatives for every local *sangat i.e.,* congregation. For their guidance he prepared a *hukmnama* containing the essential teachings of Baba Dayal and he is referred to as 'the true *guru*'. He realized that Sikhism could only be preserved in all its purity by complete break from Brahmanical influence. He was of the view that Sikhs had drifted away from the fundamental teachings of the Gurus because their social rites and customs had all been dominated by Brahmanical interference. The Sikhs were Sikhs only in name. The *Gurbani* was being recited like the Hindu *Mantras* without understanding. The changes that Baba Darbara Singh wanted to effect expressed the purpose of strengthening faith in and dedication and devotion to Guru Nanak's teachings. He wanted a complete break with the prevalent superstitions and meaningless rituals. His first act was to raise the banner of revolution and change. He summoned a large conference of his followers to the Nirankari Darbar at Rawalpindi on Tuesday 13th March 1855. He performed the marriage of a young couple by the Anand Marriage by circumambulating the *Guru Nanak Sahib* four times with the tunes of the hymns (*Santan Ke Karaj Ap Khaloya*). Thereafter four *Lavan* composed by Guru Ram Das and *Shabads* were recited. The *Ardas* (prayer) was offered and *Karah Parshad* distributed. In history this may be first *Anand Marriage.* Baba Darbara Singh got all the Sikh ceremonies codified in a *Hukamnama* issued by him in the year 1857. On his death in 1870, Sahib Rattaji succeeded him. He transformed the Nirankari mission into an impersonal institution in 1903. The mission was joined by the *Khatri, Arora* and *Bhatia* traders, bankers and shopkeepers of the towns and villages and their number rose to thousands. They professed to propagate the true mission of Guru Nanak but they insisted on complete reliance on *Nirankar.* They read *Gurbani* and sing *Shabad* on the occasions of births, marriages and deaths. At the time of *Ardas,* the Nirankaris do not invoke the blessing of *bhagoti,* but use the word *Nirankar* instead of it. They believe along with the *Guru Granth,* the existence of a living teacher and a guide.[76]

The *Namdhari* or *Kooka* Movement (so called because the devotees shout and scream the—*Kook*—when they are in ecstasy) grew up as a religious and social movement and was the first movement, which emphasized the importance of the identity of the *Khalsa* under colonial rule. Baba Ram Singh, the founder of the *Namdhari* movement enlisted himself in the *Khalsa* army in the year 1836, three years before the death of Maharaja Ranjit Singh. He left the army in 1845. Baba Ram Singh was a disciple of Baba Balak Singh, the founder of the movement. He had invoked the authority of the Sikh scriptures, emphasized the importance of the Name *(Nam)* for salvation. Baba Ram Singh was one of the three most prominent disciples of Balak Singh and was chosen to succeed him. He gave new direction to the movement and worked in the central districts of the Punjab. The nomenclature of *Namdhari* was given by Baba Ram Singh himself because he enjoined upon his people to practice *Nam*. The movement was launched at Bhaini Sahib on 14 April in 1857. Baba Ram Singh instituted the *Sant Khalsa* in 1862, the year of Baba Balak's death. Prayer followed recitation of Guru Granth Sahib. Five Sikhs were baptized into the new sect according to the ceremony prescribed by Guru Gobind Singh called *khande ki pahul*. The disciples were ordained to observe the code of conduct laid by Guru Gobind Singh and wear five Ks. The Guru whispered secret word '*waheguru*'—the Gurmantar, into the ears of new converts. The disciples were enjoined to read Guru Granth Sahib and lead a pure life of devotion to one God only. Every *Namdhari* was to live by the fruit of his own labour. Baba Ram Singh had also invoked the Goddess *Chandi* when he instituted the *Khalsa*. A book of *Sau Sakhis*—100 prophecies—believed to have been written by Guru Gobind Singh fore told the end of British rule in the Punjab under a carpenter named Ram Singh and this prophecy was known to British administrators in 1863.[77] On 28th June 1863, the Punjab Government interned Baba Ram Singh in his village Bhaini. The internship continued upto the end of 1866. It gave a great fillip to the *Kooka* movement and number of its followers increased to a large extent. According to the British, Baba Ram Singh was opposed to the British rule in the Punjab and he was hoping if not actually working for the return of Sikh rule. He was sent to Rangoon. The devotees of Baba Ram Singh established contact with him at Rangoon and letters began to exchange between Burma and the Punjab with increasing frequency till 1880 when he was removed to Mergui where he died five years later. Earlier, in 1885, his followers were eagerly looking forward to Dalip Singh's visit to the Punjab, hoping that 'this would be followed by the release and the return of their exiled Guru Ram Singh'.[78] The *Namdharis* believed that Guru Ram Singh was a re-incarnation of Guru Gobind Singh, the tenth Guru of the Sikhs, the founder of the *Khalsa*. By the end of the 19th century, the *Namdharis* had discarded militancy and stuck to the ideal of personal piety and earnest living. They developed the idea of a living *Guru*. However, the *Namdhari* idea of a living personal *Guru* could not be reconciled to the doctrines of *Guru-Granth* and *Guru-Panth*. If *Guru-gaddi* had not been accepted and propagated as a part of their creed, the movement would have been a marvellous success and would have found favour with a much larger population of the Sikhs.[79]

Another revivalist, more widespread and accepted wholeheartedly to the Sikh orthodoxy, was launched immediately after the deportation of Baba Ram Singh was known as the *Singh Sabha* Movement. It was felt that the attempt at reform in the *Khalsa* made in the shape of *Namdhari* movement had not been successful owing to the want of common feeling among the Sikhs, which could be engendered only by education. Contrary to the previous movements, *Singh Sabha* was the first movement among the Sikhs, which possessed a definite constitution to regulate its affairs and to carry out its programmes and policies.

Sri Guru Gobind Sabha was founded at Amritsar in 1873. It was attended by the *Pujaris*, *Mahants*, *Gyanis*, *Granthis*, *Udais*, *Nirmalas*, besides prominent Sardars including Thakur Singh Sandhanwalia, Baba Sir Khem Singh Bedi, a descendant of Guru Nanak, and Kanwar Bikram Singh of Kapurthala. The *Singh Sabha* undertook to (i) restore Sikhism to its pristine purity; (ii) edit and publish historical and religious books; (iii) propagate current knowledge, using Punjabi as the medium and to start magazines and new papers in Punjabi; (iv) reform and bring back into Sikh fold the apostates; and (v) interest the high placed Englishmen, in and ensure their association with, the educational programme of the Sikhs. The *Dasam Granth* was subjected to a close examination for the purpose of discovering how much of it was Guru Gobind Singh's own composition, and how much came from other writers. Many Sikh scholars volunteered to join the ranks of the *Singh Sabha.* Thirty two versions were collected to work upon. The work of collecting the different texts was completed in 1896, and its report was published in 1897. Inspired by these researches other works of great importance were prepared, such as Gyani Gyan Singh's *Panth Parkash* and *Twarikh Khalsa,* Pandit Tara Singh's *Guru Granth Kosh* and *Tirath Sangrah,* etc. In 1894, Bhai Kaur Singh and Bhai Vir Singh established the *Khalsa* Tract Society, Amritsar. Through the influence of Professor Gurmukh Singh, in 1877 classes were opened in the Oriental College for teaching Punjabi as the only modern Indian language, besides the classical languages. On 2nd November 1879, a *Singh Sabha* at Lahore was founded and was affiliated to the *Sikh Sabha* of Amritsar, which became the *Khalsa Diwan*, Amritsar. The job of publishing the *Janamsakhis* and the *Gurparnalis* was also undertaken. It was provided in the fundamental rules that nothing against the government could be discussed in the *Singh Sabha* meetings. A number of books in Punjabi were published on the lives of the Sikh Gurus, the institution of the *Khalsa*, and the political struggle of the Sikhs against the Mughals and the Afghans. Bhai Vir Singh, by far the most important literary figure among the Sikh reformers, recreated the heroic age of the *Khalsa* in his *Sundari, Bijai Singh, Satwant Kaur, Baba Naudh Singh,* etc. producing historical fiction far more attractive than history. The process was continued to the early twentieth century.[80] Moreover, the English education and western science and technology were appreciated, but the idea of Christian instruction and no religious instruction were not appreciated. Along with the western sciences and literature, they wanted to teach Sikh tenets and Sikh history to their boys and girls. This Anglo-Sikh system of education was an important plank of reform. Equally symbolic of Sikh reform was the *Kanya Mahavidyalaya* founded at Ferozpur by Bhai Takht Singh in 1892, followed by the girls schools at Lahore, Amritsar, Rawalpindi and Ropar.[81] As such, the process of reforms in the *Khalsa* which had been initiated by the *Singh Sabha* movement in the 19th century continued to work with the same spirit during the 20th century.

The *Khalsa*, which had been retrenched from the army after the first Anglo-Singh Sikh War and virtually disbanded after the annexation, came to form nearly a third of the 60,000 troops raised from the Punjab during 1857-58. At the time when the other recruiting grounds were fighting against the British, the *Khalsa* were called out to 'save the Empire'. They successfully 'fulfilled their mission'.[82] Ever since the revolt of 1857, the *Khalsa* became Great Britain's best friend. When the major portion of India was threatening the British power in this country, the *Khalsa* helped the English to weather the storm and steer the British baroque out of troubled waters. When there was the hour of peril for the British, the *Khalsa* saved the situation for their erstwhile enemies, a fact which all imperial records unhesitatingly affirm.[83] Henceforth, the *Khalsa* were to hold the positions of honour. The *Khalsa* fought in nearly all major wars fought by the British in all the three continents of the world. The percentage of the Sikhs in the Indian army was significantly larger than the percentage of the Sikh population in India. The 'gallant and faithful service' provided by the *Khalsa* made them the 'pride of the Punjab'[84]

At the end it can be maintained that the *Khalsa* during the 19th century had to see number of ups and downs. It saw the partial fulfillment of the aims of the *Khalsa* in the form of the establishment of Ranjit Singh's empire but everything seemed to have got nullified immediately after the death of the Maharaja. It certainly goes to the credit of determination of the *Khalsa* that, unlike the Mughals after their downfall, it did not remain in depression for a long time and soon recovered. Moreover, different social and religious reform movements could have brought the dismemberment of the *Khalsa* but the good sense prevailed and it took the refuge of all round education and social reforms, which once again brought them into the forefront.[85]

References

1. McLeod, W.H., *The Evolution of the Sikh Community: Five Essays*, OUP, Delhi, 1975, pp. 71&77.
2. See, Treaty of Amritsar (1809) between 'The Raja of Lahore' and the East India Company, Aitchison, Sir Charles, *A Collection of Treaties, Engagements and Sunnuds Ralating to India and Neighbouring Countries*, Calcutta, 1892, 4th edition, vol. vii. The first article of the Treaty stipulates that 'the British Government will have no concern with the territories and subjects of the Raja to the northward of the river Sutlej'. There was hardly any interference from the British East India Company in the affairs of the Maharaja on the north of the Sutlej for more than two decades.
3. Dua, J.C., *British Historiography Eighteenth Century Punjab: Their understanding of the Sikh struggle for power and role of Jassa Singh Ahluwalia*, New Delhi, 1992, p. 1.
4. *Ibid.*, p. 2. Also Grover, BR, 'Presidential Address', *Punjab History Conference*, XIX, 1985, pp. 7-58.
5. Chopra, Gulshan Lall, *The Panjab as a Sovereign State (1799-1839)*, 2nd edition, Hoshiarpur, 1960, p. 4.
6. Dua J.C., *op. cit.*, p. 2.
7. Muzaffar Alam, *The Crisis of Empire in Mughal North India; Awadh and Punjab, 1707-48*, OUP, New Delhi, 1986, pp. 315-16.
8. Ganda Singh, *A Brief Account of the Sikh People*, Delhi Sikh Gurdwara Board, Delhi, 1971, p. 35.
9. Jit Singh Sital, 'Tradition and Customs of Nihangs', *The Spokesman Weekly*, 13th February 1978.
10. B.R. Grover, 'Relationship between the Sovereign State (the Mughal and the Afghans) and the Punjab Hill Chiefs during the 17th and 18th centuries; A Case Study of Chamba Chieftainship based on Bhuri Singh Museum, Chamba Documents', *Proceedings of Punjab History Conference*, XVI Session, March 12-14, 1982, pp. 94-1032; 'Relationship between the Lahore Darbar and the Punjab Hill Chiefs during the first half of the 19th century till 1848', *Proceeding of Punjab History Conference*, XVII Session, October 8-10, 1982, pp. 230-24.
11. Gurcharan Singh, *Sultan-ul-Qaum Baba Jassa Singh Ahluwalia*, Baba Jassa Singh Ahluwalia Bi-centenary Committee, Delhi, 1984.
12. Ram Sukh Rao, *Sri Fateh Singh Partap Prabhakar*, (ed.), J. Kaur, Patiala, 1980, pp. 284-99.
13. Ram Sukh Rao, *Sri Jassa Singh Binod*, Panjab State Archives, Patiala, ms./772, fols. 64a-66a, b; 71a-72b.
14. B.R. Grover, 'Presidential Address', *Punjab History Conference*, XIX session, March 22-24, 1985.
15. The boundaries of *subah* Punjab or *subah* Lahore or *Wilayat-i-Punjab* or Darul Saltanat Lahore extended from the river Sutlej in the east to the river Indus (Sind) in the north-west. The whole *subah* comprised of five *doabs* or *sarkars* *viz.*, Bet Jalandhar, Bari, Rechna, Chenhat and Sind Sagar. Moreover, some hilly regions to the north of Bet Jalandhar not covered in the *doabs* entitled as *Berun-i-Panjnand* also formed part of the *Subah*. The mountainous regions (*parganas*) to the north of the *doabs* formed the respective *doabs* or *sarkars*.

However, the core of the Punjab was the Bari *doab* with headquarters at Lahore. By the end of the 17th century, five *parganas* of *subah* Multan were also transfered to *subah* Punjab. At the same time, Bari, Rechna and Sind Sagar *doabs* with *mahals* beyond the five rivers of Multan territories continued to form the part of *subah* Multan.

16. Maharaja Ranjit Singh also possessed forty-five *t'aaluqas* in the *cis*-Satluj territory. These territories broadly included Ludhiana and Ferozepur as well as areas lying between river Satluj and Beas inclusive of the hilly regions. The Lahore Darbar, as per the treaty of 9th March 1846, perpetually ceded these territories to the English East India Company. Aitchison, C., *Collection of Treaties Engagements and Sunnuds Relating to India and Neighbouring Countries,* Calcutta, 1892, Vol VIII, p. 160.

17. However, depending upon the political situation, the family status, the geographical and strategic position of the chieftainship and, above all, the terms and conditions of submission, their revenues might be taken as fixed or might be assessed from time to time. B.R. Grover, 'Relationship between the Lahore Darbar and Punjab Hill Chiefs during the first half of the 19th century till 1846', *Punjab History Conference,* 17th session, 8-10 October 1982, pp. 230-240. *Sri Fateh Singh Partap Prabhakar, op. cit.,* pp. 339-342. *Sri Fateh Singh Prabhakar,* while describing the revenues to be realized from the chieftains of Kotlehr (Kotal Hari, Kangra, Mandi, Kulu, Nur Mahal and Rajauri, etc., refers to the revenues as *muamala* and *baj (baju)* as well as *lawazmat (lawajme).* Joginder Kaur in introduction to the text, pp. 25-31, has used the English term 'tribute' and has not correctly translated the term *nazrana, muamala, baj* etc. Muamla stood for land revenue and this term was current under the Marathas in many a portion of northern India.

18. Punjab State Archives, Patiala, *Khalsa Darbar Records,* Bundle 3, vol. IV, 109 and 189. Indu Banga, *Agrarian System of the Sikhs, Late Eighteenth and Early Nineteenth Century,* New Delhi, 1978, pp. 39-62; J.S. Grewal, *The New Cambridge History of India II.3 The Sikhs of the Punjab,* Hyderabad, 1990, p. 105 and 'Passage to Vassalage' in *From Guru Nanak to Maharaja Ranjit Singh,* Guru Nanak Dev University, Amritsar, 1982 (2nd Ed), 160-68. Both these scholars have used the term 'tribute'. However, based on the study of above records, though after some speculation about the connotation of the term *muamala-i-qadim* does ultimately concede the "possibility that the term *mu'amala* refers to the amount of the revenue taken by the suzerain from a vassal in addition to the stipulated annual tribute." In general it is correct statement if here 'tribute' simply stands for *nazarana.* In fact, as during the Mughal age, the term *peshkash* in revenue terminology in relation to the chieftains comprised *nazarana, mu'amala* and other customary dues etc. Under the *Khalsa* rule, as often put by the chroniclers, the amount *nazarana* (if at all translated as tribute) in general terminology comprised *nazarana, mu'amala* and other customary dues etc. See B.R. Grover, *Ibid.*

19. Deborah E., Klimburg-Slater (ed.), *The Silk Route and the Diamond Path, Esoteric Buddhist Art on the Trans-Himalayan Trade Routes,* UCLA Art Council, USA, 1982, pp. 19-51, 83-90, 112-119, 153-156, 205-208; Irfan Habib, *The Atlas of the Mughal Empire,* Delhi, 1982, pp. 1-16.

20. William Moorcraft and George Trebeck, *Travels in Himalayan Provinces of Hindoostan and the Punjab, in Ladakh and Kashmir, in Peshawar, Kabul, Kundus and Bokhara (1819-1825),* London, 1841, I, p. 111; *Foreign Frontier,* National Archives of India, New Delhi, no. 5, July 30, 1842.

21. B.R. Grover, Presidential Address, *Punjab History Conference,* XIX session, March 22-24, 1985, pp. 17-18; 'An Integrated Pattern of Commercial Life in the Rural Society of North India during the 17th and 18th centuries, *IHRC, Proceedings,* 37th session, Delhi, 1966, pp. 121-153; Reeta Grewal, 'Polity, Economy and Urbanization: Early Nineteenth Century Punjab', *Journal of Regional History,* 4 (1983), pp. 56-72; Bayly, C.A., *Rulers, Townsmen and Bazaars: North Indian Society in the age of British Expansion, 1770-1870,* Delhi, 1992, pp. 29, 68-73, 157-160.

22. B.R. Grover, Presidential Address, 1985, *op. cit.*

23. Joginder Kaur (ed.), *op. cit.,* pp. 284-99.

24. For more details in this regard see, Daljinder Singh Johal, 'Heroic Literature in Punjabi (1800-1850); 'Punjabi Literature: Late Eighteenth—Early Nineteenth Century', *Journal of Regional History,* 2 (1981), pp. 57-84 and 20-42 respectively; Ganda Singh, *A Bibliography of the Punjab,* Patiala, 1966.

25. Grewal J.S., *The New Cambridge History . . .,* *op. cit.,* p. 112.

26. Mufti Ali-ud-Din, *Ibrat Namah,* (1854 AD), Lahore, 1961, I, pp. 220-222,

27. Bhai Kahan Singh Nabha in his *Encyclopaedia of Sikh Literature: Mahan Kosh* (in Punjabi), (1999 edition) has defined the word *Akali*'s as *'Akaal naal hai jis da samband',* a devotee of Akal i.e. The Timeless One, God. According to this work, *Akali* or Nihang stands for "freedom from fear of death, readiness for action and non-attachment to the worldly possessions. There are three different accounts current about the origin of the *Akalis* or Nihangs according to the above *Encyclopaedia.* After the creation of the *Khalsa* in 1699 by the tenth master Guru Gobind Singh, a new set of bodily symbols of Five Ks began to represent the *Khalsa* oriented variety of the Sikh and hence added a significant dimension of 'Singh' to the multi-layered concept of a 'Sikh' (Piyara Singh Padam, *Sikh Samprdavali* (in Punjabi), Patiala, 2000). Guru Gobind Singh, thus, selected a devoted band of followers from these *Khalsa* Singhs and named them *Akalis.* (Kailash Chander Gulati, *The Akalis Past and Present,* Delhi, 1974, p. 17.)

28. A.C. Banerjee, 'Evolution of Sikh Kingship and Ranjit Singh' in Fauja Singh and A.C. Arora (ed.), *Maharaja Ranjit Singh: Politics, Society and Economy,* Punjabi University, Patiala, 1984, p. 151.

29. Sita Ram Kohli, *Maharaja Ranjit Singh* (in Punjabi), Delhi, p. 54.

30. Osborne, W.G., *The Court and Camp of Ranjit Singh,* London, 1840, p. 63.

31. Banerjee, Indubhushan, *Evolution of the Khalsa,* Calcutta, second edition, 1962, II, p. 117.

32. Bhagat Singh, *Sikh Polity in the Eighteenth and Nineteenth Centuries,* New Delhi, 1978, p. 180.

33. Gupta, Hari Ram, *History of the Sikhs,* Delhi, 1984, edition, II, p. 93.

34. Gordon, General John, *The Sikhs,* London, 1904, p. 73.

35. Louis E. Fenech, *Martyrdom in the Sikh Tradition: Playing the 'Game of Love',* OUP, 2000, p. 260.

36. Uberoi, J.P.S., *Religion, Civil Society and the State: A study of Sikhism,* OUP, Delhi, 1997, p. 100.

37. Malcolm, John, *Sketch of the Sikhs: Their Origin, Customs and Manners,* (first Printed, London, 1812), reprint, Chandigarh, 1981, p. 157.

38. Grewal J.S., *Sikh Polity and Political Institutions,* New Delhi, 1979, p. 105.'
39. Banerjee, A.C., *The Khalsa Raj,* New Delhi, 1985, p. 120.
40. Bhagat Singh, *op. cit.,* p. 31.
41. Sinha, N.K., *Ranjit Singh,* Calcutta, 1966, p. 138; Sukhdayal Singh, 'Maharaja Ranjit Singh's Relations with the *Akalis*' (in Punjabi) in Fauja Singh and A.C. Arora (Eds.), *Maharaja Ranjit Singh,* pp. 380 & 382.
42. Sita Ram Kohli, *op. cit.,* p. 31.
43. Nayar, Gurbachan Singh, *Sikh Polity and Political Institution,* New Delhi, 1979, p. 95; Grewal, J.S., *Sikh Ideology...,* p. 132.
44. Banerjee, A.C., *The Khalsa Raj,* New Delhi, 1985, p. 165.
45. However, they would not like their holy shrines to become a battleground. This contention is evident from the situation, which arose in January 1848. Some armed Nihangs had occupied the "burjis" (towers) of the Golden Temple, with the intent of capturing its custodianship, and the *Khalsa* Durbar, under Maharaja Dalip Singh, had sent in an army detachment to clear them by force. The Nihangs immediately surrendered, saying "we do not want the holiest of our shrines to become a battle ground!" See Dr. Gopal Singh, *A History of the Sikh People (1469-1988),* New Delhi, 1998 print, pp. 765-66.
46. Founder of four branches of Udasis, the Adi Udasis were Almast, Balu, Hasna and Goinda who are believed to have lived and worked in the seventeenth century. See Grewal, J.S., *The New Cambridge History. . ., op. cit.,* p. 117n.
47. *Ibid.,* p. 117. Sulakhan Singh, 'The Udasis in the Early Nineteenth Century', *Journal of Regional History,* 2 (1981), pp. 35-42.
48. Sulakhan Singh, 'Udasi Establishment Under Sikh Rule', *Journal of Regional History,* I, (1980), pp. 70-87; 'State Patronage to Udasis under Maharaja Ranjit Singh', *Maharaja Ranjit Singh and His Times* (Eds.) J.S. Grewal and Indu Banga, Guru Nanak Dev University, Amritsar, 1980, pp. 103-116.
49. Grewal, J.S., *The New Cambridge History..., op. cit.,* pp. 117-118.
50. *Ibid.,* p. 118.
51. Sinha, N.K., *op. cit.,* p. 191.
52. Quoted in Rait, R.S., *The life and campaigns of Hugh, 1st Viscount Gough,* 2 volumes, London, 1903, II, p. 108.
53. Fortescue, J.W., *History of the British Army,* London, 1927, XII, p. 390; Mahajan, Jagmohan, *Circumstances Leading to the Annexation of the Punjab 1846-1849 (A Historical Revision),* Allahabad, 1949, p. 33.
54. Aitchison, Sir Charles, *A Collection of Treaties, Engagements and Sunnuds Relating to India and Neighbouring Countries,* Calcutta, 1892, 4th edition, vol. VIII, p. 160.
55. B.R. Grover, 'Political and Social Situation of Punjab after Ranjit Singh Era', Punjabi Academy, Delhi, Maharaja Ranjit Singh Memorial Lecture, 9th October 1992.
56. Aitchison, *op. cit.,* VIII, pp. 166-170.
57. Proclamation declaring the Punjab to be "a portion of the British Empire in India," March 29, 1849, *Parliamentary Papers relating to the Punjab, 1847-1849,* (1849) Encl. 22 in No. 52.
58. For more details see, Sanaullah Khan, *A History of Education in the Punjab,* Lahore, 1932.

59. Prof. Teja Singh, *Essays in Sikhism,* Lahore, 1944.
60. Dr. Gopal Singh, *A History of the Sikh People (1469-1988),* Delhi, 1998 print, pp. 606-07n. He further writes, "The Gurmukhi type was first got manufactured by the Christian Missionaries and the first Punjabi work in the Gurmukhi script was the Christian Bible published at Sirampur and presented to Maharaja Ranjit Singh (1835). The first grammar in Punjabi and the first English-Punjabi dictionary were also the creations of the Christian missionaries."
61. Thorburn, S.S., *The Punjab in Peace and War,* (first published 1904), Punjab Language Department, Patiala, 1970, p. 252.
62. Grewal, J.S., *The New Cambridge History. . . op. cit.,* pp. 130-131; Master Hari Singh, *Agrarian Scene in British Punjab,* I, New Delhi, 1983, pp. vi-vii, 34-41.
63. Master Hari Singh, *op. cit.,* II, New Delhi, 1984, pp. 1-2.
64. Dr. Gopal Singh, *op. cit.,* p. 602.
65. On 1st January 1877, Queen Victoria was proclaimed Empress of India in a magnificent Darbar held by the Viceroy, Lord Lytton at Delhi. Dayanand was present as the guest of one of the native princes, and met some Hindus from Lahore, who gave him a pressing invitation to visit the Punjab. Shortly after he visited Ludhiana and Lahore.
66. Farquhar, J.N., *Modern Religious Movements in India,* London, 1924, p. 111.
67. Dayanand Saraswati, *English Translation of the Satyartha Prakash, being a guide to Vedic Hermeneutics* by Durga Prasad, London, 1908, pp. 203-204, 207.
68. Bhagat Lakshman Singh, *An Autobiography,* (ed. Ganda Singh), Calcutta, 1965, p; 58.
69. Kahan Singh, Bhai, *Hum Hindu Nahin,* Panch *Khalsa* Diwan, Bhasaur.
70. Bhagat Lakshman Singh, *op. cit.,* p. 133.
71. Kanal, S.P., 'The Dev Samaj' in Ganda Singh (ed.), *The Singh Sabha and other Socio-Religious Movements in the Punjab,* Punjabi University, Patiala, pp. 268-181.
72. Smith, Wilfred Cantwell, *Modern Islam In India,* London, 1946, pp. 298-302.
73. Spencer Lavan, 'Communalism in the Punjab: The Ahmadiyah Versus the Arya Samaj During the Life Time of Mirza Ghulam Ahmad', *The Punjab Past and Present,* Vol. 5, Part 2 (October 1971), pp. 320-42.
74. The Nirankari movement was initiated by Baba Dyal and strengthened by Baba Rattan Chand (or Baba Ratta). The Namdhari Baba Ram Singh was the disciple of Baba Balak singh of Hazro (Campbellpore) who was in turn inspired by Bhagat Jawaharmal of Rawalpindi. The *Singh Sabha* movement initially was inspired and controlled by Baba Khem Singh Bedi (who discarded nothing that was Hindu in origin) and the *Akali* movement, which was the most dynamic of all, was dominated from 1920 to 1962 by Master Tara Singh, a Hindu convert from Sikhism. See Dr. Gopal Singh, *op. cit.,* p. 603.
75. *Annual Report of Lodiana Mission,* Lodiana, 1853, pp. 22-23.
76. *The Nirankari Philosophy,* Sant Nirankari Mandal, Delhi; Dr. Man Singh Nirankari, 'The Nirankaris' in Ganda Singh (ed.), *The Singh Sabha... op. cit.,* pp. 1-12; John C.B. Webster, *The Nirankari Sikhs,* Delhi, 1979, pp. 9-11, 19-43; W.H. Mcleod, *Who is a Sikh? The problem of Sikh Identity,* OUP, pp. 116-121.

77. Nahar Singh, *Gooroo Ram Singh and the Kuka Sikhs,* Amrit Books, New Delhi, 1965.

78. Ganda Singh (ed.), *Maharaja Dalip Singh Correspondençe,* Patiala, 1977, pp. 387-88.

79. Grewal, J.S., *The New Cambridge History..., op. cit.*, 141-144; Bhagat Singh, 'The Kuka Movement', in Ganda Singh (ed.), *The Singh Sabha*...op. cit., pp. 170-179; Master Hari Singh, II, *op. cit.*, pp. 1-15; Bajwa, Fauja Singh, *Kuka Movement,* Delhi, 1965, pp. 1-100.

80. J.S. Grewal, 'The Emergence of Punjabi Drama: A Cultural Response to Colonial Rule'. *Journal of Regional History,* Guru Nanak Dev University, Amritsar, vol. 5 (1984), pp. 115-55.

81. Harbans Singh, 'Origins of the Sikh Sabha'; Teja Singh, 'The *Singh Sabha* Movement'; Gurdarshan Singh, 'Origin and Development of *Singh Sabha* Movement: Constitutional Aspects' in Ganda Singh (ed.), *The Singh Sabha Movement..., op. cit.,* pp. 23-65.

82. Khushwant Singh, *A History of the Sikhs,* OUP, 1978, II, p. 114, n 47.

83. Saint Nihal Singh, 'The Sikh's Struggle Against Strangulation', in *Fortnightly Review,* January-June, 1912 (97), pp. 82-90.

84. Reginald Hodder, 'The Sikhs and the Sikh Wars', *The Punjab Past and Present,* vol. 3, part 1 (April 1970), pp. 75-77.

85. Some historians have emphatically pointed out that right from the 16th century down to at least the mid-19th century, the *Nanak Panth* was regarded as an integral part of the Hindu society. Even though distinct from the other Hindu faiths viz. The Brahmanical order, Vaishnavism, Shaivism other Bhakti cults and the socio-religious orders like the Jains, Jogis (*faqirs, Kanphattas* and *Augars* etc.), it remained within the Hindu socio-religious structure. At the close of the 18th and the early 19th century, Mirza Qatil, a converted Sikh-Muslim, in *Halft Tamasha* while giving an account of the creeds, traditions and sects of the Hindus, and of the Muslims of India, regarded the "the Sikh disciples of Peshwa Nanak Shah Punjabi as part of the Hindus of the Punjab". The Hindu and Muslim writers maintain both this concepts in the reigns of Maharaja Ranjit Singh and his successors. It is only after the annexation of Punjab that the British administrators while writing their memoranda and reports in the English language that they gave connotations to the existing aspects of socio-religious orders so as to make Sikhism as distinct from Hinduism. Prior to the annexation of the Punjab (1849), both Lord Hardinge and Lord Dalhousie, considering the viability of the annexation of Punjab, in their correspondence and respective Minutes had considered the Lahore government as a Hindu government. When after the first Anglo-Sikh War, Lord Hardinge advocated the non-annexation of Punjab, his main argument was that this being the last Hindu state in India could well serve as a buffer between 'the Sutledge and the Khyber' i.e. between the English and the Muslim states of Afghanistan and Iran etc. Both Hardinge and Dalhousie considered the 'Lahore Court', '*Khalsa* State', 'Hindu Government' and the 'Lahore Government' as co-terminus and identical. As a matter of fact, it is only the late 19th and 20th century that in the changed political circumstances, the Sikhs have come to be viewed as a separate religious entity as distinct from the Hindu society. For Example see, B.R. Grover, 'Political and Social Situation of Punjab after Ranjit Singh Era', *Maharaja Ranjit Singh Memorial Lecture,* Punjabi Academy, Delhi, 9th October,12 1992.

2

Eighteenth Century Punjab Polity: Power, Position and Achievements of Sardar Ala Singh*

Eighteenth Century Punjab needs to be studied in terms of its own structure, by and large, disregarding what preceded and followed this period and without being overwhelmed by the fate of the Mughal power. The province of Punjab had its own strategic importance. For commercial, cultural and ethnic intercourse, the Punjab served as a link between the Mughal Empire and Persia and Central Asia. It had its own unique significance because of being—(i) conveniently situated for watching the movements of armies beyond Kabul and Qandhar, as well as, the hill chiefs in control of the Himalayan range from Kishtawar and Jammu to Srinagar, Garhwal; (ii) rich in agricultural and non-agricultural production; (iii) a convenient route for Central Asian and Persian horses, Kabul fruits and Kashmiri Shawls; and (iv) close proximity to the Imperial capital.[1] Moreover, eighteenth-century Punjab has a unique distinction of being an era of political turmoil and turbulation and the Sikh struggle for power. This period witnessed the disintegration of the Mughal Empire, the foreign campaigns of Nadir Shah and the Durranis, the attempts made by Rohillas, Rajputs, Jats and the Afghans to establish their respective regional governments and the emergence and rise of the Marathas and the Sikhs.[2]

As is clear from the Persian sources that during this period a large number of *zamindars* of different denomination besides the well known categories of so-called *mufsids* (disturbers)—Sikhs, Jats, Marathas and Afghans, struggled for greater share in the revenues and in power over the region, ultimately aiming to establish sovereignty in different parts of

---

* Paper presented at the seminar on *"The Achievements of Khalsa During the 18th century with special reference to Baba Ahla Singh*, organized by the Divinity Society, Mata Sundari College, University of Delhi, New Delhi, 30th November 2000, and published in Dr. Mohinder Kaur Gill (ed.), *Khalsa Trai Statabdi: Lekha-Jokha*, (Punjabi), New Delhi, 2001, pp. 164-186.

the *subahs* of Punjab and Delhi.[3] In the Punjab, the Sikh Sardars, during this period not only confronted the political powers, especially like the Mughals and the Durranis but were able to carve out their own independent/semi-independent territories (zamindaries) for the purposes of revenue realization and administration. The most significant feature of the Sikh history during the course of the 17th and the 18th centuries is that the Sikh Community/*Nanak Panth* which originally was socio-religious in character gradually transformed into socio-religious-cum-political force comprising members from various clans and castes. The Sikh Community which was originally composed of mainly the *khatris*, artisans, craftsmen, petty traders, low caste Hindus and poor peasantry, especially from the *Majha* areas, started attracting, as is indicated in the various *Hukamnamas* of the Gurus, the prosperous commercial classes and other sections of the peasantry as well. Another noteworthy change in the character of the Sikh community during the 17th and the 18th centuries was that they were no more drawn only from the regions of Punjab alone but also from cis-Sutlej territories, the regions around Delhi and other places in India which was basically due to the conversion of the new dominant class in the landed structure especially the peasantry into Sikhism in these areas. But the emergence of the Sikh as a political force cannot be studied in isolation rather the dissolution of the Mughal empire and the rise of the Marathas, Bundelas, Rajputs, the Jats and Afghans in other parts of India have also to be taken into consideration. The Mughal empire which, for its governance and stability during the 16th and 17th centuries, had depended upon its alliance with the Rajputs and its own nobility had been shaken to the point of dismemberment due to its fight with other socio-political forces during the 18th century. Inspite of considerable element of continuity in the traditional form of regional polity, administration and economic system, the above event had great impact on the social, economic and political developments during the 18th century which transformed the Sikhs, not only into a mere political force but a force to reckon with.[4]

A critical examination of the Punjab politics during the 18th century shows that there were as many as four main political powers *viz.*, the Mughals, the Marathas, the Sikh Sardars and the Durranis of Kabul who fought for supremacy there. Of course, during the first half of the century the struggle was basically confined between the Mughals and the Sikhs whereas during the second half, after the Marathas had been defeated at Panipat and the Mughal sovereign rights over the Punjab territories had practically vanished, and the Durranis had claimed political sovereignty and started realizing *peshkash,* it mainly became a tussle between the Sikhs and the Durranis. Again, during the last three decades of the 18th century, even though the Durranis continued to claim *de jure* political sovereignty, the Sikh Sardars had started asserting their *de facto* power over the Punjab territories. The successful invasion of the Durrani Chief, Nadir Shah (1739-40) and the capture of Delhi shook the foundation of the Mughal Empire. It not only led to desolation of many a town in Punjab but also brought a period of uncertainty and serious financial crisis. Mughal Emperor Muhammad Shah was forced to cede to the Durrani Chief a vast area of the Mughal empire comprising Peshawar, Bangash, the *subah* of Kabul along with Ghazni, the Afghan hills, Hazrat-Jat as well as the *parganas* of Baluchistan, *subah* Jhatta to the west of the river Indus inclusive of its ports. Nadir Shah also claimed *peshkash* from the *subadar* of Lahore and Multan. Moreover, revenues amounting to Rupees twenty lakhs from the four mahals i.e., Aurangabad, Gujarat, Sialkot and Pasrur were permanently assigned to him.[5] The situation provided a big encouragement to the activities of the Sikh Sardars of which Sardar Ala Singh was amongst the first who had already been recognized as a *Chaudhary* by the Mughal Emperor.

Ala Singh, Ala Singh Jat, Sardar Jassa Singh, Raja Ala Singh, Baba Ala Singh, Maharaja Ala Singh, Shri 108 Maharaja Baba Ala Singh are some of the names by which one of the most powerful Sikh Chiefs not only of the *cis*-Sutlej region but also of the Punjab proper during the 18th century was known to and addressed by different persons. The absence of any dramatic episodes or decisive events in the career of Ala Singh is partly responsible for the lack of appreciation of his achievements. As is true of his contemporary chiefs in case of Ala Singh also ambition was the dominant trait of his character, but cool calculation and caution always restrained his ambition. His striking power and achievements can be explained in a very suggestive statement of Qazi Nur Muhammad author of *Jang Namah.* He wrote, "In the country of Sirhind there was a chief, nay a commander of an army, who was a *zamindar* in that land and also a ruler, *Hakim,* a Governor, *Zabit,* and a Commissioner, *Amin.* Nobody else is so resourceful in the countries of Punjab, Lahore and Sirhind as he is."[6]

In this paper an attempt has been made to highlight important aspects of Sardar Ala Singh's life, achievements, position and place in the history of 18th century Punjab. The important sources consulted include Documents (*Taliqachas* i.e. Orders, Farmans, *arzdashts* i.e. letters etc.) preserved in the Punjab State Archives, Patiala; P. Saran (ed.), *Persian Documents; Selections from the Peshwa Daftar,* ed. G.S. Sardesai; *Persian records of Maratha History I: Delhi Affairs: (1761-1788) News Letters from Persian Collection,* Dr. J.N. Sarkar, Bombay, 1953. Some of the contemporary or near contemporary works like, *Tarikh-I-Patiala* by Khalifa Sayyid Mohammed Hasan (Prime Minister of Patiala State); *Jang*

Namah by Qazi Nur Mohammed; *Kitab-i-Qissia-i-Tahmas Miskin* by Tahmas Khan Miskin (popularly known as *Tazkira-i-Tahmas Maskin*); *Ebratnamah* by Mufti Ali-ud-Din; *Tarikh-i-Kunjpura* by Asar Nayaz; *The Rajas of Punjab...*by Lepel H. Griffin. And some of the recent works e.g. *Ahmad Shah Durrani, Father of Modern Afghanistan* by Ganda Singh; *Maharaja Ala Singh of Patiala* by Kirpal Singh; *History of Sikhs,* Vol. II *(1754-1771)* and *Evolution of the Sikh Confederacies (1739-1768)* by H.R. Gupta; *Baba Ala Singh* by Karam Singh; several articles on Punjab History by Professor B.R. Grover; and *British Historiography Eighteenth Century Punjab* by present writer.

Ala Singh, son of Sardar Rama and grandson of Sardar Phul, was born in 1691 at a village called Rampura in the *chakla* Sirhind, *subah* Delhi; Sardar Phul had received a *Farman* from Shah Jahan (1627) confirming to him the office of *Chaudhuri,* which had been held by his family for so many years. On *Chaudhuri* Phul's death two of his sons, Tilokha (from whom the houses of Nabha, Jhind and Malod descended) took the lead in the family. Though Tilokha, the elder of the two succeeded to the office of *Chaudhuri,* both he and Rama remained in close association for a number of years[8]. While Ala Singh was in his teens, both his father (Rama) and uncle (Tilokha) were men of local eminence. He inherited the legacy of both and also a little more. From the death of his father in 1714 till his death in 1765 Ala Singh was busy with increasing his power, resources and influence under changing circumstances. The present paper is likely to give a deep insight into the processes of political and administrative changes that were taking place in the northwestern parts of the Mughal Empire during the eighteenth century.

Hitherto many prominent historians, e.g., J.N. Sarkar[9], H.R. Gupta[10], G.S. Sardesai[11], Ganda Singh[12], Kirpal Singh[13], Karam Singh[14], Bhagat Singh[15], G.S. Nayyar[16] and many others have worked on this phase of Punjab history. They have made extensive use of many Persian, Marathi, English, and Punjabi sources. They have made extensive use of many Persian, Marathi, English and Punjabi sources. They have mostly highlighted the campaigns of Ahmad Shah Abdali against the Mughals and Marathas as well as Afghan-Sikh struggle for supremacy in the Punjab and in *cis*-Sutlej areas (of *subah* Delhi) during the second half of the 18th century.[17] They have given an excellent narrative of political and military aspects. However, there is no significant mention of the fact that with the annexation of the *subahs* of Lahore, Multan Kashmir in 1752 and *chakla* Sirhind (*subah* Delhi) in 1757, not only the Afghan empire had extended from Afghanistan to Karnal (*Chakla* Sirhind), a new administrative set up, both for the purposes of governance and realization of the revenue, had also been established.[18] The *chakla* Sirhind was detached from the Mughal *subah* of Delhi and put under the direct Durrani administration. The Afghan Rule, undoubtedly prior to the third battle of Panipat (January 1761) experienced considerably instability due to the Maratha operations and it is on the record that the Marathas were able to realize the revenues from the Punjab and the *cis*-Sutlej territories at least during the period April 1758 to October 1759.[19]

The defeat of the Marathas at the battle of Panipat (January 1761) paved the way for the regional forces leading to the rise of the power of Sikh Sardars. Based on kinship and local territorial proximity, many a *groh* of the Sardars were able to carve out territorial jurisdictions in various parts of the Punjab and also established superior *zamindari* rights. There followed a continual tug of war between the Durrani forces and the Sikh Sardars. Even though the contemporary Persian, Marathi, and English sources do not use the term *misl*[20], the establishment of such an institution under a Sardar fundamentally altered the character of armed struggle against the Durranis. The Sikh Sardars also claimed a share in the surplus produce from the traditional landed intermediaries and the local *zamindars.*[21] Moreover, in 1761, the management of the revenues and administration was vested with Mughal Amir-ul-Umra Bakshi-ul-Mulk Najib Khan Bahadur (Naijib-ud-daula) who acted as the *wakil* of the Durrani Government.[22]

Ala Singh was twenty-three years of age when his father died in 1714 and inherited a few villages—Barnala, Tapa and Tajo and half of Akalia. Ala Singh's wife (Bibi Fatto) belonged to village Kaleke, not a distant place from his own villages. He started founding villages on his own initiative and also with the support of his wife's relations. In 1722, Ala Singh rebuilt and shifted to Barnala.[23] This marks the beginning of his independent career and ultimately attained the position of one of the most distinguished Sikh Chiefs of his day. He was gallant, and at the same time prudent, and was responsible for laying the foundations of one of the most important of the *cis*-Sutlej States, and was probably the most powerful chief, south of the Sutlej. At the same time, as is evident from the contemporary records, he does not appear to have formed any intentions of an open revolt against the Mughal Government. All through his career, political expediency was the guiding principle of Ala Singh's apparently contradictory relations with different political powers. He was quite aware of the limitations of his own resources. That is why he consistently and readily temporized with all the powers of the day, and was successful in turning their presence in his neighbourhood to his own advantage.

The period, during which Sardar Ala Singh lived, was period of political instability. The Mughal Empire was at this time falling to decay, and could, with great difficulty, maintain its authority in the outlying areas beyond the river Jamuna. The Durranis, Sikhs and Marathas were making their best to take advantage of the prevailing situations. The only law that prevailed during this period was the law of force. The keen sword and strong hand were in great demand. Every village was being converted into a fort, built on a high mound to overlook the movements of the enemy forces. Every neighbour was synonymous with an enemy, and the cultivators ploughed their fields with their matchlocks by their sides. No man could consider his land, his horse, or his wife safe unless he was strong enough to defend them. Although the Sikh leaders were happy to capture the spoil of the Mughal Emperor or an imperial convoy, the historian like Griffin would say that "they were more robbers than patriots, and plundered with much impartiality...The *Jatni* girls had been taught to consider courage and strength the only qualities to desire in a husband and was quite ready to yield herself a prize to the man who had won her in fair fight, and who would make her his lawful wife, though he had killed her brothers and burnt their village."[23a] All that a Sikh chief asked, in those days from a follower, was a horse and a matchlock. All that a follower asked was protection and permission to plunder in the name of God and the Guru, under the banner of the chief.[24] Surprisingly, the movements of different political chiefs were seldom guided by any religious considerations and their friendships or enmities were all dictated by the exigencies of the moment.

The Mughal Emperor Muhammad Shah in his *Farman* dated 3rd June 1725 A.D. recognized Ala Singh as a *chaudhuri* and as a landed intermediary. He was reckoned as one of the chief *zamindars* responsible for the realization of the revenues from the territories (villages/*parganas*) assigned to him in *zamindari.* He was asked to take up residence at Sirhind, stamp out dacoity and turbulence as well as to safeguard the (trade) route from Lahore to Delhi. He was, as such, responsible for the maintenance of law and order in the Mughal territories. In lieu of these services, he enjoyed revenue free *jagir* lands as well as *Chaudhuri/Zamindari* perquisites. The *Farman* also ensured the subordination of the other *jagirdars* and Rajas to him and in lieu of services, also promised the conferment of the title of *rajgi* upon him.[25]

In an attempt to extend his influence further and in neighbouring areas Ala Singh, in 1731, defeated the combined forces of Asad Ali Khan, the *faujdar* of Jullunder and *zamindars* of Malerkotla, Halware and Malsian in the battle of Barnala. He, thus, attained a position of undisputed eminence in a region, which was rather far from Sirhind and Hissar, the important administrative centres of Mughal Government.[26] Barnala continued to serve as his headquarters for nearly twenty years.

It is significant to note that as *chaudhuri/zamindar* and also with hereditary rights over certain villages, Ala Singh was not independent of the government and was responsible to the Mughal *faujdar* of Sirhind, then Ali Muhammad, and a Rohilla Sardar. He was not only given authorization for the realization of the revenue of the assigned areas but was also to submit regular payments to the Mughal officials. His failure to do so before the invasion of Nadir Shah in 1738-39 and reluctance to do after that, brought him into conflict Ali Muhammad Rohilla in 1745. Ala Singh was detained for non-payments of the arrears of revenues since the invasion of Nadir Shah in the fortress of Sunam for nearly two years. In 1747, his supporters succeeded in securing his escape.[27]

As a result of the support provided by Ala Singh to the Mughals against the Afghans army under Ahmad Shah Abdali during the battle of Manupur in 1748, the Crown Prince Ahmad rewarded him with a robe of honour along with a caparisoned horse.[28] This recognition encouraged Ala Singh and his activities and began to extend his control over administrative units of the *Sarkars* of Sirhind and Hissar. Within less than a decade of the battle of Manupur, Ala Singh was successful in paralyzing the power of the Bhatti Chiefs (Allahadad Khan Bohewala, Inayat Khan and Vilayat Khan of Budhlada and Bahar Khan of Hariaho). The important towns like, Sunam, Samana, Sanaur and Tohana, were now occupied by the Sikh Sardar. The Bhattis were his most formidable rivals in the region. The Bhatti Chiefs did not halt their fight against Ala Singh and joined hands first with the Mughal *faujdar* of Hissar and then with Afghan *faujdar* of Sirhind. Ala Singh's loyalty was obviously to himself and his primary objective was to increase his own power, influence and territories for which he did hesitate to fight the Mughal *faujdar* of Hissar (defeated the combined forces of the *faujdar* of Hissar and Muhammad Amin Khan Bhatti in the battle of Khudal in 1755).[29]

With the occupation of the *cis*-Sutlej territories by Durranis in 1757, Ala Singh shifted his loyalties to the Durranis and accepted their sovereignty. He was not only combined with the position he had already been enjoying as the chief *zamindar* but was also bestowed larger territories (villages/*mahals*) for the revenue administration. He was now responsible to the Durrani administration of *chakla* Sirhind.[30] All the petty *zamindars, chaudharies* as well as the *qanungos* and the *ria'aya* in these territories were now obliged to serve him in the collection of the state revenues. Apart from the privileges conferred upon him, Ala Singh was equally responsible for the maintenance of law and order as well as safeguarding the interests of Durranis, both internally and externally.[31]

The records pertaining to the years 1761 and 1763 specially mention about an enhanced status of Ala Singh Jat. He was recognized as *zamindar* that had the *jagirs* in the category of *wukala-i-ali (jagir-i-wukala-i-ali)*. In other words the Durrani State appointed him as *wakil-i-ali* (chief representative). Moreover, the villages/*mahals/taluqas* assigned in *jagir* to Ala Singh were detached from the direct administrative jurisdiction of the *chakla* authorities (*subadar/faujdar/darogha* etc.) and put under the revenue administration of Ala Singh as the *jagirdar*. By March 1761 A.D., Ala Singh's *jagir* as the *zamindar* and *wakil-i-ali* comprised 726 villages from the *parganas* of Sunam, Gharam, Sanwar and Mansurpur and that not a single *en block (darobast) pargana* was assigned to him.[32]

After the great disaster (*Wadah Gahllughara,* 1762) and suppression of the Sikhs, Ala Singh was also arrested for having been in connivance with the former and was presented before Ahmad Shah Abdali at Lahore. However, on the intervention of Shah Wali Khan (the *Wazir*) he was pardoned on the plea that he was revenue paying chief *zamindar*. Ala Singh was to pay penalty of Rupees One lakh twenty five thousand. Moreover, having been reinstated in his *zamindari,* Rupees five lakh p.a. was fixed as *malia* for payment to the Durrani Chief.[33] About the further events, there are at least three different versions. Griffin is of the view that when Ala Singh was captured and taken before Ahmad Shah, a ransom of Four lakh of rupees was demanded for his life and the money was paid. Ahmad Shah thought it to be wiser to conciliate the Sikhs and being convinced of Ala Singh's power, embraced him and gave him a dress of honour, with the title of Raja (March 1762).[34] According to *Tarikh-i-Kunjpura,* Ala Singh gave six lakh of rupees to Shah Wali Khan and was bestowed the title of *rajgi* along with a *sanad* for the management of *chakla* Sirhind (as *faujdar*) by Huzur-i-Maulla-Ahmad Shah Abdali.[35] However, *Tarikh-i-Patiala* states that after Ala Singh took over the management of *chakla* Sirhind, he undertook to pay Rupees three and a half lakh as annual *malguzar* and was bestowed the *khillat* and the title of *rajgi* by Ahmad Shah Abdali. Out of the above amount, Ala Singh paid Rupees two lakhs and eighty thousand from Lahore by way of *hundis* to Kabul.[36] Moreover, regarding the conferring of title of 'Raja' on Sardar Ala Singh, different reasons have been put forth by the English writers. Joseph Davey Cunningham and Sir Lepel Henry Griffin are unanimous on the point that the Durranis wanted to follow the policy of conciliation. However, the former has asserted that behind this step the idea was to widen the differences between "a Malwa and a Majha Singh,"[37] Griffin, on the other hand, opined that through such type of peaceful means the Durrani Chief wanted to enlist at least some of them (Sikhs) on his side, "first against the Delhi Government and then against the Marathas."[38]

However, neither *Tarikh-i-Kunjpura* nor *Tarikh-i-Patiala* gives the year in which Ala Singh was bestowed with the title of *rajgi.* All the same one thing is quite clear from the available sources that by 1762 Ala Singh was in possession of *zamindari* with enhanced revenues than held by him earlier.

The honour given to Ala Singh by Ahmad Shah resulted in the jealousy and great indignation of the contemporary Sikh Sardars who "declared that he had betrayed them, and that the title was the price of his treachery; and it was unworthy for a Sikh to bear a title conferred by a Mohammedan, a foreigner, and an enemy."[39] Immediately, after Ahmad Shah returned to Kabul, the confederacies of the Sikh Sardars, both north and south of Sutlej, united to make one joint effort against Sirhind and Ala Singh also joined the expedition (December 1763). Ala Singh joined this expedition, as he wanted to prove by his actions that he was not a servant of the Durrani King. He wanted to clear his name and his character in the eyes of his fellow beings. Apparently, the confederacies, both north and south of the river Sutlej, at least for the time being, laid aside their feuds and jealousies, and united to make one great effort against Sirhind. Incidently, Sirhind had an important significance for the Sikhs, as it was here that the two sons of Guru Gobind Singh had been put to death by the orders of the Mughal Emperor. In this expedition Zain Khan, the *faujdar* of Sirhind was killed and his force utterly routed. The Sikh Sardars made over the town and the neighbourhood to Ala Singh.[40]

In 1764 Ahmad Shah again invaded India and did not experiment of placing another *faujdar* in Sirhind to succeed Zain Khan and entrusted the management of *chakla* Sirhind to Ala Singh (as *faujdar*). In lieu of the honour, Ala Singh paid Rs. Six lakhs, which apparently included both *nazarana* and *malia.* The total amount of the revenues (*jama*) of the entire *chakla* Sirhind was fixed at Rupees Eighteen lakhs, which also included some *cis*-Sutlej territories of same *talluqdars* who paid *nazrana/ malia* revenues directly to the Durrani State. Moreover, Ala Singh, after he had acquired the *Sanad* for appointment as *faujdar,* got the right to fix the revenues to be paid by other *zamindars.* During another campaign (1765) the revenues of *chakla* Sirhind was effected and Ala Singh under took to pay Rupees Eight lakh as *muamala-i-muqarrari* to Durrani states. It may here be pointed out that *muamala-i-muqarrari* was always subject to revision. It was based upon actual seasonal assessment of the crops (*fasl ba fasl*) and revenues realized (*hal-i-hasil*) after having taken into consideration the remission afforded on account of calamities (*aft*) and the *zamindari* perquisites of Ala Singh and other *zamidars.*[41] Raja Ala Singh accompanied Ahmad Shah on his return journey as far as Lahore, and then returned to Patiala, where he died in August 1765. Before his death, Ala Singh had founded a new capital, Patiala, at the centre of possessions, which henceforth were to serve as the core dominions of his successors.

There are certain important aspects of Ala Singh's career, which need our careful attention to assess the power, position and achievements made by him.

The institutional relationship for the payment of *muamla/peshkash* on the part of the Patiala chiefs (as *zamindars*) to the Durrani state continued during the periods of Maharaja Amar Singh and to lesser degree even of Raja Sahib Singh all through eighteenth century.[42]

One of the symbols of the extension of Ala Singh's power was the system of *rakhi* adopted by him. The exact details of this system are not clear from the available evidence. However, some of the English writers have asserted that *rakhi* was regularly levied in the areas which the Sikhs subdued but did not annex to their territories, and the amount of *rakhi* varied from about "a fifth to a half of the rental or government share of the produce."[43] What was implied in *rakhi* was "protection" against other individuals or authorities. Ala Singh could not offer it before he had come to command sufficient force to meet the counter claims of his rivals or opponents. *Rakhi* also implied certain concessions to "the protected", including possibly a lenient collection of revenues. Ala Singh's ability to afford effective protection and his leniency would partly explain the popularity of this system amongst a considerable number of peasantry in the region. The system was also suitable to Ala Singh as it required no direct assumption of administrative control.[44] The collection of *rakhi* has been rightly clubbed with the Maratha system of the collection of *Chauth.* As a matter of fact, *rakhi, chauth* and *peshkash* are all synonymous terms and have the same meaning. It was an established practice of the Mughals to collect *peshkash* or tribute from the protected areas.[45] It had been a general practice in the medieval age that a budding political power establishing its chieftainship by bringing certain areas under its direct administration, would attempt to establish its overlordship on some neighbouring or even far flung regions. It may or may not be a preclude to the attainment of supremacy in those regions. The establishment of overlordship would invariably result into the demand of share in the revenue of areas. The percentage/amount thus demanded, despite having common nomenclature varied and depended upon the geographical situation of the areas, position of the submitting chief and the extent to which the subduing power could not exert continuous pressure for maintaining sustained submission. Sometimes, a well-established political power would also allow the erstwhile chief of a newly acquired territory to retain a fixed percentage/portion of the revenues of the areas. Moreover, the idea of the establishment of protectorate was also current and powerful rulers used to take tribute, *nazrana* or *muamla* before annexing a particular territory or not annexing it at all, as the case might be. The payment or allowance made by an inferior to a superior power, and superior to an inferior or even a subordinate in consideration of ones political authority or services or the nuisance value was an accepted norm during the period. No doubt in ancient India also such type of examples could be traced. A levy called *bali* or *deya,* which apart from other meanings, also, meant 'the tribute to a king' was received from the subdued rulers and people. It could be a fixed cash payment or even in the forms of fruits etc. payable regularly for a definite period. An area would be exempted from the payments of *bali* or *deya* by the King's order or after annexing it and collecting regular revenue known as *bhaga.*[46] The transactions of the above mentioned dues had been carried on in the course of the Indian history under different nomenclatures though with certain variations in the matter of details. Apart from the two possible names *bali* and *deya* in ancient India, during the medieval period, when the collection/payment seems to have become more widespread, several names, *viz., peshkash, nazrana, muamla, banth, malikana, do-biswi, chauth, rakhi, kaveli russom* and *karah parshad*[47] have been ascribed to these transactions. Apart from the *rakhi/nazrana, Dal Khalsa* of Sardar Jassa Singh Ahluwalia, as well as other Sikh Sardars, after successful incursions realized dues in the lieu of *karah parshad* from the Patiala chieftainship as well as the Durrani and Mughal territories of Jamuna-Ganga *doab.* This realization could be with or without the *rakhi/nazrana.* The amount which was fixed after taking into consideration the total realized revenues of the area concerned, could be paid either in lump sum or in installments as per the settlement.[48] It is a different matter that in regard to the percentage of the state demand thus demanded, the division of the money thus collected and in other details, there was, of course, no similarity. This would depend upon the various circumstances and there could be variations in the same system. All the same, it is correct that the Sikh Sardars had followed the Mughal practice and had not invented anything new.[49] The term *rakhi* has been described by the English writers as "blackmail"[50] and have described the Sikh Sardars as "robbers"[51], "committing depredation" and "highway robbery"[52] It is right when they club the collection of *rakhi* with the Maratha system of the collection of *chauth,* but it is wrong on their part to describe both of them as "blackmail". In this regard it can safely be pointed out that this is a concept usually used from the imperialist viewpoint. Whenever, the revolting *zamindars* or Sardars realized the revenue of a particular area after occupation, from the imperialist angle it was described as plunder, loot, pillage, etc. It is true about the Mughal description about the Marathas and the British description about the Sikh Sardars in the Punjab and the palegars in the South India.[53]

Some of the contemporary Persian records are evident to the fact that the Sikh Sardars used to realize dues in lieu of *Karah Parshad* from the Patiala chiefs/*zamindars,* the *faujdars* of *Chakla* Sirhind under Durrani rule, as well as the Mughal territories of Jamuna-Ganga *doab* (*chakla* Saharanpur).[54] At the time Ala Singh occupied *qasba* Sirhind along with a few villages, he paid an amount of Rupees Twenty five thousand on account of *Karah Parshad.* In certain circumstances the *Karah Parshad* could also be equated with *nazrana* or *muamala.*[55]

However, Ala Singh was seldom guided by any religious considerations. This contention can be very well understood by his attitudes towards the other Sikh Sardars, as well as the Mughals, the Marathas and the Afghans. Political expediency was the guiding principle of Ala Singh's relations with the contemporary political powers. His political friendship was dictated by the exigencies of the moment. Unless the basic trait of Ala Singh's political outlook are clearly understood, we the students of history are likely to misunderstand his attitude towards contemporary leaders of the *Khalsa.* They were inspired by purely political motives in their attempts to form their respective kingdoms. The use of religion, whenever made, however, denoted popular regional feelings current during seventeenth-eighteenth centuries. They resorted to persuation and suppression for welding together of scattered elements of their community. Moreover, to attribute religion as the dominant factor either with the Sikh or for that matter the contemporary Maratha movement, or with Sikh or Maratha Chiefs' military leadership, and to attribute the attempt to create Sikh/Hindu state as a counter blast against Islam, or against Muslim monarchs' religious intolerance is to overlook their great military and political gift and qualities of opportunism for creating their respective new states.[56]

The contemporary documents reveal that the incursions of Sikhs (*Sikhan*) or Singhs (*Singhan*) in his territories (*Chakla* Sirhind), Ala Singh used these terms (*Sikhan* and *Singhan*) with utter contempt. It suggests that in the 18th century, the term Sikh or a group of Sikhs did not essentially connote belonging to a particular religious faith. Both Raja Ala Singh and Maharaja Amar Singh were the followers of the Gurus and had been even baptized after performance of the ceremony of *Pahul.*[57] It seems the Sikhs and *Singhan* denoted those militant followers of the *Nanak Panth* and Guru Gobind Singh who had taken to arms against the Mughals or the

Durranis for the vindication of their religious rights and temporal power. Both Raja Ala Singh and Maharaja Amar Singh, while narrating their difficulties due to the activities of the Sikhs, have used very contemptuous words about them. They described the large groups or troupes of the Sikhs as 'contemptible' (*amboh-I-groh-i-nakbat pizhuh*) or 'large number of wretched infidel troupes (Sikhs) destined to be vanquised, (*groh-i-amboh-I-maghurran shagwat pizhuh*) or 'vanquishable infidels' (*maghurran, jama-i-maghur* or *jumhur-i-maghur*) or 'multitude of the Sikh troups—the infidels destined to the vanquished' (*ma'al jamai Sikhan Shakwat mishan*) or the contemptible and infidel armies destined for utter destruction (*magahir nakbat*), 'mean', 'vagrants', 'rioters' and 'impious groups.'[58] As a matter of fact, in the medieval period, the adversaries were usually mentioned with contempt and the adjectives used for them were rather derogatory in character. It is a question of terminology used for the activities the Sikhs, the Marathas, and the Palegars. Actually they all were fighting for a cause.[59]

The information provided by some of the sources, especially *Tarikh-i-Patiala* and *Jang Namah* have tried to make us convinced that Ala Singh became virtually a sovereign ruler by the early 1760's. According to *Tarikh-i-Patiala,* Ahmed Shah Abdali recognized Ala Singh as the ruler of over seven hundred villages, independent of the jurisdiction of the Afghan Governor of Sirhind.[60] Whereas according to *Jang Namah,* Ahmad Shah invested him with a *Khillat,* Kettle drums, and banners, and installed him in the independent chieftainship of Sirhind.[61]

The conferment of the title of Raja to Ala Singh or even *Raja-i-Rajgan* (Maharaja) to Amar Singh was compatible with *zamindari* pattern of administration. The titles only recognized the services rendered by the chiefs to the Durrani State. Timur Shah's *Farman* dated 11 *Rajab* AH 1192/5 August 1778 recognized the services rendered by *Raja-i-Rajgan* Amar Singh to the Durranis and also clearly shows that apart from the Patiala Chief, the other Rajas in the *cis*-Sutlej territories equally owed allegiance to the Durrani sovereign.[62] In the eighteenth century, apart from Sardar Ala Singh, some of the other Sikh Sardars were able to establish *de facto* power over some of the areas of Punjab. However, the *Durranis always claimed the de jure political sovereignty.* They continued to appoint their own *subahdar*/administrators/*vakeel* in different parts of Punjab and *cis*-Sutlej territories for general political control, more so for the realization of the revenues. It is a different matter that they could do so with varying success. There were times when they were either not able to collect that full revenue or not in all the regions. Sardar Ala Singh and even Maharaja Amar Singh were not the sovereign or independent chiefs but only *vakeel* and *zamindar*-cum-*jagirdar.* The *cis*-Sutlej territories were formally ceded by the Mughal state to Ahmed Shah Durrani in 1757 A.D. and in 1761, Durrani *wazir-i-mumalik* recognized Ala Singh as one of the administrators of *chakla* Sirhind. The nature of *Chaudhuri-zamindari, faujdari* and *jagir* assignments bestowed on him in the named villages was also specified.[63] In 1764, Sardar Ala Singh was conferred the powers of *naib-faujdar/faujdar* in two *parganas* and was well entrusted with the collection of the revenues therein on the payment of stipulated amount to the Durrani government.[64] Despite the titles, both Sardar Ala Singh and Maharaja Amar Singh were representatives of the Durrani state, in other words the royal authority. They were to uphold the legitimacy of Durrani sovereignty in the *cis*-Sutlej territories. It may here be pointed out that despite the capture of Lahore by Sardar Jassa Singh Ahluwalia/ Sikhs (1758 A.D.) and their incessant campaigns and incursions in the *cis*-Sutlej and Haryana territories (*subah* Delhi), regular *subedars* (of *subahs* Lahore, Multan and Kashmir), *faujdars* and *vakeels* were appointed by the Durranis. The contemporary Persian records preserved in Punjab State Archives, Patiala; grant of *madid-i-maash* and *aima* grants on behalf of the Durrani Kings (original preserved in Patiala and Chandigarh); Sheikh Rahim Ali's *Tarikh-i-Manzal-i-Kabul;* and above all, some of the coins preserved in the Moti Bagh Palace, Patiala[65] are some of the irrefutable evidences.[66] It would certainly not be necessary for the Durrani rulers to come to India every time for the collection of the revenues when they had their own representatives in the form of *subedars* and *vakeels* etc. Even the collection of the *rakhi* by the Sikh Sardars in these areas would hardly mean any evidence proving the establishment of their sovereignty in those areas. *The Calendar of Persian Correspondence* also vouch for the fact that Shah not only claimed political sovereignty but also realized *peshkash* in the Mughal patterns.[67] However, in *cis*-Sutlej areas there were some brief phases when the Sikh Sardars never paid any revenues from the local Durrani administration itself. Otherwise like the Mughals, the Durranis State equally claimed and exercised the right to decrease or increase or even confiscate the *zamindari* possessions. The Patiala Chieftain as the chief *zamindar* in lieu of his services and status enjoyed precedence in the hierarchical *zamindari* pattern in *chakla* Sirhind. The Durrani Government at Kabul was apparently in correspondence with chiefs and kept itself fully informed about the political developments through the second half of the eighteenth century. Letters written by Raja Ala Singh and Maharaja Amar Singh as faithful *zamindars* and representatives of the Durrani State confirm the traditional tone representing the royal authority and legitimacy of Durrani sovereignty. It was Maharaja Ranjit Singh who, after the occupation of Lahore in 1799, realized the necessity of expelling the Afghans from the different territories for the establishment of his sovereignty and consolidation of his power. The credit of ousting the Durranis from the Punjab goes to Maharaja Ranjit Singh when he ousted them during the closing years of the eighteenth century and the first two decades of the nineteenth century (1799-1819), and conquered Multan (January 1818), Peshawar (November 1818) and Kashmir (July 1819) [68], and the English East India Company which eventually ousted the Durrani influence and established its own protectorate over the Chieftains of the *cis*-Sutlej territories by the early 19th century.[69] However, it is extremely doubtful that Ala Singh ever took his vassalage seriously. The *de jure* appearances were immaterial so long as he could possess the *de facto* power in his own hands.

References

Note:— I am highly grateful to Professor B.R. Grover former Chairman I.C.H.R. for allowing me to utilize some of the most important Persian records/works, along with the translations done by him and helping me in their interpretation.

1. Dua, J.C., *British Historiography Eighteenth Century Punjab: Their understanding of the Sikh struggle for the power and role of Jassa Singh Ahluwalia,* New Delhi, 1992, p. vii.
2. *Ibid.* p. 1.
3. *Ibid.* p. vii.
4. *Ibid.* p. 2; also Grover, B.R. 'Presidential Address', *Punjab History Conference,* XIX session, 1985, p. 8.
5. *Ibid.* p. 3, 6. Also, Punjab State Archives, (Patiala) Mirza Muhammad Mehndi, *Tarikh-jahan Kusha-i-Nadiri,* (completed in 1757 A.D.) No. M/716, fols. 148b-191b; 197 a-b.
6. Nur Muhammad, Qazi, *Jang Namah,* edited by Ganda Singh, Khalsa College, Amritsar, 1939. Also see, Kirpal Singh, *Maharaja Ala Singh of Patiala,* Khalsa College, Amritsar, 1954, p. 150.
7. A *chakla* was a territorial division and was often identical with a *sarkar,* but in general a *chakla* was a smaller unit than a *sarkar.* In Bengal, however, a *chakla* consisted of a group of *sarkars* in the eighteenth century. Alam, Muzaffar, *The Crisis of Empire in Mughal North India: Awadh and the Punjab, 1707-48,* Delhi, 1986, p. 33n. During the Mughal period, the *faujdar* was in charge of the *sarkar* administration. With the formation of *chakla,* comprising numerous *sarkars/parganas,* the *faujdar* remained the administrative in charge of the *chakla.* He was usually vested with the functions of *amin.* The office was, however, considered distinct and subordinate to *nazim/subadar* of a *subah. Sarkar/Chakla* Sirhind formed a part of *subah* Delhi. The position of *chakla* Sirhind remained the same prior to the Durrani campaigns or rather till 1757 when it was ceded to the Durrani emperor. Many modern scholars use the designation of governor for the *faujdar/amin* of Sirhind, which is rather loose in expression. Dua, J.C., *op. cit.* pp. 124-125.
8. Ala Singh was one of the six sons—Duna, Subha, Ala Singh, Bakhta, Ladha and Dudha of Sardar Rama. Ala Singh was not the eldest son but the third, and

Duna, the eldest one would have been the head of the family, had primogeniture been then the rule. Sardar Phul had three sons, Tilokha, Rama, and Raghu and one daughter Rani Ram Kaur from his second wife Rajji. Griffin, Lepel H., *The Rajas of the Punjab being The History of the Principal States in the Punjab and their Political Relations with the British Government.* 1873, reprint 1970, Patiala, pp. 7-15.

9. *Fall of the Mughal Empire,* vol. ii (1754-1771), Calcutta, 1934.

10. *History of the Sikhs, (1739-99),* vol. I, *Evaluation of the Sikh Confederacies, (1739-68),* revised ed. Simla, 1952; vol. ii: *cis-Sutlej Sikhs,* Lahore, 1944; *Marathas and Panipat,* Punjab University, Chandigarh, 1951.

11. *New History of the Marathas,* vol. ii, *The Expansion of the Maratha Power,* Bombay, 1948.

12. *Ahmed Shah Durrani, Father of Modern Afghanistan,* Bombay, 1959; *Sardar Jassa Singh Ahluwalia* (Punjabi), Punjabi University, Patiala, 1969.

13. *Maharaja Ala Singh of Patiala and His Times,* Amritsar, 1954.

14. *Baba Ala Singh,* Patiala, 1918.

15. *Sikh Polity in the Eighteenth and Nineteenth Centuries,* New Delhi, 1978.

16. *Sikh Polity and Sikh Institutions,* New Delhi, 1979.

17. However, with the notable exceptions, (I) B.R. Grover, 'An Analysis of the Contemporary Durrani Revenue Documents and Correspondence Pertaining to the Patiala Chieftainship (Zamindari) during the Later Half of the 18th century', *Punjab Past and Present,* Vol. XXIV—I April 1990, pp. 196-233; and (ii) Dua, J.C., *British Historiography Eighteenth Century Punjab: There understanding of the Sikh struggle for power and role of Sardar Jassa Singh Ahluwalia,* Delhi, 1992; 'The British understanding of the Sikh Struggle for power during the 18th century, *Punjab Past and Present,* Vol. XXIV-1 April 1990.

18. *Selections from the Peshwa Daftar,* ed. G.S. Sardesai. II, p. 71; XXI. Letters No. 53 and 55. Punjab State Archives, Patiala, copies of *Farmans, Sanads* vide Register D1 fols. 20a, 22b-23b. These records indicate that henceforth in the territories of *chakla* Sirhind, all *sanads* relating to the land grants, fresh or renewed, in respect of *madad-i-maash* and *aimma* were issued under the seal of Ahmad Shah Durrani.

19. Tahmas Khan Miskin, *Kitab-i-Qissa-Tahmas Miskin* (popularly known as *Tazkira-i-Tahmas Miskin*) written in 1780, fols. 83b-90a. Mufti Ali-ud-Din, *Ebratnamah* (*Ebratnamah wa Umadut-ul-Tawarikh*), 1854, Ed. By Muhammad Baqir, Lahore, 2 vols. 1961, pp. 218-23. Also, B.R. Grover, *op. cit.* pp. 211-12.

20. The *misl* denoted a group of Sikhs under the leadership of a prominent Sardar. The *misls* were both big and small in size. As such, there was no uniformity in their territorial extent. The character of the *misl* was not essentially clannish and the Sikhs or the other castes were free to join it with all rights and obligations on their part. The *misl* was generally associated with a locality or a caste rather than with a particular Sardar. Despite being cohesive in character, there was no bar on any influential member to leave a *misl* on the death of the Sardar and form an independent *misl* of his own. However, the end of the eighteenth century witnessed the principle of heredity gaining ground for the assumption of *Sardari* of the *misl.* Moreover, for the specific military campaign a few *misldars,* though without any permanent allegiance, would combine under the leadership of a *misldar,* denominated as a Chief Sardar. The acquired

territories, the amount of revenues, and *rakhi* was divided by the *misldars* in proportion to their respective military strength and the effective military service rendered. However, this allegiance, being purely temporary, could be transferred from one to another Chief Sardar. Dua, J.C., *op.cit.;* B.R. Grover, 'General President Address', *Punjab History Conference Proceedings,* 19th Session, March 22-24, 1985, Patiala.

21. Asar Nayaz, *Tarikh-i-Kunjpura* (written in 1823 A.D.) ed. Muhammad Baqar, Lahore, 1973, pp. 87-94.

22. In this regard it may be pointed out that after him, even *wakil-i-mutalik* Najaf Khan (d. 1782) as well as the Marathas as *wakil-i-mutalik* (Mahadaji Sindhia w.e.f. November 1784) of the Mughal State continued to discharge this responsibility on behalf of the Durrani Government.

23. Karam Singh, *Baba Ala Singh,* Patiala, 1918, pp. 79, 82, 107-8; Kirpal Singh, *Maharaja Ala Singh of Patiala,* Khalsa College, Amritsar, 1954, pp. 34, 36, 77 and 86. However, Griffin has written, "In 1718 he left Bhadour to his elder brother Duna, and rebuilt Barnala, which had fallen into ruins, and where he took up his residence," Griffin, *op. cit.,* p. 15.

23a. Griffin, *op. cit.,* p. 17.

24. *Ibid.,* pp. 16-17.

25. Punjab State Archive, Patiala, Document No. D142-A Mughal *Farman* dated 21 *Ramazan,* A.H. 1137/3 June 1725 A.D.; Also *Tarikh-i-Patiala* by Khalifa Sayyid Muhammad Hasan (Prime Minister Of Patiala State), Safir Hind Press, Amritsar, 1878, pp. 44-45. The latter work confirms that the *Farman* was conveyed to Ala Singh through Mir Mannu (son of Qamar-ud-Din Khan) and Samai Yar Khan.

26. Kirpal Singh, *op. cit.,* pp. 49.

27. *Ibid.* pp. 59-66. However, the circumstances leading to Ala Singh's detention in the fort of Sunam are not very clear. It appears that he was detained there as a hostage and his family was made to pay. But there is no reason to suppose that they were rendered destitute. It is likely that his sons and associates had, in his absence, kept his possessions largely intact. For after Ala Singh escaped from the fort of Sunam, he was helping Mughal armies encamped near Manupur. There is another version given by Griffin. He writes, "... Ali Muhammad Khan, a Hindu convert of Rampur in Rohilkhand, who had been adopted by a Mohammedan officer and who, founded a Rohilla State in the country between the upper Ganges and the hills. In 1741, however, Ali Muhammad was a servant of the Empire, and had charge of the sub-division of Sirhind. Ala Singh accompanied him on several expeditions...But the Sikh Chief was too independent to be long in good terms with any Imperial Officer; and he soon saw that his residence at the Court of Ali Muhammad would be dangerous, and asked for his dismissal. This the Governor refused, arrested him and threw into prison..." Griffin, *op. cit.* p. 19.

28. Kirpal Singh, *op. cit,* p. 70.

29. *Ibid.* pp. 53-54, 79-83, 88-90.

30. Punjab State Archives, Patiala, Foreign Ministry Case 2A/147 of 1174 A.H. *Sacred Documents pertaining to the reign of Shri 108 Maharaja Baba Ala Singh Surgbashi,* Document No. 2A/147(E) of 1174 A.H., dated 22 Shaban A.H. 1174/29, March, 1761 A.D. Also, see B.R. Grover, *op. cit.,* p. 216.

31. *Tarikh-i-Kunjpura, op. cit.,* p. 78.
32. *Sacred Documents... op. cit., taliqachas* (orders) of Shah Wali Khan, the Durrani Prime Minister, Documents no. 2A/147 (A) dated 22 *Shaban* A.H. 1174/29 March 1761 A.D. and 2A(C) dated *Shaban* A.H. 1174/12 Feb. 1763 A.D. It seems that after annexation, the Durrani government had recognized many a chief *zamindar* as its chief representatives (*wukala-i-ali*) and clearly demarcated areas assigned in *jagirs* to them under the category *jagir-i-wukala-i-ali.*
33. *Ebratnamah, op. cit.,* p. 230.
34. Griffin, *op. cit.,* p. 24.
35. *Tarikh-i-Kunjpura, op. cit,* p. 78.
36. *Tarikh-i-Patiala, op. cit.,* p. 62.
37. Cunningham, Joseph Davey, *A History of the Sikhs from the Origin of the Nation to the Battles of the Sutlej* (edited by H.L.O Garrett with an additional notes by R.R. Sethi), Delhi, 1955, 'Author's Preface to the Second Edition', p. xxvii
38. Griffin, *op. cit.,* p. 24.
39. *Ibid.*
40. *Ibid.* p. 25.
41. *Tarikh-i-Kunjpura,* p. 78-79; *Tarikh-i-Patiala,* p. 62; *Sacred Documents...op. cit.* Document No. 2A/147 (G). Also see B.R. Grover, *op. cit.* pp. 221-2.
42. B.R. Grover, *op. cit,* p. 222.
43. Cunningham, *op. cit.,* p. 95.
44. Kirpal Singh, *op. cit,* pp. 45, 144, 184.
45. B.R. Grover (Ed.), *The Punjab Polity during the Eighteenth Century (Role of Sardar Jassa Singh Ahluwalia),* New Delhi, 1991 (in Punjabi) pp. 9-40.
46. Traces of this type of levy can be found during Mauryan and Satawahna periods. As a matter of fact, King's revenue consisted of *bali s'ulka* (tolls etc.) and *bhaga.* Sircar, D.C., *Studies in the Political and Administrative Systems in Ancient and Medieval India.* Delhi, 1974, pp. 5-6.
47. A ceremonial sweet made of *Suji/Atta* and distributed as *Prasad* in the *Gurudwara* at the end of the Prayer.
48. For the imposition/realization of *rakhi, karah parshad* and *nazrana/mu'amala* by the Sikh Sardar, see J.N. Sarkar tr,. *Persian Records of Maratha History I: Delhi Affairs: (1761-1788) News Letters (from Persian Collection),* Bombay, 1953, A7-Delhi News Letters dated 24th January 1770, pp. 19-20, A10-(Delhi) News Letter to Peshwa, 20th May, 1770, p. 23 and A56 b-17th April, Second sheet; 13, 6b—Letters to Nana Sahib Shrimat, C 28th February, pp. 93 and 119 respectively; P. Saran (ed.), *Persian Documents,* Bombay 1966, p. 370.
49. Dua J.C., *op. cit.,* pp. 113-15.
50. Cunningham, *op. cit.,* p. 95.
51. Browne, Major James, *Indian Tracts: History of the Origin and Progress of the Sikhs.* London, 1788, p. 13.
52. Prinsep, Henrey T., *Origin of the Sikh Power in the Punjab and Political life of Maharaja Ranjit Singh with an Account of the Religion, Laws and Customs of the Sikhs.* 1834, reprint Patiala, 1970, pp. 2-3,7.
53. Dua J.C., *op. cit.* p. 115.

54. *Persian Records of Maratha History I: Delhi Affairs: (1761-1788) NewsLetters From Persian Collection,* Dr. J.N. Sarkar, Bombay, 1953, A7—Delhi News Letter, dated 24th January 1770, pp. 19-20.

55. *Ebratnamah, op. cit.,* p. 233.

56. Dua J.C., *op. cit.,* p. 110.

57. *Tarikh-i-Patiala, op. cit.* pp. 58, 65.

58. Punjab State Archives, Patiala, *Foreign Ministry Case,* no. 5A/H, *folios* 2a-3b, 1a-2a, 3b-5a, 6b-7a, 8a-8b. It may be stated that these letters were got translated in English by Patiala Darbar and a verified version of the same dated 1.12.1952 have been appended to the above Ms. Under title '*Copies of Letters from Raja Alha Singh and Amar Singh to Shah Vali Khan of Kabul 1765-66 A.D.*' Also see B.R. Grover, *op. cit.* No. 17, and Dua J.C. *op. cit.* pp. 115-116.

59. J.C. Dua, 'Sir Lepel H. Griffin on Sardar Jassa Singh Ahluwalia and his Place in Eighteenth century Punjab History', *Punjab History conference*, XXI, session, 1987, pp. 118-18.

60. *Tarikh-I-Patiala, op. cit.,* pp. 58, 65.

61. *Jang Namah,* p. 160.

62. Punjab State Archives, Patiala, *Farman,* No. D—143 dated 11 *Rajab* AH 1192/ 5 August 1778 issued by Timur Shah to *Raja-i-Rajgan* Raja Patiala Amar Singh.

63. Punjab State Archives, Patiala, *Foreign Ministry Case 2A/147 of 1174 A.H.,* document number 2A/147 (A) dated 22 *Shabnam* A.H. 1174/29th March 1761 A.D. Also see B.R. Grover, *op. cit.,* 17.

64. *Ibid.,* Document number 2A/147 (D), dated 2 *Safar* A.H. 1178/1st August 1764 A.D. and document number 2A/147 (F) dated 17 *Safar* A.H. 1178/16th August 1764.

65. Some of the contemporary Persian records vouch for the fact that even till 1798 A.D. the coins of the Shah (Durrani) were current in the family of Maharaja Amar Singh at Patiala and "Whosoever succeeds to the throne issues the same coins in his country and considers himself as a subject of the Durrani Emperor." The eighteenth century currency issued under the Durrani rule is still available in the collection of the coins exhibited at Moti Bagh Palace, Patiala. *Tarikh-I-Patiala, op. cit.* pp. 75-76; Ganda Singh, *Ahmed Shah Durrani, Father of Modern Afghanistan.* Bombay, 1959, pp. 371-72; *Persian Documents,* ed. P. Saran, Bombay, 1966, p. 398.

66. B.R. Grover, *op. cit.,* 17.

67. *Calendar of Persian Correspondence,* ii, 1767-69, Persian Correspondence, February 17th, 1767, pp. 26-27 and April 8th, 1767, p. 8. 79, paper of news, p. 26; and 279, from Raja Shitab Roy, p. 84.

68. B.R. Grover, 'Relationship between the Sovereign State (the Mughals and Afghans) and Punjab Hill Chiefs during the 17th and 18th centuries (A case study of Chamba Chieftainship based on Bhuri Singh Museum, Chamba Documents)', *Punjab History Conference,* 16th session, March 1982, Patiala, pp. 94-102; and '*Nuskha-I-Insha-I-Majmua al Quwanin,* ' *Punjab History Conference,* 21st session, March 1987, pp. 138-150; Sheikh Rahim Ali, *Tarikh-I-Manzal-I-Kabul, op. cit.,* Questions and Answers 4, 13, 14, 21, 22.

69. *Tarikh-i-Kunjpura, op. cit.* pp. 112-115; National Archives of India, New Delhi, *Political Consultations* 11th September 1803, Mughal Emperor Shah Alam

accepted the "protection of the British government", (ii) in pursuance of the Anglo-Maratha Treaty of Surji Arjan Gaon dated 30th December 1803, the Marathas withdrew from the Jamuna—Ganges Doab and the Delhi—Agra region along the river Jamuna; and (iii) Maratha Chief Jaswant Rao Holker not only failed in his assault on Delhi on 8th October 1804 but also in his negotiations for eliciting support from the Chiefs of the *cis*-Sutlej territories and Maharaja Ranjit Singh against the East India Company. These events encouraged its protectorate; Punjab State Archives, Patiala, Document no. 144, Letter form Mr. Seton, Resident, Delhi to Maharaja Sahib Singh dated 21st November 1808. In this letter Seton mentioned about the protection of *cis*-Sutlej territories by the English East India Company and same was intimated to Maharaja Ranjit Singh; also Spear, *A History of Delhi Under the Later Mughals.* 1937, reprint Delhi 1988, pp. 35-36.

3

Sir Lepel Henry Griffin on Sardar Jassa Singh Ahluwalia and his Place in Eighteenth Century Punjab History

The main purpose of this paper is to critically assess and analyse the motives and approach of Sir Lepel Henry Griffin towards the comparative role played by various Sikh Sardars and more especially Sardar Jassa Singh Ahluwalia who was able to establish the Fatehabad-Kapurthala State in Majha and Jalandhar Doab regions of the Punjab.

G.S.N.

Sardar Jassa Singh Ahluwalia has a unique place in a period of turmoil and turbulence in the history of eighteenth century Punjab. This period witnessed the disintegration of the Mughal Empire, the foreign campaigns of Nadir Shah and the Durranis, the emergence of the Marathas, the attempts made by the Rohillas, Rajputs, Jats and the Afghans to establish their respective regional government and above all the rise of the Sikh Sardars who confronted not only the political powers, especially, that of the Mughals and the Durranis, but were able to carve out their own independent or semi-independent territories (*Zamindaries*) for the purposes of revenue realization and administration.[1] Even though in the recent years, scholarly works have been produced on the eighteenth century Punjab Polity,[2] there is still a considerable scope for undertaking micro-scopic study of activities, territorial set-up and achievements of the Sikh Sardars who, to a considerable extent, were primarily responsible for the liberation of the Punjab from the Durrani occupation. Apart from the Sikh organisation of the informal confederacy or *sarbat Khalsa* and execution of its plans through the decisions called *gurmatas* and their implementation with the help of the armed units, the (*dal Khalsa*), the twentieth century writings have equally emphasised the *misl* system. The British historians of the late eighteenth century and the period of

---

Paper presented at *Punjab History Conference*, Patiala, 1987.

Maharaja Ranjit Singh, even when they offer detailed description of the activities of the eighteenth century Sikh Sardars on regional basis, do suffer from some limitation owing either to their own prejudices or the ethnic complexities prevalent at the time. It is rather interesting to trace the historiographical trends in this regard, more especially when, by this time, we are also in possession of the archival source material for the eighteenth century as well as for the first half of the nineteenth century before the British occupation of the Punjab.

Sir Henry Lepel Griffin, the administrator historian, ranks quite high among the writers of the same category like Charles Aitchison, W.H. Hunter, Alfred Lyall, F.J. Stephan and Henry Maine, though the former, by and large, concentrated on the history of the Punjab and the Sikhs covering the period of their immediate past. His appointment in the Punjab in various capacities for a number of years, including as Assistant Commissioner and then Chief Secretary in the Punjab and Superintendent of the Kapurthala State[3] provided him an opportunity to know and write about the Punjab and the Sikhs.

Griffin's notable works on the Punjab include : (1) *The Punjab Chiefs : The historical and biographical notices of the principal families in the territories under the Punjab Government:* Lahore, 1865; (2) *The Law of Inheritance of Chiefships as observed by the Sikhs previous to the Annexation of the Punjab,* Lahore, 1869; (3) *The Rajas of the Punjab: Being the History of the Principal States in the Punjab and their Political Relations with the British Government,* Lahore, 1870; and (4) *Ranjit Singh,* Oxford, 1892.

The nature of Griffin's writings on Sikh history illustrates a mixture of his possession of historical vision coupled with biographical style and his own thinking and views. Despite his denial, most of Griffin's works are mainly biographical in style. Apart from attempting to quench the ever increasing thirst of the English to acquire knowledge about the people and the history of the Punjab, Griffin has tried to offer a convincing reply to hostile criticism on the British Policy towards the *cis* and trans-Sutlaj territories.[4]

Besides consulting the books written on the Punjab and the Sikhs by the English and the Indian writers, Griffin, since he wrote his first book in as late as 1865, had enough sources at his command. He consulted the official Records including *Official Correspondence; Political Records of Government,* and of the *Agencies of Delhi, Ambala and Ludhiana; Punjab Land Revenue Settlement Reports;* and his interviews with the chieftains and members of aristocracy, their family and state records. Moreover, commenting on the availability of records, he says, "The material for an historical record of the seventy two years which this period covers (1708-1780) is meagre and unreliable so far as the Manjha Sikhs are concerned."[5]

Griffin's three books viz., *The Punjab Chiefs; The Rajas of the Punjab;* and *Ranjit Singh,* provide a vivid account of the activities of the Sikhs and different Sikh sardars during the 18th Century; their mutual relations and *vis-a-vis* the Mughals and the Durranis. Among the other Sikh sardars, Sardar Jassa Singh Ahluwalia, contrary to the books of other English writers, has been discussed in greater details and, as such, has figured quite prominently in the books of Griffin.

Like other eighteenth and nineteenth century British historians, Griffin is also of the view that every man who had energy and courage gathered a band of marauders around him and plundered the country[6], seizing and holding whatever land he could.[7] But he has also defended their activities especially against the Muhammadans "who had so long trampled them under foot, who had killed their prophets and thrown down their altars, gave them a certain dignity, and to their objects and expeditions an almost national interest."[8] At the same time, the Sikhs bore no love to the Afghans as well for former had no wish to aid the latter " in building up at Delhi an Empire stronger than that which preceeded it."[9]

Griffin has remarked that "all the great families, north or south of the Sutlej, have the same origin." The Malwa chiefs were "more cultivators of the lands"; the Majha chiefs—"scarcely more than a hundred years ago the majority of them were cultivators of the soil"; and "The Brar Jats were originally Bhatti Rajputs".[10]

Describing the Sikh chiefs as barons, Griffin has opined that "they fought against each other more often than against the common enemy, the Muhammadans." Because of the "constitution of Sikhism", they did not acknowledge "Vassalage or feudal superiority" and as such "resisted all attempts at diction by one central authority." Of course, Maharaja Ranjit Singh changed the whole concept of Sikh movement from religious to the political expediency.[11]

Griffin has defined the Sikh Army as "the *Dal Khalsa,* the Army of God, sometimes the *Bhuda Dal* or Veteran Army."[12] Ahmad Shah Abdali; according to Griffin, wanted to adopt a conciliatory attitude towards the Sikhs and the Sikh chiefs "and would have been glad to enlist them on his side, first against the Delhi Government and then against the Marathas."[13]

Griffin has appreciated the role of Sardar Jassa Singh Ahluwalia in solving the problem created by Ala Singh of Patiala who has accepted the Durrani suzerainty in 1762 and the assignment of the territories of Sirhind in 1763 form Ahmad Shah Abdali. He has remarked that but for Sardar

Jassa Singh Ahluwalia "who was far more influential than Ala Singh himself, the Sikhs were ready to turn upon the latter."[14]

Of all the English writers Griffin is the only writer who has given a very detailed, though, more or less, biographical account of Sardar Jassa Singh Ahluwalia, describing him as "the leader of the *Khalsa*, and the most distinguished of all the Sikh chiefs north of Sutlaj."[15] He has given a vivid picture of his role in the extension and consolidation of the Sikh power in the parts of Punjab, Delhi, Western Utter Pradesh and Rajasthan.

Regarding the origin of the Ahluwalia family, Griffin has described that though it was founded by Sadho Singh, "a Jat of the Kalal or distiller caste, an enterprising Zamindar" and the founder of "four villages in the vicinity, Ahlu, caused the family to be known by the distinction of Ahluwalia"; "the true founder of the confederacy was Sirdar Jassa Singh Ahluwalia, fifth in the descent."[16]

Griffin has made a critical appraisal of the position enjoyed by Sardar Jassa Singh Ahluwalia *viz-a-viz* other military leaders of the time. He recognises him as "the leader of the *Khalsa*" and says that by sheer intelligence and bravery he had made himself a "leading contemporary of Nadir Shah and Ahmad Shah."[17] As early as 1749, Kaura Mal, the Governor of Multan, rewarded him "with a share of the booty and a title of honour" for assisting him against Shah Nawaz Khan. In 1755, Adina Beg Khan was compelled to "cede to him Fatehabad on the Beas.[18]

Undoubtedly, in 1761, opines Griffin, Sardar Jassa Singh Ahluwalia was "the Chief leader among the Sikhs north of the Sutlaj" and "among his own followers he was known as 'Sultan-ul-Kaum"; but this title was not acknowledged by the Sikh nation, and there is no proof that he was generally acknowledged as *Padshah* or King." Though, at times, he was accepted as "Chief among the Sikh leaders" and occasionally allowed a nominal command of the joint attack, he was never acknowledged as the Chief Commander of the Sikh forces. Of course, he was respected because of being a man of ability and for saintly as well as orthodox qualities.[19] It was because of the above qualities that the most powerful Raja Amar Singh of Patiala received the *pahal* or Sikh baptism from his hand.[20]

Griffin does not agree with earlier English writers, like Browne, Cunningham etc., regarding the occupation of Lahore by the Sikhs under the leadership of Sardar Jassa Singh Ahluwalia and subsequent coining of money by him in 1758. He says, "He is said to have struck the first coin...though this is more than doubtful." He is perhaps the only English writer who says, "Nor were these coins struck before 1762..." Moreover, accepting the version of Ganesh Dass, the author of the *Char Bagh-i-Punjab,* Griffin does not believe that these coins were ever struck by the

Sikhs. He has opined that they were only twenty one in number, struck by the *Qazis* and *Mullahs* and sent to Ahmad Shah to incite him against the Sikhs. He is of the opinion that the first coin struck by the Sikhs was the *Nanak Shahi* rupee in 1765.[21]

Griffin has very much appreciated the role of Sardar Jassa Singh Ahluwalia in consolidating the disorganised Sikh power and forcing it into cohesion. Of course, for that, on many occasions, he formed alliances and counter-alliances to face and fight against different Sikh chiefs. There were occasion when, at one time or the other, he formed alliance with the Sikh Sardars of Phulkian, Singhpuria, Karota Singhia, Bhangi, Shahid, Kanihya *Misl* and Bhais of Kaithal.[22] But, at the same time, Griffin believes that "the Patiala Chief always showed great jealousy", though with Amar Singh, "there was more sincere friendship between them than had existed in the time of Ala Singh." No doubt, in due course of time, Raja Amar Singh had also started viewing "the increasing influence of Jassa Singh with the greatest suspicion" and had not allowed the latter to retain the territories in the neighbourhood of Delhi.[23] Notwithstanding this Jassa Singh Ahluwalia maintained, by and large, cordial relations with him. Whereas, barring aside a couple of occasions when he joined hands with Jassa Singh Ramgharia, both would not see eye to eye with each other.[24]

Regarding the extent of empire and the centres of political activities, Griffin has opined that though, even as late as 1775, the "name of the Empire (Mughal) was still a word of power with the Sikhs", Sardar Jassa Singh Ahluwalia did not remain confined to the Punjab alone, but "crossed the Sutlaj and ravaged the country to the very gates of Delhi."[25] As such he covered the Haryana and certain areas of U.P. as well.

Starting with the four ancestral villages of "Ahlu, Hallu-Sadho, Tor and Chak", Sardar Jassa Singh Ahluwalia in 1743 had "seized Lakhumalanwala, Boggoki, Hicharwal and other Dogar villages"[26] on the south of river Sutlaj. In 1748, he seized large portion of Amritsar District. In 1755, he had "extended his conquests to the edge of the Beas" getting "the Fatehabad *pargana*" from Adina Beg. In 1760, he temporarily captured Jandialah, plundered Sirhind, captured Dayalpur and thence in Ferozepur, seized the Dogar *pargana* of Multanwala and Nypal *pargana* of Makhu. Then he seized Kot Isa Khan, Hoshiarpur, Bhirog, and Naraingharin Ambala, and exacted tribute from Rai Ibrahim, the Jagirdar of Kapurthala. In 1761, Jassa Singh Ahluwalia along with other Sikhs "crossed the Sutlaj and made a raid as far south as Shikarpur, Mahammadpur, and Haipur to the south of the Jamna." But after a brief debacle, known as the *Ghalughara* in February 1762, he captured Kasur, plundered Sirhind and also "seized twenty four villages forming the *ilaqua* of Suhoran" in the

Ambala District. Griffin has also made mention of the defeat of Najib Khan near Shahjahanabad in 1764 at the hands of Jassa Singh aligning himself with the Marathas and Jats, and "Delhi, would probably have fallen had not the besiegers heard that Ahmad Shah was approaching." In 1766, Jassa Singh Ahluwalia, along with Raja Amar Singh, ravaged Jhajjar, Rewari, Bhagpat and captured Payal and Isru. In 1768, the neighbourhood of Delhi, Ghaziuddin, Anupshahr and the fort of Sukhan were overrun. But he was, however, not able to retain any country as far south as this due to the opposition of his ally, Raja Amar Singh. After capturing Rai Kot from the Pathans and Berowal from the Rajputs in 1771, Sardar Jassa Singh Ahluwalia, in 1772, marched against Rai Ibrahim, holding Kapurthala. But he could manage to seize the town only in 1780 and continued to reside there till his death in 1783. Of course, in the year 1776, he had also captured the possessions of Ramgharia Sardar in the Punjab.[27]

The Study of the Griffin's writing shows that the Sikh chiefs, including Sardar Jassa Singh Ahluwalia, were originally deeply religious and peaceful, then took to the profession of arms, developing military instincts of a high order. This change correspondingly reflected upon their motives as well and under the thin veil of religion, their real motives changed into self-interests and self-aggrandisement.

Griffin has almost refrained from using the term *misl* and has used the word "confederacy." A scientific study based on the eighteenth century Persian and English records reveals the absence of the term *misl* during the 18th century territorial set up and the administrative organisation of the Sikh Sardars. This term was used by some writers only during the first half of the 19th century. In this context Cunningham has also pointed out that, "Captain Murray seems to have been the first who perceived and pointed out the Sikh system of Misls."[28]

No doubt, it is quite controversial whether, at all, the coins were stuck in 1758 but those were not struck in 1762 either as stated by Griffin and most of the writers believe that they were struck in 1761. Contrary to Griffin's version that Sardar Jassa Singh Ahluwalia resided only in Kapurthala from 1780 to 1783, other sources, especially the British Secret Proceedings, show that he was in or around Delhi in 1783.

One thing most commonly noticed in the writings of almost all the British writers, including Griffin, is that the Sikhs and the Sikh Sardars have been called the 'robbers' committing 'depredations' and 'highway robbery'. In this regard it can be stated that plunder, depredations or highway robbery is a concept usually used from the imperialist angle. When the revolting zamindars or sardars realized the revenue of a particular area after occupation, from the imperial point of view, it was described as plunder, loot, pillage etc. Same is true of the Mughal description about the Marathas and the British description about the poligars in the South India and the Sikhs in the Punjab etc.

References

1. For details see, B.R. Grover, Presidential Address', *Punjab History Conference,* XIX Session, 1985, pp. 7-58.
2. Gupta, Hari Ram, *A History of the Sikhs,* Vol. I. (*Simla,* 1952); Ganda Singh, *Sardar Jassa Singh Ahluwalia,* (Patialia, 1969), (Punjabi); Bhagat Singh, *Sikh Polity in the Eighteenth and the Nineteenth centuries,* (New Delhi), 1978.
3. For details about his life see, *Dictionary of National Biography,* Supplement Vol II (Tewntieth Century, 1901-1911), (Oxford Reprint, 1963), pp. 167-169.
4. *The Rajas of the Punjab,* i, pp. 7-10.
5. *Ranjit Singh,* p. 72.
6. *The Rajas of the Punjab,* i, p. 17.
7. *Ranjit Singh,* p. 24.
8. *The Rajas of Punjab,* i, p. 17.
9. *Ibid.,* p. 23.
10. *Ibid.,* p.vi; *Ranjit Singh,* pp. 23-24, 84
11. *Ranjit Singh,* p. 77.
12. *Ibid.,* p. 85.
13. *Ibid.,* pp. 24, 75; and *The Rajas of the Punjab,* i. p. 24.
14. *Ranjit Singh,* p. 76; *The Rajas of the Punjab,* i. pp. 24-25.
15. *The Rajas of the Punjab,* ii, p. 453.
16. *Ibid.,* pp. 452-453; *Ranjit Singh,* pp. 78-79; *the Punjab Chiefs,* ii, p. 496. The other three villages were, Hallu-Sadho, Tor and Chak. For further clarification in this respect, see, Joginder Kaur (ed.), *Ram Rao's Fateh Singh Partap Prabhakar* (Amritsar, 1978).
17. *The Punjab Chiefs,* ii, pp. 496-497.
18. *The Rajas of Punjab,* ii, pp. 457-58.
19. *Ibid.,* pp. 462-466, Ram Sukh Rao's *Jassa Singh Binod* has also referred him as *Panth ke Malik.'*
20. *Ibid.,* pp. 468.
21. *Ibid.,* pp. 460-61.
22. *Ibid.,* i, 24-25; ii, pp. 460-460 and *The Punjab Chiefs,* ii, p. 497.
23. *The Rajas of the Punjab,* i, pp. 27 and 31; ii, ii, pp. 466-467.
24. *Ibid.,* ii, pp. 457-58, 460, 463, 467, 473.
25. *Ibid.,* i, p. 41; *Ranjit Singh,* p. 24
26. *The Rajas of the Punjab,* ii, p. 456.
27. *Ibid.,* pp. 456-497; *The Punjab Chiefs,* p. 497.
28. Cunningham, Joseph Davy, *A History of the Sikhs* (Delhi, 1955), p. 97. f.n.

4

Life and Works of Sardar Jassa Singh Ahluwalia

18th century Punjab has a unique distinction of being an era of political turmoil and turbulation and the Sikh struggle for power. During the early 18th century, Punjab witnessed a stiff resistance from the local chiefs (both religious and political), the zamindars, and peasants to the local officials in their exercise of imperial control. As is clear from the Persian sources that this and the subsequent period of the 18th century witnessed the disintegration of the Mughal empire, the foreign campaigns of Nadir Shah and the Durranis, the attempts made by the Rohillas, Rajputs, Jats, and the Afghans to establish their respective regional governments and the emergence and the rise of Marathas and the Sikhs. These powers and a large number of zamindars of different denominations struggled for greater share in the revenues and in power over the region, ultimately aiming to establish sovereignty in different parts of the *subahs* of Punjab and Delhi.[1]

Sardar Jassa Singh Ahluwalia, *Jassa Singh 'Kalal', Nawab* Jassa Singh Ahluwalia, *Sultan-ul-qaum* Jassa Singh Ahluwalia, *Afsar-i-Khalsa* Jassa Singh Ahluwalia, *Sardar-i-Umda* Jassa Singh Ahluwalia, *Sarkhail-i-Sikhan* Jassa Singh Ahluwalia, *Padishah* Jassa Singh Ahluwalia and above all Baba Jassa Singh Ahluwalia are some of the names by which a great leader of the *Panth* was addressed by the people during the 18th century history of Punjab. Sardar Jassa Singh Ahluwalia was the elected supreme commander of the Sikh Federation or '*Misls*' during the struggle of Sikh people for freedom and survival at a time when the Punjab was passing through one of the darkest periods of its history. Inspired by the heroic deeds of Guru Gobind Singh and his followers like Baba Banda Singh Bahadur, the Sikhs waged a relentless struggle during the 18th century

---

Paper presented at *Mata Sundari Divas Celeberations*, Mata Sundari College, (University of Delhi), New Delhi, 2001 and published in *Khalsa Trai Shatabdi:Lekha-Jokha*, (Punjabi), edited by Dr. Mohinder Kaur Gill, New Delhi 2001, pp. 187-199.

for the liberation of the Punjab, which at that time extended from Attock to the Jamuna.[2] In short, the edge of the Mughal Sword had sharpened and the government of the day was determined to exterminate the Sikhs route and branch.[3] The need of the hour, therefore, was a united front under a capable, resolute and sagacious leadership, which the Sikhs finally got in Sardar Jassa Singh Ahluwalia. He played a remarkable role in the history of the Sikhs and the Punjab, leading the *Khalsa* from victory to victory and clearing for the Sikhs a path towards national glory and political power.[4]

After the death of Banda Singh Bahadur the Mughal rulers of the day made all out efforts to extirpate the Sikh community. The Mughal emperors Bahadur Shah (1708-1712) and Farrukh Siyar (1713-1719) (the later had issued a general addict in 1716) ordered a general massacre of the Sikhs—men, women and children—and money awards were offered for the head of every Sikh brought to Lahore, dead or alive. The execution of captured Sikhs in Lahore was a common site. They were generally broken on the wheel, flayed alive or cut up limb by limb. George Forster, a European traveller later recorded, "an addict was issued by Furruck Sir (*sic.*) directed that every Sicque falling into the hands of his officers, should . . . be put to sword. A valuable reward was also given by the Emperor for the head of every Sicque; and such was the keen spirit that animated the persecution, such was the success of the executions that the name of the Sicque no longer existed in the Mughal domineer." Sardar Jassa Singh Ahluwalia along with other Sikh Sardars successfully saved the infant nation from onslaught at a time when royal forces were going from village to village to arrest Sikhs and send them to the *Nakhas* (horse market) at Lahore to be tortured and put to death.

The main reliance of this Paper is on the various Persian, Punjabi and English sources, Ram Sukh Rao's *Jassa Singh Binod* and *Sri Fateh Singh Pratap Prabhakar,* Gian Singh's *Twarikh-i-Guru Khalsa*, Ramjas' *Tarikh-i-Riast Kapurthala,* Khushwaqat Rai's *Tarikh-i-Sikkhan,* Sohan Lal Suri's *Umdat-ut-Tawarikh,* Rattan Singh Bhangu's *Prachin Panth Prakash,* Kanahya Lal's Tarikh-i-Punjab and Mufti Alau-ddin's *Ibratnama,* apart from some of the published books on the subject have been used.

Sardar Jassa Singh Ahluwalia hailed from the family of Sardar Dewa Singh who had been baptized by the closest associates of the 10th master Guru Gobind Singh. He was born on May 3, 1718 (Baisakhi Sudi 15, Puranmashi, Samvat 1795) in a small village Ahlu near Lahore, now in Pakistan. His father Sardar Badr Singh died when he was just 5 years old. It is really interesting to know that Badr Singh who was married to the sister of Sardar Bhag Singh of Hallo and a petty *zamindar* of the Lahore district had no issue for many years. Both the husband and the wife went to Guru Gobind Singh to seek his blessings. He blessed them: "Meditate upon God and serve the saints. Remember Guru Nanak. Your son will be Guru's son."[5]

ਵਾਹਿਗੁਰੂ ਅਕਾਲ ਪੁਰਖ ਦੀ ਅਰਾਧਨ ਕਰੋ, ਸਾਧ ਸੰਗਤ ਦੀ ਸੇਵਾ ਕਰੋ,
ਗੁਰੂ ਨਨਕ ਦਾ ਧਿਆਨ ਧਰੋ, ਗੁਰੂ ਅੰਗ ਸੰਗ ਹੈਂ, ਤੁਹਾਡਾ ਪੁਤਰ ਗੁਰੂ ਦਾ ਲਾਲ ਹੋਵੇਗਾ।

After the death of his father in 1722, his mother, a noble lady of deep religious convictions, with the help of her brother Sardar Bhag Singh, brought up Jassa Singh. They took young Jassa Singh to Delhi in 1723 to seek the blessings of Mata Sundariji[6]. Mata Sundari looked after Jassa Singh as her own child. He had intense love for religion for which she became attached to him. Here he learnt Persian, Arabic and Gurumukhi and became proficient and adapt in the use of arms. He also learnt music and loved to sing hymns of Holy *Granth* along with his mother. Jassa Singh's stay of about seven years in Delhi was a God-sent opportunity indeed, for it brought him in touch with important personalities in the Sikh *Panth*. In 1729 Sardar Bhag Singh, who was keen to take his nephew back to the Punjab, requested Mata Sundari to spare Jassa Singh to succeed him. Mataji after some reluctance acceded to the request an allowed him and his mother to go to Bhag Singh's house[7]. At the time of his departure, Mataji blessed the young boy, predicted his future greatness, gave him a silver mace, some other weapons and said that Jassa Singh and mace-bearer would attend his descendents[8]. The prediction came true, as he became the progenitor of the ruling House of Kapurthala.

The time, when Jassa Singh came to Punjab, coincided with the terror let loose by the Mughal forces, and Lahore and its surroundings were not safe for the Sikhs. Sardar Kapur Faizullahpuria and members of *Dal Khalsa* were camping near Kartarpur. Bhag Singh used to go to see him, and once Jassa Singh also accompanied his maternal uncle. Kapur Singh and other chiefs of the *Dal Khalsa* were much impressed by the well built physique and manners[9] of this young boy and requested Bhag Singh to leave him and his mother for a month there. Finally Sardar Kapur Singh adopted Jassa Singh as his son. It was under his guidance that Jassa Singh got his early training in the art of warfare and statecraft, thereby, shaped his life on stern discipline. After some time Sardar Kapur Singh and four other Sikhs baptized him. His baptism and Sardar Kapur Singh's instructions inspired young Jassa Singh, who soon tried to put in hard labour to keep *Dal Khalsa* in perfect trim[10]. Sardar Kapur Singh entrusted him with the job of feeding the horses of the *Dal Khalsa*. Though Jassa Singh resented that duty but he was told that in future he would be assigned much greater responsibility[11]...

Soon Sardar Jassa Singh became the right hand of Sardar Kapur Singh. Impressed by his spirit of service, once Kapur Singh said, "Young man I am very happy with you, you are so obedient and smart at this age, I feel highly impressed."[12] Jassa Singh fought courageously in the encounters of the Sikhs against the Afghans and the Mughals. In 1739, he robbed Nadir Shah's rear of the plunders they were carrying[13]. The "political talents, religious zeal and loftly aspirations combined, rendered him one of the most powerful federal chiefs of the Punjab[14]. The Sikhs under Jassa Singh became more and more bold and understood that they could carry on their operations with perfect impunity. They organized themselves near a village called Dallewal on the river Ravi, from where they carried savages and plunder into the countryside.

The Sikhs consolidated their power under Sardar Jassa Singh Ahluwalia who was acclaimed as a very able leader and who commanded high respect from all Sikhs. He had remarkable power of organization. In fact, the *Panth* needed solidarity and union. Sardar Kapur Singh named the entire body of Sikhs the *Dal Khalsa Jio*. On the sacred day of *Baisakhi*, 29th March 1748, the Sikhs assembled at Amritsar. Sardar Kapur Singh who was now very old relinquished the leadership of the *Dal Khalsa,* which now fell on Jassa Singh's shoulders. He became the leader of the entire Sikh community and made efforts to organize it. He was the real architect of the disciplined political system of the Sikhs. The Sikhs started meeting twice a year at Amritsar. The assemblage was known as the *Sarbat Khalsa.* The foundation of the *Dal Khalsa* united the Sikhs into a compact body[15].

After the death of Sardar Kapur Singh in 1753, Jassa Singh Ahluwalia was acclaimed as the natural leader of the *Panth* and was hailed as the *'Padishah'.* The *de-facto* authority exercised by Jassa Singh over the *missals* of the Sikh confederacy was a direct corollary of the veneration in which he was held for his valour and piety. He continued to lead the *Panth* during the next thirty years till his death in 1783[16].

The leadership of the *Panth* at that critical juncture involved ceaseless struggle against frequent invasions of Ahmad Shah Abdali on the one hand and the tyranny of the local Mughal government on the other. None of the dangers dampened his spirit, but on the contrary made him more determined leader. It goes to his credit and devoted comrades-in-arms that they carried on the struggle on both the fronts. He combined in him the qualities of chivalry, humanity and tolerance. He liberated Amritsar in 1748. It was, however, in their fight against Ahmad Shah Abdali that the Sikhs had to suffer the most especially after he had defeated the Marathas in the famous third battle of Panipat in January 1761, had turned his full attention towards them. Sardar Jassa Singh Ahluwalia captured Lahore in September 1761, and challenged Abdali's authority. He declared the establishment of the *de-jure* sovereignty of *Khalsa* over the Punjab by issuing coins in the fashion of the times. Sardar Jassa Singh Ahluwalia was hailed as *'Sultan-ul-Qaum'* of the Sikhs after this conquest. This challenge made Ahmad Shah Abdali pounced upon the Sikhs near village Kup in the neighbourhood of Malerkotla, on 5th February 1762. It was estimated that about sixty thousand men, women and children were hopelessly besieged by Abdali's hordes. It goes to the credit of resourcefulness, military skill and determination of Sardar Jassa Singh Ahluwalia that he successfully faced this attack and succeeded ultimately salvaging quite a number of men, women, children and equipment. The Sikhs, however, lost about 20,000 in this bloody encounter. This great holocaust is remembered as '*Wadda Ghallughara*' in Sikh history. In his efforts to extirpate the Sikhs, Ahmad Shah Abdali attacked Sri Harmandir Sahib on 9th April 1762, and got the holy temple raised to the ground. But with remarkable resilience and determination the Sikh forces under the leadership of Jassa Singh reassembled to recapture their lost position. In 1764, he conquered both Sirhind and Lahore and there by announced the future plans of liberation of India. The same year Jassa Singh took upon himself to work for reconstruction of Harmandir Sahib, the holy shrine, which was demolished and defiled by Ahmad Shah Abdali in 1762[17].

From 1779 to 1783 Jassa Singh attempted to outmaneuver the advances of British influence over Mughal kings. He established firm relations with like-minded chiefs of Gangetic Doab including the Raja of Bharatpur. As a result, he was successful in conquering Delhi in the year 1783. Jassa Singh's political career was cut short by his sudden death while he was on his way to Harmandir Sahib in Amritsar in October 1783.

There are several things which make Jassa Singh Ahluwalia a 'Sardar', 'Padishah', 'Sultan-ul-Quam', 'Baba' etc.

- Sardar Jassa Singh Ahluwalia though a unique liberator of the downtrodden was a contended man and was never very ambitious. Even after the conquest of Sirhind and Lahore he kept for himself a very small area and neither did show any lust for territory nor did he take advantage of his being the leader. He would never help any of his relatives out of the way. After the territory of Rai Ibrahim was captured in 1773-74, the Rai had promised to send the revenue in time and submitted him. But he did not observe the *jagirdari* tradition of formal mourning on the death of Sardar Mehar Singh, son-in-law of Jassa Singh Ahluwalia, who had gone to Kapurthala to collect revenue and was killed from a shot from inside the fort[18]. Even so, when Jassa

Singh occupied Kapurthala in 1780, he would treat Rai kindly and personal house was left to him. Not giving any punishment to Rai shows his kindness[19].

- Though Jassa Singh Ahluwalia was a successful general in the field, it was rather as the most sainty and orthodox leader that the Sikhs respected him. His contemporaries regarded it as an act of great merit to receive *'Pahul'* at his hands. "It was rather as the most saintly and orthodox of their leaders that the Sikhs respected him and the most powerful Sirdars received the *'Pahul'* or Sikh Baptism from his hands." Baba Ala Singh, the founder of the House of Patiala and two of his successors, Raja Amar Singh and Sahib Singh also received the *'Pahul'* from him[20]. The *Rajas* of Patiala, Jind, Jammu, Kangra, Bilaspur and Nalagrah stood before him in all reverence and humiliating. The *Nawabs* of Malerkotla and Kunjpura paid him homage but this did not turned his head. He always considered himself as a humble and docile devotee and disciple of the 10th master.
- Neither he nor his *misl* were the biggest, nor was he an acknowledged commander of the Sikh forces, yet influence of Jassa Singh was great. Whenever any combination of the *misls* took place, he was made the commander-in-chief. He played a greater role than any other chief to consolidate the Sikh power and paved the way for the Sikhs to achieve their ultimate goal. He was an enlightened and liberal minded man. He was not an enemy of Muslims. A larger number of Muslims were in his services and were allowed to follow their own religious practices. The officials appointed by him both for revenue collection and maintenance of law and order were drawn from all religions-Hindus, Sikhs as well as Muslims[21].
- His hospitality was extended to all who asked for it, and hundreds were fed daily at his *langar* or the public kitchen. He would never keep a visitor waiting and called him at once without any consideration of time at his hands[22].
- Fatehabad was conquered by Sardar Jassa Singh Ahluwalia in 1749 A.D./*Samvat 1806*[23]. He established his position as one of the chief Sardars (*Sarkhil-i-Sikhan*) with Fatehabad as his *watan* and *maskan* (headquarters with permanent residence/*makan*)[24]. As such, Sardar Jassa Singh Ahluwalia made Fatehabad as the headquarters of his newly acquired and consolidated chieftainship. Not with standing the fact that Kapurthala was incorporated in the directly administered territories of the state in 1780 A.D./*Samvat 1837,* Fatehabad continued to remain the official headquarters.

- Based mostly on the English and other secondary sources of the later half of the 19th century onwards it is believed that Sardar Jassa Singh Ahluwalia after the final annexation of Kapurthala in 1780 A.D. shifted his state headquarters from Fatehabad to Kapurthala. But Kapurthala remained under the direct administration of Sardar Jassa Singh Ahluwalia for only about three years. During this period too he continued to reside at Fatehabad—his official capital. However, Kapurthala became second seat of power with Kunwar Bhag Singh—the heir apparent to the *gaddi* as administrator[25].
- For Sardar Jassa Singh Ahluwalia the protection of women was as much a part of his chivalrous character as that his concept of *Dharma.* In 1757 A.D. during his operations against the Jalandhar *doab,* he recovered a number of Hindu women who were returned to their relatives. The Sikh volunteers fighting for the honour of their religion and country under the leadership of Sardar Jassa Singh Ahluwalia maintained the Indian traditions of valour and moral values. One such act of valour was the liberation from the clutches of Durrani general Jahan Khan at Lahore of about 2200 women and children from the *Toshakhana* in April 1761. They were being carried away from Delhi as captives to Kabul. Sardar Jassa Singh personally led a surprise attack on the invading Afghans and succeeded in liberating the unfortunate victims. He not only freed them from captivity, but also had them escorted back to their homes. This earned him the popular appellation of *Bandichhor* (liberator)[26]. According to the Marathi folk songs, many of these women hailed from Maharashtra who had been captured after the Maratha defeat at the battle of Panipat (1761).
- Sardar Jassa Singh gave grants to a number of institutions like *Thakurdwaras, Masjid* and *Khanqahs.* Amongst the individuals who received the grants and patronage from the state were *Sheikhs, Sayyids, Brahmins* as well as *faqirs* and *bairagis*[27].
- Sardar Jassa Singh Ahluwalia possessed political acumen of a high order. When Raja Ala Singh of Patiala had accepted insignia of royality, kattles, drum and banner from Ahmad Shah Abdali, several members of the *Dal Khalsa* wanted to punish the former. Jassa Singh realized that this internecine war would go against the interests of the entire *Khalsa*. He intervened and with a strong sense of political sagacity was able to persuade both sides not to fight each other and there by weaken themselves[28].
- When Ahmad Shah Abdali had completely demolished Harmandir Sahib, Sardar Jassa Singh Ahluwalia got started its reconstruction. An amount of Rupees Fourteen lakh was spent on the reconstruction,

of which Rupees Nine lakh was given by Sardar Jassa Singh and the balance of Rupees Five lakh by other Sikh sardars, who were asked by the former to contribute towards this purpose. He also constructed *Katra Akal Bunga* renamed as *Guru Ka Katra.* Sardar Jassa Singh also deputed Kunwar Bhag Singh for the construction of a fort at Amritsar. As he did not consider that the holy place of the *Khalsa* (Amritsar) should remain under mortgage with Chaudhuri Sahib Rai of Naushehara, he got it released against payment. He constructed his own *Katra* and *Bunga,* Katra Ahluwalia still retains the same name in Amritsar. He also settled shopkeepers, *sahukars, sarafs* etc. whereby Amritsar became a thickly populated and a city of composite culture[29]. Jassa Singh's act of restoring the holy *Darbar Sahib* (the present holy Golden Temple) is recorded in Sikh history as '*Guru ki Chaddar*'. Because of these services to the *Panth,* Bhai Kan Singh has rightly given him the appellation of '*Dharamvir*' (Defender of Faith).

- Since, Ahmad Shah Abdali along with Najib-ud-Daulla had desecrated *Anandpur Sahib* and the temple of Naina Devi in 1768, Sardar Jassa Singh took the earliest opportunities to go there for pilgrimage. He got a *'Bauli'* (with fresh water) constructed at *Darbar Sahib* and got constructed five *Bungas* and *Havelis* at Anandpur Sahib. He gifted 65 villages to the Sodhis and also got a fort constructed for them. All these steps were taken for the future security and the management of that area[30].
- Sardar Jassa Singh Ahluwalia was a great lover of art. In the reconstruction of the *Harmandir Sahib* at Amritsar though based on the original late 16th/early 17th centuries model the contemporary craftmanship of Kangra, Rajasthani and Islamic architecture in its manifold aspects was blended very skillfully. Same is true of the construction work carried out at *Anandpur Sahib.* The construction of the *Bungas* as advised by Sardar Jassa Singh added a great deal of symmetry in the growth of Amritsar city[31].
- Sardar Jassa Singh Ahluwalia regarded the defence of the country as his *Dharma* and made an appeal to his soldiers that he along with them would sacrifice their lives for the sake of *Dharma*[32]. *Dharma* in this context, may be interpreted a political fight and not essentially in the religious sense, a war between the Hindu and Muslim rulers. This gives a complete reorientation of Jassa Singh's own concept as a ruler for fighting the titular government at Delhi representing the alien suzerainty of Ahmad Shah Abdali.
- One of the cardinal principals of Jassa Singh's policy was the protection of the cow. It was brought to his notice that the Hindu's of the Qasur

were being harassed due to the practice of cow slaughter there. Sardar Jassa Singh Ahluwalia led two expeditions against the cow slaughter practice at Lahore and chastised the cow slaughterers of *Kasai Mohalla.* The Pathan chief Jalal Khan of Qasur, on being defeated by Sardar Jassa Singh, apologized and gave an undertaking to stop slaughter in his territory. He also presented two horses and Rs. 25,000 in cash as *nazarana.* The Pathan chief also undertook to pay *malia.* In 1771 A.D./*1828 Samvat* he led another campaign against the Pathan chief and again reprimanded the chief against cow slaughter, harassment of the Hindus and ensured the payment of the arrears and the future regular payment of *malia*[33].

- Sardar Jassa Singh would visit Amritsar at the time of *Deepmala* (Diwali). In 1783 A.D., while on his way from Fatehabad to Amritsar for pilgrimage, he died at Bundal. Sardar Jassa Singh realizing that his end was near summoned the *Pandits, Purohits* and the *Rishis* for rendering *Paths* (offering prayers). He bestowed on them elephants, horses and land in charity. He also desired that he should be cremated at Amritsar. He told the *granthis* also to offer *Path* (prayer) of *Sukhamani Sahib.* With *'Ram, Ram'* on his lips he passed away[34]. As a rare gesture of the recognition of his services to the *Panth*, his mortal remains were cremated in the holy precincts of Burj Baba Atal Sahib, Amritsar, where his *'Samadh'* exists to this day.

It would not be out of place to quote Dr. Hari Ram Gupta's work *History of the Sikhs, Volume-I, (1739-1768),* wherein he mentions how a hostile chronicler Nur Mohammed was forced to pay a handsome tribute. He wrote, "Do not call the Sikhs 'dogs', because they are lions. If you cherish a desire of learning the art of war, come before them in the field... you may know that their title is 'Singh' (Lion) and it is unjust to call them 'dogs'. In fact they are lions at the time of battle and when in festivities they surpass *Hatim*. Besides their fighting, one thing more in which they excel all other warriors. They never kill a coward... they do not rob a woman... adultery also does not exist with them"[35].

Paying tribute to Sardar Jassa Singh Ahluwalia, Dr. J. N. Sarkar writes, "The Romantic role of Jassa Singh in the Sikh struggle for independence deserves to be written in letters of gold. The Sarbat *Khalsa* invariably nominated the brewer's son a commander. A born general, he justified his selection... In the battlefield he stood out clearly from the rest and he did not require a separate badge. Indeed he towered head and shoulders above others. Possessing patriotism, courage, industry, firmness, temperate and fixed determination to resist, he became the soul of many a successful operation..."[36].

Knowing the Sikh strong instinct for individuality and independence, it was by no means an easy task for Sardar Jassa Singh Ahluwalia to keep them welded together. It speaks volumes for the remarkable personality who was unanimously acclaimed '*Sultan-ul-Qaum*' for the first time in the annals of history. The routes of the future *Khalsa* rule in the Punjab were firmly laid by the creative genius and leadership of Jassa Singh. It was under him that the Sikh cry, which forms part of their daily prayer, '*Raj Karega Khalsa*' first came true. It may, however, be emphasized that the struggle of the Sikhs under Sardar Jassa Singh Ahluwalia was not for any narrow objectives or for capturing personal power but it was for the defence of India and its culture.

References

1. Dua J. C., *British Historiography Eighteenth Century Punjab,* New Delhi, 1992, pp. 1-2.
2. Forester, George, *A journey from Bengal to England through North India, Kashmir, Afghanistan and Persia into Russia, 1783-1784,* 2 vols., London 1789, i, p. 271.
3. Ramjas, *Tawarikh-i-Riast Kapurthala,* vol. I (ed. 1897), 97-98.
4. Syed Muhammad Latif, *History of the Punjab,* Delhi, 1964, 314.
5. Ganda Singh, *Jassa Singh Ahluwalia* (Punjabi), Patiala, 1969, 25.
6. Gian Singh, *Twarikh-i-Guru Khalsa* (ed. 1970), 722.
7. Ramjas, *op. cit.,* 100-02; Rai, Khushwaqat, *Tarikh-i-Sikkhan* (MS Dr. Ganda Singh Collection, Patiala), 66; Gian Singh, *op. cit.,* 77.
8. Dr. Ganda Singh, *op. cit.,* 23-25.
9. Bhangu, Rattan Singh, *Prachin Panth Prakash* (ed. 1939), 204; Kanahya Lal, *Tarikh-i-Punjab* (ed. 1877), 99; Mufti Alau-ddin, *Ibratnama,* i, 310.
10. Bhangu, Rattan Singh, *op. cit.,* 204; Kanahya Lal, *op. cit.,* 99; Ramjas, *op. cit.,* 104; Mufti Alau-ddin, *op. cit.,* 310.
11. Bhangu, Rattan Singh, *op. cit.,* 204.
12. Syed Muhammad Latif, *op. cit.,* 314.
13. Gian Singh, *op. cit.,* 718.
14. Syed Muhammad Latif, *op. cit.,* 314.
15. Gupta, Hari Ram, *A History of the Sikhs,* Simla, 1952, 11-12.
16. Rai, Khushwant, *op. cit.,* 89.
17. Ganda Singh, *Ahmad Shah Durrani,* Bombay, 1959, 274-75; Teja Singh and Ganda Singh, *A Short History of the Sikhs,* vol. I, Bombay, 1950, 184.
18. Ram Sukh Rao, *Jassa Singh Binod,* and Ms no. M/772, Punjab State Archives, Patiala, written in twenties of the 19th century, fol. 205-224.
19. Rattan Singh, *op. cit.,* 481-88; Syed Muhammad Latif, *op. cit.,* 316.
20. Lepel Griffin, *The Rajas of the Punjab,* 1873, 468.
21. *Jassa Singh Binod,* 159a; *The Minor Phulkian Families* (Department of languages, Patiala, 1970), 468.

22. *Ibid.*, 469; Ramjas, *op. cit.*, 110.
23. *Jassa Singh Binod,* M 772.
24. Ramjas, *op. cit.*, 295-299.
25. Grover, B. R. (ed.), *Sardar Jassa Singh Ahluwalia,* 1990, 158-172.
26. *Jassa Singh Binod,* 86a-b, 123b.
27. *Foreign/Political consultations,* National Archives of India, New Delhi, 31st December, 1858, no. 1053; *Jassa Singh Binod,* 132a, 134b, 223a.
28. *Ibid.*, 151a.
29. *Ibid.*, 151, 109b, 210a, 211a. Ram Sukh Rao has given a detailed description about the reconstruction of *Harmandir Sahib,* the town planning of the city of Amritsar comprising *Katras, Bungas* as well as arrangements made for the administration of the city.
30. *Ibid.*, 195b, 196a. Ram Sukh Rao has provided a detailed account about the measures taken by Sardar Jassa Singh Ahluwalia for the maintenance and security of Anandpur Sahib.
31. *Ibid.*, 109b, 210a-211a.
32. *Ibid.*, 150a-152b; *Sri Fateh Singh Partap Prabhakar*, ed. Joginder Kaur, Patiala, 1980, 140a-b.
33. *Ibid.*, 107a-b, 119b-120b, 198a-199a.
34. *Ibid.*, 249a-250b.
35. Gupta, Hari Ram, *op. cit.*, 119.
36. Sarkar J.N., *Fall of the Mughal Empire,* vol. II, Calcutta, 1966, 27.

5

The British Historiography on Sardar Jassa Singh Ahluwalia and His Place in Eighteenth Century Punjab History*

Introduction

Eighteenth century Punjab has unique distinction of being an era of political turmoil and turbulation and the Sikh struggle for power. In the Punjab, the Sikh Sardars, during this period not only confronted the political powers, especially like the Mughals and the Durranis but were able to carve out their own independent/semi-independent territories (*zamindaries*) for the purposes of revenue realization and administration. A critical examination of the Punjab politics during the 18th century shows that there were as many as four main political power viz., the Mughals, the Marathas, the Sikh Sardars and the Durranis of Kabul who fought for supremacy there. Of course, during the first half of the century the struggle was basically confined between the Mughals and the Sikhs whereas during the second half, after the Marathas had been defeated at Panipat and the Mughal sovereign rights over the Punjab territories had practically vanished, and the Durranis had claimed political sovereignty and started realizing *peshkash,* it mainly became a tussle between the Sikhs and the Durranis. Again, during the last three decades of the 18th century, even though the Durranis continued to claim *de jure* political sovereignty, the Sikh Sardars had started asserting their *de facto* power over the Punjab territories.

The execution of Banda Bahadur (1716) along with his 1300 disciples, killing of his three year old son, forcible conversion of this wife to Islam and her enlistment as one of the slaves of the royal seraglio,[1] and the

---

* Revised version of the Paper Presented at *International Seminar on Baba Jassa Singh Ahluwalia as a National and Seculiar Hero*, New Delhi, 1986.

general atrocities committed on the community as a whole left a deep scar on the heart of the Sikhs. At this juncture a new leader, Sardar Kapur Singh (1697-1753), son of Dalip Singh, a Virk Jat of the village of Faizullahpur, emerged on the scene. He has been described as *"Dar mazhab-e-sihan daramadah Chande Bakhidmot Bagh singh quzranid."*[2] On the behest of Zakarya Khan, the then governor of Lahore, who wanted to adopt conciliatory policy towards the Sikhs, the Mughal government in the year 1733, offered a *jagir* worth of one lakh of rupees in revenue comprising the *parganas* of Dipalpur, Kanganwal and Jhabal to them. The offer was reluctantly accepted by Sardar Kapur Singh who was, as such, nominated as *jagirdar* and given the title of Nawab.[3]

The Sikhs had, meanwhile, organized themselves into small *Jathas,* one of which was headed by him. The multifarious activities of these *Jathas* included the forcible occupation of villages, seizing of the revenues from the village zamindars and plundering the commercial carvans passing through the territories of Punjab and Sirhind.[4] He divided the Sikhs into two groups viz., and *Budha Dal* and *Taruna Dal.*[5]

The successful invasion of the Durrani Chief, Nadir Shah (1739-40) and the capture of Delhi shook the foundations of the Mughal Empire. It not only led to desolation of many a town in the Punjab but also brought a period of uncertainty and serious financial crisis. Mughal Emperor Muhammed Shah was forced to cede to the Durrani Chief a vast area of the Mughal empire comprising Peshawar, Bangash, the *subah* of Kabul along with Ghazni, the Afghan hills, Hazara-Jat as well as *parganas* of Baluchistan, *subah* Jhatta to the west of the river Indus inclusive of its ports. Nadir Shah also claimed *peshkash* from the *subahdars* of Lahore and Multan. Moreover, revenues amounting to Rupees twenty lakhs from the four *mahals* i.e., Aurangabad, Gujrat, Sialkot and Pasrur were permanently assigned to him.[6] The situation provided a big encouragement to the activities of the Sikh *Jathas.* They fully exploited the weak position of the Mughals and accelerated this aggressive policies of plunder and forcible realization of the revenues from the Mughal and some of the newly ceded/acquired territories by the Durranis.

Closely associated with Sardar Kapur Singh was another remarkable man of the 18th century Punjab, Sardar Jassa Singh Ahluwalia.

As traditionally chronicled, Jassa Singh was the son of Badar Singh,[7] a *kalal,* a distiller, of village Ahlu, near Lahore, and born in 1718. It is said that he was born with the blessings of Guru Gobind Singh, though nearly ten years after the death of the latter. Badar Singh had died in 1722, leaving his five years old son and his widow in the care of his brother-in-law, Bagh Singh. As Badar Singh had got the blessings of Guru Gobind Singh on the condition that the son, thus born, would become his disciple, the widow went to Delhi in the service of Mata Sundri, the widow of the Guru. They spent the next seven years in the service of Mata Sundari, who became much attached to both mother and son. Griffin has opined that "when Jassa Singh was twelve years old, his uncle, Bagh Singh, urged his return to the Punjab. . . Sardar Kapur Singh Faizullapuria was at Jalandhar when the little party arrived there, and to this Chief's protection Jassa Singh's mother commended her son." Other traditions point out that in 1728, when he was a lad of ten or eleven years, Sardar Kapur Singh who had gone to Delhi to pay homage to Mata Sundari, was deeply struck by the physical appearance, piety, affable manners and intelligence of Jassa Singh, offered to adopt him as his foster son. On his departure with Sardar Kapur Singh, Mata Sundari blessed him, "predicted his future greatness, and gave him a silver mace, saying that saying that he and his descendants would have mace bearers to attend them". Sardar Kapur Singh formally initiated Jassa Singh, then a boy of 15, into the 'Sikh fold, administered *pahul* or the Sikh baptism and appointed him to feed the Sikh horses with grain.[8] Jassa Singh, well versed in Persian and *Gurumukhi*, got training in the arts of warfare and statecraft under Sardar Kapur Singh and occupied a very prominent position among the various Sikh Sardars. On the sacred day of Baisakhi, 29th March 1748, at the meeting of the Sarbat *Khalsa* at Amritsar, "it was resolved to merge the independent *jathas* into one army, the *Dal Khalsa.* Jassa Singh Ahluwalia, who had gradually taken over the leadership from the ageing Kapur Singh and who had come to be addressed as the *padsah* (king) of the Sikhs, was made the Supreme Commander."[9]

Other significant landmarks which, apart from affecting the course and nature of the struggle and designs of the Sikh Sardars, including Sardar Jassa Singh Ahluwalia, also brought fundamental changes in the political and economic spheres, included incursions by Ahmed Shah Abdali from 1747-48 onwards, the Maratha in roads in the 1750s and the emergence of English as a political power. As a result of various campaigns of the Durrani chief, the *subahs* of Punjab, Multan and Kashmir and part of *subah* Delhi (covering the area-Chakla Sirhind upto Karnal)[10] were lost to the Mughal State for ever and became part of the Afghan empire.[11] However, for political and revenue purposes, by and large, the old Mughal administrators/*subahdars/faujdars* etc. were recognized and allowed to function as Afghan Chief's own representatives. The Maratha inroads in the *subahs* of Delhi and Punjab brought them into conflict with the Durranis and their defeat at Panipat (1761). Despite their defeat they continued to play a significant role in the political and economic activities in the *subahs* of Punjab and Delhi. However, their defeat had certainly provided an opportunity to the English East India Company. The English administrators not only appointed their political agents in these areas, especially at the Mughal Court, but also, in order to gain their own political superiority, played different political powers against each other. The Sikh Sardars in their struggle for power during the eighteenth century, however, had to deal with the Durrani in the *subahs* of Multan and Punjab and the *chakla* of Sirhind and with the Mughals in the regions of *subah* Delhi.

Even though in the recent years, scholarly works have been produced on the 18th Century Punjab polity,[12] there is still a considerable scope for undertaking microscopic study of the activities, territorial set-up and achievements of the Sikh Sardars who, to a considerable extent, were primarily responsible for the liberation of the Punjab from the Durrani occupation. Apart from the Sikh organization of the informal confederacy (*sarbat Khalsa*) and execution of the plans through the decisions (*gurmata*) and their implementation with the help of the armed units (*dal Khalsa*), the twentieth century writings have equally emphasized the system and the role of the Sikh *misls* in the Punjab in which Sardar Jassa Singh Ahluwalia, the leader of the Ahluwalia *misl,* "was selected a *mukhi sardar* and was bestowed the title of Nawab and *Panth ke Malik* by the *Panth* itself."[13]

After the death of Maharaja Ranjit Singh and more especially after the British occupation of the Punjab, a number of works in Punjabi,[14] depicting the eighteenth century history of the Punjab were also produced. It is also true that for the accomplishment of their mission the Sikh Sardars, at times, took, more or less, united action and sometimes, a combination of the few Sardars undertook expeditions and campaigns for the expulsion of the Abdali as well as for the establishment of their territorial rule in specified regions. The British writers of the late eighteenth century; of the period of Maharaja Ranjit Singh and of post annexation period, even when they offer detailed general description of the activities of the eighteenth century Sikh Sardars on regional basis, do suffer from some limitations owing to either their own prejudices or the ethnic complexities prevalent at the time. The British administrator-scholars/historians were very much tempted to write on the history of the Punjab earlier and after they had seized the power from the Sikhs. Whereas Ranjit Singh and post Ranjit Singh periods have been very well looked after by the historians, on eighteenth century comparatively less work has been done. As such, it is very imperative not only to know the motivation and purpose of the English writers, but also to see as to how far were they correct in their analysis in contrast to other contemporary source, which are being unearthed. The main purpose of writing the present paper is to make an attempt to analyze the motives and approach of the British writers towards the comparative role played by Sikh Sardars and more especially Sardar Jassa Singh Ahluwalia who was able to establish the Fatehabad-Kapurthala state in the *Majiha* and Jalandhar *Doab* regions of the Punjab. It is rather interesting to trace the historiographical trends in this regard, especially when, by this time, we are also in possession of the archival source material for the eighteenth as well as for the first half of the nineteenth century before the British occupation of the Punjab.

The English writers, taken for the present study, have been divided into three categories, viz., (i) Eye witness or, more or less, contemporary accounts of the late eighteenth century like the *Calendar of Persian Correspondence,* English *Foreign Department/Secret Proceedings,* the writer James Browne and traveller George Forster; (ii) those who wrote during the life time of Maharaja Ranjit Singh e.g., John Malcolm, Henry T. Prinsep; and (iii) those who wrote after Maharaja Ranjit Singh's death and even after the annexation of Punjab. e.g., W.L. M'Gregor, Joseph Davey Cunningham and Sir Lepel Henry Griffin. The idea behind this division is to highlight the aims, objectives and insight of the English writers and government during the three different phases of the Punjab history and also to pinpoint significant changes in their motives and outlook that occurred during the intermittent periods.

Finally, an attempt has been made to analyse and coordinate these writings with other sources namely, Punjabi, English, and Persian, relating to the eighteenth and the first half of the nineteenth centuries concerning the Sikh regime of Maharaja Ranjit Singh and his successors.[16]

Contemporary and Near Contemporary Accounts

(i) Calendar of Persian Correspondence

(ii) Foreign Department/Secret Proceedings

(iii) Major James Browne

(iv) George Forster

The main objective behind the accounts in the first category seems to be, more or less, identical. It was, for all practical purposes, the political motive which was foremost in the minds of these writers and those at the helm of affairs. The political situation in this part of India, more especially fast growing political importance of the Sikhs must have perturbed the English East India Company. The Company was *anxious* to make itself akin to the political situations in the region, especially of Delhi and Punjab, and the military strength of various chiefs and factions, including different Sikh Sardars, who were fighting for hegemony in those areas. As a matter of fact, Company's future course of action largely depended upon these reports/accounts. There is evidence to show that soon the Company had started hobnobbing with the affairs of the cis-Sutlej territories/Chiefs culminating in bringing under their protection the Chiefs of Nabha, Malwa and Sirhind first after the defeat of Sindhia in 1803 and then, barring the period of George Barlow (1805-07), finally in the period of Lord Minto in 1809.

The *Calendar of Persian Correspondence*[17] being letters which passed between some of the East India Company's servants and Indian rulers and notables, gives minute details and throws considerable light on the position, especially, of the Sikhs, the Afghans, the Mughal Emperor, the Marathas, the Rohillas and other notable political Chiefs, their inter-relations and above all the interest and attitude of the English towards the problems particularly created by the activities of the Durranis and the Sikhs in then *Subah* Punjab and in the other outlying regions covering the territories of then *Subah* Multan as well as *cis*-Satluj and Jamuna-Ganges regions which formed a part of *Subah* Delhi during the second half of the eighteenth century. The name of Sardar Jassa Singh Ahluwalia has also appeared several times in this *Correspondence.*

This *Correspondence* has given two different versions regarding the position of the Sikhs at the time of Ahmad Shah Abdali's invasion of India in December 1766. On the one hand it has described the Sikh power weak enough to face the challenge of Ahmad Shah Abdali and has stated that the Sikhs were not well-versed in the art of pitched battle and because of their mutual quarrels, the Sikh Sardars were not cooperating with each other nor were they prepared to fight under a common command. It has been mentioned that the "Sikhs are taken up with intestine quarrels" and "not a single Sikh chief appears to oppose the Shah."[18] Since "these people are under no command", they "have not made any attempts to bring on a general engagement with the Shah," "nor does unanimity reign in their counsels sufficiently to make them resolved on a pitched battle" with him.[19] When the Shah had come as far Fazilabad, "about 12 *kos* from Aminabad and 6 *kos* on the other side of Lahore", several Sikh Sardars who "were in the city of Lahore with a body of 8,000 horse, on the approach of Shah, abandoned the fort and town with precipitation." The result was that the Afghan generals "passing over the river Ravi at Razi Ghat took possession of the city of Lahore."[20]

On the other hand, the *Correspondence* has also narrated the weak position of Ahmad Shah Abdali *vis-a-vis* the Sikhs and the English during the same period and his inability to establish himself firmly in India. It is very much clear that inspite of the success of the Abdali's forces at Lahore "he will not advance beyond Shahjahanabad, nor does it appear possible that he will be able to put Lahore under a proper form of

Government or disperse the Sikhs within the compass of two years."[21] Another letter has also corroborated the same view and states that "as soon as he (Abdali) crossed the river at Sirhind, the Sikhs took possession of Lahore and the country between the rivers Ravi and Sutlej, and placed garrisons there. In the writer's opinion, the Shah will not be able either to bring the Sikhs to punishment or expel then from the country between the two rivers."[22] It has also been opined in one of the letters that Ahmad Shah Abdali must have got very much disheartened because of the difficulties and the losses that he suffered during his earlier campaigns. It further states, "It is by no means his intention to settle in this country. Besides he has no claim to it. All he wants is to amass money". Under the circumstances it would at least be impossible for him to go beyond Delhi as the "fame of the victories of the English must have reached his ears."[23] During this period the fortunes of Ahmad Shah Abdali seems to have taken a dramatic change for the worse. It is revealed in one of letters dated 30th March, 1767 which shows that he "will probably wage war for two or three months, at the end of which he will either fall a sacrifice to his own troops through his inability to discharge their pay, or to the sword of the Sikhs or seek shelter in his own dominions."[24] Moreover, a letter written by General Barker to Jhanda Singh indicates that by the year 1771, the English had also recognized the importance of the Sikh Army. He wrote, "...rumour of Shah Abdali's approach, but he cannot cross the Attock for fear of the *Khalisah* army.... It is clear that as long as the *Khalisah* army is on the watch, no one can march upon Hindustan unopposed."[25]

It is quite interesting to note that due to the hostile and adverse atmosphere, Ahmad Shah Abdali, either on the advise of his advisers or on his own accord, tried to adopt conciliatory attitude towards the Marathas, Sikhs and the Rohillas. As regards the Marathas, Abdali was persuaded by his Wazir, Shah Vali Khan, to recognise the authority of the Peshwa by presenting him with "the *tika* of Rajaship, the impression of his palm dipped in saffron (*Kesha-e-Panja*), robes, jewels, horses and an elephant."[26] But there is hardly any reference of the Marathas joining hands with the Afghans. On the contrary they were always "ready in their allegiance to His Majesty (Mughal Emperor)."[27] Moreover, the *Correspondence* shows that some of the Sikhs were helping a Jat group "with the object of exterminating the Mahrattas"[28] while the English never wanted that the Marathas should ever cross the river Narbada.[29]

During Ahmad Shah Abdali's campaign of 1766-67, Najibu'd-Daulah, the Rohilla Chief strongly desired that the former "should advance and seat himself on the throne of Delhi" and was prepared to join him, but the Shah was "not in readiness."[30] Najibu'd-Daulah, in order to earn the favour of the Shah, had gone to the extent of saying that "if the Shah gives him orders he will raise for him two crores of rupees from the Chiefs of Hindustan, and seat Timur Shah, Ahmad Shah's son, on the throne of Delhi."[31] But it was only after he had "settled the *peshkash* for the Shah at 25 lakh of rupees," that he was given the "charge of Sirhind and the country between the Bias and Sutlej."[32]

There are several references in the *Correspondence* which depict that apart from Raja Amar Singh some of the other Sikh Sardars were also sympathetic towards the Durranis and even joined hands with them in fighting against other Sikh Sardars. At the time of Ahmad Shah Abdali's invasion during 1766-67, it has been pointed out, "Amar Singh's *Vakil* is at Birdawal and preparing to join the Shah's army."[33] When Ahmad Shah had crossed Attock and entered Rohtasgarh, it was reported that, "A pair of *qasids* have come from the grandson of Allah Singh"[34] and when his army had reached the neighbourhood of Chak, "The *Vakil* of Amar Singh and Himat Singh, grandsons of Allah Singh, came and made his obeisance to the Shah and presented him on behalf of his masters with Rupees 5,000/- and 2 horses as a *nazr.* To Shah Vali Khan and Jahan Khan, he presented Rupees 2,000/- each."[35] Due to the unfavourable circumstances, when Shah was determined to retreat to his country, though outwardly he was proposing to remain "a year longer at Lahore to complete the destruction of the Sikhs," Raja Amar Singh was "called upon to pay 9 lakhs, which sum became due during his management of the Sirhind country."[36]

Some of the other Sikh Sardars not only paid their respects to Ahmad Shah Abdali, at least two of them, Gujar Singh and Laltha Singh "were introduced to him by Shah Vali Khan and were each presented with a *Khil'at.* The Shah took them into service and sent them to the Subah of Lahore.[37]

On the other hand, Sardar Jassa Singh Ahluwalia, along with likeminded Sikh Sardars, gave stiff resistance to the Durrani forces. He fought with the Shah's troops in December 1766 near Chak, "being wounded went to the village of Chak Ranwah" and thence to the jungles. After a futile chase, "the Shah returned from pursuing them and encamped."[38] Then, later in the same month, Shah had another encounter with Jassa Singh and his fellow Sikh Sardars "who were encamped at village of Kalsah, which is about 35 Kos on this side of Lahore and is at the same distance from the Bias."[39] Though on the 29th December, Shah's forces had gained control over Lahore and it was "evacuated by the Sikhs,"[40] not only Sardar Jassa Singh Ahluwalia and others remained unrouted, the control over Lahore also proved temporary. The Sikhs once again took possession of

Lahore immediately after Shah had crossed the river at Sirhind.[41] It seems that Ahmad Shah Abdali ,recognizing Sardar Jassa Singh Ahluwalia as one of the most important Sikh leaders and his invincibility, wanted to bring him round either by love or threats. On 15th of January 1767 he wrote to him and two of his fellow Sikh Sardars, Khumda Singh and Khushal Singh, "to the effect that if they were desirous of entering his service, they should come and join him, but that if they had any hostile intentions, they should meet him in the field."[42] But it had no impact on Jassa Singh and the Sikh forces kept on "hovering all round the Shah's army."[43]

The *Correspondence* has given a different version regarding the attitude of, at least, some of the zamindars towards the Sikh Sardars, including Sardar Jassa Singh Ahluwalia, who were fighting against Ahmad Shah Abdali. At the same time, it is also established that the Shah, not only claimed political sovereignty in the Punjab territories, but also, realized *peshkash* from the different zamindars on the Mughal pattern and the latter were also eager to settle the payments. Contrary to the view point of different writers, the local zamindars, out of fear, would not cooperate with the Sikh Sardars even in emergency. When Sardar Jassa Singh Ahluwalia was wounded while fighting against the Shah's troops in December, 1766 and had taken shelter in the village of Chak Ranwah, "upon the zamindar of Chak Ranwah representing to Jassa Singh that the village would be plundered on his account, he went towards the jungles."[44] Moreover, when "Shah, on the 20th January (1767), was encamped at Shiver Theley" and chiefs like Raja Amar Singh and Himmat Singh, grandsons of Alah Singh had paid their respects to the former, the *Correspondence* states, "The other zamindars of that quarter are likewise ready, and are settling the payments of their respective districts", whereas, "the neighbouring zamindars are coming to him and settling their payments through the mediation of Shah Vali Khan."[45]

It is quite evident from the *Correspondence* that the Sikhs were always ready in their allegiance to the Mughal Emperor[46] and the latter also sought their help, though with all the precautions, on several occasions either out of fear or for helping him and the English against the Rohillas. It was reported in the *Correspondence* of March 2, 1768 that the Sikhs were "actually committing hostilities and depredations"[47] in and around Agra, whereas the *Correspondence* of July 13; 27; and December 19, 1774 show that the Sikhs had "plundered and burnt Shahdara"[48] after usurping Karnal, Panipat and Sirhind; were "preparing to march towards Indri,"[49] and made their "Appearance in the neighbourhood Shahjahanabad."[50] The Mughal Emperor first summoned Samru in 1774[51] and then invited Nawab Asafu'd-Daulah in 1775[52] to assist him in fighting against the Sikhs. On the one hand Nawab Najibu'd-Daulah "had taken possession of the Royal revenues of the province of Delhi" and declared that "if he had not done so, the Sikhs would have usurped the revenues"[53] and on the other, "the Sikh rising and the drought have further stopped the collections of several of the *parganas.*"[54]

One of the unconfirmed reports, dated 13th January, 1768, indicates that some of the disturbances apparently created by the Sikhs were due to the fact that the Mughal Emperor Shah Alam had "commanded them to see to the expulsion of Najibu'd-Daulah." Otherwise "they would have been contented with exacting a chauth after the example of the Marathas."[55] But the future correspondence did confirm that the Mughal emperor was certainly anxious in getting the help of the Sikh Sardars against the Rohillas.

In a letter, apparently written by Sardar Jassa Singh Ahluwalia, sometime in early 1768, to the Mughal emperor, it was proposed that "His Majesty should advance in his fortunate and propitious person to the Capital, assuring His Majesty that the whole empire will be again united and restored to him."[56] In reply to the above proposal, the Mughal emperor, who had been "perpetually awaiting the opportunity when he may illuminate Shahjahanabad with his presence and purge the Empire of profanations,"[57] replied, "If the addressee and the whole body of the Sikh Sardars can form a binding confederacy and accompany his fortunate stirrup, the Empire will be easily restored to order and obedience and the tyrants of the realm confounded."[58] But, apart from giving due regards to the "representations" made by Jassa Singh Ahluwalia, since, it seems, he could not take the Sikhs for granted, the Mughal emperor wanted to "associate all the Sardars together and making it a general cause."[59] He wrote, "The addressee should then send an *arzi* under the seals of the whole body of Sardars by the hands of a Sardar of eminence and character, chosen from amongst them,.. .and His Majesty will advance his standards with a proper and well ordered army. Will take the addressee along with his stirrup and enter on the affairs of his Government."[60]

The *News* of May 18, 1774 reveals that the Mughal emperor had sent *Khil'ats* for the Sikh chiefs invited them to enter his service with a body of 10,000 horse and offered to allot to the *pargana* of Shahbazpur[61] for their support.[62] Since there is no further reference in this context, it is difficult to presume whether this offer was accepted or rejected by the Sikhs.

It is very interesting to note that the Sikhs during this period had no permanent friends or enemies and always formed alliance taking into consideration the political and/or economic expediency. The

Correspondence indicates that the Sikhs in alliance with Zabitah Khan, during early 1775, were "creating disturbances near the capital (Delhi)"[63] and there was a proposal from the Mughal emperor "to buy up the Sikhs by giving them 50,000 rupees.. but as no reliance could be placed upon them, the proposal had to be given up."[64] When Zabitah Khan, along with the Sikhs, after having totally defeated the Royal army, was advancing towards Shahjahanbad, the Vazir, Nawab Asafu'd-Daulah sought the cooperation of the latter with him (Nawab *Vazir*) and the English for expelling the former and the other Rohillas from *Doab*. Even though the Sikhs were already in alliance with Zabitah Khan, when they were offered 10 lakhs of rupees, one-half to be paid on their entering into alliance and other half on the defeat of Zabitah Khan, alongwith annual payment of half the revenues of the *Doab,* the Sikh chiefs "threw off their connections with Zabitah Khan and entered into an alliance with the Nawab *Vazir* on the aforesaid terms."[65] Another conjecture that can be made from the *Correspondence* is that apart from the Mughal emperor, the English, who by that time had become an important Indian power, were also equally, if not more, keen in overpowering the Rohillas for which they wanted to make use of the Sikhs, either by making them an ally or by just disuading them from the Rohillas, through the good offices of the Nawab *Vazir.* Another agreement proposed to the Sikhs, for expelling other Rohillas, gave clear indication that the English were not mere spectators but were, as a matter of fact, party to it, though the proposal was made on behalf of the *Vazir*. The Sikhs were offered 7 lakh of rupees in two instalments—"One to be paid in advance and the other to be paid on their expelling the Rohillas." The *qabuliat* was executed "in favour of the *Vazir.*" The other details of the *qabuliat* showed that in future the Nawab *Vazir* would get, through the English, every year a sum of Rs. 26 lakhs, where as the Sikhs would be paid every year a sum of Rs. 4 lakhs from the *Kharif* harvest and Rs. 3 lakh from the *Rabi* harvest.[66] It is, however, not clear whether the Sikhs would also receive the above amount through the English or through the Nawab *Vazir*. Moreover, it is quite intriguing that the King was not only congratulated for his victory over Zabitah Khan but also over the Sikhs as well and was sent a *"nazr* of 101 gold *mohurs.*[67]

The fact that the English were seriously concerned about the activities of the Sikhs and wanted to put a check on them is firmly established by other evidence given in the *Correspondence.* When they came to know that Mir Qasim Ali was thinking of invading Bengal by "inviting the Sikhs and the Marathas in his cause," not only the proposed allies were blamed for instigating the former, but also declared, "It is necessary for the well-being of Hindustan that the Sikhs should not be allowed to cross the frontier of Sirhind."[68]

Foreign Department/Secret Proceedings have provided significant contemporary information and insight regarding the position and activities of the Sikh Sardars including Sardar Jassa Singh Ahluwalia during the later half of the eighteenth century. Of course, some of the accounts are similar to that of furnished in the above discussed, *Calendar of Persian Correspondence,* but this fact has made these *Proceedings* all the more important and indispensible. Apart from giving the information about the terror that had been created by the Sikhs in the areas of Delhi and around, these *Proceedings* have also described about the concern of both Mughal emperor and the English regarding that and their eagerness to come to an agreement with the Sikhs to overcome the problem. Above all, little information concerning some aspects of the administrative framework of Sardar Jassa Singh Ahluwalia is also available in the above *Proceedings.*

It is very interesting to note that it was after "several conferences of the *Khalsa Seick* Chiefs"[69] with the representatives of the Nawab *Vazir* that the former could be persuaded to break their alliance with the Rohilla Chief Zabitah Khan and come to an, above discussed, agreement with the latter (Nawab *Vazir*) in September 1776.[70] The *Proceedings* of the same date also show that the Sikhs had assumed friendship with the English as well.[71] But it seems that the above agreement had not provided any respite to the Mughals and the Sikh attacks had continued uninterrupted. The Mughal emperor, who was staying at Lucknow, "alarmed at the accounts he daily receives of the ravages of the Sikhs about the environs of Delhy," desired, "he might immediately return to oppose the incursion of the Sikhs."[72]

The intelligence reports of 6th/8th March 1783 point out that the Sikh forces had extended their areas of attack to the Jamuna-Ganga regions, covering the parts of present Uttar Pradesh, Haryana and Delhi. After fighting on the banks of river Ganga, they, on 6th March, 1783, were reported to have moved "towards Anoopshear, Ali Ghur, Kass Gunge and Khoorjah."[73] and on 8th of the same month they were placed enroute "towards Furrockabad."[74] It is quite probable that in these attacks Sardar Jassa Singh Ahluwalia, who has been described as the "Chief of the *Seiks*,"[75] along with other principal Sikh Sardars, had played a prominent role.

The intelligence report of the same date stated that the Sikhs under their chiefs, namely, Jassa Singh, Hasa Singh, Karam Singh, Dewan Singh and others were found in the vicinity of Delhi and it was apprehended that they might attack Delhi. It was reported that they "marched from village Shemsheer and laid waste and plundered 8 towns in the district of Bangh Putt, then proceeded to Buran which stands the banks of the

Jamna, 7 *kos* from Delhi."[76] After this, a party of them "crossed over the Jamna and plundered the Rookoolla Khan and the Town of Buderpoor, which is on the West bank of the Jamna." When the Sikhs sent "a pair of Hercarras to the Nabob Mujid Dowulah to demand the Rakhi for the city"[77] and there were great apprehensions that they might attack the city of Delhi, the Mughal emperor is reported to have got panicy. He "despatched orders to Merza Shuffi Khan and to Afraisial Khan to march towards Delhi with all their forces immediately."[78] It is quite evident from Warren Hastings' Minute about Sikhs dated 4th December, 1784 that they had been collecting *rakhi* either from the city of Delhi itself or at least from its suburbs.[79] He stated, "they (Sikhs) carried their depredations to the very suburbs of Delhi, where two of their officers actually reside in a quarter called '*Subzee Mundee*,' which is chiefly occupied by shroffs and shopkeepers, for double purpose of levying their *rauky* and of protecting the inhabitants from the marauders of their own nation."[80] Thereafter the Sikhs had "proceeded to Naziff Gur which is 10 kos from Delhi."[81]

A letter from Lt. Col. Christian Knudson to Colonel Sir John Cumming, dated April 12, 1783, shows that the English were also feeling very much concerned about the activities of the Sikhs and wanted to take protective measures against them. When they had received the intelligence of a body of Sikhs having passed the Jamuna under the command of one of their sardars, Jassa Singh, they apprized Khawaja Ain-ul-Din the *amil* of Rohilkhand about the situation. They wanted him to keep them informed about "the motion of the Sikhs"[82] to enable them "to take such steps, as may be necessary for the protection of it (Rohilkhand) against the incursions of the *Seiks*."[83]

The Sikhs, presumably under Sardar Jassa Singh Ahluwalia, also suffered a defeat at the hands of the Mughal forces "at the Battle of Cas Gunge".[84] It is also reported that "the brother of Jassa Singh, Chief of the Seiks was killed.. by a ball he recieved, as he was sitting on his elephant."[85] Another letter gave the name of the Sikh Sardar, thus killed, as, "Jeshru."[86]

Some indirect inferences, regarding the administrative structure of Sardar Jassa Singh Ahluwalia, can also be drawn from these *Secret Proceedings*. No doubt, because of continuous increase or decrease in the territories under the influence of Jassa Singh Ahluwalia, the size of the units, in which the territories were divided could not remain static. It could be safely presumed that the smallest unit was the *mauza* or a village and the primary units were the *ta'alluqas*.[87] The system of granting *jagirs,* for the maintenance of horsemen, also comes to light from the study of these *Proceedings*. For instance, Diwan Singh was granted Nurmahal worth 50,000 rupees on the condition of maintaining 150 horsemen.[88]

Moreover, the *Proceedings* also reveal that Sardar Jassa Singh Ahluwalia, at the time of his death in 1783, had about 7,500 horsemen and 2,500 foot soldiers and his total resources amounted to about 8 lakhs of rupees a year.[89]

Another contemporary/near contemporary English writer, *Major James Browne*, the author of *'Indian Tracts, History of the Origin and Progress of the Sicks'*, is perhaps the first European to write on Sikhs and his book was published from London in 1788. His appointment as Agent and Envoy of the Governor General in the court of the Mughal Emperor, Shah Alam not only provided him and the East India Company an opportunity to understand the day to day political affairs at the Imperial Court at Delhi but also made them akin to the situation in the region, especially of Delhi and Punjab, and the military strength of the various chiefs and factions, including the different Sikh Sardars, who were fighting for hegemony in these areas.[90]

It is quite clear from the forwarding letter,[91] dated 17th September 1787, submitted, along with the above work, to John Motteux, Chairman of the Hon'ble Court of Directors that, in view of the fast growing political importance of the Sikhs, the English must have got anxious to obtain an authentic account about them. It seems that Warren Hastings must have conveyed this desire of the Court of Directors to Major James Browne.

The first portion regarding the "rise" of the Sikhs is, as a matter of fact, the translation (translated by Major Browne, who himself was a good Persian scholar) of a Persian manuscript, prepared at the instance of James Browne himself, by Budh Singh Arora of Lahore and Ajaib Singh Suraj of Malerkotla. But though he wanted the account "without injuring the essential purpose of information," he found it "extremely defective in a regular continuation of dates."[92] Though he had no ready means to check and eliminate the inaccuracies, he cannot escape the responsibility of committing errors in translating and paraphrasing the Persian text. Inspite of that, Browne has provided, though brief, quite a useful and systematic account of the Sikhs, their polity, society, institutions and practices during the eighteenth century. Moreover, his book has thrown considerable light on the political activities of the Sikh Sardars including Sardar Jassa Singh Ahluwalia during that period.

James Browne is of the opinion that every Sikh Sardar or chief had many petty chiefs under him which constituted his confederacy and the number of latter chiefs has been computed to something like 400 to 500. All these chiefs of higher category enjoyed distinct authority in their respective districts uncontrolled by any superior power and would assemble together only on particular occasions. No doubt, a leader, to command their joint forces, was chosen from amongst those chiefs whose *zamindaris* were most considerable, by a majority vote, he would invariably be ill-obeyed by his fellow, comparatively, smaller chiefs and would barely allow him, during his temporary elevation, the dignity of *primus inter pares*. He has further opined that the Sikhs "confederated for the purpose of conquest" and that "they have called their confederacy, *Khalsa Gee,* or the State." He has defined the *Dal Khalsa* as "the grand army" and as "the army of the state," and *Gurmatta* as "the grand Diet of the Sikh Chiefs."[93] But to the political activities of the Sikhs, Major Browne has described them as "depredations" and "highway robbery."[94] He has spoken very high of the Sikh chiefs regarding their attitude towards those *zamindars* who accepted to pay *Rakhi*, to which he has called "tribute". He says, "Whenever a zamindar has agreed to pay this tribute to any Sick Chief, that chief not only himself refrains from plundering him, but will protect him from all others; and this protection is by general consent held so far sacred, that even if the grand army passed through a *zamindari* where the safeguards of the lowest Sick chief are stationed, it will not violate them."[95]

Browne has written about the plight of Ahmad Shah Abdali during his campaign of December, 1756, when the Sikhs plundered the stragglers from his camp and had cut off his supplies. Though greatly enraged, Ahmad Shah could only threaten them with punishment on his return journey. But the very next year the Sikhs were defeated at the hands of Jahan Khan at Amritsar.[96] Ahmad Shah Abdali once again felt helpless when in 1761, after the third battle of Panipat, his army, loaded with plunder, was attacked by the Sikhs immediately after it had crossed the river Sutlej. Browne wrote, "Every night he had to throw up a slight work round his camp and in this manner he continued his march to Attock, the Sicks following him all the way. When the Afghans crossed the Attock, the Sicks returned to blockade Lahore."[97]

Sardar Jassa Singh Ahluwalia, to whom James Browne has considered "a chief of considerable weight and abilities, having been chosen commander of their (Sikhs') grand army (*Dal Khalsa*),"[98] has been given reasonably prominent place in this book. Browne has, of course, taken a critical view of Jassa Singh's operation in Sirhind in 1761. It was under his leadership that the Sikhs had defeated Zain Khan's deputy and "began to devastate the accursed city against which their wrath knew no bounds."[99]

The most controversial thing that Major James Browne has opined in his book is that the Sikhs under the chief command of Sardar Jassa Singh Ahluwalia alone expelled the Afghan forces under Timur Shah and Jahan Khan from Lahore in 1758, occupied the provincial capital and declared their 'sovereignty.' Jassa Singh, as per the usual practice of the time, struck the coins in his own name on that occassion. Narrating the above incident, Browne wrote, "The Sicks collected together under chiefs from all quarters, and blockading the city of Lahore, collected the revenues of the country all around for their own use. Jehan Khan with the prince, marched out to give the battle, but after several actions, finding the Sicks too numerous for him to contend with, he retreated to Kandahar. Upon this occasion, Jassa Singh Kelal, who was at the time Commander-in-Chief of the Dul, struck rupees in his own name, at the royal mint at Lahore with the following inscription,

'Jassa Kalal conquered the country of Ahmed, and struck this coin by the grace of God."[100]

The Persian inscription on the above coin reads,

"Sikka zad dar Jahan bafazal-i-Akal,

Mulk-i-Ahmad garift Jassa Kalal."[101]

Major Brown, who is the earliest English author and who compiled his book nearly thirty years after that incident, has tried to explain the circumstances under which these coins had totally disappeared. He wrote. "after they had been current about fifteen years, the Grand Diet of the Sick Chiefs (*Gurmatta*), determined to call in all those rupees, and to strike them in the names of Guru Nanak and Guru Gobind Singh."[102]

Browne has also written about the coins struck for the second time in *Samvat* 1822 (A.D. 1765), popularly known as '*Gobindshahi*' coins, after the Sikh conquest of Lahore in that year, about which there is hardly any controversy. He wrote, "Soon after the last expulsion of the Aumils of the Durrani Shah, the Sicks held a general diet (*Gurmatta*) at Amritsar, in which they determined to call in the rupees which were struck in the name of Jassa Kalal and to strike them for the future in the name of their Gooroos, with an inscription to their effect, 'Gooroo Gobind Singh, received from Nanak, the *Daig*, the sword and rapid victory', which coin is current throughout their dominions to this day."[103]

The Persian inscription on the obverse of these coins reads:

"Deg O tegh O fatah O nusrat bedirang

Yaft az Nanak Guru Gobind Sinh."[104]

George Forster, though a near-contemporary writer and technically a traveller, was very close to Major James Browne in his objective and approach regarding his writings on the Sikhs. Of course, for the contemporary period, former's account, being based on personal observations, is of greater dependability. Inspite of being a civil servant on the Madras establishment of the East India Company, his accounts reveal that he was also a scholar of considerable merit. Since he left for a long and strenuous overland journey from Bengal to England on May 23, 1782, a little more than a year before the death of Sardar Jassa Singh Ahluwalia, he could not give much of the first hand information regarding the activities of the Sikhs during and before the active political lifetime of the Sardar. As is borne out by one of his letters written to Mr. Gregory at Lucknow in 1783 that for the knowledge regarding the above period he was obliged to Colonel Polier of the Honourable Company's service (1757-75, 1782-89) "for having furnished me with large historical tracts of the Siques." With this he also added his own observations, information and impressions about the Sikhs and the Punjab that he gathered during the course of his travels. His book, *A Journey from Bengal to England through North India, Kashmir, Afghanistan, Persia, into Russia (1782-83),* is actually a travelogue comprising the compilation of a series of letters written during his journey which were published in two volumes in London in 1798.

There is no doubt that his account regarding the origin and early history of the Sikhs, probably due to the paucity of material, is extremely sketchy and replete with factual errors. In view of the great political achievements of the Sikhs, his motive was to acquaint the English East India Company with them and their activities during the eighteenth century.

George Forster is one of those English writers who has very rarely mentioned about the names of different Sikh Sardars and their respective activities. He has mainly written about the Sikhs in general and several important aspects of their society and polity, *viz*., their "aristocratical" government, their armed forces, their guerilla mode of fighting, their concern for the welfare of the people under their rule, their religion and their struggle against the Mughal and the Afghan armies. Nor has he, like any of the three different English writings discussed above, specifically mentioned about the organisation or the term *Misl*. He has certainly referred to the Mughal governors/*faujdars,* Nadir Shah and Ahmad Shah Abdali. But even without making any particular reference to Sardar Jassa Singh Ahluwalia, or for that matter any other Sikh Sardar, his description of certain important incidents of the period is really valuable.

George Forster's book reveals that for nearly a decade after the death of Banda Bahadur, the Sikhs experienced the worst possible time. Due to the action taken by the Mughal emperor, while some of them had sought shelter in northern hills, Malwa desert and Lakhi jungles, there were others who trimmed their hair and went back into the Hindu fold and were known as *"Khulasas"* or irregular Sikhs.[105] In the words of Forster, the "name of a sicque no longer existed in the Mughal dominion."[106]

At the time of Nadir Shah's attack, the Sikhs, as is clear from the account of Forster, had once again gained strength and had become quite bold. Narrating the incident of the Afghan leader's return journey after his success in Delhi, Forster wrote, "the *Sicque* forces appeared in arms at the period of Nadir Shah's return from Delhi, when the Persian army, encumbered with spoils, and regardless of order, was attacked in the rear by detached predatory parties of *Sicque* cavalry, who occasionally fell upon the baggage guards, and acquired a large plunder."[107]

Forster has praised the conciliatory policy of Diwan Kaura Mal, "who was himself of the Khualasah sect" towards the Sikhs in their fight with the forces under Muin-ul-Mulk, the *Subedar* of Lahore in 1748-49.[108]

He has also given an account of the great defeat of the Sikhs in February, 1762 known as *Ghallughara* and estimated that as many as 25,000 Sikhs lost their lives in that.[109]

But the revenge taken by the Sikhs in the same year in the month of October has been well described by Forster who has spoken very high of the frantic enthusiasm evoked by the religious sentiment of sacrifice amongst the Sikhs which forced Ahmad Shah to flee from Amritsar."[110]

Again without making any mention of the role played by any particular Sikh Sardar, Forster has written about the conquest of Lahore by the Sikhs in early 1763, after which, they are stated to have taken full revenge of the outrages committed by the Afghans, the previous year and they were also "compelled to excavate the reservoir at Amritsar."[111]

Forster has also estimated the combined strength of the Sikh forces in 1783 at 3,00,000.[112]

From the above discussion certain interesting and revealing facts come to light. For instance, despite the fact, the above four accounts discussed are contemporary or near contemporary ones and have also given the description of the military and territorial structure, word *misl* is conspicuously absent in all of them. That is perhaps the precise reason that even the names of different Sikh Sardars, if at all mentioned, have been mentioned without adding the names of their respective *misls*. Of course, there is an instance when Amar Singh and Gajpat Singh have been described as "Chiefs of Patiala."[113] Sardar Jassa Singh Ahluwalia has been mentioned as "Jassa Singh"[114] or "Jesa Singh Gulal"[115] or 'Jesah Singh, the elder"[116] or "Jessa Singh, a Sikh Sardar"[117] or "Jesa Singh, Chief of the Seiks"[118] or "Jessa Singh Kalal,"[119] This shows that either the sovereignty of the Sikh Sardars in their respective areas was not recognised or the term *'misl'* was not current during this period.

In contrast to the above discussion, one learns from the writings under review that in 1758, with the occupation of Lahore, the then capital of *Subah* Punjab, under the leadership of Sardar Jassa Singh Ahluwalia, the Sikhs declared their 'sovereignty'. In pursuance of the usual practice of the time the coins were also struck in the name of the leader.[120] It is, of course, besides the point whether the incident of coining the money is correct or not, or whether it was contrary to the wishes/practices of the *Panth,* or whether it was a mischief on the part of the *Qazis* and *Mullahs*. Moreover, there are several references of the collection/demand of *Rakhi* from different areas by the Sikh Sardars. But there is hardly any evidence to prove that they had been able to establish their sovereignty in those areas or the chiefs/*zamindars* who paid the *Rakhi* accepted them as their sovereign. As a matter of fact, collection/demand of *Rakhi* and the establishment of sovereignty are two different things altogether.

The Politico-military activities of the Sikhs and the Sikh Sardars have been described as 'depredations' and highway robbery.'[121]

It is wrong to presume that all the local *zamindars* were sympathetic to the cause of the Sikh Sardars and their *zamindaris* could be used as hideouts in emergency.[122] There were atleast some who, either out of fear of Ahmad Shah Abdali or due to other reasons, would not give shelter even to Sardar Jassa Singh Ahluwalia. It is, however, correct that the Sikh Sardars would, by and large, refrain from plundering the areas of the local *zamindars*/chiefs if the latter accepted to pay *Rakhi*, called tribute.[123]

These writers have highlighted the religious sentiments of sacrifice amongst the Sikhs in their fight against the Mughals and Durranis, thereby giving unduly religious colour to their struggle.[124]

It will be suicidal to use any of the above accounts, though contemporary or near contemporary, in isolation for no right conclusion can be drawn in that manner. These accounts can be useful if studied in co-ordination not only with the above four accounts but with the other contemporary documents and later sources as well. Most of the times, the term 'Sikhs' or Sikh Sardars' has been used in general and the name of a particular Sikh Sardar under whom they fought, suffered defeat or demanded *Rakhi* etc., is left to a mere conjecture of the reader. Moreover, if even the writings under discussion alone are studied in co-ordination, one can draw inferences that Sardar Jassa Singh Ahluwalia had also the practice of granting land in *in'am* for bringing waste land under cultivation; certain *muqaddams* and *chaudharis*, irrespective of their religion, were also among the recipients of *in'am* grants; and land was granted even to the religious persons, again, not necessarily to his co-religionists alone.[125]

Above all, it is quite evident, especially from the *Calendar of Persian Correspondence*, that Sikhs were unaware of the political and imperialistic designs of the English East India Company which had gained considerable power by that time. They, like the other contemporary Indian political powers, *e.g.*, Nizam-ul-Mulk, Nawabs of Carnatic, Awadh and Bengal etc., also failed to realize that the English were the most aggressive and expansionist power of the time. Owing to their ignorance and lack of contact with the rest of the world, the Sikhs did not know about the devastation caused by the English and the other Western trading companies in Africa, South-East Asia and Latin America. This was the precise reason that they had fallen prey to their political manoeuvres and allied with the English along with the Mughals against the Rohillas.[126] They were not far sighted enough to resist the temptation of a temporary material gain[127] and thereby restricting the growing political power of the English, who, on the other hand, not only wanted to check the growth of Sikh power beyond the river Sutlej[128] but had even congratulated the Mughal Emperor for defeating the Sikhs.[129]

English Writers of Maharaja Ranjit Singh's Period

(i) John Malcolm

(ii) Henry T. Prinsep

In the second category of English writers, *John Malcolm's* amongst other books, *Sketch of the Sikhs* (London, 1812) has to be viewed in the light of number of political changes that had occurred especially in regard to Punjab. Notwithstanding, the rise of Ranjit Singh's power, the political designs of the English had also started becoming clearer and clearer. Due to the English apprehension of a combined attack of the French monarch Napolean Bonaparte and Afghan Chief Zaman Shah on India, the former tolerated for some time Ranjit Singh's interference in the affairs of *cis*-Sutlej states, though they could successfully persuade him not to help the Maratha Sardar, Jaswant Rao Holkar. Meanwhile, the English had started creating a strong political front in the *cis*-Sutlej territories by bringing Nabha, Jind, Patiala etc. under their protection after the defeat of the Maratha Sardar, Mahadji Sindhia in 1803. At the same time, the English would not accept Ranjit Singh as the ruler of the Sikhs as a reward for a proposed defensive treaty between the two against the French. However, the new developments like, the entanglement of Napolean in the Peninsular War in Europe and friendly relations between Britain and Mahmud II, the new ruler of Turkey, turned the political scales in favour of the English in India. Ranjit Singh under the circumstances, was left with no alternative but to accept humiliating Treaty of Amritsar on 25 April 1809 with the English. Despite the fact that according to the treaty Maharaja Ranjit

Singh had been apparently given a free hand in the trans-Sutlej areas, the English still wanted to gather more information about Punjab keeping in view their future course of actions and designs. As such, the job before John Malcolm was to write with the conviction and motive that "every information regarding the Sikhs is of importance."

The scholar, statesman, John Malcolm, who had held various important military, political, diplomatic and administrative positions, including the prize post of the Governor of Bombay Presidency (1827-30), authored several books of considerable merit and information. Apart from his *Sketch of the Sikhs* (London, 1812), he has the distinction of writing the works like *History of India,* his *Memoirs*, his report on the General Provinces and the English translation of Bakhat Mal's *Khalsa Nama.*

John Malcolm is one of those English writers who, instead of writing about the activities and role played by the different Sikh Sardars in their fight against the Mughal and the Durrani forces, wrote about the Sikhs as a whole and has left it to the mere conjecture of the reader to make out the names of the Sikh leaders leading the Sikh forces at a particular juncture. But inspite of this and certain in-accuracies, his work seems to be more objective, richer in information and of better quality than the earlier works and many a thing written by him during the first decade of the nineteenth century in the brief treatise on the Sikhs remained unchallenged for quite some time.

For his *Sketch of the Sikhs*, Malcolm is believed to have been guided by George Forster's *A Journey from Bengal to England; Siyar-ul-Mutakharin* (in Persian) and several tracts written by Sikh authors in the Punjabi and Dogri dialects provided to him by Dr. Leyden supplemented, of course, by his own close personal observations during his Punjab tour in 1805 accompanying Lord Lake in pursuit of the Maratha Sardar, Jaswant Rao Holkar.

Since he was writing at a time when the curiosity of the English East India Company about the rising Sikh Community knew no bounds and "every information regarding the Sikhs is of importance", the motivation behind this work could be in no way different from that of earlier English writers like Major James Browne and George Forster etc.

John Malcolm has opined that the Sikhs who had spent nightmarish period for more than a decade after the death of Banda Bahadur had started asserting their political superiority simultaneously with the disintegration of the Mughal empire. Especially, the invasion of Nadir Shah in 1739, which had damaged the remnant power, wealth and prestige of the Mughal empire beyond redemption, provided lot of encouragement to the Sikhs. They had not only constructed a small mud fort at Dallewal[130] to serve them as a place of retreat and refute, the more daring amongst them had begun to visit Amritsar more freely even at the risk of death.[131] Apart from giving due importance to the above factors, Malcolm has also cited the ardour of the spirit of the Sikhs which led to their ultimate triumph.[132]

Without making any specific reference to Sardar Jassa Singh Ahluwalia, John Malcolm has mentioned about the constituting of the *Dal Khalsa.*[133] He has, of course, described it as "combined forces of the Sikh Sardars at a certain place and time."[134]

Like Forster,[135] John Malcom also wrote about the help rendered by Diwan Kaura Mal, a *"Khulasa"* Sikh[136] (*i.e.* believer in the Sikh religion but without having adopted the tenets of Guru Gobind Singh) to the Sikh forces in 1748-49 against the forces of Muin-ul-Mulk, the *Subedar* of Lahore.[137]

Malcolm has given very interesting version regarding the attitude of Adina Beg Khan towards the Sikhs. He is of the view that the former, especially in 1752, looked upon the continuing political activities of the Sikhs as the means of his personal advancement and, as such, was not only interested in not reducing them altogether rather entered into a secret understanding with them, which indirectly helped them in gaining further strength.[138]

The Sikhs, in due course, had become so formidable that they could even dare attack Ahmad Shah Abdali on his way back to Afghanistan in early 1757 and were successful in acquiring a part of the enormous booty that he was carrying to his country. Ahmad Shah on his part being unable to do anything but to order his experienced general Jahan Khan, deputy to the newly appointed governor of Lahore, Timur Shah, to take vengeance on the Sikhs. Jahan Khan apart from defeating the Sikhs later in the same year destroyed and polluted all their places of worship at Amritsar.[139]

John Malcolm narrating the activities the Sikhs, apparently under the Chief Command of Sardar Jassa Singh Ahluwalia, in and around Lahore during the early 1758 writes, "They (Sikhs) all assembled at Lahore and not only attempted to cut off the communication between the fort and the country, but collected and divided the revenues of the towns and villages around it."[140] He agrees with Major Browne regarding the seizure of Lahore by the Sikhs in 1758 and subsequent striking of the coins by them.[141]

Malcolm, while giving the description about the *Ghallughara* in 1762, believes that upward of 20,000 Sikhs lost their lives in this bloody carnage and in Amritsar their sacred buildings were destroyed by the Abdali forces.[142] But he has hesitated in believing the authenticity of the version given by George Forster[143] regarding the subsequent revenge taken by the Sikhs later in the same year which forced Ahmad Shah Abdali to escape from Amritsar to Lahore.[144]

Though published in 1812, the *Sketch of the Sikhs*, like any of the previous English writings, does not contain any reference to the existence, organisation or the term *Misl*. Moreover, Malcolm has opined that it was Guru Gobind Singh who directed the assemblage of '*Gurumatta*' and himself convened it for the first time. But he has not cited any authority for believing that Guru Gobind Singh ordained any formal or particular institution.[145]

By the time other English writer of this category, *Henry T. Prinsep,* published his work in 1834 a lot more political developments had taken place in the national and international arena, especially on the north-western parts of India. Maharaja Ranjit Singh had not only captured Attack, Kashmir, Dera Ghazi Khan, Dera Ismail Khan, Bakhar, Leh, Mankera and above all Peshawar but was trying to increase his political influence in Afghanistan through its fugitive ruler, Shah Shuja. Afghanistan had become a prey to the politics of Europe because of the growing differences between Britain and Russia. Russian influence had so much increased in Persia and Central Asia that English had started feeling *Rus-Phobia* and was considered dangerous for the security of latter's empire in India. Maharaja Ranjit Singh was being considered as a stumbling block. As such, though Prinsep has given his object of writing his work as to give a narrative of the occurrences leading to the rise of Ranjit Singh, the brief but useful information about the activities and political, social and economic fabric of the Sikhs show that the English were preparing for the take off at an opportune time.

Henry T. Prinsep's book entitled, *The Origin of the Sikh Power in the Punjab and the Political Life of Maharaja Ranjit Singh with an Account of the Religion, Laws and Customs of the Sikhs* (1834) was another serious attempt by the English on Punjab history after more than two decades of the publication of John Malcolm's *Sketch of the Sikhs*. Starting his career as a writer in the East India Company at the age of sixteen, on 20th December 1808, Henry Prinsep remained in close contact with the Indian affairs by holding various important positions. He was the Persian Secretary to the Government, member of the Governor General's Council, elected member of the British Parliament, elected member of the Court of Directors and, after the transfer of power in 1858, was also offered membership of India Council, which he held till 1874.[146] Apart from his *Origin of the Sikh Power*...he has the credit of writing several other works of historical importance.[147]

It is quite probable that Henry Prinsep wrote the book on the Sikhs while he was the Persian Secretary to the Government. It is also evident from the book that notwithstanding his own discretion regarding the facts and events of the period covered[148] *i. e.* roughly from 1742 to 1833,[149] Prinsep has largely depended upon Captain Murrary, "who has the merit of being the first to collect and put together in a consistent narrative, the lose fragments and materials that exist, in respect to the events in the Punjab at this period"[150] and Captain Wade, "Whose information as to the origin of the family of Ranjit Singh, will have been derived from the most authentic sources."[151] Moreover, the chapter on 'Notes' clearly shows that Prinsep also made use of Khushwant Rai's monumental Persian work *Tarikh-i-Sikhan* which provided an account of the Sikhs upto 1811.[152]

Since, as admitted by Prinsep himself that his objective of writing this book was to give a narrative of the occurrences leading to the rise of Ranjit Singh[153], he has given a little but useful information 'about the activities and some aspects of the administrative structure of the Sikhs and different Sikh Sardars during the eighteenth century from the invasion of Nadir Shah onward. However, as compared to other Sikh Sardars like Alha Singh, Amar Singh, Jhanda Singh, Jassa Singh Ramgarhia, Charat Singh and Maha Singh, Sardar Jassa Singh Ahluwalia has not figured so prominently in this account. Certain indirect inferences, however, can certainly be drawn about him.

Writing about the circumstances leading to the rise of the Sikhs and the nature of their activities around the middle of the eighteenth century, especially when Yahya Khan held the viceroyalty of Lahore, Prinsep has opined that the "Jat Zamindars of Punjab" who had been empoverished due to "long extortion" by the Mughal government, in desperation, "took to repine and plunder for the support of themselves and families, and as a bond of union and excitement against their oppressors revived in their customs and ceremonies, the latent flame of the Sikh ritual."[154] The Sikhs, discarding "the more peaceable doctrines of the *Vedas* and *Shastras* of pure Hinduism" and following "the maxims and precepts of the *Granth* of Guru Govind" began their activities "at first in secret-association and isolated acts of depredation."[155] The initial groups of 'armed men, in tens and twenties, called *Dharwi* in the dialect of the province, that is, highwaymen.....were united by common, no less than by the profession of a new faith; and system of general confederation for defence, or for operations requiring more than single efforts, was early arranged between the chiefs."[156] The associations, thus formed, "were called *Misals*, implying that they were confederacies of equals, under chiefs of their own selection."[157]

Moreover, the invasion of Ahmad Shah Abdali around this period, as opined by Prinsep, also proved "favourable to the further rise of the Sikhs." The preoccupation of the Mughal and the Durrani forces "in the struggle for empire on the plains of Sarhind"[158] provided the Sikhs an opportunity of making unchecked "depredations" and "ventured even to satisfy their religious prejudices by stolen visits to the shrines of their faith at Amritsar."[159] "A small party of Sikhs had the audacity to throw up a mud work which they called Ram-Rauni, in the district and immediate vicinity of Amritsar, and the Sikh plunderers scoured the country in all directions."[160]

Prinsep has written about Adina Beg Khan's success in persuading the Sikhs along with the Marathas to help him against the Durrani forces under Prince Timur and Jahan Khan. Adina Beg was able to enrol a considerable number of Sikh and Maratha soldiers in his payroll. The strength of the combined forces was powerful enough to occupy Lahore and forced the Durranis to retire "precipitately to the Indus."[161] In this regard Prinsep has definitely mentioned the name of Maratha leader Malhar Rao Holkar but has failed to give the names of Sikh leaders under whose leadership the Sikhs had agreed to help Adina Beg. Some of the Persian sources[162] do point out that the Mughal General Adina Beg Khan won over Sodhi Barbhag Singh and Jassa Singh Ahluwalia by payment of a heavy tribute, besides granting them many concessions of loot due to which the whole *Dal Khalsa* had got ready to fight on his side. Moreover, Prinsep's assertion of the occupation of Lahore by the Mughal-Sikh-Maratha joint forces is contrary to that of earlier English writers who had asserted that the Sikhs alone expelled the Afghans from Lahore and their leader Jassa Singh Ahluwalia also struck coins in his own name. Nor has Prinsep mentioned about the capture of Lahore by the Sikhs in 1761.

Prinsep has made reference to the incidence "*Ghalu-Ghara* or bloody carnage" in 1762 in which he has estimated that 25,000 to 30,000 men had been killed. He has also stated that according to Captain Murray "the entire killed and wounded of the Sikhs in this battle did not exceed 12,000."[163]

Henry Prinsep has also written about the conferring of the title of '*Raja*' on Alha Singh of Patiala in 1762[164] and the title of '*Maharaja Rajgan-Mahendar Bahadur*' on his grandson Amar Singh in 1764 by Ahmad Shah Abdali.[165] However, Prinsep is absolutely quiet regarding the attitude of the Sikh Chief towards Allah Singh when he accepted the honour from the Durrani Chief. Nor has he mentioned the role of Sardar Jassa Singh Ahluwalia in pacifying the situation.

Prinsep is of the view that after 1764 neither Ahmad Shah Abdali nor, after his death in 1773, his son Timur Shah made any "attempt to recover Lahore, and the Punjab." These along with the province of Sirhand and the area on the east as far as the Jamuna "fell into the possession of the (Sikh) chiefs and associations" and the movements of the Sikhs were " by any further interference from the west."[166]

Inspite of the fact that every Sikh Sardar, according to his strength, seized whatever fell in his way, and acknowledged no superior, nor submitted to the control of any body, nor to any constituted authority whatsoever, but still, as Prinsep has opined, "Most of these looked upon themselves as partners and associates in each enterprise"[167] and regarded the lands, thus "acquired as a common property."[168] All these associates or confederacies, divided into twelve principal *misls*, had their own distinguishing titles and "together could bring into field about 70,000 horse."[169]

About the Ahluwalia *Misl*, Prinsep writes that it was then headed by "Jassa Singh, *Kalal*, or mace-bearer".[170] Jassa Singh Ahluwalia, according to Prinsep, "rose to great eminence amongst the Sikhs, and by his followers was honoured with the title of *Badshah*."[171] Whereas regarding his extent of territories, the author without giving any details, has simply mentioned that "His possessions lay on both sides of the Satluj...[172]

From the description of the various land tenures created by different Sikh chiefs due to the circumstances arising out of the establishment of their power and from the nature of their association with those who composed their *misl*, certain inferences can be drawn regarding the aspects of Sardar Jassa Singh Ahluwalia's administration.

Whenever the joint forces of several *misls* fought collectively or collected "*Rakha* (Black Mail)",[173] the army assumed the denomination of a "*Dal* of the *Khalsa Ji*."[174] From every conquest made in common or "*Shamil*",[175] every "*Sarkarda* or the leader of the smallest party of the horse",[176] who was otherwise not on the regular payroll, was granted his share, "in proportion to the degree in which he had contributed to the acquisition."[177] Without giving the respective percentage of the different recipients of the share in the above system, described by Prinsep as *Pattidari* tenure, he writes, "The *Sirdari* or chief's portion being first divided off, the remainder was separated into *Pattis* of parcels for each *Sarkarda*"[178] which would be further apportioned to "every associate in the *Misal* of less rank than a Sardar, down even to the single horseman, who equipped and mounted himself...."[179] Every one of them took ones portion "as a co-sharer, and held it in absolute independence"[180] enjoying only the right to mortgage or transfer it but without any right "to sell his tenure to a stranger."[181] Even though "the service was gratuitous, and the plunder was the reward", it was also customary for the chief "to pay a rupee per *kathi* or saddle."[182]

Besides the *Pattidari*, Prinsep has also made mention of the creation of three other types of tenures, *e.g.*, "the *Misaldari*, the *Tabadari* and the *Jagirdari*."[183]

Under the *Misaldari* tenure, different petty chiefs and their followers, who would attach themselves to a *misl* without subscribing to any conditions of association or dependence, were assigned land which "would be considered as the free reward of their co-operation"[184] without any sort of subordination. They, along with their possessions, would, of course, be free to transfer their services to any other chief.[185]

In the *Tabadari* tenure, on the other hand, a *Tabadar* was "a retainer", in other words, "one completely subservient." The lands, rewarded under such tenure, were always on the pleasure of the Sardar and "liable to forfeiture for any act of disobedience or rebellion."[186]

The *Jagirdari* tenure, as can be understood from the description given by Prinsep, was, more or less, on the Mughal pattern. The lands, given in *jagirs*, were, no doubt, "part of the allotment set apart for the *Sirdari*" and were even hereditary, but only according to the pleasure of the Sardar. As under the Mughals, "the holders were liable to be called upon for their personal services at all times, with their quotas or contingents, equipped and mounted at their own charge, according to the extent of the grant."[187]

Moreover, as opined by Prinsep, lands were also assigned for religious, charitable and endowment purposes as was done by the Mughal and other rulers all over India. In this case, the beneficiaries were not only "Sikh Gurus, Sodhis and Bedis", or the temples but also "*Musalman Pirzadas*."[188]

Apart from this, except a brief reference of the Ahluwalia, *misl*, under the leadership of Sardar Jassa Singh Ahluwalia, instrumental in ousting Sardar Jassa Singh Ramgarhia from his possessions in the Punjab,[189] Prinsep has mainly focalized on the political events leading to the assumption of power by Ranjit Singh.

The unique feature of the writings of the two English writers above discussed is that one comes across a new trend in the English writing.

These English writers have given greater stress on the economic factors rather than the political and religious ones for the rise of the Sikh Sardars as a political force during the eighteenth century. The extortions of the *Jat zamindars* by the Mughal *faujdars* forced them to take to rapine and plunder. However, in order to get a bond of union amongst the Sikhs the use of religion was made.[190]

The term *misls*', 'implying that they were confederacies of equals, under chiefs of their own selection', figured for the first time in Prinsep's book. He has also given the number of the principal *misls* as twelve.[191]

The activities of the Sikhs and the Sikh Sardars, whether for political, religious or economic reasons, have been described as 'depredations'. The earlier comparatively smaller groups, called *Dharwi* have been termed as 'highwaymen'. Another thing, which has been stressed upon in this regard, is that the political activities were also combined with the means to satisfy their prejudices.[192]

The above two English writers have also asserted that it was a joint Adina-Sikh-Maratha venture which had forced the Durranis to retire 'precipitately to the Indus' in 1761 and not, as opined by the earlier English writer, James Browne, that it were only the Sikhs under the leadership of Sardar Jassa Singh Ahluwalia who had expelled the Durranis on that occasion. It is certainly notwithstanding the fact that it had indirectly helped the Sikhs in gaining further political strength. It is a different question altogether that by seeking the help of the Sikhs and the Marathas and even by successfully enrolling number of Sikh and Maratha soldiers in his pay roll, Adina Beg Khan wanted to achieve his personal political advancement.[193]

These authors do not see any opposition from the Durranis to the Sikhs and Sikh chiefs, especially after 1764, in the latter's attempt to the establishment of political sovereignty in the Punjab and the territories between Sirhind and river Jamuna.[194] This assertion on the part of these authors seems to be quite contradictory. The same English writers have also written about the conferring of the title of '*Raja*' on Alha Singh of Patiala in 1762 and of '*Maharaja Rajgan-Mahendar Bahadur*' on his grand son, Amar Singh in 1764.[195] However, it is difficult to rule out completely the possibility of the Sikhs having established some sort of political sovereignty in certain areas. It might be a *de-facto* power, otherwise how could Sikh Sardars introduce different land tenures along with the conditions attached with them, that find mention in the writings under discussion? Moreover, lands were also assigned for religious charitable and endowment purposes[196] as was done by the Mughals and other rulers all over India.

Another noteworthy thing that one comes across is that the term *Rakha (Rakhi)* has been termed as 'Black Mail'.[197] No attempt has, however, been made to explain the amount/ percentage collected/ demanded as *rakhi* and the nature of relations between the Sikh Sardars and the Chief/*Rajas*/*Zamindars* and the people and cultivators of the areas concerned. It has also been mentioned by Prinsep that whenever the joint forces of several *misls* fought collectively or collected *rakhi*, the army assumed the denomination of a '*Dal* of the *Khalsa Ji*'.[198]

Post Ranjit Singh and Post Annexation Period

(i) W.L. M'Gregor

(ii) Joseph Davey Cunningham

(iii) Lepel Henry Griffin

The period during which the English writers in the third category, W.L. M'Gregor, Joseph Davey Cunningham and Lepel Henry Griffin published their respective works, there was a sea change in the Indian and international compulsions on the part of the English government in India and in Britain. In the Indian context the policy of 'Divide and Rule' on the religious lines seems to have stated taking shape in the minds of the English administrators. In the international context, they had both political and commercial interests. They had their political interests towards Central and West Asia. As regards their commercial interests, they wanted to give a practical shape to their long cherised desire of opening the navigation of the Indus and thereby bringing Turkestan and Khorasan within their commercial influence. The books written by the above English writers provided, both the practical and theoretical foundations to the English policies. M'Gregor was instrumental in preventing the annexation of Sind by Ranjit Singh. Through his writings he provided information pertaining to the nature of the Sikh struggle during the eighteenth century as well as general information about the Sikhs and also gave suggestions regarding the English future policy towards Punjab and Afghanistan. Cunningham vehemently attributed a positive role to religion in the history of the Sikhs and described their as a 'natural and important result of the Muhammedan conquest'. He also aimed at involving the English 'in the web of their policy for opening the navigation of the Indus.'

Griffin's main endeavour was to justify the British policy towards the Punjab and *cis*-Sutlaj states and offer a convincing reply to the hostile criticism. Moreover, in an attempt to serve the English political interests, he also highlighted the political, social and economic advantages bestowed upon the Sikh chiefs for their services rendered, especially during the war against the Gurkhas, the Anglo-Sikh wars, revolt of 1857 etc.

Dr. W.L. M'Gregor, the author of *The History of the Sikhs; containing the Lives of the Gooroos ; The History of the Independent Sirdars, or Missuls, and The Life of the Great Founder of the Sikh Monarchy, Maharajah Ranjeet Singh* (Two volumes, London 1847), may not be technically an administrator, but he was not, pure and simple, a medical surgeon either. He had gone to Lahore in 1836 to cure Maharaja Ranjit Singh of the after effects of a paralytic stroke.[199] His mission was more of a diplomatic nature and of a political agent in the court of the Maharaja to serve the interests of the East India Company of which he was an employee. It was, he, who, by his sheer diplomacy, had prevailed upon Ranjit Singh and got "the annexation of Sciende (Sind) prevented"[200] by the latter. His intimacy with the Maharaja provided him enormous opportunities to wean the latter away from the influence of his French employees.[201] Moreover, he would often officiate "for the Political Agent, during the temporary absence of the functionary."[202] Before publishing his book on the history of the Sikhs, in the second half of 1846, M'Gregor also wrote a paper on Maharaja Ranjit in 1838 for Lord Auckland, the then Governor General of India.[203] But for both these works he had presumably identical aims and intentions by which he intended to provide the English information on the Sikhs and suggestions for a right policy towards the Punjab and even towards Afghanistan.[204]

But by the treatment given to the history of the Sikhs during the pre-Ranjit Singh period, it seems that M'Gregor's main objective was to write a detailed account of the period of the Maharaja and the events that took place after his death, whereas the narration the earlier period looks like an introduction to the main body of the book. As such, the discussion regarding the history of the Sikh *misls* including that of the Ahluwalia *misl* and its Sardar, Jassa Singh, though significant, is very brief.

As is evident from the narrative and foot-notes given by M'Gregor in his book that inspite of consulting several English books written by different writers, more especially, Malcolm, Thornton, Forster and Prinsep etc. and even some of the Persian writings for most of the chapters, it is difficult to establish the nature of source material on which he has based his information on the *misls*. In all probability, he banked, more or less, upon the anecdotes heard from the descendants of those Sikh Sardars who had been active when the *misls* were engaged in fighting either amongst themselves or the Mughals and the Durranis. Despite giving comparatively better description of the Sikh *misls* on the north of river Satluj, M'Gregor, on the whole, looks quite tentative in his approach and does not seem to have mastered the subject before attempting to write on it. Besides, most of the important incidents being devoid of any date, it, at times, creates lot of confusion.[205]

Regarding the relative position of the Sikhs and the Durranis, first under Ahmed Shah and later under Timur Shah, M'Gregor has opined that the latter were quite alarmed at the daring attacks of the former and that they even felt helpless in settling the affairs and disputing their claims to the Punjab.[206] The Sikhs ultimately succeeded in assuming overlordship of the land and building up a workable policy to become "a friendly nation, divided into what was called the *missuls*".[207]

M'Gregor has praised the valour of the Sikhs and their Sardars. He has, however, used identical expression for the first leader of every *misl. e.g.*, "He took, like the rest, to robbing",[208] "he was, like the rest, a robber"[209];or he "became a famous robber,"[210] etc. Every Sikh Sardar after appropriating a portion of the territories won, named it after his native village or his habit, *viz.*, Ramgarhia, Ahluwalia or Bhangi etc. They did not encroach upon the others territories and in case a *pargana* or a district was divided between two, each received half the revenue of the whole.[211]

Inspite of an outward expression of "a friendly nation" and signs of peace, friendship and harmony when they met at Amritsar, M'Gregor has opined that hostilities between different Sikh Sardars for the extension of their respective political power, had started emerging. After "repeated contests the country became the property of a few of the most powerful[212] ones, paving way for the establishment of monarchy under Ranjit Singh. In this regard, the role of the minor Sikh chiefs who had the "option of prolonging or curtailing their services according to circumstances,"[213] was also quite significant.

M'Gregor is of the view that in the *Majiha* area many of the local *zamindars*, being related to the Sikh soldier, would give full support to the latter in emergency and would conceal and protect them "when pursued by the Musulmans.[214] But this help would be forthcoming "unless when they (*zamindar*) chose to provide for themselves by robbery and pillage."[215]

M'Gregor's description about Sardar Jassa Singh Ahluwalia, though brief, is full of praise of his activities, position and as a man. A sketch of life and deeds of Jassa Singh, as a matter of fact, forms the part of a brief history of the Ahluwalia *misl* given by M'Gregor in his book.

The early history of Sardar Jassa Singh Ahluwalia, who has been described as "The first man of note" in the Ahluwalia *misl*, it has been stated that he "lived at the village of Mulma Sadhoo, in the *Manja* country", and he was "by trade a *kulal*, or distiller, of the Toolse tribe."[216] It is quite confusing that in the very next line, M'Gregor writes, "This Jassa Singh supported his father and mother at the village of Alloo, near Mulma Sadhoo",[217] whereas other sources, including the English ones,[218] do mention that Jassa Singh's father had died when the former was nearly a five years old boy. Besides, Sardar Kapur Singh Faizullahpuria has been called as "the head of this *Missul*"[219] under whom Jassa Singh, his uncle (Sardar Bagh Singh) and other relatives had stated serving.[220]

M'Gregor, contrary to the earlier English writers, has given comparatively, a better description of Jassa Singh Ahluwalia's political career especially his political relations with other contemporary Sikh Sardars and the extent of his territories. After his mother had placed him "under the charge" of Sardar Kapur Singh, Jassa Singh, after sometime, himself "became a sirdar" by collecting his own followers. But it was only after the death of Sardar Kapur Singh, as stated by M'Gregor, that Jassa Singh, along with his followers, had separated himself, earned a distinguished position amongst the different Sikh Sardars and "became a famous robber, and seized on different portions of land."[221]The most interesting part of the description is that for the first time has been named as "Jassa Singh, Allowalya" who "became the greatest Sirdar in the Bist Jalindhur."[222] Repeating what Prinsep also wrote, M'Gregor writes, he "was called "*Badshah*" by his dependents and followers. [223]

Whereas there were occasions when he joined hands with some of the Sikh *misls* against their common enemy *i.e.* the Durranis, on other occasions he is also said to have fought against a few of the same Sardars. He says, "on the death of Ahmed Shah, a coalition was formed among the *Missuldars* for pillaging, and becoming masters of the Punjab; the chief of these were Jye Singh, Ghuneeya (Khanhaya) : Jassa Singh, Ramghureea ; Jussa Singh, Allowalya; Tara Singh Ghueba; and Khooshyal Singh, Fyzoolapooreea. All these joined their forces, and proceeded towards Kussoor...At length, the whole fort was taken and divided among the *Missuldars.*"[224] At the same time M'Gregor, mentioning about the differences and fight between Sardar Jassa Singh Ahluwalia and other Sikh Sardars, has opined that the successors of Kapur Singh of Faizullahpuria *misl*, Budh and Sudh Singh "were constantly at war with Alloowalya Surdar."[225] At times Jassa Singh did not have cordial relations with the Ramgarhia *misl* and joined hands with Jai Singh Kanhaya against the latter.[226]

Without giving any date and, in most of the cases, with whom did he fight, M'Gregor has given the details of the places conquered by Sardar Jassa Singh Ahluwalia which formed the part of his *misl.* After taking possession of "the villages of Alloo and Seereeala", he writes that Jassa Singh "seized on Futtehiabad, Lilliana, Govindwal, Silleeala and Bhopala, as far as Turuntara. After this, he possessed himself of Gograwal and crossing the Beas he seized on Sultanpore and Tilwundee."[227] Thereafter, he "attacked Raee Ibrahim of Kapoorthullah, who gave up his country to him" and then "crossing the Shutlej, he became master of Eese Khan and Jagraon."[228] M'Gregor writes, "Kapoorthullah was the chief town in the possession of the Alloowalya Sirdar, in the Bist, "which was, later on, greatly enlarged and beautified by Futteh Singh."[229]

In M'Gregor's opinion Sardar Jassa Singh Ahluwalia was a man of "liberal disposition" and a very kind hearted person who "never wore a suit of clothes twice, giving them away to his dependents."[230] Besides, though M'Gregor has not elaborated much, it can be conjectured that he had a secular outlook as well, as he was not only "friendly to the Mussalmans" but had employed many of them "in his service."[231]

Joseph Davey Cunningham, author of *A History of the Sikhs from the Origin of the Nation to the Battles of the Sutlaj*, London, 1849[232] held a brilliant and successful career, which included civil, military and diplomatic assignments of even very delicate nature.[233] He chartered a new philosophy and approach to the study of the history of the Sikhs which was quite different from those of late eighteenth and the early nineteenth century British historians of India. Cunningham attributed a positive role to religion in the history of the Sikhs which developed them or "disciples" into "a nation."[234]

Hailing from the family which possessed a great flair for writing,[235] J.D. Cunningham, as has been indicated in his *A History of the Sikhs*, seems to have gone through books on various subjects like, history, literature, philosophy, science, geography and geology before developing a taste for the critical study of the Indian history, more especially, the history of the Sikhs and the Punjab. The foot-notes in the book clearly show that he had made a careful and critical study of the works written by the English authors on Indian history,[236] particularly History of the Punjab;[237] Persian works[238] and the books on the Sikh religion.[239] Besides, he also consulted published and unpublished public records, Memoirs etc. within his reach and the articles on Sikhs published in the Journals like the *Asiatic Researches;* the *Calcutta Monthly Journal;* and *the Journal of Asiatic Society of Bengal.*

It is quite evident from the 'Preface to the second edition' of the book in question, that Cunningham had two-fold objectives in writing this book. His "main endeavour was to give Sikhism its place in the general history of humanity, by showing its connexion with the different creeds of India, by exhibiting it as a natural and important result of the Muhammadan Conquest, and by impressing upon the people of England the great necessity of attending to the mental changes now in progress amongst their subject millions in the East...."[240] He attempted to achieve the above objective in the first four chapters of his book. In the last five chapters, which incidently, cover the contemporary history of his own times, Cunningham aimed at achieving the other object which "was to give some account of the connexion of the English with the Sikhs, and in part with the Afghans, from the time they began to take a direct interest in the affairs of these races, and to involve them in the web of their policy for opening the navigation of the Indus, and for bringing Turkestan and Khorasan within their commercial influence."[241]

In the chapter III and part of chapter IV, Cunningham has made a critical appraisal of the rise of the Sikh Sardars, their mutual relations and their struggle with the Durranis, the Mughals and the Marathas leading to the establishment of the Sikh supremacy in the Punjab. Despite attributing some of the achievements of the Sikh Sardars during the eighteenth century to Sardar Jassa Singh Ahluwalia, contrary to the writings of some of the earlier English writers, he has not figured so prominently in Cunningham's *The History of the Sikhs.*

Making almost an identical version to what had been made by the earlier British historians, Cunningham attributed the beginning of the rise of the Sikh Sardars to the defeat of the Mughals at the hands of Nadir Shah (1738-39). This incident provided so much encouragement to the Sikhs that they not only became bolder to "visit Amritsar openly instead of in secrecy and disguise", some of them even "succeeded in establishing a small fort at Dalhwal on the Ravi."[242] Moreover, inspite of the fact that on some occasions the Sikhs have been described as "marauders"[243] or "as predatory bands"[244], he, unlike his predecessors, has not succumbed to the temptation of calling them 'robbers' committing 'high way robbery', though, at times, they did "levy contributions"[245] in different areas.

Explaining the attitude of Ahmad Shah Abdali towards India and particularly towards the Sikhs, Cunningham has opined that the Durrani Chief "looked to India as the most productive field of conquest or incursion."[246] He has been described as "hardy and enterprising, fitted for conquest, yet incapable of empire, seemed but to exist for the sake of losing and recovering provinces."[247] The main idea behind conferring of the title of '*Raja*' on Sardar Alha Singh by Ahmad Shah in 1762, was to widen "the difference between a Malwa and a Manjha Singh."[248] Later on in 1767, giving due credit to the then predominantly strong Sikh power in the Punjab and leaving the idea of the reconquest of Lahore, the Durrani Chief "endeavoured to conciliate when he could no longer overcome."[249] He bestowed "the title of *Maharaja* and the office of military commander in Sirhind"[250] upon the successor of Raja Alha Singh, Amar Singh, the new chief of Patiala.

Despite making scanty reference about Sardar Jassa Singh Ahluwalia in the *History of the Sikhs*, Cunningham has given him full credit for achieving the first major break through in the process of the establishment of Sikh supremacy in the Punjab and has described him as "one of their most able leaders."[251] Coinciding with the first invasion of Ahmad Shah

Abdali (1747-48), it was "Jassa Singh Kalal, a brewer or distiller, who boldly proclaimed the birth of a new power in the state—the '*Dal*' of the '*Khalsa*', or army of the theocracy of '*Singhs.*'"[252] Within a few years after this incident, precisely by 1752, according to Cunningham, the Sikhs "had virtually possessed themselves of the country lying between Amritsar and the hills."[253] Inspite of the fact that they suffered defeat at the hands of Adina Beg Khan in the same year, the latter without underestimating their position and rather recognising their *de facto* power, not only took "many of them into his pay"[254] but also "came to an understanding with them that their payment of their own rents should be nominal or limited and their exactions from others moderate or systematic."[255] Quoting and agreeing with the earlier English writers like Major James Browne and John Malcolm, etc., Cunningham hailed the temporary occupation of Lahore in 1758 by the Sikhs under the leadership of Sardar Jassa Singh Ahluwalia and coining the money by the latter in his own name, thereby giving the '*Khalsa*' "another symbol of substantive power."[256]

After this, despite the victory of Ahmad Shah Abdali upon the Marathas in early 1761 at Panipat, the absence of any regular government on the part of the Durranis or the Mughals, gave the Sikhs "additional strength, and they became not only masters of their own villages, but began to erect forts for the purpose of keeping stranger communities in check."[257] As an immediate repercussion of this move, the Sikhs, according to Cunningham, did suffer "a total defeat"[258] at the hands of the Durranis near Ludhiana in 1762. He further stated, "The Sikhs are variously reported to have lost from twelve to twenty five thousand men, and the rout is still familiarly known as the '*Ghula Ghara*', or great disaster."[259] However, thereafter, of course, without referring the role of any particular Sikh Sardar, they have been described to have taken over not only Kasur and "the plains of Sirhind" from the Sutlej to the Jamuna"[260] but had even become masters of Lahore in 1764. The different Sikh chiefs, on that occasion, "assembled at Amritsar, and proclaimed their own sway and the prevalence of their faith, by striking a coin with an inscription to the effect that Guru Gobind had received from Nanak '*Deg, Tegh,* and *Fath*', or Grace, Power, and Rapid Victory."[261] Cunningham has made little deviation in this respect first, by ascribing the year 1764 to the issue these coins, secondly by translating the word '*Deg*' inscribed on them as 'Grace'.[262]

The lone direct reference in the *History of the Sikhs* regarding the extent of the territories of the Ahluwalias, who had "derived their title from the village in which Jassa, who first proclaimed the existence of the army of the new theocracy, had helped his father to distil spirits,"[263] simply states that they "occupied the left bank" of the river Beas.[264] In this respect,

Cunningham has further opined that "the *Shahibs* and *Nishanias* along with those of *Manjha*, who captured Sirhand, *viz*, the *Bhangis*, the *Ahluwalias*, the *Dallahwalas*, the *Ramgarhias*, and the *Krora Singhias*, divided among themselves the plains lying south of the Sutlej and under the hills from Ferozepore in Karnal"[265] Giving another aspect of the political career of Sardar Jassa Singh Ahluwalia, he writes that in 1774 Jai Singh Kanhaya entered into a league with the former "for the expulsion of the other Jassa Singh the Carpenter" who "was at last beaten, and he retired to the wastes of Hariana to live by plunder."[266] But the fall of Kangra to the Kanhaya *Misl* about the same year aided its leader (Jai Singh) "in his usurpation of Jassa Singh's authority over the surrounding Rajas and Thakurs."[267] It is quite intriguing to note that Amar Singh Phulkia, described to have got control over the Haryana between 1768-78, not only helped Jassa Singh Ramgarhia in establishing himself in the country near Hissar,"[268] had even "acquired Sirsa and Fatehabad."[269]

Cunningham is of the view that by 1767[270] "The Sikhs had mastered the upper plains from Karnal and Hansi to the banks of Jhelum" and not only Ahmad Shah Abdali, who crossed the Indus in the same year, "avoided Lahore and advanced no farther than the Sutlej"[271] even Timur Shah, who succeed him in 1773, "seems to have had no thought of a reconquest of Lahore."[272] At the same time he has also cited a change in the attitude of the Sikhs and the Sikh Sardars from 1767 onwards. He says, "The necessity of union was no longer paramount, and rude untaught men are ever prone to give the rein to their passions, and to prefer their own interests to the welfare of the community."[273]

Cunningham has made very important observations on the political system of the Sikhs during the period under study, of which Sardar Jassa Singh Ahluwalia was obviously a party. In his view the *Misl* organisation or the Sikh political system "resolved itself into a theocratic confederate feudalism, with all the confusion and uncertainty attendant upon a triple alliance of the kind in a society half-barbarous."[274] It was theocratic because, "God was their helper and only judge, community of faith or object was their moving principle, and warlike array, the devotion to steel of Gobind, was their material instrument."[275] It was confederate because, "Year after year the "*Sarbat Khalsa*' or whole Sikh people, met once at least at Amritsar."[276] It was feudalism because, "the obvious feudal, or military notion of a chain of dependence, was acknowledged as the law, and the federate chiefs partitioned their joint conquests equally among themselves, and divided their respective shares in the same manner among their own leaders of bands, while these again subdivided their portions among their own dependents, agreeably to the general custom of subinfeudation."[277] Explaining the system further, Cunningham opines,

"In theory such men were neither the subjects nor the retrainers of any feudal chiefs, and they could transfer their services to whom they pleased, or they could themselves become leaders, and acquire new lands for their own use in the name of the *Khalsa* or Commonwealth."[278]

Another significant aspect on which Cunningham has commented upon, though briefly, is the system of *'Rakhi'* practised by the Sikh Sardars during this period. This is an aspect on which, of course, he does not seem to have done much research. He is of the view, "From the tracts of country which the Sikhs subdued but did not occupy, '*Rakhi*' (literally, protection money) was regularly levied. The '*Rakhi*' varied in amount from perhaps a fifth to a half of the rental or government share of the produce."[279] Corresponding it with Mahratta system of '*Chowth*', he says, "both terms meant 'black-mail', or, in a higher sense, tribute."[280]

Of all the administrator historians hitherto discussed, the information on the activities of the different Sikh Sardars in the Punjab during the eighteenth century, more especially that of Sardar Jassa Singh Ahluwalia, provided by *Sir Lepel Henry Griffin* is more graphic and detailed one, covering almost all the aspects of their lives and work. He has, by and large, concentrated on the history of the Punjab and the Sikhs covering the period of their immediate past. Griffin ranks quite high amongst the English administrator historians like, Charles Aitchison, W.W. Hunter, Alfred Lyall, F.J. Stephan and Henry Maine.

Starting his career as Assistant Commissioner in the Punjab from 17th November, 1860, after successfully appearing in the Indian Civil Services Examination in 1859, Griffin rose to the position of permanent Chief Secretary in the same state in November 1878.[281] In between he also had a brief but academically rewarding stint of nearly three and a half years as Superintendent of the Kapurthala State from April, 1875 to November, 1878. As a matter of fact, his important official assignments in the Punjab for nearly two decades provided him ample time and opportunity to know and write about the Punjab and the Sikhs.[282]

Griffin's notable works on Punjab include *(i) The Punjab Chiefs : The Historical and Biographical Notices of the Principal Families in the territories under the Punjab Government*, Lahore, 1865. (This book was revised and enlarged by Charles Francis Massey bringing the histories to date, in two volumes, Lahore, 1890); *(ii) The Law of Inheritance to Chiefships as observed by the Sikhs previous to the Annexation of the Punjab,* Lahore, 1869; *(iii) The Rajas of the Punjab: Being the History of the Principal States in the Punjab and Their Political Relations with the British Government*, Lahore, 1870 ; and *(iv) Ranjit Singh (Rulers of India Series),* Oxford, 1892. It shows that except the last above-mentioned major work all other works on the Punjab had been written and published before his retirement in 1889.[283]

The nature of Griffin's writings on the Sikh history illustrates a mixture of his possession of historical vision coupled with biographical style and his own thinking and views regarding the then prevailing customs, attitudes and social institutions. Despite his claims that his "object has not been to record the biographies of reigning families"[284] and that is why he chose to discuss about only a few of the "many Chiefs in the territories administered by the Punjab Government, bearing the title of *Raja*"[285] and that his main motive was "to give a Connected account of the political relations of the British Government with the Independent States of the Punjab from the commencement of the present century,"[286] all his major works, except *The Law of Inheritance...*, are mainly biographical in style.

Moreover, apart from attempting to quench the ever increasing thirst of the English of acquiring more and more knowledge about the people and the history of the Punjab, Griffin also tried to offer a convincing reply to the hostile criticism of the British policy towards the *cis* and trans-Sutlej territories. The critics, according to Griffin, "believed that the country was won by the most unjustifiable means, that each new province added to British India signified new crimes, and that the conquerors were only successful because they were unscruplous."[287] Justifying the British policy towards the *cis*-Sutlej states, Griffin writes, "A sufficient answer to hostile criticism on the Government of India is found in the political history of the *cis*-Sutlej States for the last sixty five years,"[288] (roughly 1805-70). The administration of Ranjit Singh in the trans-Sutlej areas, he writes, "was certainly a favourable specimen of a Native State. Yet the revenue system of Ranjit Singh was but an organised system of pillage..."[289] Approving the establishment of British rule, he has further opined that inspite of "the preference of the people for the rule of their hereditary Chiefs, the simple fact remains that whenever an opportunity has been afforded them, the people have accepted British rule with the most unfeigned satisfaction."[290]

Since the very first book that Griffin wrote was published in, as late as, 1865, he had an opportunity of consulting not only the printed books,[291] but also had an "enormous mass of materials in the shape of official correspondence"[292] and other sources at his command. Notwithstanding his personal experience and knowledge of the subject, he seems to have made an extensive use of the Official Records like *(i) Official Correspondence ; (ii) Political Records of Government;* and *(iii) of the Agencies of Delhi, Ambala and Ludhiana; (iv) Punjab Land Revenue Settlement Reports;* and *(v)* his interviews with the Chieftains and members of aristocracy ; *(vi)* their family and state records. It is very interesting to note the observations made by Griffin on the availability and reliability of the records pertaining, especially, to the *Majiha* Sikhs covering the period from 1708 to 1780. He writes, "The material for an historical record of the seventy-two years (1708-1780) is meagre and unreliable so far as the *Manjha* Sikhs are concerned. More is known of the Southern Sikhs. As to the Muhammadan records, it is full of great and varied interest, and includes the invasions of Nadir Shah, of Ahmad Shah, and the gradual decline and disintegration of the Mughal empire; whose governors and lieutenants threw off the authority of the Emperors and declared themselves independent."[293]

Lepel Griffin, particularly, in his three books *viz., The Punjab Chiefs; The Rajas of the Punjab* and *Ranjit Singh*, has not only provided a vivid and detailed description of the activities of the Sikhs and different Sikh Sardars during the eighteenth century, but, at the same time, has given an account of their mutual relations as well as with especially that of the Mughals, the Marathas and Durranis. Amongst the different important Sikh Sardars, contrary to the books of earlier English writers, Sardar Jassa Singh Ahluwalia has been discussed in greater details and, as such, has figured quite prominently in the books of Griffin.

Despite being critical of the means adopted by the Sikhs for achieving their objective, Griffin is quite sympathetic to the Sikh cause and has gone to the extent of calling it of national interest. Like other eighteenth and nineteenth centuries English historians, Griffin is also of the view that "the Sikhs were undoubted robbers"[294] and "every man who had energy and courage gathered a band of marauders around him and plundered the country, seizing and holding whatever land be could."[295] But defending, in no uncertain words, their attitude towards the Mughal rulers, he says, "their enthusiasm for their faith, their hatred to the Muhammadans who had so long trampled them under foot, who bad killed their prophets and thrown down their altars, gave them a certain dignity, and to their objects and expeditions an almost national interest."[296]

They were, as a matter of fact, according to Griffin, "hoping for a Sikh republic, and a time when all Northern India would be the heritage of the *Khalsa*; when all hostile creeds should have fallen before the sword of the Guru."[297] In their desire to achieve their objective, inspite of having hatred towards the Mughals and the Mughal rule, "they bore no love for the Afghans"[298] either, for they had "no wish to aid in building up at Delhi an Empire stronger than that which preceded it, and to bind the yoke more firmly on their own necks."[299]

Apart from giving a narration of the political activities of different Sikh Chiefs, Griffin has also dabbled into their origin as well. Whereas "all the great families, north or south of the Sutlej, have the same origin."[300] The hill chiefs bearing the title of *Raja*, in his opinion, were "mostly of Rajput descent and whose pedigrees stretch back in unbroken succession for several thousand years."[301] The Malwa chiefs were "mere cultivators of the land on which, as immigrants, they had settled; the owners of the same lands. Next came the period of conflict with the Muhammadan power, during which the chiefships grew up gradually and naturally.[302] The *Majiha* chiefs also "scarcely more than a hundred years ago the majority of them were cultivators of the soil, enjoying none of the consideration which the *cis*-Sutlej chiefs had, for long, received from the court of Delhi."[303] "The Brar Jats were originally Bhatti Rajputs and in former days were wild and unruly race addicted to cattle-stealing and dacoity."[304] But "the law of force, the keen sword and the strong hand were the foundations upon which the Sikh society was founded. To attract followers by his power and success was the main desire of every Sikh chief..."[305]

It is quite significant that Griffin has expressed two divergent views about the nature of the Sikh chiefs. He has described them as 'barons' but at the same time they were supposed to adhere to the constitution of Sikhism under which, according to him, "no such thing as vassalage or feudal superiority was acknowledged."[306] Moreover, as opined by Griffin, the democratic nature of the Sikh faith and the natural sentiment of the people resisted all attempts of dictation by one central authority.[307] This shows that the Sikh chiefs enjoyed a different position in theory and in practice and worked either according to their whims or as the time demanded. The multiplicity of the chiefs did not make them in any way different from other medieval political chiefs. Without caring much about the ideal of brotherhood and the democratic nature of Sikh faith, they, too, were more interested in their personal political and economic gains rather than for the community as a whole. Commenting upon this type of situation and its repercussions, Griffin has also opined that they "fought against each other more often than against the common enemy the Muhammadans"[308] and "had they known how to put aside private jealousies and unite... they would have become as formidable and irresistible in North India as the Marathas in the South and West."[309] It was only after Maharaja Ranjit Singh came into the picture, and the whole concept of the Sikh movement had undergone a dramatic change from religious to the political expediency, that he "broke down opposition and reduced rivals and enemies to a common obediency."[310]

According to Griffin, Ahmad Shah Abdali, "who was a man of great sagacity,"[311] recognising the position of the Sikhs in the Punjab and "thinking that it would be wiser to conciliate"[312] them, not only wanted to win over, at least, some of them through peaceful means but would have been rather "glad to enlist them on his side, first against the Delhi Government and then against the Marathas.[313] It was in all probability due to the above policy that the Durrani chief bestowed on Alha Singh of Patiala a dress of honour with the title of '*Raja*' in March 1762 and in 1763 was assigned the district of Sirhind on an annual revenue of three and a half lakhs of rupees.[314] Later on, Raja Amar Singh, the grandson and successor of Raja Alha Singh, was not only allowed to continue to enjoy the title of '*Raja*' but was also granted the additional honour in the form of an additional title of "*Raja-i-Rajgan Buhadur*" in 1767.[315] It is certainly quite doubtful whether this policy of Ahmad Shah Abdali brought the desired and expected results. As a matter of fact, with the acceptance of the title by Raja Alha Singh all the other Sikh chiefs not only felt betrayed, but according to Griffin, had created "jealously", "indignation" and "anger" in all of them.[316] They termed it "unworthy" and thought "that the title was the prize of his treachery, and it was disgraceful for a Sikh to accept an honour conferred by a Muhammadan, a foreigner and an enemy."[317] At this juncture it was left to Sardar Jassa Singh Ahluwalia, who, in the words of Griffin, "was at this time far more influential than Alha Singh himself,"[318] to diffuse the situation and pacify the Sikhs, who "were ready to turn upon Ala Singh."[319] Inspite of taking "his side in the dispute," Jassa Singh Ahluwalia made it "necessary for Ala Singh to prove by his actions that he was not a servant of the Durrani King."[320]

The works of Lepel Griffin show that Sardar Jassa Singh Ahluwalia has been considered by the author as "the leader of the *Khalsa*, and the most distinguished of all the Sikh chiefs "north of Sutlej"[321] especially after the death of Sardar Kapur Singh Singhpuria. Despite the account being, by and large, biographical in style, Griffin has provided considerable details regarding Jassa Singh's activities and role in the extension and consolidation of the *Khalsa* and/or Sikh power since the time of Nadir Shah's invasion to the former's death in 1783. It can also be gathered that the areas of political activities of the Ahluwalia Sardar did not remain confined to the Punjab and Haryana alone but had even extended to the parts of Delhi, Western Uttar Pradesh and Rajasthan.

Regarding the origin of Ahluwalia family, Griffin is of the view that it was founded by Sadho Singh, "a Jat of the Kalal or distiller caste", "an enterprizing zamindar" and founder of "four villages[322] in the vicinity of Lahore" during the sixteenth century, of which one of the villages, "Ahlu, caused the family to be known by the distinguishing name of Ahluwalia."[323] But "the true founder of the confederacy was Sardar Jassa Singh, fifth in the descent."[324]

Sir Lepel Griffin has made critical appraisal of the position enjoyed by the Ahluwalia Chief *vis-a-vis* other contemporary Sikh leaders and his rise to the enviable place in the eyes of the rival Chiefs/administrators of the time. Recognising him as "the leader of the *Khalsa*", Griffin has opined that by sheer intelligence and bravery Jassa Singh had made himself "the leading contemporary of Nadir Shah and of Ahmad Shah."[325] As early as the year 1749, Sardar Jassa Singh Ahluwalia, "whose reputation had now become great for bravery and ability"[326] was invited by Kaura Mal, the governor of Multan, not only to assist him against Shah Nawaz Khan but was even rewarded "with a share of booty and a title of honour."[327] In 1775, no less person than Adina Beg Khan was also compelled to concede "that friendship was better than enemity with so powerful a Chief" and "ceded to him Fatahabad on the Beas."[328]

Undoubtedly, by the year 1761, as per Griffin's own assessment, apart from being the chief leader among the Sikhs north of the Sutlej, Sardar Jassa Singh Ahluwalia was also "the equal of any chief south of that river.[329] But inspite of accepting it that he was known as *Sultan-ul-Qaum* among his own followers, Griffin has positively asserted that "this title was not acknowledged by the Sikh nation, and there is no proof that he was generally acknowledged as *Padshah* or King, which his descendants allege to have been the case."[330] If he was accepted as "Chief among the Sikh Sardars" or occasionally allowed a nominal command of joint attack and even commanded the army which earned victories in the areas near Delhi in 1764 and 1768, it was mainly because of his being "man of greatest ability" and more so because of the respect that the Sikhs had for him for being "the most saintly and orthodox of their leaders."[331] Recognising the above qualities, "the most powerful Sirdars, Amar Singh Patiala included, received the *Pahal* or Sikh baptism from his hand."[332] Moreover, the character and the constitution of the *misls* or the individual fighting capacity of the Ahluwalia *misl* did not warrant Jassa Singh to achieve the supreme political command of the Sikhs during this period. While the confederacies were "independent and hostile to each other, although they occasionally combined to attack some common enemy," the Ahluwalia *misl*, which did not have "more than 4,000 fighting men, could never have stood alone in the field."[333] Inspite of an occasional combined attack under the command of Sardar Jassa Singh Ahluwalia, "each body of troops fought under its own leaders, and seized whatever territory or plunder it could for itself."[334]

Contrary to the opinion expressed by earlier English writers like Browne, Cunningham etc. Griffin has nowhere mentioned about the occupation of Lahore by the Sikhs under the leadership of Sardar Jassa Singh Ahluwalia in 1758. According to him the above incident took place in the year 1761. Nor does he agree with the subsequent striking of the coins bearing the name of 'Jassa Kalal'. He simply says "He (Jassa Singh Ahluwalia) is said to have struck the first Sikh coin though this is more than doubtful."[335] Even if the coins were struck, Griffin opines, it did not happen "before 1762 ; not in 1757-58, as stated by Cunningham ; and it is very doubtful whether they were struck in large numbers at all."[336] Referring to the contemporary circumstantial evidence, he further says, "The Raja of Kapurthalla has none in his possession, nor do I know any one who has seen one."[337] In support of his views Griffin has also given the reference of the *Tawarikh-i-Punjab* of Ganesh Dass, according to which he says, "Sikhs did not strike this coin, but the Kazis and Mullahs in 1764, after the famous *Nanakshahi* rupee had been struck, and desiring to anger Ahmad Shah against the Sikhs, coined twenty one rupees, with this inscription, and sent them to the Shah Kabul, who was as indignant as they anticipated at the insolence of the Distiller, "Kalal", who claimed to have seized his country '*Mulk-i-Ahmad*.'"[338] But there seems to be a contradiction in it. While it is clear from the above statement that the '*Nanakshahi*' rupee was struck before 1764 or at least before the *Qazis* and the *Mullahs* had done their job, Griffin, later in his book, has himself ascribed the year 1765 to the issue of the above coins."[339] Surprisingly he has failed to take note of it.

Griffin has very much appreciated the role of Sardar Jassa Singh Ahluwalia in consolidating the disorganised Sikh power and forming it into cohesion, though, on many an occasion, it had necessitated the formation of alliances and counter alliances to face and fight against different Sikh chiefs. This shows that he had no permanent friendship or enemity with any of the Sikh *misls* and his relations with them changed according to the needs of the time either due to the political considerations or for the interests and the unity of the *Panth*. There were occasions when he formed alliances or had cordial relations with the Sikh Sardars of Phulkian, Faizalahpuria, Singhpuria, Karore Singhia, Bhangi, Shahidi, Kanihya and the Bhais of Kaithal, whereas on other occasions he also fought with some of them."[340] Illustrating this point and the instances when the joint fronts were taken, Griffin has opined that in February 1761, when Ahmad Shah Abdali had left the Punjab, "Jassa Singh, with the Phulkian, Faizullahpuria, and other Sirdars, again ravaged Sirhind, and the Governor of Lahore, Ubed Khan, was shut up within the walls of city."[341] In 1762, the Sikh confederacies, *viz.*, "All the Phulkian Chiefs, the Singhpurias, the Faizullapurias, the Bhais of Kythal, Jassa Singh Ahluwalia, and many others, had collected to oppose"[342] Ahmad Shah Abdali, though were defeated first near Barnala and then near Sirhind.[343] Again, Jassa Singh Ahluwalia came to the rescue of Alha Singh after the latter had been conferred with the title of '*Raja*' by Ahmad Shah. Because of his influence he successfully 'prevented an open quarrel" and "tried to persuade his fanatical co-religionists that Ala Singh had no option as to his acceptance of the obnoxious title."[344] Incidentally, as Griffin has pointed out that such title "had not till then been known among the Sikhs; the greatest of them being known only as "*Sardar*" or Baron."[345] But, Griffin, is of the view that inspite of Jassa Singh's soft and friendly attitude, "the Patiala chief always showed great jealousy" towards the Ahluwalia Sardar which despite "the remembrance of his (Jassa Singh's) good offices with the Sikhs...did not dispel."[346] As an evidence to his contentions, he has narrated that in 1762 after the conquest of Sirhind by the joint forces of the "Karora Singhias, Bhangis, Shahidis, Kanheyas, Nihangs, Phulkians and Ahluwalias", Jassa Singh had "seized twenty four villages forming the ilaqua of Suhoran" (in the Ambala district); of these he had retained only eight for himself.[347] But no sooner did he recross the river Sutlej than "Ala Singh seized his share of the plunder, eight villages, and held them inspite of protests and force."[348] However, a temporary change in the attitude of the Phulkian chief has been noticed by Griffin when Raja Amar Singh became the chief of that *misl* and he says, "there was more sincere friendship between them than had existed in the time of Ala Singh."[349] The new chief along with other chiefs of renown were not only proud to accept *pahul* or Sikh baptism from the hands of Jassa Singh Ahluwalia, both together even successfully fought against the Kotla Afghans in 1766.[350] However, this phase of friendship was over immediately after Raja Amar Singh was conferred an "additional honour" in 1767 by Ahmad Shah Abdali which, according to Griffin, was done with a specific motive. He believes that the Durrani chief, by conferring the new title, "endeavoured to recover the country rather by intrigue than by force, and was so far successful that he showed jealousy and suspicion between the Sikh chiefs."[351] The result was that the relations between the two did not remain the same. Raja Amar Singh started viewing "the increasing influence of Jassa Singh with greatest suspicion" and did not allow the latter to retain the territories in the neighbourhood of Delhi.[352]

Regarding Jassa Singh Ahluwalia's relations with some of the other important Sikh chiefs, Lepel Griffin's writings show that despite an unsuccessful expedition against Charat Singh Sukerchakia, grand father of Maharaja Ranjit Singh, in 1761,[353] both, by and large, maintained quite cordial relations. Mohan Singh Sukerchakia, who succeeded Charat Singh in 1773, certainly assisted Jassa Singh Ramgharia, with whom Sardar Jassa Singh Ahluwalia and his successors had, more or less, perpetual enemity, in regaining his territories in the Punjab.[354] Barring aside a couple of occasions when both the Jassa Singhs joined hands against the common enemies, they would not see eye to eye with each other and ultimately in 1776 the Ahluwalia Sardar, with the assistance of the Bhangis, Kanheyas, Sukerchakias and others, was able "to expel Jassa Singh Ramgharia from the Punjab, and seize his possessions."[355] The Ramgharia Sardar was forced to flee "to Sirsa and Harriana, where he supported himself by plunder and by selling his services to whoever would buy them"[356] and remained there until after the death of Jassa Singh Ahluwalia in 1783.

Griffin's writings contain very interesting and informative details regarding the centres of political activities of the different Sikh Sardars and their extent of empire more especially that of Sardar Jassa Singh Ahluwalia.[357] Despite the fact that till as late as 1775 A.D. the name of the Mughal empire "was still a word of power with the undisciplined Sikhs, who knew their inability to stand against regular troops in the field,"[358] they were "hoping for a Sikh republic, and a time when all Northern India would be the heritage of the *Khalsa*."[359] In their attempt to achieve the objective, Sardar Jassa Singh Ahluwalia, so also many of the Sikh chiefs, even "crossed the Sutlej and ravaged the country to the very gates of Delhi."[360] thereby extending the dimensions of their activities from Punjab to Haryana, parts of Western Uttar Pradesh and Eastern Rajasthan.

The life sketch of Sardar Jassa Singh Ahluwalia given by Griffin has incidentally provided a detailed narration of his political activities till the year of the Sikh Sardar's death in 1783. Starting with the four ancestral villages of "Ahlu, Hallusadho, Tor, and Chak, in the neighbourhood of Lahore,"[361] the Ahluwalia Sardar had, as early as 1761, earned the recognition of an exceptionally important Sikh chief. It was right after the departure of Nadir Shah from the Punjab in May 1739 that Jassa Singh came into the lime light who in the same year "built the fort of Daliwal, on the banks of the Ravi, where he set up his headquarters."[362] In 1743, when Zakira Khan was the governor of Lahore, Jassa Singh, with a large body of horse made a successful attack on "Diwan Lakhpat Rai, who was escorting treasure from Imanabad to Lahore, and killed him, carrying off the spoil."[363] Being something unbearable for the Mughals, Adina Beg Khan "was sent against the Sikhs, whom he defeated with great slaughter."[364] Jassa Singh Ahluwalia, at this juncture, escaped to the Sutlej and 'seized Lakhumalanwala, Baggoki, Hicharwal, and other Dogar villages"[365] on the south of that river. For a few years he along with his allies viz., Hari Singh and Jhanda Singh Bhangi fought unsuccessful or undecisive battles and his activities were confined to Kassur, Sirhand, Lahore, Sialkot and Hoshiarpur.[366] However, in 1748 he was instrumental in successfully attacking and killing Salabat Khan, *faujdar* of Amritsar thereby seizing a large portion of it.[367]

According to Griffin, in 1752 Adina Beg Khan was successful in inducing some of the Sikh Sardars, *viz.*, Jassa Singh Ramgharia, Jai Singh and Kaushal Singh "to join him and attacked the Ahluwalia, Kaneya, and Sikerchakia forces at Makhowal, inflicting upon them a severe defeat."[368] No doubt, "this defection of the clan was terribly avenged by Jassa Singh on the Ramgharias a few years later."[369] The years 1753 to 1755 witnessed perpetual contests between Jassa Singh Ahluwalia and the Mughal forces with varying success. During this period he "defeated Aziz Khan, commanding the Lahore forces, plundered Rao Jagaron and Raikot" and in November 1755 he had extended his conquest to the edge of the Beas, defeating Adina Beg, governor of the Jullundur *Doab*."[370] This success of the Ahluwalias not only compelled the latter to cede "the Fatehabad pargana" but as Griffin points out, even forced the Mughal chief to sue for peace with Jassa Singh Ahluwalia "believing that friendship was better than enemity with so powerful a chief."[371] The combined forces were instrumental in defeating Sarbuland Khan, who had been appointed by Ahmad Shah Durrani as incharge of Jalandhar, "of which place the allies took possession."[372] However, Adina Beg, being susceptible about the effectiveness of the Sikh Sardar against the Durrani monarch, also "invited Mala Rao and Ragho Rao, two famous Maratha Chiefs, to join him."[373] The terror of this combination of the forces was such that "Prince Timur and Jahan Khan, his minister, fled to Afghanistan, and the conquest of Ahmad Shah seemed for ever lost."[374] However, Griffin has made no mention of the temporary occupation of Lahore by the Sikhs under the leadership of Jassa Singh Ahluwalia alone or together with the Marathas in the year 1758.[375]

In 1760, while Ahmad Shah Abdali was engaged in fighting with Marathas, Jassa Singh Ahluwalia, according to Lepel Griffin, concentrated his activities on both north and south of river Sutlej and enjoyed fairly successful military career. He temporarily captured Jandialah from Sarran Das, plundered Sirhind, captured Dayalpur from Gajja Singh, giving half share in the latter to the Sodhis of Kartarpur.[376] "He then marched into the Firozpur district, seized the Dogar *ilaqua* of Mullanwala and Nypal *ilaqua* of Mukku, in both of which he built fortified posts, and they were held by the Ahluwalia Chief till the Satlej campaign, when they were confiscated by the British Government."[377] Thereafter, Jassa Singh "seized the neighbouring estate of Kot lsai Khan from Qadir Baksh Khan... Hoshiarpur, Bhirog and Naraingar in Ambala."[378] He, then exacted tribute from Rai Ibrahim, the Muslim *jagirdar* of Kapurthalla, "who saved himself from destruction by becoming a feudatory of the successful Sikh.[379] But during his expedition from the south of Lahore to Jhang, he had to face a comparatively stronger opposition in Inayatullah Khan, the Sial Chief of the area, who proved strong enough to hold his own and, as such, success deserted the Ahluwalia Sardar, so was the case in his expedition to Gujranwala against Charat Singh Sukerchakia and the former had to retire "with the loss of his guns and baggage.[380] However, in the very next year Jassa Singh has been described to have assisted "the Bhangis and Sukarchakias to repulse Ubed Khan from Gujranwala."[381]

Without giving exact geographical locations of the places attacked, Lepel Griffin is of the view that in 1761, Jassa Singh Ahluwalia and other Sikhs "crossed the Satlej, and made a raid as far south as Shikarpur, Mohammadpur, and Raipur to the south of Jamna."[382] However, despite a fair amount of successes achieved and the foremost position acquired by him, "he was more than once on the verge of losing all he had acquired."[383] A severe jolt of this nature was witnessed in February 1762 when the Sikhs belonging to different confederacies were utterly defeated near Barnala by Ahmad Shah Abdali, with the loss of many thousands killed and wounded. Almost immediately after this incident, "named the *Ghalu Ghara*, or great defeat," the Sikhs were again badly beaten or rather utterly routed near Sirhind. The Sikh forces had to flee and Jassa Singh along with his brother chiefs "found themselves obliged to seek refuge in the Kangra hills."[384]

The Sikhs could recoup from this hopeless position and had their revenge shortly after the departure of Ahmad Shah Abdali from India. They did so first "in the capture and plunder of the strongly fortified town of Kasur. Thence, under the leadership, as usual, of the brave Jassa Singh,"[385] they successfully attacked Sirhind, the place which by that time, according to Griffin, had earned the reputation of "a well-gnawed bone of contention between the Sikhs and the Muslims."[386] Here it is very interesting to mark the expression conveyed by the term 'as usual' written by Griffin, which is contrary to the thesis hitherto presented by him. It shows that due whatever reasons, political or religious, Sardar Jassa Singh Ahluwalia, if not all, at least, in most of the cases, though of course, in a limited way, as envisaged in the accepted constitutional framework, was allowed to lead the Sikh forces against the common enemies.

Lepel Griffin has also referred to Jassa Singh Ahluwalia's "strict alliance" with the Jat rulers of Bharatpur, first with Suraj Mal and then his son and successor Jawahar Singh, and was also in league with the Marathas. All these three political powers made a common cause especially against the Rohilla Chief Najib-ud-daulah in 1764 and "the allies gained a victory near Shahjehanabad."[387] The city of Delhi, where Najib had taken refuge and which was, as opined by Griffin, invested by the Sikhs and the Marathas, "would probably have failed had not the besiegers heard that Ahmad Shah was approaching, and this induced them to accept a large sum of money and raise the siege."[388] Thereafter the scene of Jassa Singh's military activities had temporarily shifted back to the Punjab. Moreover, because of the growing age and the mutinous behaviour of his forces, the Durrani monarch did not come beyond Sirhind and retired to Qabul, "not without molestation from the Sikhs, who captured almost the whole of his baggage at the passage of the Chanab."[389]

It seems that other Sikh chiefs, more especially the Bhangi chiefs were more powerful and dominating in the western Punjab than the Ahluwalia Sardar. The Bhangi, as per Griffin's version, not only captured Lahore in 1764, but the very next year even Gujrat and "the whole country between the Chenab and the Jhelam fell into their hands."[390] Jassa Singh Ahluwalia along with the chiefs of Patiala and Jind marched Southwards in 1766 ravaging Jhajjar, Rewari, Bhagpat and capturing Payal and Isru from the Kotla Afghans. In 1768, despite the fact that the Ahluwalia chief had overrun "the neighbourhood of Delhi, Ghaziuddin and Anupshahr, defeating Mirza Sukhan, who was sent against him by the Emperor, and capturing the fort of Mehtab" but because of the opposition of his ally, Raja Amar Sigh, who had by now become very powerful, did not allow the former to retain any area as far south as this.[391] However, in 1771, after capturing Raikot from the Pathans and Berowal from the Rajputs, he marched against Kapurthala, held by Rai Ibrahim. As already discussed Rai Ibrahim had agreed to pay annual tribute to Jassa Singh, but the latter found it difficult to realize the same, "it was only after reducing thirteen forts in the neighbourhood of Kapurthalla, and investing the town itself, that the Rai paid what was due.[392] Despite all this "Jassa Singh's authority was not really restored, and it was in 1780, "taking the advantage of the tribute again falling into arrears," that he could seize the town. According to Griffin, after seizing Kapurthala, Jassa Singh Ahluwalia continued to reside there till his death in 1783 and had made it his headquarters.[393]

In between the above success, the Ahluwalia Sardar, by forming a coalition "with several powerful confederacies, the Bhangis, Kanheyas, Sukerchakias, and others" also succeeded in defeating and seizing the possessions of Sardar Jassa Singh Ramgharia and forcing him "to try into Harriana, where he remained in great poverty" till 1783.[394]

The military system of the Sikhs, the composition of the army, the methods of their warfare and the types of arms preferred by the Sikhs during the period of Sardar Jassa Singh Ahluwalia have, though briefly, also figured in the writings of Lepel Griffin. He is of the opinion that the Sikh army was commonly known as the *Dal Khalsa* or "army of God" and surprisingly has also called it as *Budha Dal* or the army of old men. Most of the battles fought by the Sikhs during this period "were invariably cavalry actions" and while they "possessed scarcely any artillery", the infantry was considered "an inferior branch of the service...used only for garrison and sentry duty."[395] Artillery was the branch of the service which, as opined by Griffin, was "hated by every true Sikh" and even during the period of Maharaja Ranjit Singh, who, "with the aid of French and Italian officers", had formed a "very powerful and well-appointed artillery," it was "principally filled by Mohammadans.[396] Whereas the Sikh or foot was known to be "one of the bravest and most steady of soldiers," a very interesting and practical reason for the preference to cavalry during the time of Sardar Jassa Singh Ahluwalia, as can be understood from the writings of Griffin, was most likely due to the inability of the Sikhs to fight pitched battles. The clouds of horsemen, he writes, "hung on the skirts of the army of Ahmed Shah Durrani, afraid to venture an attack upon regular troops, but cutting off convoys and endangering the communications of the enemy.[397]

The major portion of the cavalry was consisted of "*Kathiwand*", i.e. those soldiers who found their own horses, and received a double share of all prize-money. Besides, each Sikh chief also furnished horses and arms, to his retainers according to his means and these soldiers were called "*Bargirs*"[398]

Griffin has also made mention of certain set principles followed by the Sikh Sardars in their dealings with the fellow soldiers. First of all the plunder and the "prize-money" was equally shared among the combatants. Moreover, in case a soldier was wounded, "he invariably received compensation" and if killed, "his son, or nearest male relate, was entertained in his place."[399]

As regards the weaponary of the Sikh soldiers, Griffin is of the view that while sword was the principal weapon of the cavalry, bows and arrows were used by the infantry, the use of the matchlocks was "little loved by the Sikhs." "Nor were the Sikhs fond of fighting behind walls; and Sardar Jassa Singh only maintained the two forts of Daliwal and Werowal."[400] However, after Jassa Singh Ahluwalia and more especially during the period of Maharaja Ranjit Singh, Griffin has positively maintained that the character, constitution and the composition of the Sikh army had almost entirely changed. In that period, the cavalry "ceased to be the chief part of the force, and the infantry became the favourite service."[401]

Apart from all other things, Griffin has also touched upon the personal ideas and life of Sardar Jassa Singh Ahluwalia. He has been described as very generous, enlightened and liberal but firm in his religious ideology. Inspite of being "far in advance of the majority of his countrymen" and had a very large number of Mohammadans employed in his service who "were allowed to follow their own religious observances", he forbade the "call to prayer of the *Muwazzin*" and on the question of the killing of cows "Jassa Singh was a thorough bigot." Twice he made "expeditions to punish contumacious cow-killers, once at Kassur and once at Lahore."[402]

Describing about the generosity of Jassa Singh Ahluwalia., Griffin is of the opinion that he, in a great measure, not only beautified and rebuilt the city of Amritsar and the great temple, the Darbar Sahib after they had been destroyed by Ahmad Shah Abdali, but also, "at great expense, constructed a large reservoir at Anandpur." Jassa Singh's hospitality was "extended to all who asked it, and hundreds were fed daily at his *Langar*, or public kitchen."[403]

Comparing the role, nature and capabilities of the two great Sikh leaders of the Punjab, Griffin has opined that Jassa Singh's "death was a calamity which might have seriously affected the future of the new faith had not the gap been speedily filled by a ladder still more able, though not more brave and beloved, the redoubtable Maharaja Ranjit Singh. Of two men, it may be said that Jassa Singh was a Sikh by honest conviction, while Ranjit Singh supported the movement, because it was politically advantageous to do so."[404]

In the writings of some of the later English writers, like George Batley Scott,[405] the only Sikh Sardar referred by name before Ranjit Singh, is Sardar Jassa Singh Ahluwalia.[406] About him and the role played by him, Scott wrote, "At length one, *Jassa Singh*, a distiller, became a noted leader," who "proclaimed that the *Khalsa* were no longer free lances, but an organised military body, the Dal, a belligerent nation."[407] Scott has further pointed out that "several states in confederacies were known as *Misls*", and whereas in theory "the lands occupied belonged to each and every number of the *Khalsa*", in practice, "the boldest leaders formed principalities, nominally twelve," leading to "a mutual struggle for supermacy" which, "to the west of the Sutlej ended in Ranjit Singh welding the whole into a *Khalsa* Kingdom."[408]

It is quite evident from the writings of the above British administrator writers on Sikh history that despite maintaining the identical objective of providing the English rulers a detailed information of the Sikhs, circumstances leading to the rise of Maharaja Ranjit Singh and suggestions regarding the policy to be adopted towards Punjab and even Afganistan, the nature and scope of their writings kept on changing, maintaining a pace with the growth of British power in India and their interests in the Punjab before, during and after Ranjit Singh's period. Despite the treaty of 1809 with Maharaja Ranjit Singh, the English policy towards the Punjab was quite tentative and they, as is clear from John Malcolm's book, were very curious to know about the rising Sikh community about whom every information was of great importance to them. Prinsep, apart from coming roughly upto 1833, has, though briefly, dealt with the religion, laws, customs of Sikhs and various land tenures created by different Sikh Sardars under the prevailing circumstances. M'Gregor, who first wrote a Paper on Ranjit Singh in 1838 before publishing his book in 1847, though mainly concentrating on Maharaja Ranjit Singh and the events that took place after his death but has, at the same time, counselled the English government regarding the policy to be adopted towards the Punjab and Afghanistan which corresponded the events that took place in 1838-39 and after Cunningham's book (published in 1849), attributing a positive role to religion in the history of Sikhs, contained fore-warning and suggestions to the administrators regarding the future course of action to be taken towards the Punjab after the second Anglo-Sikh war. Griffin's writings starting with, more or less, biographical sketches of more important Sikh Sardars developed into postmortem like treatment to the British relations with the Punjab and tried to justify the English policy towards *cis* and trans Sutlej Sikh chiefs.

The information derived from the writings of these English writers, especially Griffin's, has some similarity with that of *Calender of Persian Correspondence* and the *Secret Proceeding*. For instance they mention about Ahmad Shah Durrani's invitation to the Sikh Sardars like Jassa Singh Ahluwalia to enter his service.[409] These writings also mention about the extension of the influence and activities of the Sikhs in Delhi and areas in its neighbourhood.[410] However, it is not correct to compare the power of the Marathas during the eighteenth century with that of the Sikh Sardars.[411] It would be more appropriate if the Maratha power during the mid-seventeenth century is compared with that of the Sikh power during the period under study.[412] Though not fully united, they had become a power to reckon with and had become a terror for the Mughal and the Durrani powers. They were collecting *rakhi*, though not on regular basis, from many an area and were enjoying *de facto* power in major portion of Punjab. Moreover, as is evident from the above as well as from the other contemporary accounts, the major powers in the region were eager to enlist them on their respective sides.[413]

Of the above English writers, Cunningham has refrained from calling the Sikh Sardars as 'robbers' committing 'high way robbery', though it hardly makes much difference if he calls them as 'marauders' or 'as predatory bands'.[414] It is also quite noteworthy that he is the one who tried to interpret the reason behind conferring the title of '*Raja*' on Alha

Singh by Ahmad Shah Abdali.[415] It is quite significant to note his opinion that the Durrani Chief wanted to widen the gulf between the *Majiha* and the Malwa Sikhs. It is equally significant that the above writers do not have the same opinion about the introduction of the coins by Jassa Singh Ahluwalia.[416] Moreover, Cunningham's view about the nature of the Sikh state, as 'a theocratic confederate feudalism', has not been endorsed by Griffin or M'Gregor in so many words.[417] It is also a pity that though Griffin has given a more detailed account about the Sikhs during the period under study he has not worked on the percentage of the amount charged as *rakhi* by the Sikh Sardars nor has he commented on the percentage mentioned by Cunningham.[418] It is also quite surprising that despite giving so much importance to Sardar Jassa Singh Ahluwalia, as a man and as a political/military leader and as head of Ahluwalia *misl*, he has been named as Jassa Singh or Jassa Singh Kalal or occasionally Sardar Jassa Singh and never as Sardar Jassa Singh Ahluwalia, of course, with the exception of M'Gregor, who occasionally writes him 'Jassa Singh, Allowalya'.[419]

References

1. Rajasthan Archives, Bikaner, *Akhbart-i-Darbar-i-Maula,* dated 26 *Zulhijia,* A.H. 1127, 4th R.Y.F.S./12 December, 1715. A.D. (Banda captured): 1 *Rajab,* A.H. 1128, 5th R.Y. FS./10 June, 1716 A.D. (Banda executed); for details of execution, Shiv Das Lakhnawi, *Shah Nama Munawar Kalam,* tr. S.H. Askari, Patna, 1983, *Waqai,* pp. 15-18 Quoted by B.R. Grover (ed.), *Sardar Jassa Singh Ahluwalia (Against the 18th century Background of Punjab Polity)* (New Delhi, 1991) in Punjabi 'Introduction'.
2. Khushwaqt Rai, *Kitab-i-Tawarikh-i-Punjab,* Persian MSS, State Archives, Patiala, p. 159.
3. Ratan Singh Bhangu, *Prachin Panth Prakash,* Amritsar (4th edition), 1962, pp. 213-14.
4. Punjab State Archives, Patiala, *Mughal Farman* dated 21, *Ramazan* A.H. 1137/ 3 June 1725 A.D. (addressed to Ala, zamindar) (Chaudhary of Padau) directs him to take up his residence (*Jaisakunat*-Headquarters) in the Sirhind territories for its administration which otherwise were in turbulent condition because of the highway robbery on the main Delhi-Lahore route. It also promises the conferment of the title of *Rajgi,* on Ala Singh; also Saiyid Muhammed Bilgrami, *Tasirant-un-Nazirin,* Ms. Faristya Akhbar No. 204, Aligarh Muslim University, Maulana Azad Library, fols. 82a and 61b.
5. Ratan Singh Bhangu, *op. cit.,* pp. 210-18, Gyan Singh Gyani, *Panth Prakash,* Amritsar, 1880, pp. 500-550, 556.
6. Punjab State Archives, (Patiala) Mirza Muhammad Mehdi, *Tarikh-Jahan-kusha-i-Nadiri,* (completed in 1757 A.D.) No. M/716, fols. 148b-191b; *Tazikara-i-Waqai*-Anand Ram Mukhils, MS 94, pp. 59-61.
7. Dr. Hari Ram Gupta has given the name of Jassa Singh's father as Dyal Singh, Gupta, Hari Ram, *A History of the Sikhs from Nadir Shah's Invasion to the Rise of Ranjit Singh (1739-1799),* Vol. I, Simla, 1952, p. 51, f.n. 1.

8. Griffin, Lepel Henry, *The Rajas of the Punjab: Being the History of Principal States in the Punjab and their political Relations with the British Government*, Lahore, 1870, ii, pp. 454-455; Ratan Singh Bhangu, *op. cit.*, pp. 265-66; Gyan Singh Gyani, *op. cit.*, p. 571.
9. Khushwant Singh, *A History of the Sikhs*, Vol. I: 1469-1839, Princeton and London, 1963, p. 132.
10. B.R. Grover, 'Presidential Address: *Punjab History Conference*, XIX Session, 1985, pp. 7-58.
11. *Selection from the Peshwa Daftar*, ed. G.S. Sardesai, XXI, Letters Nos. 53, 55 and 71.
12. Especially the works like: Gupta, Hari Ram, *A History of the Sikhs from Nadir Shah's invasion to the Rise of Ranjit Singh (1739-1799)*, Vol. I, Simla, 1952; Khushwant Singh, *A History of the Sikhs*, Vol. I: 1469-1839, Princeton and London, 1963; Ganda Singh, *Sardar Jassa Singh Ahluwalia* (in Punjabi), Patiala 1969; Bhagat Singh, *Sikh Polity in the Eighteenth and the Nineteenth Centuries*, New Delhi, 1978; Nayyar, G.S., *Sikh Polity and Political Institutions*, New Delhi, 1979; and Muzaffar Alam, *The Crisis of Empire in Mughal North India: Awadh and the Punjab, 1707-48*, (O.U.P. Delhi) 1986.
13. Grover, B.R., *op. cit.*, and Ram Sukh Rao, *Sri Fateh Singh Partap Prabhakar*, (ed.), Joginder Kaur, Patiala, 1980, pp. 294-99.
14. The most important works on 18th Punjab history in Punjabi are: Ram Sukh Rao, *Jassa Singh Binod*, Ms. Punjab State Archives, Patiala, written sometimes during the late twenties of the 19th century; Ram Sukh Rao, *Sri Fateh Singh Partap Prabhakar*, Ms. Punjab State Archives, Patiala, written sometime after 1827. This has also been edited by Joginder Kaur, Patiala 1980; Ratan Singh Bhangu, *Prachin Panth Parkash*, written about 1830 and printed, Amritsar, 1914; Gyan Singh Gyani, *Panth Parkash*, Amritsar, 1880; and Karam Singh, *Maharaja Alha Singh*, Amritsar, 1918.
15. Of course, scholarly article has been written by Professor J.S. Grewal, entitled, 'The Historians of Maharaja Ranjit Singh', J.S. Grewal and Indu Banga (ed.), *Maharaja Ranjit Singh and His Times*, Amritsar, 1980, and various scholars have contributed scholarly articles on different British Writers in Dr. Fauja Singh (ed.), *Historians and Historiography of the Sikhs*, New Delhi, 1978. But whereas the former has, more or less, concentrated particularly on Maharaja Ranjit Singh, the latters have, by and large, concentrated on the Sikhs in general. The present writer proposes to focus on Sardar Jassa Singh Ahluwalia and as such, an attempt has been made to look into the writings of the English writers in a different angle.
16. The writer is extremely grateful to Professor B.R. Grover, former Chairman, Indian Council of Historical Research, New Delhi for the help and guidance provided in understanding and analyzing the Persian sources.
17. The author has consulted volume i. 1759-1761; vol. ii, 1767-1769; vol. iii, 1770-1772; vol. iv, 1772-1775;: and vol. v, 1779-1780 of the *Correspondence*.
18. 120. News of Friday, the 9th December, p. 8, *Calendar of Persian Correspondence (C.P. C.)*, vol. ii, 1767-69. *Persian Correspondence*, Feb. 4, 1707, pp. 7.8.
19. 16A. 'Paper of news, Abdali crossing the Attock', pp. 10 and 12, *C.P.C.*, ii, 1767-69, *Persian Correspondence*, February 4, 1767, pp. 9-12.
20. *Ibid.*, p. 11.

21. 251. 'From Muniru'd-Daulah,' p. 75, *C.P.C., ii, 1765-69, Persian Correspondence, April 1, 1767, pp. 74-76.*

22. 213. 'From Muniru'd-Daulah,' p. 59. *C.P.C.*, ii, 1767-69, *Persian Correspondence*, March 26, 1767, pp. 59-60.

23. 184. 'To Muniru'd.Daulab,' p. 50, *C.P.C.*, ii, 1767-69, *Persian Correspondence*, March 20, 1767, pp. 50-51.

24. 377. 'From the Vazir', p. 105, *C.P.C.*, ii, 1767-69 *Persian Correspondence*, April 30, 1767, pp. 104-107.

25. 868. 'General Barker to Jhanda Singh', August 19, 1771, *C. P.C.*, iii, 1770-72, p. 236.

26. *1532, C P.C.*, i, 1759-67, June, 1762.

27. 1008 'Ali Naqi Khan to the King', p. 279, *C.P.C.*, ii. 1767-69, *Persian Correspondence*, June, 176, p. 279.

28. 129. 'From Raja Shitab Roy, Naib Nazim of Behar,' March 17, 1770, p. 35, *C.P.C.*, iii, 1770-72.

29. 94. 'To Daudi Khan', February 20, 1770 (February 24, according to the volume of copies), p. 23, *C.P.C.*, iii, 1770-72.

30. 251. 'From Muniru'd-Daulah'. *pp. 74-75*, *C.P.C.*, ii, 1767-69, *Persian Correspondence*, April 1, 1767, pp. 74-76.

31. 36. 'News of the 9th January', p. 16, *C.P.C.*, ii, 1767-69, *Persian Correspondence*, February 6, 1767, pp. 16-17.

32. 279. 'From Raja Shitab Roy', p. 84, *C.P.C.*, ii, 1767-69, *Persian Correspondence*, April 8, 1767, p. 8.

33. 16A. 'Paper of news, Abdali Crossing the Attock', p. 12, *C.P C.*, ii, 1767-69, *Persian Correspondence*, February 4, 1767, pp. 9-12.

34. 120. News of Friday, the 9th December, p. 8, *C.P.C.*, ii, 1767-69, *Persian Correspondence*, February 4, 1767, pp. 7-8.

35. 65. 'Another paper of news', January 1767, p. 22, *C.P.C.*, ii, 1767-69, *Persian Correspondence*, February 16, 1767, pp. 22-23; also 79. 'Paper of News', p. 26, *C.P.C.*, ii, 1767-69, *Persian Correspondence*, February 17, 1767.

36. 310. 'Papers of intelligence', p. 89, *C.P.C.*, ii, 1767.69, *Persian Correspondence*, April 15, 1767, pp. 89-90.

37. *Op. cit.* ,f.n. 35.

38. 65. 'Another Paper of news', p. 22, *C.P.C.*, ii, 1767.69, *Persian Correspondence*, February 16, 1767, pp. 22-23.

39. *Op. cit.*, f.n. 31.

40. *Ibid.*

41. *Op. cit.*, f.n. 22.

42. 50. 'Paper of news', p. 19, *C.P.C.*, ii, 1767-69, *Persian Correspondence*, February 13, 1767, pp. 19-20.

43. *Ibid.*

44. *Op. cit.*, f.n. 38.

45. 79. 'Paper of news', p. 26. *C.P.C.*, ii, 1767-69, *Persian Correspondence*, February 17, 1767, pp. 26-27.

46. *Op. cit.*, f.n. 27.

47. 835. 'The Vazir to the King', p. 234, *C.P.C.*, ii, 1767-69, *Persian Correspondence*, March 2, 1768, pp. 234-35.
48. 1152. 'The King to Col. Champion', July 13, 1774, *C.P.C.*, iv, 1772-75. pp. 206-207.
49. 1184. 'Extracts from news', July 27, 1774, *C.P.C.*, iv, 1772-75, p. 214.
50. 1493. 'From Mirza Najaf Khan', December 19, 1774, *C.P.C.*, iv, 1772-75, pp. 265-66.
51. *Op. cit,* f.n. 48.
52. 2058. 'From Nawab Asafu'd—Daulah', November 23, 1775, *C.P.C.* iv, 1772-75, p. 359.
53. 200. 'News from Akbarabad' (*i.e.* Agra), May 9, 1977, *C.P.C.*, iii, 1770-72, p. 61.
54. *Op. cit.*, f.n. 48.
55. 776. 'Papers of intelligence', dated the 13th January, *C.P.C,* ii, 1767-69, *Persian Correspondence*, January 27, 1786, p. 216.
56. 849. 'The King to Jassa Singh, a Sikh Sardar', p. 240, *C.P.C.*, ii, 1767-69, *Persian Correspondence*, March 10, 1768, pp. 240-41.
57. *Ibid.*
58. *Ibid.*
59. *Ibid.*
60. *Ibid.*
61. The author has been able to locate only one Shahbazpur which was situated in the *Subah* Bengal, vide, Habib, Irfan, *An Atlas of the Mughal Empire, Political and Economic Maps with Detailed Notes, Bibliography and Index,* Delhi, 1986 print, p. 11A. It is quite interesting that the Sikhs were offered a jagir in as far as *Subah* Bengal.
62. 1026. 'News', dated May 18, 1774, *C.P.C.*, iv, 1772-75, pp. 183-84.
63. 1733. 'From Mir Murtaza Khan', dated April 30, 1775, *C.P.C.*, iv, 1772-75, p. 31.
64. 2033. 'The King to Saiyad Murtaza Khan', November 1775, *C.P.C.*, iv, 1772-75, p. 355.
65. 279, 'An account of the Vazir's (Nawab Asafu'd—Daulah's) overtures to the Khalisa Sikh Chiefs for an alliance against the Rohillas', dated September 20, 1776, *C.P.C.*, v, 1778-80, pp. 41-42.
66. 280. 'From Nahar Singh, Chief of the Gujars', dated September 20, 1776, *C.P.C.*, v, 1778-80, pp. 42-43.
67. 687. 'To the King', dated October 5, 1777, *C.P.C.*, v, 1778-80, p. 101.
68. 79. 'From the Vazir', dated February 16, 1770; and 94. 'To Dandi Khan', dated February 20/24, 1770, *C.P.C.*, iii, 1770-72, pp. 18 and 23.
69. *Foreign Department/Secret Proceedings*, 23 September, 1776, Translation.
70. *Ibid.*
71. *Foreign DepartmentlSecret Proceedings*, 23 September, 1776, No. 10, 'To General John Clavering, C. in C.'
72. *Foreign Department/Secret Proceedings*, 5 March, 1779, 'To Warren Hastings, Mr. Middleton, the British Resident at Lucknow.'
73. *Foreign Department/Secret Proceedings*, 23 June, 1783, No. 23, 'Extracts of Intelligence, Darangur, 6th March, 1783, signed by W.M. Swainston'.

74. *Ibid.*, Agra, 8th March, 1783.

75. *Foreign Department/Secret Proceedings*, 23rd June, 1783, No. 42B, Translation of the copy of an Arzee from Azimoldeen Khan and Sheik Keramuttulla addressed to Elmas Ali Khan wrote the 25th of *Rebee ul awel* of the present year of the *Hizira*, translated by Ralph Browne, Persian interpretter.

76. *Op. cit.*, f.n. 73, 'Extracts of Intelligence from the News Papers arrived from Delhi dated 8th March, 1783.'

77. *Ibid.*

78. *Ibid.*

79. *Ibid.*

80. *Foreign Department/Secret Proceedings*, 14th December, 1784, 'Warren Hastings' Minute about Sikhs presented to his Council on 4 December, 1784.'

81. *Op. cit.*, f.n. 76

82. *Foreign Department/Secret Proceedings*, 23rd June, 1783, No. 43, 'Letter from Lt. Col. Christian Knudson to Colonel Sir John Cumming, Jehangareebad, dated April 12th, 1783'.

83. *Ibid.*

84. *Op. cit.*, f.n. 80.

85. *Ibid.*

86. *Foreign Department/Secret Proceedings*, 23rd June, 1783, No. 42B, 'Translation of the copy of an Arzee from Sheik Azomalden Khan and Keramuttola to Elmass Ali Khan, under date the 29th of *Rebuil awel* of the present year of the *Hezira*'.

87. *Foreign Department/Secret Proceedings*, 24 June, 1809, No. 7.

88. *Ibid.*

89. *Ibid.*

90. Major James Browne worked as *aide-de*-camp to Warren Hastings; Collector of the Jungle Terai district; and Agent and Envoy of the Governor General in the imperial Court at Delhi.

91. He wrote, "Conformably to the wish you were pleased to express, that I should furnish with an account of the rise and present State of the tribe of the people called Sicks, I now beg leave to submit to your perusal, the following translation which I have made of a Persian manuscript, written by my desire while I resided at the Court of Delhy."

92. Browne, Major James, *Indian Tracts: History of the Origin and Progress of the Sicks*, London, 1788, 'Introduction', pp. iii-iv. This book has been reproduced and edited with critical remarks in Ganda Singh (ed.), *Early European Accounts of the Sikhs*, Calcutta, 1962.

93. *Ibid.*, ii, p. 8.

94. *Ibid.*, ii, p. 13.

95. *Ibid.*, 'Introduction', p. vii.

96. *Ibid.*, ii, pp. 19-20

97. *Ibid.*, ii, p. 22.

98. *Ibid.*, 'Introduction', p. vii.

99. *Ibid.*, ii, p. 23.

100. *Ibid.*, 'Introduction', p. vii and ii, p. 19. According to other authors like Chopra, Gulshan Lall, *The Panjab As A Sovereign State (1799-1839)*, Hoshiarpur, 2nd edition, 1960, p. 152, the English translation of the Persian inscription on the coin in question is, "By the grace of God, the coin is struck in the world, Jassa Kalal having captured the country of Ahmed."

101. Chopra, Gulshan Lall, *op. cit.*

102. Browne, Major James, *op. cit.*, 'Introduction', p. vii.

103. *Ibid.*, ii, p. 27. Chopra. Gulshan Lall, op. cit , p. 153, has, translated the Persian distich written in poetry on the obverse of the coin as: "Festivity (Abundance), Sword, Victory without delay, Guru Gobind Singh received from Nanak." The reverse side has been translated as "Struck in Lahore, the seat of Government in the auspicious *Samvat* , year 1822". He has also stated that "rupees of this type were struck also in Samvats, 1825, 26, 27, 28, 30, 31, 32, 33 and 34."

104. Chopra, Gulshan Lall, *op. cit.*, p. 153. Major James Browne is conspicuously silent about the word '*Deg*' inscribed in these coins and has left it meaningless.

105. Forster, George, *A Journey from Bengal to England through North India, Kashmir, Afghanistan, Persia, into Russia (1782-83)*, London, 1798, i, p. 271.

106. *Ibid.*, i, pp. 312- 13.

107. *Ibid.*, i, p. 313.

108. He wrote, "It is supposed that their forces would then have been annihilated, had not this people found a strenous advocate in his minister Korah Mal who was himself of the Khualasah sect and diverted Meer Munnoo from reaping the full fruits of the superiority he had gained." *Ibid.*, i, p. 314.

109. *Ibid.*, i, p. 319.

110. He wrote, "This event is said to have happened in October 1762, when the collected body of the Sicque nation, amounting to sixty thousand cavalry had formed a junction at the ruin of Amrutsir for the purpose of performing some appointed ceremony, and where they resolved, expecting the attack, to pledge their national existence, in the event of a battle. Ahmad Shah at that time encamped at Lahore, marched with a strong force to Amrutsir, and immediately engaged the Sicaques; who roused by the fury of a desperate revenue, in sight also of the ground sacred to the founders of their religion, whose monuments, had been destroyed by the enemy they were then to combat, displayed during a bloody contest, which from the morning until night, an enthusiastic and fierce courage, which ultimately, forced Ahmad Shah to draw off his army and retire with precipitation to Lahore." *Ibid*, i, pp. 321-22.

111. He wrote '...they committed violent outrages. The mosques were demolished with every mark of contempt and indignation; and the Afghans, in chains, washed the foundation with the blood of hogs. They were also compelled to excavate the reservoir at Amrutsir, which in the preceding year they had filled up.. .and though the Afghan massacre and persecution must have been deeply imprinted on their minds; they did not, it is said, destroy one prisoner in cold blood." *Ibid.*, i, p. 321.

112. *Ibid.*, i, p. 333.

113. 376. Mirza Najaf Khan to Major Hannay, *C.P.C.*, v, 1778-80, Nov. 7, 1776, p. 60.

114. *Op. cit.*, f.n. 38, 73 and 82.

115. *Ibid.* and *op. cit.*, f.n. 42.

116. *Op. cit.*, f.n. 31.

117. *Op.cit.*, f.n. 56.

118. *Op. cit.*, f.n. 75.

119. *Op. cit.*, f.n. 96.

120. Browne, *op. cit.*, f.n. 95, 96.

121. Browne, *op. cit.*, f.n. 94.

122. *Op. cit.*, f.n. 38.

123. Browne, *op. cit.* '*Introduction*', p. vii.

124. *Ibid.*, ii p. 8 ; also Forster, *op. cit.*, pp. 321-22.

125. For example see *Foreign Department/Political Proceedings*, 5 September 1856, No. 114; 26 September 1856, No. 114; and 28 November 1856, No. 113 and 135.

126. *Op cit.*,f.n.65.

127. *Ibid.* Also *op. cit.*, f.n. 66.

128. *Op. cit.*, f.n. 68.

129. *Op. cit.*, f.n. 67.

130. Malcolm, John, *Sketch of the Sikhs*, London, 1812, p. 68.

131. *Ibid.*, p. 88. He writes, "According to a contemporary Mohammadan author (most likely *Siyar-ul-Mutakharin*) the Sikh horsemen were seen riding, at full gallop, towards their favourite shrine of devotion. They were often slain in making this attempt, and sometime taken prisoners; but they used, on such occasions, to seek, instead of avoiding, the crown of martyrdom; and the same authority states, that an instance was never known of a Sikh, taken on his way to Amritsar, consenting to adjure his faith."

132. *Ibid.*, pp. 102-03. He writes, "The Sikh nation, who have throughout their early history, always appeared, like a suppressed flame, to rise into higher splendour from every attempt to crush them, had become, while they were suppressed, as formidable for their union, as for their determined courage and unconquerable spirit of resistance."

133. *Ibid.*, p. 89.

134. *Ibid.*, pp. 122-23.

135. *Op. cit.*, f.n. 108.

136. Malcolm, John, *op. cit.*, p. 91.

137. *Ibid.*, 91-92.

138. He writes, "That able but artful chief considered this turbulent tribe in no other light than as the means of his personal advancement, he was careful not to reduce them altogether; but, after defeating them in an action, which was fought near Makhoval, he entered into a secret understanding with them, by which, though their excursions were limited, they enjoyed a security to which they had been unaccustomed, and from which they gathered strength and resources for future efforts." *Ibid.*, p. 92.

139. *Ibid.*, pp. 93-94.

140. *Ibid.*,p.94.

141. *Ibid.*, pp. 94-95.

142. *Ibid.*, p. 98.

143. Forster, George, *op. cit.*, i, pp. 321-22.

144. Malcolm, John, *op. cit*, pp. 100-101.

145. *Ibid.*, p. 52; also see Cunningham, Joseph Davey, *A History of the Sikhs* (London, 1839), Delhi, 1955, p. 95.

146. For further details of his life sketch see *Dictionary of National Biographies* (London, 1886) Oxford, reprint 1959-60), Vol. XVI, pp. 392-95.

147. His other works are

(i) *A History of the Political and Military Transactions in India during the Administration of Marquis of Hastings* (1813-23).

(ii) *The Historical Facts Deducible from Recent Discoveries in Afghanistan* (1844).

(iii) *Social and Political Conditions of Tibet, Tartary and Mangolia* (1852).

(iv) A Pamphlet on Indian Question.

(v) Brought out Ram Dasa's '*Registrar of Bengal Civil Servants*' and also wrote commentaries and translations of classical works.

148. He seems to have made an extensive use of the manuscript prepared by Captain Murray which was later published under the title '*Ranjit Singh*' in two volumes in 1846.

149. Prinsep, Henry T., *Origin of the Sikh Power in the Punjab and Political Life of Maharaja Ranjit Singh with an Account of the Religion, Laws and Customs of the Sikhs,* 1834. Reprint, Patiala, 1970. (The present author has used its second impression published by the Language Department, Punjab, Patiala, 1970), pp. 31-32 foot-note.

150. *Ibid.*, p. 1, n.

151. *Ibid.*, p. 17, n.

152. No doubt Khushwaqt Rai's *Tarikh-i-Sikhan* was completed in 1839 and Prinsep's book was published in 1834, it seems either the former showed his manuscript to the latter or both were in close contact.

153. He writes "It is the object of the following pages to collect and exhibit in continuous narrative, the occurrences of this description in the Punjab, and to trace the rise of the chief (Ranjit Singh) who now sways the destinies of that province, and of a large bordering territory, with a vigour of authority, unknown to any other part of India, not subject to the dominions of Europeans." Prinsep, Henry T., *op. cit.,* p. 2.

154. *Ibid.*

155. *Ibid.*

156. *Ibid.*, pp. 2-3.

157. *Ibid.*, p. 23.

158. *Ibid.*, p. 7.

159. *Ibid.*

160. *Ibid.*

161. He writes, Adina Beg "strengthened himself by association with the Sikhs, of whom he took a considerable body into pay,... He applied to the Mahrathas

...stipulated for the payment of a daily sum for their aid, and pointed out the rich harvest of spoil that was within their reach." *Ibid.*, p. 13.

162. Ganesh Dass, *Rislah-i-Sahib Nama or Char Bagh-i Punjab*, Ms. 1855 (Khalsa College, Amritsar), p. 156 and Sayyid Ghulam Hussain, *Siyar-ul-Mutakherin*, Calcutta, 1836, iii, p. 64.

163. Prinsep, Henry T., *op. cit.*, p. 20.

164. *Ibid.*

165. *Ibid.*, p. 22. Citing the authority of Khuswaqt Rai, Prinsep writes, "the title of *Mahendra* was obtained from Shah Alam in the time of Sahib Singh (successor of Amar Singh), and the style *Maharaja Rajagan Bahadur* was that conferred on Amar Singh by Ahmad Shah." *ibid.*, p. 172. But both Prinsep and Khushwaqt Rai seem to be partially incorrect as Amar Singh on this occasion was conferred with the title of "*Raja-i-Rajagan Bahadur*" and the title of *Maharaja* was granted later, by Akbar II, in 1810, on the recommendation of General Ochterlony.

166. *Ibid.*, pp. 22-23.

167. *Ibid.*

168. *Ibid.*, p. 23.

169. *Ibid.*

170. *Ibid.*, p.24.

171. *Ibid.*

172. *Ibid.*

173. *Ibid.* p. 26.

174. *Ibid.*

175. *Ibid.*

176. *Ibid.*

177. *Ibid.*

178. *Ibid.*

179. *Ibid.*, pp. 27-28.

180. *Ibid.*,p 26.

181. *Ibid.*, p. 28.

182. *Ibid.*, p. 27.

183. *Op. cit.*, f.n. 181.

184. *Ibid.*

185. *Ibid.*

186. *Ibid.*

187. *Ibid.*, pp. 28-29.

188. *Ibid.*, p. 29.

189. *Ibid.*, p. 35.

190. *Ibid.*,p.2.

191. *Ibid.*, p. 23.

192. *Ibid.*, pp. 2, 3, 7.

193. *Ibid.*, p. 13; Malcolm, *op. cit.*, p. 92. Same views have been expressed in 1184. 'Extracts from News', *Calendar of Persian Correspondence*, July 27, 1774, iv, 1772-75, p. 214.

194. Prinsep, *op. cit.*, pp. 22-23.

195. *Ibid.*, p. 20.

196. *Ibid.*, pp. 26-29.

197. *Ibid.*, p. 26.

198. *Ibid.*

199. M'Gregor, W.L., *The History of the Sikhs containing an account The War between The Slkhs and the British in 1845-46, Vol. II*, London, 1847. (Second edition, Patiala, 1970), p. 2 (The titles of both the volumes are different).

200. M'Gregor, W.L., *The History of the Sikhs containing the Lives of the Gooroos'; The History of the Independent Sirdars, or Missuls, and The Life of the Great Founder of the Sikh Monarchy, Maharjah Runjeet Singh*, Vol. I, London, 1847 (Second edition, Patiala, 1970). p. 280.

201. M'Gregor, *op. cit.*, Vol. II, pp. 87 and 278.

202. *Ibid.*, p. 281 and f.n.

203. *Ibid.*, p. 202.

204. *Ibid.*, p. 267.

205. For instance, M'Gregor writes (op. cit., Vol. I, p. 116), "The Shah was alarmed at this daring attack, on the part of the Sikhs, and leaving Juhan Khan as governor of Lahore, he proceeded to Sealkote." From the above statement, it is difficult to make out the year and date of the above incident. Moreover, since Jahan Khan was never appointed the Governor of Lahore, whether the author is referring to the former's appointment as Deputy Governor under Timur Shah in 1757 ; or his appointment as the *zamindar* of Rachna and Singh Sagar (the territory between the Indus and Ravi) in 1762 ; or his appointment as the Commander-in-Chief of the Durrani's forces. Of course, since the very next incidence mentioned by M'Gregor is about Jahan Khan's defeat in Lahore which apparently took place in 1758. It seems that he is referring to latter's appointment as Deputy Viceroy.

206. He Writes, "On the death of Ahmad Shah Douranee, his son Timoor Shah succeeded to the Musnud.. .it was out of his power to settle the affairs of the Punjab, or dispute the claims of the Sikhs to the country." M'Gregor, *op. cit.*, Vol. I, p. 117.

207. M'Gregor, *op. cit.*, Vol. I. p. 118.

208. M'Gregor, *op cit.*, Vol. 1, p. 128.

209. M'Gregor, *op. cit.*, Vol. I, p. 138.

210. M'Gregor, *op. cit.*, Vol. I, p. 147.

211. He writes, "Every Sirdar appropriated a portion to himself, and named it after his native village, such as Ramghureea, Alloowalya; and other from their habits, as Bhunjeea. Each Sirdar, therefore, kept his own followers, and took possession of his own district, taking under his protection those zamindars who revolted from Timoor Shah. Each independent Sirdar kept possession of his own territory, nor encroached on that of his neighbour. In some instances, pergunnahs, or districts, were divided between two, and each received half the revenue of the whole." M'Gregor, *op. cit.*, Vol. I. p. 117.

212. M'Gregor, *op. cit.*, Vol. I, p. 118.

213. *Ibid.*

214. M'Gregor, *op. cit.*, Vol. 1, p. 114.

215. He writes, "Many of the Zamindars in the Manja tract were related to his Sikhs, and concealed the latter when pursued by the Musulmans; and in every village of this jungly tract, there were two or three Sikh horsemen quartered, and supported by the Zamindars, unless when they chose to provide for themselves by robbery and pillage." M'Gregor, *op. cit.*, Vol. I pp. 114-115.

216. M'Gregor, *op. cit.*, Vol. I, p. 146.

217. *Ibid.*

218. See for example, Griffin, Lepel Henry, *The Rajas of the Punjab*, Lahore, 1870, (Second edition Patiala, 1970), p. 454.

219. M'Gregor, *op. cit.*, Vol. I, p. 146.

220. *Ibid.*

221. M'Gregor, *op. cit,*, Vol. I, p. 147.

222. *Ibid.*

223. *Ibid.*

224. M'Gregor, *op cit.*, Vol. I, p. 140.

225. M'Gregor, *op cit.*, Vol. I, p. 129.

226. M'Gregor, *op cit.*, Vol. I, p. 147.

227. *Ibid.*

228. *Ibid.*

229. M'Gregor, *op. cit.*, Vol. I, p. 149.

230. *Op. cit.*, f.n. 228.

231. *Ibid.*

232. The present writer has used the edition published by S. Chand and Company, Delhi, 1955 which has been edited by H.L.O. Garrett and contains additional notes by R.R. Sethi.

233. For the details of his biographical sketch see, *Dictionary of National Biography*, London, 1886, pp. 309-318 and '*Biographical Note on the Cunningham Family*' in Cunningham, Joseph Davey, *A History of the Sikhs from The Origin of the Nation to the Battles of the Sutlej*, Delhi, 1955, pp. XIX-XXI.

234. Cunningham, Joseph Davey, *op. cit.*, p. 1.

235. *Op. cit.*, f.n. 233.

236. The works of the authors like, Elphinstone, Mill. Auber, Thornton and Harlon etc.

237. Especially written by Browne, Malcolm, Lawerence, Murry, Steinback and Osbourne etc.

238. The works like, *Debistan, Siyar-ul-Mutakhrin, Jahangir's Memoir, Mirat-i-Aftab Nama* and *Memoirs of Amir Khan.*

239. Especially *Adi Granth* and Guru Gobind Singh's *Gur Ratnavali.*

240. Cunningham, Joseph Davey, *op. cit.*, 'Author's Preface to the Second edition', p. XXVIII.

241. *Ibid.*

242. *Ibid.*, pp. 83-84.

243. *Ibid.*, p.84.

244. *Ibid.*, p. 91.

245. *Op. cit.*, f.n. 243.

246. *Ibid.*

247. *Ibid.*

248. Cunningham, Joseph Davey, *op. cit.*, p. 92.

249. *Ibid.*, p. 101.

250. *Ibid.*

251. Cunningham. Joseph Davey, *ibid.*, p. 85.

252. *Ibid.*

253. *Ibid.*, p. 87.

254. *Ibid.*

255. *Ibid.*

256 He wrote, "Lahore was temporarily occupied by the triumphant Sikhs, and the same Jassa Singh, who had proclaimed the '*Khalsa*' to be a state and to possess an army, now gave it another symbol of substantive power. He used the mint of the Mughals to strike a rupee bearing the inscription, "Coined by the grace of the "*Khalsa*" in the country of Ahmad, conquered by *Jassa* the *Kalal.*" *Ibid.*, p. 89.

257. *Ibid.*, pp. 90-91.

258. *Ibid.*, p. 91.

259. *Ibid.*, p. 92.

260. *Ibid.*

261. *Ibid.*, p. 94.

262. For example, see, Griffin, Sir Lepel Henry, *The Rajas of the Punjab: Being the History of the Principal States in the Punjab and their Political Relations with the British Government*, Lahore, 1870 (Second edition, Patiala, 1970), ii, p. 460. f.n.

263. Cunningham, Joseph Davey. *op. cit.*, pp. 96-97.

264. *Ibid.*, p. 98.

265. *Ibid.*

266. *Ibid.*, p. 103.

267. *Ibid.*, pp. 103-104.

268. *Ibid.*, p. 105.

269. *Ibid.*, p. 104.

270. *Ibid.*, p. 101.

271. *Ibid.*

272. *Op. cit.*, f.n 269.

273. *Op. cit.*, f.n. 270.

274. *Op. cit.*, f.n. 261.

275. *Ibid.*

276. *Ibid.*

277. Cunningham, Joseph Davey, *op. cit.*, p. 95.

278. *Ibid.*

279. *Ibid.*, f.n.

280. *Ibid.*

281. For the details of Griffin's biographical sketch see, *Dictionary of National Biography, Supplement*, Vol. II (Twentieth Century, 1901-1911), Oxford Reprint, 1963, pp. 167-169. Also see Eric Stokes, "The Administration and Historical Writings on India" in C.H. Philips' *Historians of India, Pakistan and Ceylone* (London 1961), p. 385.

282. For his successful negotiations with Abdur Rehman in Kabul as assistant of Sir Fredrick Roberts in 1880, the former gave Griffin a well deserved epithet of 'Lord of Kabul'. In recognition of his services, he was also conferred with the titles, respectively, of *C.S.I.* in July, 1879 and *K.C.S.I.* in May 1881 by the British government. Moreover, besides Punjab, Griffin was also sent in the Central India by Lord Ripon to reform the state of affairs in the princely states of Gwalior, Indore, Bhopal etc., from where he took retirement in January 1889 on medical grounds.

283. Besides, some of his other works also include, *(i) Our North West Frontier*, Allahabad, 1881, printed 27 pages for private circulation, *(ii) The Great Republic*, London, 1884; *(iii) Famous Monuments of Central India*, London, 1886, *(iv) Women's Influence in the East, with an introduction by Sir Lepel Griffin*, (1892); and (v) "*Sikhism and the Sikhs*", an article contributed to the book, *Great Religions of the World*, London 1905.

284. Griffin, Lepel H., *The Rajas of the Punjab Being the History of the Principal States in the Punjab and Their Political Relations with the British Government*, Lahore, 1870 (Second Edition, 1970) (heretofore Griffin, *The Rajas of the Punjab*), Preface to the First Edition, p. v.

285. *Ibid.*

286. *Ibid.*

287. *Ibid.*, p. vii.

288. *Ibid.*, pp. vii-viii.

289. *Ibid.*, p. ix.

290. *Ibid.*

291. Various books evidently consulted by Lepel Griffin include : J.D. Cunningham, *A History of the Sikhs*; Radha Kishan, *Gosha-i-Punjab*; W. Franklin, *The Military Memoirs of George Thomas*; Moorcroft, *Travels in the Himalayan Princes* (1819-25); William Murray, *History of the Punjab*; Ganesh Dass, *Tawarikh-i-Punjab*; Col. Sleeman, *Rambles of an Indian Official*; Ernest Trumpp, *Adi Granth*; Denzil Ibbetson, *Census Report of 1881*, etc.

292. Griffin, *The Rajas of the Punjab*, 'Preface to the first edition'. p. xii.

293. Griffin, Lepel, *Ranjit Singh* (Rulers of India Series, edited by W.W. Hunter), Lahore, 1870 (Indian Reprint, Delhi, 1957), p. 72. (heretofore, Griffin, *Ranjit Singh*)

294. Griffin, *The Rajas of the Punjab*, p. 17.

295. Griffin, *Ranjit Singh*, p. 24.

296. *Op. cit.*, f.n. 294.

297. Griffin, *The Rajas of the Punjab*, p. 23.

298. *Ibid.*

299. *Ibid.*

300. Griffin, *Ranjit Singh*, p. 84.

301. Griffin, *The Rajas of the Punjab*, Preface to the first edition', p. vi.

302. Ibid. also Griffin, *Ranjit Singh*, p. 123.

303. Griffin, *Ranjit Singh*, p. 24.

304. Griffin, *The Rajas of the Punjab*, p. 547.

305. Griffin, *Ranjit Singh*, p. 84.

306. *Ibid.*, p. 83.

307. *Ibid.*, p. 77.

308. *Op. cit.*, f.n. 306.

309. *Op. cit.*, f.n. 307.

310. *Ibid.*,

311. *Ibid.*, p. 75.

312. *Ibid.*

313. Griffin, *The Rajas of the Punjab*, p. 24.

314. Griffin, *Ranjit Singh*, pp. 75-77 also *Ibid.*, pp. 24-26.

315. Griffin, *The Rajas of the Punjab*, p. 31. Here it may be pointed out that Griffin does not agree with Cunningham as far as the latter's version that Raja Amar Singh on this occasion received the title of *Maharaja* is concerned. As explained in the foot-note No 1 of the above page he says, 'this was granted later, by Akbar II, in 1810, on the recommendation of General Ochterlony. The *sanad* is still in possession of the family."

316. *Op. cit.*, f.n. 314.

317. *Ibid.*

318. Griffin, *The Rajas of the Punjab*, p. 25.

319. *Op. cit.*, f.n. 314.

320. *Op. cit.*, f.n. 318 and Griffin, *Ranjit Singh*, p. 76.

321. Griffin, *The Rajas of the Punjab*, p. 453.

322. The four villages were: "Hallu-Sadho, Tor, Chak and Allu."

323. Griffin, *The Rajas of the Punjab*, pp. 452-53 ; *Ranjit Singh*, pp. 78-79; also Griffin, *The Punjab Chiefs, Historical and biographical notices of the principal families in the territories under the Punjab Government*, Lahore, 1865 ; New edition bringing the histories down to date by Charles Massey, two volumes, Lahore, 1890; Appendix Revised pedigree of the families in Griffin and Massey, *Chiefs and Families of Note in the Punjab*, two volumes, Lahore, 1911, (The present author has made use of the last mentioned edition), ii. p. 496. (heretofore *Chiefs and Families of Note in the Punjab*). Denzil Ibbetson, writing about the *Kalals*, says that they were "notorious for enterprise, energy, and obstinacy." "Death may budge, but a Kalal won't". It was Sardar Jassa Singh Ahluwalia, he further writes, who "adopted the title of Ahluwalia from his ancestral village Ahlu, the title is still borne by the Kapurthala royal family, and a Sikh Kalal will commonly give his caste as Ahluwalia." Ibbetson has considered him as the most powerful and influential chief that the Sikhs ever possessed till the rise of Ranjit Singh. *Punjab Castes*, 1883, p. 325.

324. Griffin, Ranjit Singh, p. 79; and *Chiefs and Families of Note in the Punjab*, ii, p. 496.

325. *Chiefs and Families of Note in the Punjab*, ii, pp. 496-97.

326. Griffin, *The Rajas of the Punjab*, p. 496.

327. *Ibid.*

328. *Ibid.*, p. 458.

329. *Ibid.*, p. 460.

330. *Ibid.*, pp. 462-63.

331. *Ibid.*, pp. 463-66.

332. *Ibid.*

333. *Ibid.*

334. *Ibid.*, p. 468.

335. *Ibid.*, pp. 460-61.

336. *Ibid.*, *Op. cit.*, f.n. 200.

337. *Ibid.*

338. *Ibid.* Justifying the right of Sardar Jassa Singh Ahluwalia to issue the coins in his own name after taking possession of Lahore, C.T. Rodgers has stated, "The striking of coins in India is a prerogative of royalty, and which has always been exercised the moment a man sat on the throne." C.T. Rodgers, *Journal of Asiatic Society of Bengal*, 1885. Vol. Liv, p. 67.

339. *Ibid.*, p.466.

340. *Ibid.*, pp. 24-25; 460-62; also *Chiefs and Families of Note in the Punjab*, ii. p. 497.

341. *Op. cit.*, f.n. 329.

342. Griffin, *The Rajas of the Punjab*, pp. 24 and 462; also *Chiefs and Families of Note in the Punjab*, ii. p. 497.

343. *Ibid.*

344. Griffin., *The Rajas of the Punjab*, pp. 24-25 and 462.

345. *Ibid.*

346. *Ibid.*, p. 27.

347. The eight villages were; "Suhoran, Pir Suhanab, Khanpur, Bhagu Mazrah, Simbal Mazrah, Dadu Mazrah, Orijian and Bhukri." *Ibid.* p. 464.

348. *Ibid.*, pp. 27 and 464.

349. *Ibid.*, p. 31.

350. *Ibid.*, pp. 41. 456 and 463 ; *Chiefs and Families of Note in the Punjab*, ii. p. 498.

351. Griffin, *The Rajas of the Punjab*, p. 466.

352. *Ibid.*, pp. 466-67.

353. *Ibid.*, pp. 460.

354. *Ibid.*, pp. 467 and 473.

355. *Ibid.*, pp. 457-58, 463 and 467.

356. *Ibid.*, pp. 43 and 467.

357. *Ibid.*, p. 467.

358. *Ibid.*, p. 43.

359. *Ibid.*, p. 23.

360. Griffin, *Ranjit Singh*, p. 24.

361. Griffin, *The Rajas of the Punjab*, p. 453. These villages, along with some other in the Lahore district, "had been resumed (by the British government) on the death of Raja Nihal Singh in September 1852." Since "they had been the first conquests of Sirdar Jassa Singh, and included the village of Ahlu, which had been the original home of the family, and from which their name has been derived." Raja Randhir Singh had always been desires of regaining those estates. "The Government of the Punjab strongly recommended that the wishes of the Raja ("whose services had been most distinguished, was entitled to more consideration") should be complied with, and these estates were accordingly granted in perpetuity" in 1859. *Ibid.*, pp. 531-32.

362. *Ibid.*, pp. 455 and 460; *Chiefs and Families of Note in the Punjab*, ii, p. 497.

363. Griffin, *The Rajas of the Punjab*, p. 456.

364. The prisoners taken in this battle were executed in Lahore, where Shahidganj or martyrs' memorial is still pointed out." Later on the British government had granted a small endowment to this memorial. *Ibid.*, p. 456 and n. 1.

365. "Here another force was sent against him, under Lachmi Narayan, one of the officers of Abdul Samad Khan; and he and his allies, Hari Singh and Jhanda Singh Bhangis, were again defeated, Jassa Singh being forced to take refuge in the hilly country to the north of the Satlej. This happened in 1765, in which Zakria Khan died, and after a lengthened struggle for viceroyalty between his sons Yahia Khan, and Shah Nawaz Khan, the latter, although the younger succeeded in obtaining power." *Ibid.*, p. 456.

366. *Ibid.*, pp. 456-57.

367. *Ibid.*, p. 457 and *op. cit.*, f.n. 362. Here it may be pointed out that Griffin has called Salabat Khan as 'Governor' of Amritsar whereas it should be the *faujdar*'.

368. *Ibid.*, p. 458.

369. *Ibid.*

370. *Ibid.* and *Chiefs and Families of Note in the Punjab*, ii. p. 497. Captain G. Birch in a brief note has also stated that Sardar Jassa Singh Ahluwalia had captured the territories of Jagraon, Bharog, Fatahgarh and Naraingarh. He appointed his servant Mirza Singh of Sultanwind, a village near Amritsar, as his *thanadar* in Fatehgarh and his two horsemen, Hakumat Singh and Dasaundha Singh, who were incidently the uncles of his servant in Bharog and Naraingarh respectively. *Punjab Government Records*, Selections from note book kept by Captain G. Birch, 1818-1821, Vol. IX, No. 17, p.129.

371. *Op. Cit.*, f.n. 368.

372. *Ibid.*

373. *Ibid.*

374. *Ibid.*, p. 459.

375. Regarding the 'Dogars,' Griffin writes, "The Dogars are pastoral tribe, resident in the neighbourhood of Kussur, Firozpur, and along the south bank of the Satlej. They are now Muhammadans, but are supposed to have been originally Chouhan Rajputs, emigrants from Delhi." *Ibid.* n. 1.

376. About the 'Nypals,' Griffin says, "The Nypals are a tribe inhabiting the Firozpur district, great thieves and vagabounds. They are a sub-caste of the Bhattis, who were originally Rajputs." *Ibid.*, n. 2.

377. *Op. cit.*, f.n. 374.

378. Griffin says, "Both Bhirog and Naraingarh were in 1760, held by Muhammad Bakr, the Rais of Kotakha. On the approach of the royal army, Mirza Singh, the Lieutenant of Muhammad Bakr, took fright and abandoned Naraingarh, of which the Raja of Patiala took possession and made it over to Jassa Singh, who reappointed Mirza Singh as his deputy. When Ahmed Shah again marched southwards, Mirza Singh, a second time abandoned Naraingarh, which fell into the hands of Punjilassa Rajputs, and afterwards of Nahan Raja, the Ahluwalia chief only recovering half the estate in 1807, and the remainder in 1832." "Bhirog remained a fife of the Ahluwalias till the first Sikh war, though their supremacy was often questioned, and was the subject of many disputes." *Ibid.*, p. 460 and n. 1.

379. *Ibid.*, p. 460.

380. *Ibid.*, also *Chiefs and Families of Note in the Punjab*, ii., 497.

381. Griffin, *The Rajas of the Punjab*, p. 461.

382. *Ibid.*

383. *Chiefs and Families of Note in the Punjab*,, ii. p. 497.

384. *Ibid.*, also Griffin, *The Rajas of the Punjab*, pp. 462-63.

385. *Ibid.*, Also J.C. Dua, 'Sir Lepel Henry Griffin on Sardar Jassa Singh Ahluwalia and his place in the Eighteenth century Punjab history, '*Punjab History Conference*, XXI Session 1997, pp. 111-118.

386. *Ibid.*, pp. 463, n. 2 and 464, also *op. cit.*, f.n. 383. Regarding 'Kassur', Griffin writes, "Kassur territory was made over to Bhangi Chiefs, who held it till 1794." "In 1794, Nizamuddin Khan drove out the Sikhs ; and Kassur was again captured by Ranjit Singh in 1807"

387. In this connection Griffin has pointed out that Sardar Jassa Singh Ahluwalia "had entertained a strict alliance with Suraj Mal, the Jat ruler of Bhurtpur, and when this Chief was killed in a skirmish on the banks of Hindan, in 1764, his son Jowahir Singh invited Jassa Singh to join him and take vengenance on Sher Khan, the slayer of his father, who had found an asylum with Najib Khan. Jassa Singh and a large body of Maratha horse marched against the common enemy, who refused to give up Sher Khan, and the allies gained a victory near Shahjehanabad." Griffin, *The Rajas of the Punjab*, p. 465.

388. *Ibid.*

389. *Ibid.* However, though the Sikhs attacked and routed the lieutenants of Ahmed Shah Abdali, they feared his name greatly as long as he lived, and that it was after his death in 1773, "they commonly met the Afghan armies on equal terms." J.C. Dua, "The British Historiography on Sardar Jassa Singh Ahluwalia and his place in 18th century Punjab History." *Seminar on Baba Jassa Singh Ahluwalia as Secular and National Hero, New Delhi*, September 20-21, 1986.

390. *Ibid.*

391. *Ibid.*, pp. 466-67.

392. *Ibid.*, p. 467.

393. *Ibid.*

394. However, after the death of Jassa Singh Ahluwalia in 1783, he returned to the Punjab, and, with the assistance of Mahan Singh Sukarchakia and the Katoch Rajputs, recovered .a considerable portion of his possessions. *Ibid.*, pp. 43 n. 1 and 467, also *Ranjit Singh*, p. 157. But despite this, to some English writers, the Bhanghis, Ramgharias and Ahluwalias "were roughly recognized as the leading confederacies of the great Sikh body" on the north of the Sutlej, "all of them having their headquarters in the district lying between the Sutlej and the Chenab, known as Manjha." Gough, Charles and Innes, Aurthur D., *The Sikhs and the Sikh Wars; The Rise, Conquest, and Annexation of the Punjab State*, London, 1897, p. 22.

395. Griffin, *The Rajas of the Punjab*, pp. 468-69. also *Ranjit Singh*, p. 134. Explaining it further Griffin says, "The only infantry which enjoyed any respect were the *Akalis*. They were a fanatical bodies of devotees, who dressed in dark blue, and were round their turbans steel quoits, partly for show and partly as weapons, though they were not very effective. Their other distinctive signs were a knife stuck in the turbans, a sword slung round their neck, and a wooden club. These men, excited with a decoction of hemp, were generally the first to storm a town, and often did excellent service, but they were lawless and uncertain, and, in peaceful times, enjoyed almost boundless licence" He further writes, "The *Akalis* or Followers of the Immortal, derive the name from *Akal*, immortal, an attribute of God. They were always a turbulent race ; and Ranjit Singh, finding that he was unable to control them, used to employ them on the most desperate undertakings, in which they were successful or killed, either result being satisfactory to the Maharaja." But "towards the end of the reign of Ranjit Singh, (they) lost their old reputation for sanctity, and were only an undisciplined rabble of lawless, drunken savages. They served nominally as irregular cavalry, having being formed into a corps by Ranjit Singh. Before this they served on foot, and to the last they generally dismounted for a charge. They numbered about three thousands." Now they were generally "armed with two or three swords, a matehlock, and steel rings or quoits with sharp edges." Griffin, *The Rajas of the Punjab*, pp. 469 and n. 2 ; 470-71 n.1.

396. *Ibid.*, pp. 469-70, also *Ranjit Singh*, p. 135.

397. Griffin, *The Rajas of the Punjab*, p. 470 n. 1.

398. *Ibid.*, p. 469.

399. *Ibid.*, pp. 469 and 471.

400. *Ibid.*, p. 470.

401. *Ibid.*, n. 1.

402. *Ibid.*, p. 471. In this connection Griffin writes, "The Kassur offenders escaped, for the whole town was inhabited by Muhammadans, but the unfortunate butchers of Lahore were almost all massacred." *Ibid.*, p. 471.

403. *Ibid.*, pp. 471-72. About the daily life of Sardar Jassa Singh Ahluwalia, Griffin writes, "The life of a Sikh Sardar, in the days of Jassa Singh, was very simple. At daybreak he would rise, perform his ablutions, and dress, repeating the morning prayers or "*Sukhmani.*" He then took his morning meal, which consisted, in Jassa Singh's case, of two pounds of flour and half a pound of sugar candy, and it is not surprising to hear that he grew very fat. He then set about the business of the day, and at 3 p.m. held a *Durbar* or assembly for all who chose to attend, where all matters of general interest were discussed.

After the evening meal, musicians played and sung hymns called '*Sabdh Rahras*" and an hour after sunset all retired to rest, having repeated the "*Ardas*," or evening prayer." *Ibid.*, n. 1.

404. *Chiefs and Families of Note in the Punjab*, ii, p. 498.

405. Scott, George Bately, *Religion and Short History of the Sikhs*, 1469-1930, 1930.

406. J.C. Dua, *op. cit.*, 191.

407. Scott, George Batley, *op. cit.*, pp. 40-41.

408. *Ibid.*, also J.C. Dua, *op. cit.*, 191.

409. *Calenaer of Persian Correspondence*, *op. cit.*, Vol. II, 1767-69, Feb. 13, 1767, Paper of news, p. 19 ; and Griffin, *The Rajas of the Punjab*, p. 24.

410. *Calender of Persian Correspondence*, *op. cit.*, Vol. III, News from Akbarabad (*i.e.* Agra) May 9, 1 770; Secret Report of March 5, 1779 to Warren Hastings by Mr. Middleton, the British Resident at Lucknow ; *Foreign Department/ Secret Proceedings*, *op. cit.*, 23 June 1783, No. 23 Griffin, *Ranjit Singh*, p. 24.

411. As has been done by Griffin, see *Ranjit Singh*, p. 84.

412. No doubt, Sikhs had become a militant and fighting community since the times of Guru Hargobind Sahib (1606-45 A.D.). He had asked his followers to keep arms and fight against the Mughal tyranny. Instead of accepting money from his followers, he would ask them to offer horses and weapons to him. It was certainly not the lure of politics and glamour of arms which had led the Guru away from the true path of religion and spiritualism. It was the changing political situation due to which the policy of the Guru had perforce to be adjusted to the new environment. It was under Guru Gobind Singh Sahib (1664-1708) that the Sikhs became a political and military force. They were at constant wars against the armies of Aurangzeb and the Hill Rajas. However, there was comparatively a lull in their political activities after the death of Banda Bahadur Sahib in 1715. It was only after the invasion of Nadir Shah and later Ahmed Shah Durrani which gave the Sikhs an opportunity to rise again. Their struggle before the rise of Maharaja Ranjit Singh had a limited vision. Despite the fact that their combined power had become a force to reckon with, none of the Sikh Sardars, either due to the political circumstances or due to the lack of objective, could hope to become an independent ruler. Even the titles like '*Raja*', *Maharaja Rajgan—Mahendar Bahadur* (or *Raja-i-Rajgan Bahadur*) and '*Sultan-ul-Qaum*' etc. enjoyed by Alha Singh, Amar Singh and Jassa Singh Ahluwalia, respectively did not have the required pre-requisites of an independent ruler. It was only Maharaja Ranjit Singh who could claim to enjoy that status.

In case of the Marathas, on the other hand, the decadence of the Deccan states like Ahmednagar, Bijapur and Golconda; Mughal threats to the existence of the Deccan Muslim States; rebillious attitude of the Nayaks and palegars of the defunct Vijayanagar empire coupled with favourable geographical and cultural backgrounds provided their chieftains ample opportunities to emerge as a political force during the l6th-l7th centuries. But before the rise of Shivaji, the Maratha Chiefs had aspired only for *watan-jagir* and the *zamindaries* first under the allegience of the Muslim Sultanates and later the Mughal empire. Despite exercising sufficient local authority, both political and otherwise, none of them aspired for a separate independent Maratha state. Their then position was broadly comparable with that of the Sikh Sardars during the eighteenth century. In case of Shivaji, however, the contemporary political situation and the responsibility of Aurangzeb played a great role in his establishment of an independent state. In this respect the concept of Shivaji as well as Maharaja Ranjit Singh, differed from their predecessors and other contemporary Maratha and Sikh Chiefs. Both were inspired by purely political motives for the formation of their respective kingdoms. Even after the death of Shivaji (1680), with a minor set back in 1689 when Sambhaji was executed. Aurangzeb, till his death in 1707, could not put a check on the Maratha power. However, after the accession of Sahu (1708) on the Maratha throne the regional character of the Maratha power changed into a national one.

413. In this regard mention may be made of the powers like the Durranis, Nawab of Awadh, Mughals, Mir Qasim of Bengal and the English. See *Calender of Persian Correspondence*, *op. cit.*, Vol-II 1767-69, Feb. 13, 1767, Paper of news, p. 19 ; Vol. III, 1770-72, General Barker to Jhanda Singh, August 19, 1771 Vol. II, p. 240, Letter of Mughal Emperor dated March 10, 1768 ; Vol. III, News from Akhbarabad (Agra) dated May, 1770 ; Vol. IV, 1772-75, July 13, 1774, pp. 206-07 ; News, May 18, 1774 ; Nov. 1775, p. 208 ; Vol. III, Feb. 16, 1770 and Feb. 20, 1770. pp. 18, 22-23 ; Vol. V, Sept. 20, 1776, No. 279 and 280, pp. 41.43 ; From Nahar Singh, Chief of the Gujars, dated Sept. 20, 1776 pp. 42.43; *Foreign Department Secret Proceedings*, 23 June, 1783, No. 23, Extracts of Intelligence from the News Papers arrived form Delhi dated 8 March 1783 ; Cunningham, *op. cit.*, p. 87 ; Griffin, *Ranjit Singh* p. 75; *The Rajas of the Punjab*, p. 24.

414. Cunningham, pp. 84, 91.

415. *Ibid.*, p. 90.

416. *Ibid.*, p. 89 ; Griffin, *The Rajas of the Punjab*, pp. 460-61, n. 2., 466.

417. Cunningham, *op. cit.*, p. 94.

418. *Ibid.*, p. 95.

419. *Ibid.*, p. 85 ; M'Gregor, *op. cit.*, i, p. 147.

6

The British Understanding of the Sikh Struggle for Power During the 18th century

At the very outset, it is quite imperative to state that some of the contemporary Persian documents[1] pertaining to subject unearthed (though some of them do find passing reference in some of the academic reports[2]) and utilized by Professor B.R. Grover, have outdated the works and knowledge, pertaining to the British understanding of the Sikh struggle for power during the eighteenth century, of the students of Punjab history banking heavily on the English writings. Professor Grover's several research papers[3] have inspired or rather forced the young scholars to leave the over dependence on the English writings for interpreting and analysing the eighteenth century Punjab history and give a fresh look to this problem with the help of other contemporary sources.

Many scholars have made historiographical study of the British historians on Punjab[4]. The present writer has also, though in a very limited sense, looked into this aspect of Punjab history. But in our analysis and interpretation practically none of us has gone beyond the writing of English writers. Moreover, Ranjit Singh and post Ranjit Singh period has been very well looked after by the historians. But on eighteenth century comparatively less work has been done. As such, it is very necessary not only to know the motivation and purpose of the English writers but also to see as to how far were they correct in their analysis in contrast to other contemporary sources.

In the present analysis the English writers have been broadly categorized into three categories, namely, (*i*) those who wrote during the eighteenth century *e.g.*, Major James Browne and George Foster; (*ii*) those who wrote during the life time of Maharaja Ranjit Singh *e.g.* John

---

Paper presented at *Punjab History Conference*, 1988 Session, Patiala and Published in *The Punjab Past and Present*, XXIV-1, April, 1990.

Malcolm, Henry T. Princep; and (*iii*) those who wrote after Maharaja Ranjit Singh's death and even after the annexation of Punjab *e.g.* W.L. M'Gregor, Joseph Davey Cunningham and Lepal Griffin. The idea behind this division is to highlight the aims, objectives and insight of the English writers and government during the three different phases of the Punjab history and also to pin point significant changes in their motives and outlook that occurred during the intermittent periods.

The aim of both the writers in the first category, *i.e.* Browne and Forster in writing their respective works was identical. It was the political motive which was foremost in their minds. The political situation in this part of India, more especially fast growing political importance of the Sikhs, must have perturbed the English East India Company. It is clear from the forwarding letter (17th September, 1787) of James Browne[5], submitted along with his work[6], to John Motteux, the then Chairman of the Hon'ble Court of Directors that he was writing in response to the Directors' instructions conveyed to him through Warren Hastings.[7] The Company was anxious to make itself akin to the political situation in the region, especially of Delhi and Punjab, and the military strength of various chiefs and factions, including the different Sikh Sardars, who were fighting for hegemony in those areas. Apart from providing information on the above subject, both the writers have also dwelt on the Sikh polity, society, institutions and practices during the 18th century. Browne's appointment as Agent and Envoy of the Governor General in the Court of the Mughal Emperor Shah Alam must be viewed as an opportunity provided to him to acquaint himself and then the Company with the required information. As a matter of fact, Company's future course of action largely dependent upon his report. There is evidence to show that soon the Company had started interfering in the affairs of the *cis*-Sutlej territories culmination in bringing under their protection the chiefs of Nabha, Malwa and Sirhind, first after the defeat of the Sindhia in 1803 and then, barring the period of George Barlow (1805-07), in the period of Lord Minto in 1809.[8]

Some of the most signification things that one comes across in the writings of Browne and Forster are:

(*i*) In 1758, with the occupation of Lahore, the then capital of Punjab, under the leadership of Sardar Jassa Singh Ahluwalia the Sikhs declared their 'sovereignty'. In pursuance of the usual practice of the time the coins were also struck in the name of the leader.[9]

(*ii*) Despite the fact that both the writers have given the description of the military and territorial structure of the Sikhs, the word *'misl'* is conspicuously absent. Different Sikh Sardars have been mentioned as *'Chiefs'* of their respective areas rather than of a particular *'misl'*.[10]

This shows that either the sovereignty of the Sikh Sardars, in their respective areas, was not recognised or the term *misl* was not current during that period. As a matter of fact, the detailed study on the subject made by Professor Grover[11] shows that the 18th century Persian, Marathi and English sources do not use the term *misl.* The Sikh Sardars in the Persian sources have been referred as *Sardaran-i-Sikhan;* Sikh Sardars in groups as *Jamai-i-Sardaran* or *Sardaran-i-Jamai Sikhan;* a distinguished Sikh Sardar with his group as *Jamai* or *Jamhur* or *groh* or *fariq* or even with his *Dal* and individual Sikh Sardar as *Sardar-i-Sikhan.* The Marathi sources refer them as the *Sikhs* or their Sardars. The English sources mention only the Sikhs and their distinguished leaders as Sardars. However, the 19th century Persian and English sources do make mention of the term *misl* and *misldari* system.

(*iii*) The politico-military activities of the Sikhs and the Sikh Sardars have been described as 'depredations' and 'highway robbery'.[12]

(*iv*) The attitude of the local *zamindars* towards the cause of the Sikh Sardars has been described as quite sympathetic and later would also refrain from plundering the former if they accepted to pay *'rakhi'* called *'tribute'*.[13]

(*v*) Both have highlighted the religious sentiments of sacrifice amongst the Sikhs in their fight against the Mughals and Durranis,[14] thereby giving unduly religious colour to their struggle.

In the second category of English writers, John Malclom's amongst other books, *Sketch of the Sikhs* (London, 1812) has to be viewed in the light of number political changes that had occured especially in regard to Punjab. Notwithstanding, the rise of Ranjit Singh's power, the political designs of the English had also started becoming clearer and clearer. Due to the English apprehension of a combined attack of Napolean Bonaparte and Zaman Shah on India, former tolerated for some time Ranjit Singh's interference in the affairs of *cis*-Sutlej states, though they could successfully persuade him not to help Jaswant Rao Holkar. Meanwhile, the English had started creating a strong political front in the *cis*-Sutlej territories by bringing Nabha, Jind, Patiala etc. under their protection after the defeat of the Sindhia in 1803. At the same time, the English would not accept Ranjit Singh as the ruler of the Sikhs as a reward for a proposed defensive treaty between the two against the French. However, the new developments like, the entanglement of Napolean in the Peninsular war in Europe and friendly relations between Britain and Mahmud II, the new ruler of Turkey, turned the political scales in favour of the English in India. Ranjit Singh was left with no alternative but to accept humiliating

Treaty of Amritsar on 25 April, 1809 with the English. Despite the fact that under the treaty Maharaja Ranjit Singh had been apparently given a free hand in the *trans*-Sutlej areas, the English still wanted to gather more information about Punjab keeping in view their future course of actions and designs. As such, John Malcolm wrote with the conviction and motive that "every information regarding the Sikhs is of importance."

By the time other English writer, Henry T. Princep published his book, *The Origin of the Sikh Power in the Punjab and Political Life of Maharaja Ranjit Singh with an Account of the Religion, Laws and Customs of the Sikhs* in 1834 a lot more political developments had taken place in the national and international arena especially on the North-Western parts of India. Maharaja Ranjit Singh had not only captured Attock, Kashmir, Dera Ghazi Khan, Dera Ismail Khan, Bakhar, Leh, Mankera and above all Peshwar but was also trying to increase his political influence in Afghanistan through its fugitive ruler Shah Shuja. Afghanistan had become a prey to the politics of Europe because of the growing differences between Britain and Russia. Russian influence had so much increased in Persia and Central Asia that the English had started feeling *Russa-Phobia* and was considered dangerous for the security of later's empire in India. Maharaja Ranjit Singh was being considered as a stumbling block. As such, though Prinsep has given object of writing the above book as to give a narrative of the occurrences leading to the rise of Ranjit Singh,[15] the brief but useful information about the activities and political, social and economic fabric of the Sikhs shows that the English were preparing for the take off at an opportune time.

The unique feature of these two books is that one comes across a new trend in the English writings. Apart from religious and political nature of the Sikh struggle during the eighteenth century, the economic oppression by the Mughal government as the cause of the rise of the Jat *zamindars* of Punjab has also been given due consideration.[16]

The term *misls,* 'implying that they were confederacies of equals, under chief of their own selection[17]', has also figured for the first time in Prinsep's book. He has also given the number of the principal *misls* as twelve.[18]

The political activities of the Sikhs have been described as 'depredations' and earlier comparatively smaller groups, called *Dharwi* have been termed as 'highwaymen'. The political activities were also combined with the means to satisfy their religious prejudices.[19]

Whereas Malcolm has given the reason why Adina Beg Khan wanted to join hands with the Sikhs against the Durranis, Princep has mentioned that Adina was successful in persuading not only the Sikhs but also the Marathas to help him against the Durrani forces. Malcolm is of the view that in case of a secret understanding between the two, the continuing political activities of the Sikhs would help Adhina Beg in the personal political advancement.[20] Prinsep has even gone to the extent of saying that Adina Beg was successful in enrolling number of Sikh and Maratha soldiers in his pay roll.[21] In any case it had indirectly helped the Sikhs in gaining further political strength.

As such, it was a joint Mughal-Sikh-Maratha venture which forced the Durranis to retire "precipitately to the Indus" in 1761.[22]

Prinsep has asserted that after 1764 neither Ahmed Shah Durrani nor Timur Shah made any "attempt to recover Lahore, and the Punjab." These along with the province of Sarhind and the areas on the east, as far as the Jamuna "fell into the possession of the (Sikh) chiefs and associations" and the movements of the Sikhs were "unmolested by any further interference from the West."[23]

The conferring of the titles of *'Raja'* on Alha Singh of Patiala in 1762 and of *'Maharaja Raja-Mahender Bahadur'* on his grandson Amar Singh in 1764 also figure in the Prinsep's account.[24]

Besides, Prinsep has dwelt, for the first time, in the land problem and different land tenures created by different Sikh chiefs as per the demands of the circumstances arising out of the establishment of *de-facto* power and from the nature of their association with the those who composed their respective *misls.* The different land tenures along with the conditions attached with them, that find mention in his book are, *Sirdari, Pattidari, Misaldari, Tabadari* and *Jagirdari.*[25] Moreover, lands were also assigned for religious, charitable and endowment purposes as was done by the Mughals and other rulers all over India. The beneficiaries included "Sikh *Gurus*, Sodhis, Bedis, the temples and *Musalman Pirzadas.*"[26]

Above all, not only the term *'Rakha' (Rakhi)* has been explained as 'Black Mail',[27] but Prinsep has also stated that whenever the joint forces of several *misls* fought collectively or collected *Rakhi* the army assumed the denomination of a "*Dal* of the *Khalsa Ji.*"[28]

By the time the English writers in the third category, W.L. M'Gregor Joseph Davey Cunningham and Lepel Henry Griffin, published their respective works, there was a sea-change in the Indian and international compulsions on the part of the English. In the Indian context the policy of 'Divide and Rule' on the religious lines seems to have started taking shape in the minds of the English administrators. In the international context, they had both political and commercial interests. They had their political interests towards Central and West Asia. As regards their commercial interests, they wanted to give a practical shape to their long cherished desire of opening the navigation of the Indus and bringing

Turkestan and Khorasan within their commercial influence. These books provided, both the practical and theoretical, foundations to the English policies.

M'Gregor[29], though a medical surgeon to Maharaja Ranjit Singh, used his stay at the latter's courts for diplomatic ends and was instrumental in prevention of the annexation of Sind by him.[30] Through his works, he not only aimed at providing the English information on the nature of the Sikh struggle during the eighteenth century but also general information about the Sikhs and suggestions for a policy towards Punjab and Afghanistan.[31]

Cunningham chartered a new philosophy and approach to the study of the history of the Sikhs which was quite different from those of earlier English writers. No doubt earlier writers had given lot of stress on religion in the Sikh struggle for power during the eighteenth century, Cunningham vehemently attributed a positive role to religion in the history of the Sikhs. His "main endeavour was to give Sikhism its place in the general history of humanity, by showing its connextion with the different creeds of India, by exhibiting it is as a natural and important result of the Muhammadan Conquest..."[32] His other object "was to give some account of the connection of the English with the Sikhs and in part with the Afghans...and to involve them in the web of their policy for opening the navigation of the Indus, and for bringing Turkestan and Khorasan within their commercial influence."[33]

By the time Lepel Henry Griffin published his first book in 1865[34] lot of criticism regarding the British policy towards the *cis* and *trans* Sutlej territories had accrued. The critics in his words "believed the country was won by the most unjustifiable means, that each new province added to the British India signified new crimes, and that the conquerors were only successful because they were unscruplous."[35] Obviously Griffin's main endeavour had been to justify the British policy and offer a convincing reply to the hostile criticism. Regarding the British policy towards the *cis*-Sutlej states, he asserted that a sufficient answer could be found in the history of those states since the beginning of the 19th century. Despite "the preference of the people for the rule of their hereditary chiefs", he stated they (people) "accepted British rule with most unfringed satisfaction."[36] In order to justify the annexation of Punjab and the daring changes being introduced in the agrarian set up there[37], he dubbed the revenue system of Maharaja Ranjit Singh as "an organised system of pillage".[38] Moreover, in an attempt to serve the English political interests he also highlighted the political, social and economic advantages bestowed upon the Punjab chiefs for their services rendered, especially during the war against the Gurkhas, the Anglo-Sikh wars, revolt of 1857, etc.[39] Griffin's account of 18th century history of the Punjab, though denied by the author, is mainly biographical in style. He has, however, taken up only those chiefs who bore the title of *'Raja'*.[40] He has certainly given nature and details of the major political events, prevailing customs, attitudes and social institutions prevailing during the 18th century.

Since none of the above three writer was witness to the Sikh struggle for power during the eighteenth century, they have based their information either on the previous writings or upon the anecdotes coupled with their own views and politico-economic requirements of their government.

All the above English writers are unanimous that the Sikh Sardars had religious harmony and bondage. Griffin has highlighted their enthusiasm for their faith and hatred towards the Muhammdans and has gone to the extent of saying that they were "hoping for a Sikh republic and a time when all northern India would be the heritage of the *Khalsa.*"[41] Cunningham saw a positive role of the religion in the history of the Sikhs which developed the "disciples" into a "nation".[42] But a careful study of these works also show that despite religious harmony every Sikh Sardar was fighting for the extension of his respective political power. Repeated contests between different Sikh Sardars had converted the Punjab into a property of a few of the most powerful ones which ultimately paved the way for the establishment of monarchy under Maharaja Ranjit Singh.[43] Especially after 1767, this change in the attitude of the various Sikh Sardars was all the more glaring when the necessity of union had no longer remained paramount and would rather prefer their own interests to the welfare of the community.[44] But for the private jealousies, as has been opined by Griffin, "they would have become as formidable and irresistible in North India as the Marathas in South and West.[45] At the same time he has also asserted that atleast upto the time when Maharaja Ranjit Singh came into the picture the whole concept of Sikh movement was religious and it was only after that it underwent a dramatic change from religious to the political expediency.[46]

Regarding the attitude of the local 'zamindars, particularly belonging to the *Majiha* area, towards the Sikh struggle for power, M'Gregor is quite positive in his views that they, being related to the Sikh soldiers, would give full support to the Sikh Sardars in emergency. They would conceal and protect them "when pursued by the Musulmans.[47]

As in case of the earlier English writers, all these three writers have also asserted that the Durranis had got very much alarmed at the daring attacks of the Sikhs and had felt helpless in disputing their (Sikhs') claims to the Punjab. With their ultimate success, the Sikhs assumed overlordship of the land, built up a workable polity and divided into, what was called, the *misls.*[48] In this regard, there is a contradiction in the views of above English writers and, as such, needs further probing. These authors have also referred to the conferring of the title of *'Raja'* on Sardars Alha Singh in 1762 and the assignment of the district of Sirhind on an annual revenue of three and a half lakhs of rupees in 1763. His successor Raja Amar Singh was not only allowed to continue to enjoy the above privileges but was also given the title of *"Raja-i-Rajgan-Buhadur"* and the office of military commander in Sirhind in 1767.[49]

This group of English writers, like the previous ones, have also called the Sikhs and Sikhs Sardars as 'robbers', 'marauders' or 'predatory bands'. Even for Sardar Jassa Singh Ahluwalia the same expression has been used and stated that he "became a famous robber."[50]

Regarding the conferring of title of *'Raja'* on Sardar Alha Singh different reasons have been put forth by these English writers. Cunningham and Griffin both are unanimous on the point that the Durranis wanted to follow the policy of conciliation. However, the former has asserted that behind this step the idea was to widen the difference between "a Malwa and a Majha Singh."[51] Griffin, on the other hand, opined that through such type of peaceful means the Durrani chief wanted to enlist at least some of them (Sikhs) on his side, "first against the Delhi government and then against the Marathas."[52]

These authors have also maintained that *Rakhi* was regularly levied in the area which the Sikhs, subdued but did not annex to their territories. Its amount, however, varied from about "a fifth to a half of the rental or government share of produce."[53] The term *Rakhi* along with the Maratha system of *Chauth,* has been described as 'protection money', 'black-mail' or "in a higher sense, tribute."[54]

In the light of the contemporary source material being referred to many a view of these English writers need further probing and reconsideration.

The English writers, more especially of the post Ranjit Singh period, have unduly over emphasized the religion as the main cause of struggle. It was basically a political struggle for power. Whatever the English wrote has perpetuated and has been mostly accepted as a part of primary source material.

As a matter of fact, the Sikh community/*Nanak Panth,* which was originally socio-religious in character, had, during the course of the seventeenth and the eighteenth centuries, transformed into socio-religious-cum-political force.[55] In this new set up every Sikh Sardar was fighting for his own personal ends. This assertion is further strengthened by the fact that though Sardar Jassa Singh Ahluwalia enjoyed the title of

'Badshah' or *'Sultan-ul-Quam'*, there is no evidence that he was generally acknowledged as such. This is notwithstanding the fact that he was held in highest esteem by the *Khalsa,* and the powerful Sikh Sardars like Raja Amar Singh received the *Pahul* or Sikh baptism from his hand.[56] In this regard a parallel can be drawn with another contemporary fast upcoming political power *i.e.* the Marathas. In both the cases attempts have been to equate their struggle with their respective religions. Both the Sikhs and the Marathas were inspired by purely political motives in their attempts to form their respective kingdoms. The use of religion, however, denoted popular regional feelings current during the 17th-18th centuries. Both resorted to persuation and suppression for welding together the scattered elements of their respective communities. They believed in the expansionist policy and forcibly exacted the revenues from the Durrani/Mughal territories in the form of *rakhi* and *chauth.* Despite enjoying the titles like *Sultan-ul-Quam* and *Haindave Dharmodharak* both would not refrain from military conquest and the suppression of Sikh/Hindu chiefs side by side with Muslims. To attribute religion as the dominant factor either with the Sikh or the Maratha movement, or with Sikh or Maratha chiefs' military leadership, and to attribute the attempt to create Sikh/Hindu state as a counterblast against Muslim monarchs' religious intolerance is to overlook their great military and political gift and qualities of opportunism for creating their respective new states.

However, Sikh/Maratha attempt to carve out an independent state was bound to result in a clash with the Durrani/Mughal rulers. It goes without saying that the emergence of strong Sikh/Maratha militant community was neither solely because of Mughal religious policy nor their revenue policy. Their clash with the Durranis/Mughals was a must even if king like Akbar was there on the throne. In that case, however, he would have made an attempt to settle the issue by giving them *wattan-jagirs* and *tankhwah-jagirs* etc. as the Durrani rulers had done, though in a limited manner, in case of Alha Singh and Amar Singh. The problem was both the Sikhs/Marathas and the Mughals looked upon each other with distrust. As a matter of fact, from the political, strategical and economic considerations, the Mughal state would never tolerate the existence of strong Sikh/Maratha power at its Northern/Southern borders. That could jeopardize the safety of their trade routes, as well. At the same time, they had also enforced the practice of levying *rakhi/chauth.* This was a serious challenge to the Mughal sovereignty. Also, despite the fact that the bulk of Sikh/Maratha army came from the peasant stock, the rise of their respective power was not at all a peasants' insurrection either in origin or during its course of final development.

The English had two-fold objectives in their minds. Firstly, they wanted to fight the Islamic countries like, Afghanistan, Persia etc. Secondly, the safest way of ruling over India was to follow the policy of divide and rule on the religious lines. As such, they wanted to put Punjab/Sikhs as a barrier against *Pan Islamism.* They never wanted that Islamic political power should join hands with the Sikhs. It was perhaps with this motive in mind that Griffin, contrary to the earlier views of the English writers, asserted that it was most likely the mischief on the part of the *Qazis* and *Mullahs* and could not be the work of Sardar Jassa Singh Ahluwalia as far as striking of the coins in 1757-58 was concerned.[57] Even Raja Gulab Singh was given the *gaddhi* of Kashmir mainly because of this reason.[58] As such, especially after annexation, the English played up the religious factor for vested interests.

As has been convincingly emphasized by Professor Grover in his above mentioned different papers based on contemporary Persian records, hither to untapped, that though some of the Sikh Sardars had been able to establish *de-facto* power over some of the areas of Punjab, the *de-jure* political sovereignty was always claimed by the Durranis. They continued to appoint their own *subahdar*/administrators/*vakeel* in different parts of Punjab and *cis*-Sutlej territories for general political control and, more especially, for the realization of revenue. It is a different matter that they could do so with varying success and were not able to collect the revenue all the times and in all the regions. Even Maharaja Alha Singh and Amar Singh were not the sovereign or independent chiefs but only a *vakeel* and *zamindar*-cum-*jagirdar.* The *cis*-Sutlej territories were formally ceded by the Mughal state to Ahmed Shah Durrani in 1757 A.D. In 1761, the Durrani *Wazir-i-Mumalik* recognising Alha Singh as one of the administrators of *chakla* Sirhind specified the nature of *chaudurie-zamindari, faujdari* and *jagir* assignments to him in the named villages and *parganas.*[59] In 1764, Alha Singh was conferred the powers of *naib-faujdar/faujdar* in two *parganas* and was as well entrusted with the collection of the revenues therein on the payment of stipulated amount to the Durrani government.[60] Timur Shah's *Farman* dated 5th August, 1778 A.D. addressed to Maharaja Amar Singh confirmed him in his territorial possessions and the functions to be performed by him as per instructions.[61] Even the conferment of the titles of *Raja* and *Raja-i-Rajgan* (Maharaja) to Alha Singh and Amar Singh respectively by the Durrani rulers only meant the recognition of the services rendered by them to the Durrani state. They were representatives of the Durrani state, in other words, the royal authority, and were to uphold the legitimacy of the Durrani sovereignty in the Punjab and *cis*-Sutlej territories. Despite the capture of Lahore by Sardar Jassa Singh Ahluwalia/Sikhs and their campaigns and incursions in the *cis*-Sutlej and Haryana territories (*Subah* Delhi), regular *subahdars* (of *Subahs* Lahore, Multan and Kashmir); *faujdar* and *vakeels* were appointed by the Durranis. All those territories were claimed by the Durranis as part of their empire. The contemporary Persian records preserved in the Punjab State Archives, Patiala; grant of *madad-i-maash* and *aima* grants on behalf of the Durrani Kings (originals preserved at Patiala and Chandigarh); Persian Documents covering the period practically to the end of the 18th century preserved in Bhuri Singh Museum, Chamba; Shiekh Rahim Ali's *Tarikh-i-Manazal-i-Kabul;* and above all, some of the coins preserved in the Moti Bagh Palace, Patiala[62] are some of the irrefutable evidences to prove this assertion.[63] It would certainly not be necessary for the Durrani rulers to come to India every time for the collection of revenues when they had their own representatives in the form of *subahdars* and *vakeels* etc. Moreover, despite several references of the collection or demand of *rakhi* by the Sikh Sardars from different areas, there is hardly any evidence to prove that they had been able to establish their sovereignty in those areas. It is also clear from the *Calendar of Persian Correspondence* that the Shah not only claimed political sovereignty but also realized *peshcush* on the Mughal pattern.[64] The last of the Durrani campaigns to Lahore was led by Zaman Shah on 19 September 1798, though he had to retreat towards Multan due to the shortage of funds. The Sikhs were certainly a great barrier to the fulfillment of the Durrani aims for the reestablishment of the *de-facto* control over the territories of Punjab and *cis*-Sutlej upto Karnal over which he claimed *de-jure* sovereignty. However, till the end of the eighteenth century, the Durranis realized *peshkash/nazrana* from many a Hindu chief of the sub-Himalayan ranges like Chamba, Jammu etc. as well as from the territories of *Chach* Hazara and even at times from the *zamindaries* and *mahals* of the Gakhars and Khataks of the regions between Jhelum and Sind and from many other Muslim chiefs in West Punjab. Apart from the Punjab, the Durranis claimed revenues from the *Subah* of Multan, the Blochs and the territories on the West of Indus as well. In the *cis*-Sutlej areas there were, however, some brief phases when the Sikh Sardars never paid any revenues, specially when Sardar Jassa Singh Ahluwalia was able to realize revenues from the local Durrani administration itself. But, by and large, many a *misldar* were subjected to the payment of the revenues even during the last three decades of the 18th century. It was Maharaja Ranjit Singh who, after the occupation of Lahore in 1799, realised the necessity of expelling the Afghans from all the above territories for the establishment of his sovereignty and consolidation of his power. He, therefore, conquered Multan (January, 1818), Peshawar (November, 1818) and Kashmiri (July, 1819). As such, the real credit of ousting the Durranis from the Indian territories goes only to Maharaja Ranjit Singh.[65] It, however, cannot be denied that a sufficient ground work had certainly been done by the Sikh Sardars.

It is wrong to generalise on the part of M'Gregor that the Majiha Sikhs gave full support to the Sikh Sardars in emergency. This contention of the author can be viewed as an attempt to widen the gulf between the Majiha and Malwa Sikhs. In this regard it is important to note at least two things: (*i*) the observations made by Griffin on the nature of the records available pertaining to the Majiha Sikhs for period 1708-1780, and (*ii*) the contents of the *Calendar of Persian Correspondence.* Griffin observed that the above material was 'meagre and unreliable.[66] The later records show that the fear of Shah was so great in the minds of the local *zamindars* that on many an occasion they refused to co-operate with the Sikh Sardars, including Sardar Jassa Singh Ahluwalia, even in dire emergency.[67]

The collection of *rakhi* by the Sikh Sardars has been rightly clubbed with the Maratha system of the collection of *chauth.* But it is wrong to describe them as 'blackmail'. As a matter of fact, *rakhi, chauth* and *peshkash* are all synonymous terms and have the same meaning. It was an established practice of the Mughals to collect *peshkash* or tribute from the protected areas.[68] It had been a general practice in the medieval age that a budding political power establishing its chieftainship by bringing certain areas under its direct administration would attempt to establish its overlordship on some neighbouring or even far flung regions. It may or may not be a preclude to the attainment of supremacy in those regions. The establishment of overlordship would invariably result into the demand of share in the revenues of the areas. The percentage/amount thus demanded, despite having common nomenclature, varied and depended upon the geographical situation of the areas, position of the submitting chief and the extent to which the subduing power could put continuous pressure for maintaining sustained submission. Sometimes, a well-established political power would also allow the erstwhile chief of a newly acquired territory to retain a fixed percentage/portion of the revenues of the areas. Moreover, the idea of the establishment of protectorate was also current and powerful rulers used to take tribute, *nazrana* or *muamala* before annexing a particular territory or not annexing it at all, as the case might be. As such, the payment or allowance made by an inferior to a superior power and superior to an inferior or even a subordinate power in consideration of ones political authority or services or the nuisance value was an accepted norm during the period. No doubt in ancient India also such type of examples could be traced. A levy called *bali* or *deya,* which apart from other meanings, also, meant 'the tribute to a king' was received from to subdued rulers and people. It could be a fixed cash payment or even in the forms of fruits etc. payable regularly for a definite period. An area would be exempted from the payments of *bali* or *deya* by the King's order or after annexing it and collecting regular revenue known as *bhaga.*[69] The transactions of the above mentioned dues had been carried on in the course of the Indian history under different nomenclatures though with certain variations in the matter of details. Apart from the two possible names, *bali* and *deya* in ancient India, during the medieval period, when the collection/payment seems to have become more widespread, several names, *viz., peshkash nazrana, mauamala, banth, malikana, do-biswi, chauth, rakhi* and *karah parshad* have been ascribed to these transactions. Apart from the *rakhi/nazrana, Dal Khalsa* of Sardar Jassa Singh Ahluwalia as well as other Sikh Sardar after successful incursions realized dues in lieu of *karah parshad* from the Patiala chieftainship as well as the Durrani and Mughal territories of Jamuna-Ganga *doab.* This realization could be with or without the *rakhi/nazrana.* The amount which was fixed after taking into consideration the total realized revenues of the area concerned, could be paid either in lump sum or in installments as per the settlement.[70] It is different matter that in regard to the percentage of the state demand thus demanded, the division of the money thus collected and in other details, there was, of course, no similarity. This would depend upon the various circumstances and there could be variations in the same system. All the same, it is correct that the Sikh Sardars had followed the Mughal practice and had not invented anything new.

As far as describing the Sikhs and Sikh Sardars as 'robbers', 'committing 'depredation' and 'highway robbery' is concerned, it can safely be pointed out that this is a concept usually used from the imperialist view point. Whenever, the revolting *zamindars* or Sardars realized the revenue of a particular area after occupation, from the imperialist angle it was described as plunder, loot, pillage etc. Same is true about the Mughal description about the Marathas and the British description about the Marathas, the palegars in the South India and the Sikhs in the Punjab etc. In this regard, even Raja Amar Singh in an *arzdasht* addressed to Durrani Prime Minister (Shah Wali Khan), while narrating his difficulties due to the activities of the Sikhs, wrote that "large number of wretched infidel troops destined to be vanquished (*groh-i-amboh-maghurian shagawat pizhuh*—the Sikhs) have again created turbulence, have taken to vagrancy in the *mahals* of the *chakla* (Sirhind) and are indulging in pillage and plunder.[71] Both Raja Alha Singh and Raja Amar Singh described the large groups or troops of the Sikhs as 'contemptible' (*amboh-i-groh-i-nakbat pizhuh*) or 'large number of wretched infidel troops (Sikhs) destined to be vanquished (*groh-i-amboh-maghurran shagwat pizhuh*) or 'vanquishable infidels' (*maghurran, jama-i-maghur* or *jumhur-i-maghur*) or 'multitude of the Sikh troops—the infidels destined to the vanquished' (*ma'al jamai Sikhan Shakwat mishan*) or the contemptible and infidel armies destined for utter destruction (*magahir nakbat*) 'mean', 'vegarants', 'rioters' and 'impious groups'.[72] As a matter of fact, in the medieval period, the adversaries were usually mentioned with contempt and the adjectives used for them were rather derogratory in character. It is a question of terminology used for the activities of the Sikhs, the Marathas and the palegars. As a matter of fact, they were fighting for a cause.[73]

All the categories of English writers have referred to the utmost importance given to the *Gurmata* by the Sikh Sardars during the course of the Sikh struggle for supremacy in the eighteenth century. *Gurmata* can be defined as a joint consultative meeting of the Sikh Sardars for mutual consultations on various military, operational, territorial, economic and administrative matters. The English writers have written about the convening of the *Gurmata* regularly on every *Baisakhi* and *Diwali* at Amritsar. Various Persian and Punjabi sources[74] have also written about such meetings. However, when the English writings are studied in coordination with the Persian and Punjabi sources it is found that the *Gurmata* was not always held on *Baisakhi* and *Diwali* even at Amritsar. Whenever there was a news about the intended plan of Ahmed Shah Abdali for attacking Punjab or even entry into the Punjab, an earliest opportunity would be taken for holding such meeting at Amritsar. The deliberations of the meeting would decide about the military defensive measures to be adopted by the Sikh Sardars in different parts of Punjab and the *cis*-Sutlej territories. At the same time, it was not always necessary that the *Gurmata* would be held only at Amritsar. On some urgent matters it could be convinced at any other place as well. It could even be convened during the course of a military campaign.[75]

It has been noticed that all the English writers considered Sardar Jassa Singh Ahluwalia as one of the most prominent chief Sikh Sardars and was, to a considerable extent, a great unifying force within the Sikh community. Same conclusions can be drawn from other relevant English, Punjabi and Persian sources. For nearly three decades he remained closely associated with the *Dal Khalsa* as a Sardar. He, as a chief Sardar or otherwise, along with other Sikh Sardars, fought a number of battles against the Mughals, Durranis, the local chiefs, the Jats, the Rohillas, the Rajasthan chiefs, the Marathas and even Awadh Nawabs. His maturity of thought and action, religious and pious learnings, orthodox nature and political were *par excellence* amongst the other contemporary Sikh Sardars. The Punjabi sources have named him as *Sultan ul Quam, Badshaha-i-Singhan, Sarkar Khalsa, Panth Ke Malik* and *Panth Ke Badshaha.* Some of the

English sources mention him as '*Badshah Singh*' whereas contemporary Persian sources mention him as *Sarkhail-i-Sikhan.*[76]

The documents like, the *Calender of Persian Correspondence* also reveal that the Sikhs had also been persuaded by the English to side with them, especially against the Rehillas, on the payment of some money.[77] This shows that the Sikhs and the Sikh Sardars were in no way different from other contemporary Indian political chiefs, *e.g.* the Nawabs of Carnatic, Awadh and Bengal etc. They (Sikhs) had also failed to understand the aggressive and expansionist nature of the British, who wanted to check the growth of Sikhs as well.

References

Note: I am highly grateful to Professor B.R. Grover for allowing me to utilize some of the most important Persian records, along with the translations done by him and helping me in their interpretation.

1. These documents comprise three *talikachas* (orders) dated 1761 A.D. from the Durrani *Wazir-i-Mumalik* (Prime Minister) to the named revenue administrators of *chakla* Sirhind; two *sanads* dated 1764 A.D. issued by a Durrani official conferring the powers of *naib-faujdar/faujdar* on Alha Singh Jat in two *parganas,* as well as, entrusting him with the collection of the revenues therein on the payment of stipulated amount to the Durrani Government; one document with the two seals of the Durrani official dated 1765 A.D. as a Receipt given to Alha Singh; Timur Shah's *Farman* dated 5 August, 1778 A.D. addressed to Maharaja Amar Singh : Timur Shah's *murasala* (communication) dated 5 August, 1778 addressed to Chauhar Singh Phul; and seven *arzdashts* (Letters of obeisance), dated 1764-65 A.D of which two were written by Raja Alha Singh and five by Raja Amar Singh to Shah Wali Khan, *Wazir* of Ahmed Shah Abdali. Punjab State Archives, Patiala, 2A/H Foreign Ministry Case No. 2A/147 of AH 1174 (March 1761 A.D.) known as *Sacred Documents pertaining to the reign of Sh. 108 Maharaja Baba Ala Singh Surghashi.*

   Other important sources consulted are : Sheikh Rahim Ali, *Tarikh-i-Manazal-i-Kabul* (written in 1797 A.D. and recompiled by Abdul Qadir Khan), Regional Archives Office, Allahabad (U.P.) Ms. no. 12842. (Translated and quoted by Prof. B.R. Grover mentioned in his paper, f.n. 3 (iv and v). It's English translated version (Maulawi Abdul Kabir Khan, 'Memorandum of the Route between Delhi and Cabul, 1797 A.D.' *Punjab Past and Present,* XII, Part I, 1978) has also been used by Muzaffar Alam author of *The Crisis of Empire in Mughal North India: Awadh and the Punjab, 1707-48,* (OUP, Delhi), 1986.

2. Some of the Persian records pertaining to Patiala do find mention in Diwan Bahadur Sir Daya Kishan Kaul's (Chief Secretary, Patiala State), 'Care and Preservation of Old Records in Northern India'. *Indian Historical Records Commission,* Vol. II, January, 1920 (Lahore Session) pp. 31-39. Moreover, one administrator-scholar too has briefly referred to two of these documents (No. 2A/147 (B) of 1174 A.H. dated 22 *Shaban*—A.H. 1174/29 March 1761 A.D. and *Farman* (original) No. D-143 dated 11 *Rajab* A.H. 1192/5 August 1778 A.D. issued by Timur Shah to *Raja-i-Rajgan* Raja Patiala Amar Singh) was Khalifa Sayyid Muhammad Hasan (Prime Minister of Patiala State) in his work *Tarikh-i-Patiala,* Safir Hind Press, Amritsar, 1878. However, Ganda

Singh (author of *Ahmed Shah Durrani, Father of Modern Afghanistan,* Bombay 1959) and Kirpal Singh (author of *Maharaja Ala Singh of Patiala and His Times.* Amritsar, 1954) have not referred to any of the above documents. Incidently one administrator/scholar Sir Lepel Henry Griffin, in his book *The Rajas of Punjab...* (pp. 256-57 n. 1) has not only used but has given the translated version of at least one of the above documents. The document is '*Sanad of Timur Shah in the name of Chuhr Singh Phul,* dated 11 *Rajab,* 1192 AH'. It seems to have even escaped the otherwise very keen attention of Professor B R. Grover. However, one noticeable flaw is that while converting 1192 A.H. into A.D., Griffin has written 1779 A.D. whereas it should be 1778 A.D. The translated version of the above document is as follow:

"At this time the magnificent mandate is issued, owing to the enhanced kindness of Royalty."

"The old Taluka of Pargana Sihara, together with the Ilaka of Bhadour, which is in your possession, is granted to you as heretofore. You may realise the fees collected by the Pahuls, as were herefore collected by your ancestors. And you should pay obedience to the Raja of Patiala, and submit whatever you might have to say to the Hazur through the Raja of Patiala."

"It is also reached our ears that Hari Singh has raised a tumult in his country. You should ally yourself with the other Rajas and restrain him from injuring the creatures of God; and Muhammad Hussein Khan will be soon deputed in order to take possession of the country of Hari Singh through the Raja of Patiala, and annex it to the Royal territories."

"As Hari Singh originally came from Multan, his native country, he should return to it."

"All matters connected with yourself have been explained to Muhammad Hussain Khan; and they will be determined and executed through the Raja of Patiala."

"You should wait on us, else your country will be taken possession of by the Government."

"Hari Singh had proceeded to the Taluka of Nali. The Raja of Patiala excluded him from thence. If Hari Singh should now go to the Jungul, let him not enter it."

As of old you should remain obedient to the Raja of Patiala, and depend upon the royal favours."

3. Some of Professor B.R. Grover's most important papers are:

(*i*) 'General President Address', *Punjab History Conference Proceedings,* 19th Session, March 22-24, 1985, Patiala.

(*ii*) 'Relationship between the Sovereign State (the Mughals and Afghans) and the Punjab Hill Chiefs during the 17th and 18th Centuries—a case study of Chamba Chieftainship based on Bhuri Singh Museum, Chamba-Document', *Punjab History Conference,* XVII Session, Patiala, 1982.

(*iii*) The Importance of *Nuskha-i-Inshah-i-Majma al Qawanin* of Ganesh Dass Badehra (*Munshiat-i-Ganesh Das*) for the late 18th and early 19th centuries History of the Punjab', *Punjab History Conference,* XXI Session, March 27-29, 1987, Patiala.

(*iv*) 'An Analysis of the contemporary Revenue Documents and Correspondence pertaining to the Patiala Chieftainship (*Zamindari*). During the later half of the 18th Century', Paper presented at *Punjab History Conference* 1988 session Patiala. *The Punjab Past and Present, XXIV*—1, April 1990, pp. 196-233.

(v) B.R. Grover (ed.). The *Punjab Polity during the 18th century (Role of Sardar Jassa Singh Ahluwalia)*, New Delhi, 1991 (in Punjab), 'Introduction'. (I am obliged to Professor B.R. Grover for allowing me to go through the manuscripts of the last Two Papers).

4. Some of the important works are: (*i*) J.S. Grewal and Indu Banga (ed.) *Maharaja Ranjit Singh and His Times,* Amritsar, 1980; (*ii*) Hari Ram Gupta, *A History of the Sikhs,* Vol. I, Simha, 1952; (*iii*) *A History of the Sikhs, 5 Vols.* Delhi, 1978-82, (*iv*) Ganda Singh, *Sardar Jassa Singh Ahluwalia,* Patiala, 1969 (in Punjabi); Bhagat Singh, *Sikh Polity in the Eighteenth and Nineteenth centuries.* New Delhi, 1978; (*v*) G.S. Nayyar, *Sikh Polity and Sikh Institutions,* New Delhi, 1979.

5. Major James Browne worked as *aide-de-camp* to Warren Hastings; Collector of the Jungle Terai district; and Agent and Envoy of the Governor General in the Imperial Court at Delhi.

6. *Indian Tracts: History of the Origin and Progress of the Sikhs.* London, 1788 (hereafter, *Indian Tracts*). This book has been reproduced and edited with critical remarks in Ganda Singh (ed.) *Early European Accounts of the Sikhs,* Calcutta, 1962.

7. He wrote, "Conformably to the wish you were pleased to express, that I should furnish you with an account of the rise and present State of the tribe of the people called Sicks, I now beg leave to submit to your perusal, the following translation which I have made of a Persian manuscript written by my desire while I resided at the Court of Dehly..."

8. See for reference, Syed Muhammad Latif, *History of the Punjab From the Remotest Antiquity to the Present Time,* (1889). New Delhi, 1964, pp. 328, 330-332.

9. *Indian Tracts,* 'Introduction', p. vii and ii, p. 19.

10. *Ibid.,* ii, p. 8. Same is true about the various letters of the *Calendar of Persian Correspondence.*

11. B.R. Grover, *op. cit.* f.n. 3(v). The *misl* denoted a group of Sikhs under the leadership of a prominent Sardar. The *misls* were both big and small in size, as such, there was no uniformity in their territorial extent. The character of the *misl* was not essentially clannish and the Sikhs of other castes were free to join it with all rights and obligations on their part. The *misl* was generally associated with a locality or a caste rather than with a particular Sardar. Despite being cohesive in character, there was no bar on any influential member to leave a *misl* on the death of the Sardar and form an independent *misl* of his own. However, the end of the 18th century witnessed the principle of heredity gaining ground for the assumption of *Sardari* of the *misl.* Moreover, for a specific military campaign a few *misldars,* though without any permanent allegiance, would combine under the leadership of a *misldar,* denominated as a chief Sardar. The acquired territories, the amount of revenues and *rakhi* was divided by the *misldars* in proportion to their respective military strength and the effective military service rendered. However, this allegiance, being purely temporary, could be transferred from one to another Chief Sardar.

12. *Indian Tracts,* ii, p. 13.

13. *Ibid.,* 'Introduction', p. vii.

14. *Ibid.,* ii, p. 8. Also, George Forster, *A Journey from Bengal to England through North India, Kashmir, Afghanistan, Persia, into Russia (1782-83),* London, 1798, i, pp. 321-22.

15. He writes, "It is the object of the following pages to collect and exhibit in continuous narrative, the occurrences of this description in the Punjab, and to trace the rise of the chief (Ranjit Singh) who now sways the destinies of that province, and of a large bordering territory, with a vigour of authority, unknown to any other part of India, not subject to the dominions of Europeans." Henery T. Prinsep, *Origin of the Sikh Power in the Punjab and Political life of Maharaja Ranjit Singh with an Account of the Religion, Laws and Customs of the Sikhs, (1834),* Patiala, p. 2.
16. *Ibid.*
17. *Ibid.*, p. 23.
18. *Ibid.*
19. *Ibid.*, pp. 2-3, 7.
20. He writes, "That able but artful chief considered this turbulent tribe in no other light than as the means of his personal advancement." John Malcolm, *Sketch the Sikhs,* London, 1812, p. 92.
21. Prinsep, *op. cit.*, p. 13. Same views have been expressed in 1184. Extracts from News, *Calendar of Persian Correspondence,* July 27, 1774, iv, 1772-75, p. 214.
22. Prinsep, *op. cit.*, p. 13. It is contrary to the assertion of the earlier writers like James Browne who opined that it were only the Sikhs under the leadership of Sardar Jassa Singh Ahluwalia who had expelled the Durranis on that occasion. f.n. 8.
23. Prinsep, *op. cit.* pp. 22-23.
24. *Ibid.*, p. 20.
25. *Ibid.*, pp. 26-28.
26. *Ibid.*, p. 29.
27. *Ibid.*, p. 26.
28. *Ibid.*
29. W.L. M'Gregor wrote his work in two volumes. Both the volumes bore different titles. They are : *The History of the Sikh : containing the lives of the Gooroos; The History of the Independent Sirdars, or Missuls and the Life of the Great Founder of the Sikh Monarchy, Maharajah Ranjeet Singh,* Vol. I; and *The History of the Sikhs containing an account of The War between the Sikhs and the British in 1845-46,* vol. II (London 1847), Patiala, 1970.
30. M'Gregor, Vol. II, p. 280.
31. *Ibid.*
32. Joseph Davey Cunningham, *A History of the Sikhs from the Origin of the Nation to the Battles of the Sutlej* (Edited by H.L.O. Gerrett with an additional notes by R.R. Sethi), Delhi, 1955, 'Author's Preface to the Second edition, p. XXVIII.
33. *Ibid.*
34. Sir Lepel Henry Griffin, *The Punjab Chiefs : The Historical and Biographical Notices of the Principal Families in the territories under the Punjab Government,* Lahore, 1865. This book was, however, revised and enlarged by Charles Francis Massey and Published in two volumes, Lahore, 1890.
35. Lepel Henry Griffin, *The Rajas of the Punjab; Being The History of the Principal States in the Punjab and Their Political Relations with the British Government,* (Lahore, 1870), Patiala, 1970, 'Preface to the First edition,' p. v.

36. *Ibid.*, pp. vii-ix.

37. See for instance, J.C. Dua, 'Comparative Position of the village Headman During the Early British Rule in the Punjab and the Madras Presidency'; and 'Comparative Position of the village Patwari/Karnum during the Early British Rule in the Punjab (upto 1885), and the Madras Presidency (upto 1855)', *Punjab History Conference,* XXI Session, 1987, pp. 242-52 and XXII Session, 1988, pp. 177-88 respectively.

38. Griffin, *The Rajas...*, p. ix.

39. See for example, *Ibid.*, pp. 530-544 and Latif, *op. cit.* pp. 328-32.

40. *Op. cit.*, f.n. 35.

41. M'Gregor, *op. cit.*, i, p. 118 and Griffin, *The Rajas...*pp. 17, 23.

42. Cunningham, *op. cit.*, p.1.

43. See for example, M'Gregor, *op. cit.*, i, p. 118.

44. Cunningham, *op. cit.*, p. 101.

45. Lepel Henry Griffin, *Ranjit Singh* (Rulers of India Series, edited by W.W. Hunter) (Lahore, 1870), Delhi, 1957, p. 77, also, J.C. Dua, 'Sir Lepel Henry Griffin on Sardar Jassa Singh Ahluwalia and his Place in Eighteenth century Punjab History; *Punjab History Conference,* XXI, Session, 1987, pp. 111-18.

46. *Ibid.*

47. M'Gregor, *op. cit.*, i, p. 114.

48. *Ibid.*, pp. 117-18; Cunningham, *op. cit.*, pp. 101, 104; Griffin, *The Rajas...*, pp. 465-67.

49. Cunningham, *op. cit.*, pp. 92, 101; Griffin, *The Rajas...*, p. 31; *Ranjit Singh,* pp. 75-77. However, Griffin would not agree with Cunningham on this point. The former believed that the title of "*Raja-i-Rajgan Bahadur*" was conferred on the Patiala Chief by the Mughal Emperor Akbar II on the recommendation of General Ochterlony. But there seems to be nothing wrong in it. As long as Durranis were recognised as the sovereign, the conferring or the renewal of such titles was the prerogative of the Durrani rulers. After the take over by the British and since the Mughal Emperor was considered, though nominal, sovereign, this was to be performed by him.

50. M'Gregor, *op. cit.*, i, p. 147; Cunningham, J.D...., *op. cit.*, pp. 81, 91; Griffin, *The Rajas...*, p. 17.

51. Cunningham, *op. cit.*, p. 92.

52. Griffin, *The Rajas...*, p. 24.

53. Cunningham, *op. cit.*, p. 95.

54. *Ibid.*

55. B.R. Grover, *op. cit.*, f.n. 3(i).

56. *Ibid.*, M'Gregor, *op. cit.*, i, p. 147 and Griffin, *The Rajas...*, pp. 462-63. Explaining *Pahul* Prinsep writes:

Initiation by drinking of the *Pahul* is a rite established by Guru Govind and is thus described by Khushwaqt Rai. The candidate and the initiator wash their feet with water, and then put sugar into the liquid and stir it with a knife, while they repeat five quatrains, the first of which runs as follows:

Sarawak sidh samoh sidhank dekh phiryo ghar Jogi Jati Ke,

Sur sarawak sigh sarawak sant samoh anek mati ke—

Sare hi desko phiryo mat kooo na dekhat pranpati ke

Sri Bhagwan ki Bhaye kripa bin ek rati bin ek rati ke.

I have been round and have seen all kinds of devotees, Jogis and Jatis, Holy men, practisers of austerities, men wrapped up in contemplation of the Divinity with all their many ways and habits.

Every country have I travelled over, but truly godly I have seen no where. Without the grace of God, friend, Man's lot weighs not the lowest fraction.

The other quatrains are very nearly to the same effect, we add the whole in the original character for the benefit of the curious, but do not think it worth while to translate the remainder.

सरावक सिद्ध समोहसिद्धांक देखफिरियोधर जोगीजतीके ।
सूरसरावक सिद्धसरावक सन्तसमोह अनेकमतीके ॥
सारेहीदेसको देखफिरियोमत् कोऊनदेखत् प्रानपतीके ।
श्रीभगवानकी भाईकृपाविन ऐकरतीविन ऐकरतीके ॥
माते मतंग जड़े जरसंग अनूपउमंग सुरंग संवारे ।
कोटतरंग कुरंगसे कूदत् पवनकी गवन को जातनिवारे ॥
भारी भुजानके भूपभली वुद्ध नियावत सीस न जात विचारे ।
ईतेभयेतो कहा भये भूपत अन्त को नांगे हैपावों सिधारे ॥
जीत फिरे सब देस दैसांको वाजत ढोल मृदंग नगारे ।
गजपतको वुह गजानकेसुन्दर हेंसत हैं रब राज हजारे ॥
भूत भविख भुवान्के भूपत कौन गने नहीं जात विचारे ।
ईतेभये तो कहा भये भूपत अंतको नांगेहै पायें पधारे ॥
तीरथ थान दयादम दान सुंजमनेम शनेक विसेखे ।
वेद पुरान किताब कुरान जमीन अजोमान सभानके पेखे ॥
पवन अहार जतीजट धार सब ही शुभचार विचारके देखे ।
श्री भगवंत भजे बिन् भूपत ऐक रती बिन ऐक नः लेखे ॥
सुद्ध सिपाह दूरंत दुरवाहा सुसाज सनाह दुर्जन डलेंगे ।
भारी गुमान भरे म्न में गिर परबत पेख हिले न हिलेंगे ॥
तोर अरीं मरोर मवासन माते गजान के मान मलेंगे ।
श्री भगवान कृपातुमहरी बिन त्याग जहान निदान चलेंगे ॥

Between each quatrain the breath is exhaled with a puff, and the drunk to the toast of "*wah! wah! Gobind Sikh! ap hi guru chela.*" Hail! hail! Govind Sikh! himself preceptor and pupil." The neophyte, after this ceremony is a Sikh complete. It is said that when Guru Govind had only five followers, he went through this form with them, drinking of the water which had washed their feet, and they drinking that which had washed his.

57. Griffin, *The Rajas...*, pp. 460-61.

58. B.R. Grover, *op. cit.*, f.n. 3(iii).

59. Punjab State Archives, Patiala. *Foreign Ministry case 2A/147 of 1174 A.H.*, Document No. 2A/147 (A) dated 22 *Shabnam* A.H. 1174/29 March 1761 A.D. See B.R. Grover. f.n. 2(iv). A *chakla* was a territorial division and was often identical with a *sarkar*, but in general a *chakla* was a smaller unit than a *sarkar*. In Bengal, however, a *chakla* consisted of a group of *sarkars* in the eighteenth century. Muzaffar Alam, *op. cit.*, p. 33n. During the Mughal period, the *faujdar* was incharge of the *sarkar* administration. With the formation of *chaklas*, comprising numerous *sarkars/parganas*, the *faujdar* remained the administrative incharge of the *chakla*. He was usually vested with the functions of *amin*. The office was, however, considered distinct and subordinate to *nazim/subahdar* of a *subah*. *Sarkar/chakla* Sirhind formed a part of *subah* Delhi. The position of *chakla* Sirhind remained the same prior to the Durrani campaigns or rather till 1757 when it was ceded to the Durrani empire. Many modern scholars use the designation of governor for the *faujdar/amin* of Sirhind which is rather loose in expression.

60. *Ibid.*, Document No. 2A/147 (D), dated 2 *Safar* A.H. 1178/1 August 1764 A.D. and document No. 2A/147 (F) dated 17 *Safar* A.H. 1178/16 August 1764 A.D. B.R. Grover, *Ibid.*

61. *Ibid.*, *Farman* (original) No. D-143 dated 11 *Rajab* A.H. 1192/5 August 1778 A.D. issued by Timur Shah to *Raja-i-Rajgan* Raja Patiala Amar Singh.

62. Some of the contemporary Persian records vouch for the fact that even till 1798 A.D. the coins of the Shah (Durrani) were current in the family of Amar Singh at Patiala and "Whosoever succeeds to the Throne issues the same coins in his country and considers himself as a subject of the Durrani Emperor." The 18th century currency issued under the Durrani rule is still available in the collection of the coins exhibited at Moti Bagh Palace, Patiala. National Archives of India, *Akhbar* dated 16 *Jamuda* A.H. 1211/17 December 1796 A.D.; *Persian Documents*, ed. P. Saran, Bombay Ms. Khuda Baksh Oriental public library, Patna (written in 1798); *Tarikh-i-Patiala, op. cit.*, pp. 75-76 and Ganda Singh. *Ahmed Shah Durrani, Father of Modern Afghanistan*, (Bombay, 1959), pp. 371-72. See, B.R. Grover, *op. cit.*, f.n. 2(iv), n. 86.

63. For further details see, B.R. Grover, *op. cit.*, f.n. 3.

64. 79, Paper of news, p. 26; and 279. From Raja Shitab Roy, p. 84. *Calendar of Persian Correspondence*, ii, 1767-69, Persian Correspondence, February, 17, 1767, pp. 26-27 and April 8, 1767, p. 8 respectively.

65. B.R. Grover, 'Relationship between the Sovereign State (the Mughals and Afghans) and Punjab Hill Chiefs during the 17th and 18th centuries (A case study of Chamba Chieftainship based on Bhuri Singh Museum, Chamba Documents)'; and '*Nuskha-i-Insha-i-Majmua al Quwanim,' Punjab History Conference*, 16th session, March 1982, Patiala, pp. 94-102 and 21st session, March 1987, pp. 138-150 respectively; Sheikh Rahim Ali, *Tarikh-i-Manzal-i-Kabul, op. cit.*, Questions and Answers 4, 13, 14, 21, 22.

66. Griffin, *Ranjit Singh*, p. 72.

67. 65. Another Paper of news, p. 22, *Calendar of Persian Correspondence*, ii, 1767-69, Persian Correspondence, February 16, 1767, pp. 22-23.

68. For details see, B.R. Grover, *op. cit.*, f.n. 3(v).

69. Traces of this type of levy can be found during Mauryan and Satavahna periods. As a matter of fact, king's revenue consisted of *bali s'ulka* (tolls etc.) and *bhaga*. Sircar, D.C., *Studies in the Political and Administrative System in Ancient and Medieval India*, (Delhi, 1974), pp. 5-6.

70. For the imposition/realization of *rakhi, karah parshad* and *nazrana/mu'amala* by the Sikh Sardars, see J.N. Sarkar tr., *Persian Records of Maratha History I : Delhi Affairs : (1761-1788) News Letters (From Persian Collection)*, Bombay, 1953, A7—Delhi News Letters dated 24th January 1770, pp. 19-20, A10—(Delhi) News Letters to Peshwa, 20 May, 1770, p. 23 and A56b—17 April, Second Sheet; 13, 6b—Letters to Nana Sahib Shrimat, C28th February, pp. 93 and 119 respectively; National Archives of India, *Secret Proceedings*, Vol. 23, pp. 776, 777, 781, 783—785; *Foreign Department, Secret Proceedings*, 23, June, 1783, Nos. 23, 42B; p. Saran (ed.), *Persian Documents*, Bombay 1966, p. 370.

71. Punjab State Archives, Patiala, *Foreign Ministry Case*, No. 5A/H, *folio* 6b-7a. It may be stated that these letters were got translated in English earlier also by the Patiala Darbar and a verified version of the same dated 1.12.1952, appended to the above Ms. under title 'Copies of Letters from Raja Alha Singh and Amar-Singh to Shah Vali Khan of Kabul 1765-66 A.D.' is also available in the file. See B.R. Grover, f.n. 3(iv).

72. *Ibid.*, folios 2a-3a, 1a-2a, 3b-5a, 6b-7a, 8a-8b, B.R. Grover f.n. 3(iv).

73. J.C. Dua, *op. cit.*, f.n. 45.

74. Ram Sukh Rao, *Sri Jassa Singh Binod*, Punjab State Archives, Patiala, Ms. 772; Ratan Singh Bhangu, *Prachin Panth Parkash*, Amritsar (4th edition), 1962; Ram Sukh Rao, *Fateh Singh Pratap Prabhakar*, ed. Joginder Kaur, Patiala, 1980; *Persian Records of Maratha History I : Delhi Affairs : (1761-1788) News Letters*, (from Persian collection). tr. J.N. Sarkar, Bombay 1953. Also relevant News Letters from the Imperial Court, *Akhbarat-i-Darbar-i-Mu'alla*, Rajasthan State Archives, Bikaner quoted by B.R. Grover, *op. cit.*, f.n. 3(v).

75. See *Persian Records of Maratha History, op. cit.*, A3b-10th December 1766, Sheet 2, News about Sikh Sardars b. 6. Also B.R. Grover, *Ibid.*

76. *Prachin Panth Parkash, op. cit.*, p. 217; *Fateh Singh Pratap Prabakhar, op. cit.*, p. 214; *Jassa Singh Binod, op. cit.*, fols. 123-125; National Archives of India, *Foreign Department/Secret Proceedings*, 23rd June, 1783, No. 428; *Browne Correspondence (Indian Records Series)* ed. K.D. Bhargava, N.A.I. Delhi, 1960, Letter No. 41, pp. 71-82. Also, B.R. Grover, *Ibid.*

77. 279. An account of the Vazir's (Nawab Asafu'd—Daulah's) overtures to the Khalisa Sikh Chiefs for an alliance against the Rohillas, dated September 20, 1776; and 280. From Nahar Singh, Chief of the Gujars, dated September 20, 1776, *Calendar of Persian Correspondence*, v. 1778-88, pp. 41-42, and 42-43.

7

Maharaja Ranjit Singh : Institutional and Political Backdrop

Maharaja Ranjit Singh, a man of destiny, was one of those great rulers of India who rose to the high position of a king from a petty chief. He had to face the responsibilities of the state at a very young age. Ranjit Singh Sukerchakia was the man who liquidated the warring *misls,* nurtured the consciousness of regional nationalism to forge a unified kingdom.

When Ranjit Singh took over the reigns of Sukerchakia *misl* in 1790, Punjab was passing through an era of political turmoil and turbulation and the Sikh struggle for power. Eighteenth century Punjab had witnessed the disintegration of the Mughal empire, the foreign campaigns of Nadir Shah and the Durranis, the attempts made by the Rohillas, Rajputs, Jats and the Afghans to establish their respective regional governments and the emergence and rise of the Marathas and the Sikhs[1].

In the Punjab, the Sikh Sardars, during this period, not only confronted the political powers, especially like the Mughals and the Durranis, but were able to carve out their own independent/semi-independent territories (*zamindaries*) for the purposes for revenue realization and administration. The most significant feature of the Sikh history during the course of the 17th and the 18th centuries is that the Sikh community/*Nanak Panth* which originally was socio-religious in character gradually transformed into socio-religious cum-political force comprising members of various clans and castes[2]. The earlier Sikhs of the days of Guru Gobind Singh and Banda Bahadur were a purely religious community, suffering from great persecutions. In taking up arms, their chief object had been the defence of their religion and individual existence. Their predatory practice was merely the means of securing that object. With the later Sikhs, however,

---

Paper Presented at *Seminar on Life and Achievements of Sher-e-Punjab Maharaja Ranjit Singh*, Mata Sundrari College for Women (University of Delhi), New Delhi, 26th September, 2001 and published in Dr. Mohinder Kaur Gill (ed.), *Secular Sovereign: Maharaja Ranjit Singh*, Delhi, 2002, pp. 39-57.

the case was different. They were fighting principally for a dominion[3]. Initially, the *Nanak Panth* mostly comprised the *khatris,* artisans, craftmen, petty traders, low caste Hindus and a section of poor peasantry, more especially from the *Majiha* territories. The various *Hukmnamas* of the Gurus reveal that the *Sangat* of Guru (Sikhs) were equally drawn from the prosperous commercial classes and other sections of the peasantry as well. Another noteworthy change in the character of the Sikh community during the 17th and the 18th centuries was that they were not only drawn only from the regions of the Punjab alone but also from *cis*-Satluj territories, the regions around Delhi and other places in India. The socio-economic phenomenon involving the emergence of the new dominant clans in the landed structure in the Punjab and territories of Delhi, the conversion of these clans more especially the peasantry to Sikhism in the course of the 17th and the 18th centuries added a new dimension to the character of the Sikh community. The initiation of the *Khalsa* by Guru Gobind Singh, the armed struggle by Banda Bahadur in the territories of *Subah* Delhi, hilly and plain regions of the Punjab against the Mughal state in the early 18th century, the later division of the *Khalsa* into *Bandais* (after Banda's death) and the *Tat Khalsa,* the ultimate supremacy of the latter further moulded the militant character of the *Singhan* for the safeguarding the interest of the *Panth.* But the emergence of Sikhs as a political force cannot be studied in isolation rather the dissolution of the Mughal empire and the rise of the Marathas, Bundelas, Rajputs, the Jats and Afghans in other parts of India have also to be taken into consideration. The Mughal empire which, for its governance and stability during the 16th and 17th centuries, had depended upon its alliance with the Rajputs and its own nobility, had been shaken to the point of dismemberment due to its fight with other socio-political forces during the 18th century. Inspite of considerable element of continuity in the traditional form of regional polity, administration and economic system, the other event had great impact on the social, economic and political developments during the 18th century which transformed the Sikhs, not only into a mere political force but a force to reckon with[4].

A critical examination of the Punjab politics during the 18th century shows that there were as many as four main political powers *viz.,* the Mughals, and Marathas, the Sikhs Sardars, and the Durranis of Kabul who fought for supremacy there. Of course, during the first half of the century the struggle was basically confined between the Mughals and the Sikhs whereas during the second half, after the Marathas had been defeated at Panipat and the Mughal sovereign rights over the Punjab territories had practically vanished, the Durranis had claimed political sovereignty and started realizing *peshkash,* it mainly became a tussle between the Sikhs and the Durranis. Again, during the last three decades of the 18th century, even though the Durranis continued to claim *de jure* political sovereignty, the Sikh Sardars had started asserting the *de facto* power over the Punjab territories.

Apart from the Sikh organization of the informal confederacy (*Sarbat Khalsa*) and execution of the plans through the decisions (*Gurmata*) and their implementation with the help of the armed units (*Dal Khalsa*), the twentieth century writings have equally emphasized on the system and role of *rakhi* and Sikh *misls* in the Punjab. As such, for a better understanding of political process and the nature of the Sikh rule at the time Maharaja Ranjit Singh took over, it is imperative to understand the 'political institutions' which are believed to have been evolved by the Sikhs, viz., the *Sarbat Khalsa,* the *Gurmata,* the *Dal Khalsa,* and *rakhi* and *misls.*

The *Gurmata* literally means 'the Council of the Gurus' followers' or 'a resolution endorsed by the Guru'. The Guru was believed to be present in the *Khalsa* deliberating in the presence of *Guru Granth Sahib*[5]. It is not easy to say definitely who founded this institution. From its name, functions, procedure and other characteristics, however, it seems probable that it owed its origin to the genius of Guru Gobind Singh, the most martial of Sikh Gurus. Its early growth also is rounded in mystery. It probably ceased to exist after the Mughal repression in the beginning of the 18th century until it was revived during Ahmed Shah Abdali's invasions. It then served as the central institution of a lose confederacy formed by the *misls.* Its constitution was somewhat indefinite; for though in theory it was intended to be democratic, yet in practice it invariably consisted of chiefs of various *misls.* Within the Council, however, the members were of equal rank. The leadership of the federation was elective and the authority of the elective *Sardar* (Chief) was limited to the direction of the military policy of the *misldars.* He was in reality their chosen warlord. Thus, the main purpose of the *Gurmata* was to preserve the corporate existence of Sikh people. This fact justifies its aristocratic character and entitles it to be considered as a national institution. It was in reality so looked upon by its members in those days. They recognised its value, not only from the point of view of saving their respective possessions, but also for the safety of their theocratic commonwealth, the *Khalsa* (the Body of the chosen)[6]. The actual working of the *Gurumata* shows that it cannot be equated with any 'council' or 'general meeting' of the Sikhs[7]. That the *Gurumata* gave unity and direction to the activities of a large number of Sikh Sardars during the third quarter of the 18th century may be readily conceded, but neither the meeting of the *Sarbat Khalsa,* literally the entire body of the *Khalsa,* nor the resolutions adopted in such meetings give any indication of institutionalization. It can indeed be asserted that these decisions related almost invariably to, matters of defence[8]. It can be visualized that the Sikh *Sardars* participating in the *Gurmata* were bound to gain from executing them, but there is no reason to believe that these resolutions were formally binding on the *Sardars.* The events during the 18th century show that *Gurmata* had a very limited scope and had incomplete participation even of the important *Sardar*[9]. "...the decisions which the Sikh leaders at Amritsar took from time to time were *ad hoc* deliberation of voluntary gatherings and their scope was confined to matters concerning the preservation and augmentation of the striking power"[10]. The *Gurmata* had as well the sanction of the faith (*Guru Panth*) and was binding on all the participants. In fact, *Gurumata* meant mutual consultation (*mashwara/mashwarat/salah*) at a gathering of the Sardars for taking decision and adopting course of action regarding a particular matter. The gathered *Sardars,* as the *Khalsa,* embodied the form of the Guru. As such, after the deliberation (*masallhat*) and mutual consultation (*Mashwarat/Gurumata*), decision was taken which was mandatory (*hukm*) in character to be implemented by all the participating Sardars[11]. However, there are not more than two instances of its general convocation after 1760, and it was almost a dead letter when it was discontinued by Maharaja Ranjit Singh after 1805.

The Sikh organization of the informal confederacy, *Sarbat Khalsa,* literally means the entire body of the *Khalsa.* As discussed above, the *Gurmata* stopped short of territorial occupation, government and administration. "All this land," as written by Teja Singh, "was held in joint ownership of the whole Sikh nation, called the *Sarbat Khalsa*"[12]. Even Ranjit Singh is regarded by some historians as merely a representative of the *Sarbat Khalsa*[13].

This frequency of joint action by a combination of Sikh *Sardars* accounts for the vital role, which is commonly attributed to the *Dal Khalsa,* or the army of the *Khalsa.* The word is colloquial Punjabi expression meaning a horde; and suggests the notion of an undisciplined force. At times, for the purpose of defence or offence, more particularly at critical junctures for operation against the Durranis or the Mughals, the Chief *Sardars* (*Sardaran-i-umda*) after mutual consultation (*Gurmata*) at a joint meeting and in accordance with the decision joined together for a united action under the leadership of one of the chief *Sardars.* Such a combination on the part of the most of the chief *Sardars* and their constituent *misls* was named as *Dal Khalsa.* The 18th century Persian *Akhbars* ordinarily describe the chief Sikh *Sardars* as *Sardar-i-Sikhan* or *Sardar-i-umda* and their *Dal* as *Dal-i-Sikhan* but after the *Gurumata* was taken they were described as *Sardaran-i-Khalsa* or *Khalsa Ji* and their *Dal* was put as *Dal Khalsa*[14]. There is no denying the fact that on numerous occasions several *Sardars* joined their forces for a collective action. However, the frequency of joint action by a combination of *Sikh Sardars* accounts for the vital role which is commonly attributed to the *Dal Khalsa,* but the *Dal Khalsa* did not become anything more than an *ad hoc* combination of the forces of more than one *Sardar* for the limited purpose of offence of defence[15]. After 1773, when the danger of invasion from Afghanistan lessened, and the Chiefs began to quarrel among themselves, it became necessary for them to retain permanent armed followers, and the great days of *Dal Khalsa* were practically over.

An opportunity of collection of *Rakhi* by the Sikh *Sardars* has been considered as a step that 'supplied them with the idea of the raising themselves into territorial chieftains.'[16] In the territories where *rakhi* was imposed upon the villages, it was realized from the *zamindars* of the respective village who parted with *rakhi* amount from the surplus produce or the revenue payable to the Durrani or the Mughal administration, as the case may be[17]. It could as well be imposed upon the *jagir* lands assigned by the Durrani or Mughal government. If the Zamindar, being recalcitrant had fled or when unit of the *rakhi* composed only a village, *rakhi* could as well be realized directly from the peasant proprietors or occupancy tenants. However, the usual practice was to realise *rakhi* from the petty *zamindars* or the landed intermediaries of the villages. The incidence of *rakhi* varied from one territory to another. Ordinarily, it amounted to one-fourth, one-fifth or one-eighth of the revenues (*Jama*). It is rather significant to note that *rakhi* was not a substitute for the revenues to be realized from the *riaya*. It was essentially from the surplus produce after the payment of the customary right of the *zamindars,* landed intermediaries, jagirdars, if any, and the chieftains, as the case may be[18].

The collection of the *rakhi* by the Sikh *Sardars* has been rightly clubbed with the Maratha system of the collection of *Chauth.* But it is wrong to describe them as 'blackmail'. As a matter of fact, *rakhi, chauth* and *peshkash* are all synonymous terms and have the same meaning. It was an established practice of the Mughals to collect *peshkash* or tribute from the protected areas. It had been a general practice in the medieval age that a budding political power establishing its chieftainship by bringing certain areas under its direct administration would attempt to establish its overlordship on some neighbouring or even far-flung regions. It may or may not be a prelude to the attainment of supremacy in those regions. The establishment of overlordship would invariably result into the demand of share in the revenues of the areas. The percentage/amount, thus demanded, despite having common nomenclature, varied and depended upon the geographical situation of the areas, position of the submitting chief and the extent to which the subduing power could not pose continuous pressure for maintaining sustained submission. Sometimes, a well established political power would also allow the erstwhile chief of a newly acquired territory to retain a fixed percentage/portion of the revenues of the areas. Moreover, the idea of the establishment of protectorate was also current and powerful rulers used to take tribute, *nazrana* or *mu'amala* before annexing a particular territory or not annexing it at all, as the case might be. As such, the payment or allowance made by an inferior to a superior power and superior to an inferior or even a subordinate power in consideration of ones political authority or service or the nuisance value was an accepted norm during the period[19]. Several names, viz., *peshkash, nazarana, mu'amala, banth, malikana, do biswi, chauth, rakhi, karah parshad* and *kaveli russom* etc. have been ascribed to these transactions, though with slight difference in their actual working. It is a different matter that the percentage of the same demand, thus demanded, the division of the money, thus collected, and in other details, there was no similarity. All the same, it is correct that the Sikh *Sardars* had followed the Mughal practice and had not invented anything new[20].

The most significant institution of the eighteenth century Punjab and an important feature of political and economic order of this period is the establishment of *misldari* and *Sardari* which fundamentally altered the character of armed struggle of the Sikhs against the Mughals and the Durranis as well as the revenue administration of the agrarian society. According to Cunningham, the term '*misl*' has been derived from the Arabic word *musluhut,* which would equate it with "armed men and warlike people". He further says that *misl* might mean a file of papers of, for that matter, anything placed in ranks[21]. The term *'misl'* may be traced in *Sri Gur Sobha,* the biography of Guru Gobind Singh written by Sainapat. He has used it at two places in the sense of a group[22]. Rattan Singh Bhangu has also used the word *misl,* meant a group. It is difficult to form an estimate about the number of men this group comprised. There is neither a single connotation nor a single description of the origin, nature and working of the *misl.* George Thomas, J.D. Cunningham and Syed Muhammad Latif emphasize the religious character of the men who constituted the *misls.* They have also emphasized the 'laws' which governed them, and hold the *misl* was the supreme power of its Sardar who was "paramount in peace and war"[25]. To Wilson the organization of *misl* seemed strictly democratic, a view shared by Princep,[26] while there are others who confer upon the *misl* a confederate or a feudal character.[27] The origin of the *misl* organization may be traced to the period after the death of Banda Bahadur. A number of Sikhs, by virtue of their religious discipline, mental training and association, were convinced that defiance of "unjust rule" was their duty. To begin with, they concentrated on increasing their number and about bringing about unity in their ranks.[28] In due course of time, the conflict of the *Khalsa* with the authorities affected the nature of the *misl* organization and helped its transition from non-territorial group into a territorial power. The acquisition of the territories, later on, accounted for the change in the character of leadership as well as the nature of the organization. In the early stages, two or more *misls* could undertake a joint expedition[29] and the conquered territories could be partitioned amongst them. But as the territorial ambitions of the *Sardars* became more pronounced, the way was prepared for their own liquidation.[30] To satisfy their political ambitions, the *Sardars* often resorted to convenient matrimonial alliances, as it happened between the Kanhaiyas and Sukarchakkias.[31] It provided the ladder for the rise of Ranjit Singh. An alliance to achieve political ends could also be effected by the ceremonial exchange of turbans at the *Akal Takhat.* Such alliances could be formed against the common enemy, and also against the fellow *Sardars.*

The contemporary 18th century Persian, Marathi and English, so far known, sources don't use the term *misl.* The Persian sources make mention of Sikh *Sardars* or the Sikh *Sardars* in-groups or a distinguished sikh *Sardar* with his group or with his *Dal,* the Marathi sources simply refer to the Sikhs or their Sardars. The English sources mention only the Sikhs or some of their distinguished leaders as *Sardars.* These sources bring out the role played by the particular *Sardars* in different military campaigns as well as for their territorial acquisition on their part at different phases in the course of the later half of the 18th century. However, the early 19th century Persian and English sources do distinctly describe the *misldari* system with all the territorial, administrative and military aspects. There was no uniformity in the territorial extent of the *misls* as there were both big as well as small *misls.* The villages and *t'aaluqas* in the jurisdiction of a *misl* were divided amongst the male members of the dominant *Sardari* family as well as other distinguished co-parceners and the individuals (*Sikhan*). At the bottom, the unassigned villages were divided amongst the individual Sikhs in general. The *misl* was not essentially clannish in character, as the Sikh of other castes were free to join the group with all rights and obligations on their part. Though the overwhelming majority of then chief *Sardars* were *Jats* from the rural areas, there were castes like the Najjar (Ramgarhia-thoka), Ahluwalia who had some of the chief *Sardars* hailing from rural areas. Even though a *misl* was cohesive in character, an influential constituent member was always free to leave the *misl* on the death of the Sardar so as to form an independent *misl* of his own. By the end of the 18th century, the principal of heredity started gaining ground for the resumption of the *Sardari* of a *misl.* At the same time, with accelerated process of the establishment of a new *misl* and their multiplication the number of the *misldars* in the Punjab and the *cis*-Satluj territories ran into hundreds, estimated at about four to five hundred by some of the 19th century sources.[32]

The period from 1747-48 onwards is marked by the dominant role played by the Sikh Sardars in the agrarian and political set-up in the territories of the Punjab and *cis*-Satluj as well as Jamuna-Ganga *Doab* regions forming a part of *subah* Delhi. Moreover, Ahmad Shah Abdali claimed himself to be a successor to Nadir Shah's Indian territories acquired by the latter in 1739. After a successful operation in 1751-52, Abdali annexed the *subahs* of Lahore and Multan by a regular treaty signed by Muin-ul-Mulk which was also ratified by the Mughal Emperor on 13th April, 1752[33]. As such, *subahs* of Punjab, Multan and Kashmir became a part of the Afghan empire and were lost to the Mughal state for ever. After another successful campaign by 1757, Ahmad Shah Durrani also annexed the *chakla* of Sirhind[34]. The Mughal empire ceded the *subahs* of Punjab, Multan, Kashmir and *chakla* Sirhind (*subah* Delhi) to the Durrani Afghan empire whose borders were extended from Afghanistan to Karnal (*Chakla* Sirhind, at present Haryana) in the north India. This is not withstanding the fact that for about a year and a half (April, 1758-October, 1759), the Marathas virtually ruled over the Punjab and the *cis*-Satluj territories. Before and after this period Durrani had set up its own administration both for the purposes of governance and realization of the revenues of the territories. The Durrani recognized many a chief *zamindar* as its chief representative (*Wukala-i-ali*) and clearly demarcated territories (village/*mahals*) assigned in *jagir* to them under the category *jagir-i-wukala-i-ali.* The Durrani at Kabul was in correspondence with the Chief/ *zamindars* in the *cis*-Satluj territories, Punjab, Multan and Kashmir and kept itself fully informed about political developments and administrative problems in these regions all through the second half of the 18th century. However, even though the Battle of Panipat (January, 1761) had given a fatal blow to the Maratha supremacy in Multan, Punjab and *cis*-Satluj territories, the Durrani rule in the Punjab could not be easily consolidated due to severe opposition on the part of the Sikhs. The circumstances had enabled the Sikhs Sardars to establish themselves on an institutionalized basis. But it was only the English East India Company, which eventually ousted the Durrani influence and established its own protectorate over the chieftains of the *cis*-satluj territories by the early 19th century. The Durranis were ousted root and branch from the *subahs* of Lahore, Multan and Kashmir by Maharaja Ranjit Singh from the closing years of the 18th to second decade of the 19th century (1799-1819)[35].

When in 1799 Ranjit Singh succeeded to the leadership of the Sukerchakia *misl,* the Punjab was divided into a large number of *misls,* big and small. Some of them were, in fact, no more than a party of armed band, who depended for their maintenance on the support of some large *misls,* and thus could not be regarded as an independent organization. The more important ones were twelve in number. They were : (1) The Bhangi *Misl,* (2) the Sukerchakia *Misl,* (3) The Kanhiya *Misl,* (4) The Nakai *Misl,* (5) The Ramgarhias, (6) The Dallewalias, (7) The Ahluwalias, (8) the Faizulpurias or Singhpurias, (9) the Karorasinghia *Misl* (10) the Phulkian Misl, (11) the Nishanwalas, and (12) the Nehangs or the Shahids.

The land between the rivers, Jehlam and Satluj, or the central part of Punjab, was mostly under the *misls.* Chief among these was the Bhangis. This *misl,* besides controlling a long strip of territory along the river Jehlam, held in possession a greater part of the districts of Gujarat, Sialkot, Lahore and Amritsar. Their possessions, however, were not contiguous, for, both between Gujarat and Sialkot and between Gujarat and Lahore, were situated large tracts and several strongholds belonging to other *misls.* Wazirabad was under an independent Sikh Chief, Jodh Singh. Gujranwala formed the centre of Ranjit Singh's own *misl,* the Sukerchakia. The Sukerchakia possessions also lay around Sialkot, Gujarat and across the river Jehlam in Pind-dadan Khan and Miani. The lands between Amritsar and Ludhiana were divided among various Sardars, the most important being the *Kanhaiyas*, with their seat at Batala in the Gurdaspur district, and *Ahluwalias*, with their centre at Kapurthala and their possessions reaching in the vicinity of Jalandhar itself, however, was in the control of a separate Sardar. The *Ramgarhias*, whose possessions also lay across the Satluj, held some tracts in the districts of Gurdaspur and Amritsar, and in the Jalandhar Doab. The area, which intervenes between Lahore and Multan, was divided among the Pathans of Kasur, the Nakai Sardar of Pakpatan, and the Sials of Jhang. A number of Muslim and Rajput Chieftains administered Rajauri, Bhimbar, Jammu, and the adjoining lands. A Hindu Raja, Sansar Chand, possessed the Kangra hills; but Chamba belonged to Raja Charat Singh. The province of Multan was under Nawab Muzaffar Khan Sadozai. Beyond the Indus, Dera Ismail Khan was in the possession of Abdul Samand Khan, while Bahawalpur and Dera Ghazi Khan were in the hands of Daudputra chief, Bahawal

Khan, Jahandad Khan, the Wazir Khel chief; and Mankera, Bannu, Kohat and Tonk were under different Muslim rulers, held the fort of Attock. The valley of Peshawar was administered by Fateh Khan Barakzai, and the province of Kashmir by his brother Azim Khan. Most of the Muslim chiefs were originally feudatories of the Kings of Afghanistan, but had lately become independent by reason of the death of Ahmed Shah and the weakness of his successors. The *cis*-Satluj portion of the Punjab was divided among the ruling families of Patiala, Jind, Nabha, and several other less important Sardars. Most of these chiefs had descended originally from the Phulkian *misl.* Another *misl,* the Nishanwalas, possessed some territory between Ambala and Saharanpur. Only one small state—that of Malerkotla, was governed by an Afghan dynasty on the *cis*-Satluj side of the Punjab[36]. In the last decades of the 18th century, the Durrani administration supported by the Mughals or the Mughal-Maratha operations, exerted greater pressure over the local Sikh Sardars in the *cis*-Satluj territories and was able to maintain its sovereign rights over *chakla* Sirhind till the end of the 18th century[37].

The Sikh dominions in the last quarter of the eighteenth century are remembered more for internal strife than expansion. Not significant extension of territory is on record during this period. In fact, Multan was lost by Rai Singh Bhangi in the late 1770s and the conquest of Kangra by Jai Singh Kanhiya proved to be transitory gain[38]. There were sharp religious and racial differences among the numerous rulers/chiefs who governed the Punjab at this time. There was no unity of purpose among them. Even among the Sikh *misldars,* there was little inclination towards unified action. The Bhangi *misl* itself was divided into three armed camps, with their respective headquarters at Lahore, Amritsar and Gujarat. The *Kanhiyas* were pitted against the *Ramgarhias*, and the latter were hostile to the *Ahluwalias*. There existed also the bitterest enemity between the *Sukerchakias* and the *Bhangis*, and between the latter and the Kanhiyas. All were at war one against the other. There was a constant grouping and re-grouping of parties and factions, the balance of military strength shifting from one to the other.

Jassa Singh Ramgarhia, Jai Singh Kanhiya, Gujjar Singh Bhangi and Jhanda Singh Bhangi were fighting among themselves for supermacy. In 1774, Charhat Singh Sukerchakia and Jai Singh Kanhiya supported Brij Raj Dev against his father, Raja Ranjit Dev of Jammu, who in turn was supported by his overlord, Jhanda Singh Bhangi. During this conflict, both Charhat Singh Sukerchkia and Jhanda Singh Bhangi died. Soon afterwards, the Kanhiyas and the Bhangis fought over Pathankot. In 1776, Jassa Singh Ramgarhia was dislodged from his territories by Jassa Singh

Ahluwalia and Jai Singh Kanhiya. In 1782, the *Bhangis* and the *Kanhiyas* clashed once more over the affairs of Jammu. When they patched up their difference and turned against Brij Raj Dev, he received assistance from Mahan Singh Sukerchakia who, however, raided Jammu later on, appropriating immense booty. Around 1785, Mahan Singh joined hands with Jassa Singh Ramgarhia to defeat his erstwhile ally, Jai Singh Kanhiya, in a battle near Batala in which Gurbaksh Singh, the eldest son of Jai Singh, was killed. Around 1790, Mahan Singh was trying to wrest some of the territories of Sahib Singh Bhangi. When Mahan Singh died, the issue of ascendancy between the House of Gujjar Singh Bhangi and the House of Charhat Singh Sukerchakia was still unresolved. It was left for Ranjit Singh to settle the issue of supermacy and to unite numerous principalities into a single whole[39]. Maharaja Ranjit Singh accomplished his job in the well-marked periods and achieved definite results. From 1799 to 1809, he established himself in the central Punjab. His penetration in to the territories lying either beyond the Jhelum or Satluj was governed by the motives of extorting tributes and establishing overlordship, rather than by a desire for immediate annexation. Between 1809 and 1822, Ranjit Singh improved upon his former policy of penetration, and brought to its natural conclusion by actually incorporating into his kingdom. As such, at the end of the first period, the eastern frontier of Ranjit Singh's kingdom was established on the Satluj; and in the second, the border line was extended to its geographical limits in other directions of the conquests of Multan and Kashmir. Before his death in 1839, Ranjit Singh had been able to accomplish the control of the principal avenue by which the Punjab had been attacked by annexing the valley of Peshawar in 1834. Within next two year an advanced post was established by the occupation of Jamrud. This way Maharaja Ranjit Singh brought the scattered people of the Punjab under a uniform and consistent system of government; and thereby evolved a young and vigorous sovereign state.

References

Note—I am very grateful to late Professor B.R. Grover, who helped me in locating, deciphering, analyzing and making available translations done by him of the Persian sources/works.

1. Dua, J. C., *British Historiography Eighteenth Century Punjab : Their understanding of the Sikh struggle for power and role of Jassa Singh Ahluwalia,* New Delhi, 1992, p. 1.
2. *Ibid.*, p. 2. Also Grover, B.R. 'Presidential Address', *Punjab History* Conference, XIX, 1985, pp. 7-58.
3. Chopra, Gulshan Lall, *The Punjab as a Sovereign State (1799-1839),* 2nd edition, Hoshiarpur, 1960, p. 4.
4. Dua, J.C., *op. cit.*, p. 2.

5. Ganda Singh (ed.), 'Early European Accounts of the Sikhs', *Indian Studies : Past and Present* reprint, Calcutta, 1962, 16n9. Dr. Ganda Singh further adds that '*Mata* generally means opinion or solution and it is called Gurmata, opinion or resolution endorsed by the Guru, because the Guru is believed to be always presiding over the deliberations of the *Khalsa* held in the presence of the Holy Book, the *Guru Granth Sahib*'.

6. Ram Sukh Rao, *Sri Jassa Sing Binod*, Punjab State Archives, Patiala, Ms. 772; Ratan Singh Bhangru, *Prachin Panth Parkash*, Amritsar (4th edition), 1962; Ram Sukh Rao, *Fateh Singh Pratap Prabhakar*, ed. Joginder Kaur, Patiala, 1980; *Persian Records of Maratha History I: Delhi Affairs: (1761-1788) News Letters*, (from Persian Collection, tr. J.N. Sarkar, Bombay 1953.

7. Prinsep, Henry T., *Origin of the Sikh power in the Punjab and Political Life of Maharaja Ranjit Singh with an account of the Religion, Law and Customs of the Sikhs,* (first published 1834), Reprint, Language Department, Patiala, 1970, p. 26. Cunningham, Joseph Davey, *A History of the Sikhs from the Origin of the Nation to the Battles of the Sutlej* (First published 1848). Edited by H.L.O. Garret with additional notes by R.R. Sethi, Delhi, 1955, pp. 94 and 119.

8. The traveller George Forster in the early 1780s wrote that in the 'grand convention' called *Gurmata* 'the army met to transact the more important affairs of the nation, as the declaration of war or peace, forming alliances and detaching parties on the service of the years'; *A journey from Bengal to England through North India, Kashmir, Afghanistan and Persia into Russia (1782-1784),* 2 vols. London 1798, I, pp. 286-87.

9. Banga, Indu, *Agrarian System of the Sikhs : Late Eighteenth and Early Nineteenth Century,* New Delhi, 1978 p. 29.

10. Grewal, J.S., 'Eighteenth Century Sikh Polity', in *From Guru Nanak to Maharaja Ranjit Singh (Essays in Sikh History),* Guru Nanak Dev University, Amritsar, 1972, pp. 98-99.

11. Grover, B.R., (ed.), *Sardar Jassa Singh Ahluwalia (Atharvin Sadi di Punjab-Rajiniti de SandharbhVich) a Collection of Seminar Papers,* New Delhi, 1991, (Punjabi), Introduction, p. 19. All the categories of English writers have referred to the utmost importance given to the *Gurumata* by the Sikh Sardars during the course of the Sikh struggle for supermacy in the eighteenth century. They have written about the convening of the *Gurumata* regularly on every *Baisakhi* and *Diwali* at Amritsar. Various Persian and Punjabi sources have also written about such meetings. However, when the English writings are studied in coordination with the Persian and Punjabi sources it is found that the *Gurumata* was not always held on *Baisakhi* and *Diwali* even at Amritsar. Whenever there was a news about the intended plan of Ahmad Shah Abdali for attacking Punjab or even entry into the Punjab, the earliest opportunity would be taken for holding such meeting at Amritsar. The deliberations of the meeting would decide about the military defensive measures to be adopted by the Sikh Sardars in different parts of the Punjab and the *cis*-Satluj territories. At the same time, it was not always necessary that the *Gurmata* would be held only at Amritsar. On some urgent matters it could be convened at any other place as well. It could even be convened during the course of a military campaign. Dua, J.C., *Op. cit.*, p. 116.

12. Teja Singh, 'Historical Background', in Ganda Singh (ed.), *Maharaja Ranjit Singh; First Death Centenary Memorial Volume,* Khalsa College, June, 1939, p. 11.

13. Khushwant Singh, *Ranjit Singh, Maharaja of the Punjab, 1780-1839,* London, 1962, p. 47.
14. Saran, P., *Persian Documents,* Bombay, 1966, pp. 51, 363-68. Also Grover, B.R. (ed.), *op. cit.,* 19.
15. Banga, Indu, *Agrarian System of the Sikhs, op. cit.,* pp. 30-31.
16. Dua, J.C., *op. cit.,* p. 125.
17. Saran, P., *op. cit.,* p. 51. Sarkar, JN, (tr.), *Persian Records of Maratha History I : Delhi Affairs : (1761-1788) News Letters (From Persian Collection),* Bombay, 1953, no, 25 and 56b, 17 April, 1778 Letters to Nana Sahib Shrimant.
18. Grover, B.R. (ed.), *Sardar Jassa Singh... Op. cit.,* p. 19.
19. Traces of this type of levy can be found during Mauryan and Satavahana periods. As a matter of fact, King's revenue consisted *of bali, S'ulka* (tolls etc.) and *bhaga.* Sircar, D.C., *Studies in the Political and Administrative Systems in Ancient and Medieval India,* Delhi, 1974, pp. 5-6.
20. Sarkar, J.N., *Op. cit.,* National Archives of India, *Secret Proceedings,* vol. 23, pp. 776, 777, 781-785, 783, P. Saran, *op. cit.* 370; Dua, J.C., p. 117.
21. Cunningham, Joseph Davey, *A History of Sikhs from the Origin of the Nation to the Battles of the Sutlej.* (First published 1848). Edited by H.L.O. Garrett with additional notes by R.R. Sethi, Delhi, 1955, p. 114n.
22. *Sri Gur Sobha* (AD 1711), ed. Ganda Singh, Punjabi University, Patiala, 1967, pp. 9, 124.
23. *Prachin Panth Prakash* (ed. Bhai Vir Singh), Khalsa Samachar, Amritsar, 1962, p. 364.
24. Franklin, W., *Military Memoirs of George Thomas,* Calcutta, 1803, p. 76; Syed Muhammad Latif, *History of the Punjab,* Calcutta, 1891, p. 290; and Cunningham, *op. cit.,* pp. 112-14.
25. M'Gregor, W.L., *A History of the Sikhs,* London, 1846, pp. 118-19 : Franklin, *op. cit.* 76.
26. Wilson, H.H., 'Civil and Religious Institutions of the Sikhs' in *The Sikh Religion (A Symposium),* Susil Gupta, Calcutta, 1958, p. 61.
27. Cunnigham, *op. cit.,* 112-14.
28. Rattan Singh Bhangu, *Prachin Panth Prakash,* Amritsar, 1972, pp. 45-47.
29. Prinsep, Henry T., *Op. cit.,* pp. 26-36.
30. *Ibid.*
31. Batalia, Ahmad Shah 'Zikr-i-guruan was Ibtida-Sikhan wa Mazahab-i-Eshan', appendix in *Umdat-ul-Tawarikh,* daftar I, Lahore, 1885, p. 25.
32. Azar Nayaz, *Tarikh-i-Kunjpura,* ed. Muhammad Baqar, 1973, pp. 80-86, 89-90.
33. *Tazikara-i-Waqai-Anand Ram Mukhils,* ms. No. 12, Sikh Research Department, Khalsa College, Amritsar, pp. 265-67, 270-72; Imam-ud-din-al Husaini, *Tarikh-i-Ahmad Shahi,* (covers up to 1798 AD), pp. 7-20.
34. *Selections from the Peshwa Dafatar,* ed. G.S. Sardesai, II, p. 71.
35. *Ibid.,* XXI, Letter no., 53 and 55; Azar Nayaz, *Tarikh-i-Kunjpura,* ed. Muhammad Baqar, Lahore, 1973, pp. 80-86; Punjab State Archives, Patiala, Foreign Ministry Case 2A/147 of 1174 AH, *Sacred Documents pertaining to the reign of Shri 108 Maharaja Baba Ala Singh Surgbashi,* Document no. 2A/147 (E)

of 1174 AH. dated Shaban AH 1174/29 March, 1761. (1) It was only after the British occupation of Delhi (11 September, 1803) and withdrawals of Marathas from the Jamuna-Ganga Doab and the Delhi-Agra region along the Jamuna in pursuance of the Anglo-Maratha Treaty of Surji-Arjan Gaon (30 December, 1803), and the failure of Jaswant Rao Holkar's assault on Delhi (October 8, 1804) and later futile negotiations for eliciting support from the Chiefs of *cis*-Satluj territories and Maharaja Ranjit Singh that the East India Company penetrated into the *cis*-Satluj territories for the establishment of its protectorate. (2) Zaman Shah led his last campaign to Lahore on 19 Rajab AH 1213/19 September 1798 but had to retreat towards Multan due to shortage of funds. Notwithstanding the fact that the Sikhs were a great barrier to the fulfillment of the Durrani aims for the reoccupation of the territories of the Punjab and *cis*-Satluj upto Karnal over which it claimed sovereignty.

36. Chopra, Gulshan Lall, *The Punjab as a Sovereign State (1799-1839)*, 2nd edition, Hoshiarpur, 1960, pp. 5-6.

37. Azar Nayaz, *Tarikh-i-Kunjpura,* ed. Muhammad Baqar, Lahore, 1973, pp. 112-115.

38. Banga, Indu, *op. cit.,* p. 21.

39. Ahmad Shah Batalia, *Tarikh-i-Hind,* ms. SHR 1291, Khalsa College, Amritsar, pp. 407-420. Mufti Aliuddin, *Ibrathama,* ms. SHR, Khalsa college, Amritsar, pp. 294-464.

8

Maharaja Ranjit Singh and East India Company

Maharaja Ranjit Singh rose from a petty *Sardar*/Chief of Gujranwala to a mighty ruler of an extensive kingdom. The kingdom established by Maharaja Ranjit Singh (1799-1839 AD) covered all the territories of the erstwhile Mughal *subahs* of Punjab[1], Kashmir, Multan, some of the trans-Indus *ilaqas* of *subah* Kabul viz., Peshawar, Kohat, Bannu and few tribal kingdoms. On the eastern side, the chief of *cis*-Sutlej territories viz., the chiefs of Malwa and Sirhind being under the British protection remained outside the territorial boundaries of Ranjit Singh.[2]

The capture of the territories beyond the river Indus was all the more significant, as Ranjit Singh was the first monarch after Anangpal to do so. There was recurring stream of invasions from the northwestern covers of India around eight hundred years ago. Maharaja Ranjit Singh like Anangpal had also subdued and governed a fairly good amount of territories in that region. As such, Ranjit Singh, to a large extent, fulfilled the cherished dream of Guru Gobind Singh, viz., the unity of all the Sikhs under the "commonwealth of Gobind"[3]. He was able to bring the scattered people of the Punjab under a consistent and uniform system of administration, and was instrumental in evolving a young and vigorous nation.

As far as history of Punjab is concerned, the period of Maharaja Ranjit Singh (1799-1839) and until its annexation in 1849 have, perhaps, attracted the largest attention of the British and the Indian historians. Several historical accounts in Persian, written both by the Hindu and Muslim historians, had been produced even during the lifetime of Ranjit Singh. Since the Sikh rule was the immediate predecessor to the English

Paper presented at the *Seminar on the Life and Achievements of Sher-e-Punjab Maharaja Ranjit Singh* at S.G.T.B. Khalsa P.G. (E) College, (University of Delhi), New Delhi, 8th November, 2001.

rule, it produced a likely temptation for the British writers to produce works on the past history of the Sikh community. In fact, a large number of Indian writers have produced a fairly good number of works both in Persian and vernacular languages. Apart from the above work, we the students of Punjab history, are fortunate enough to have inherited original archival source material in the form of *Khalsa Darbar Records* as well as the Persian correspondence of various categories entitled *Bhandari Collection* preserved at State Archives, Patiala. Moreover, the English reports of various categories are immensely valuable. There are some very good works on Maharaja Ranjit Singh, his successors and on the circumstances that led to the annexation of Punjab by the East Indian Company. However, in the present Paper an attempt has been made to make critical assessment of Maharaja Ranjit Singh's relations with the East India Company.

At the time of Ranjit Singh's accession to the leadership of Sukerchakia *Misl* in 1790, Punjab was divided in to not less than a score of chief states being ruled over by Sikhs, Muslims and the Hindus. The land between the rivers Jehlam and Satluj was mostly under the *Misls* amongst which the most important of them was the *Bhangis*. This *Misl*, besides controlling a long strip of territory along the river Jehlam, held in possession the greater part of the districts of Gujrat, Sialkot, Lahore and Amritsar. This was, more or less, an outward picture and their possessions were not contiguous. Between Gujrat and Sialkot and between Gujrat and Lahore, there were large tracts as well as several strongholds belonging to other *Misls.* Wazirabad was under an independent Sikh chief while Gujranwala formed the centre of Ranjit Singh's own *Misl*, the Sukerchakias.

The possessions of the Sukerchakia *Misl* were consisted of the area around Sialkot, Gujrat, and across the river Jehlum in Pind-dadan Khan and Miani.

The lands between Amritsar and Ludhiana were divided among several Sardars. The *Kanhyas* were the most important amongst them. They had their seat at Batala in the Gurdaspur district.[4] The *Ahluwalias* had their centre at Kapurthala and their possessions reached the vicinity of Jalandhar in one direction and on the other side embraced Hoshiarpur. While Jalandhar itself was in control of a seperate Sardar. The *Ramgarhias* who had their possessions across the river Satluj also held some tracts in the districts of Gurdaspur and Amritsar, and in the Jalandhar *Doab*. The *cis*-Satluj portion of Punjab was divided among the ruling families of Patiala, Nabha, Jind, and several other less important Sardars. The *Nishanwalas* possessed some territory between Ambala and Saharanpur. However, Malerkotla, a small state, was governed by the representative of Afghan dynasty. The areas between Lahore and Multan were divided among the Pathans of Kasur, the Nakai Sardar of Pakpatan, and the Sials of Jhnag. Sansar Chand, a Hindu Raja, possessed the Kangra Hills; but Chamba belonged to Raja Charat Singh. Rajauri, Bhimbar, Jammu and adjoining areas were being administered by Muslim and Rajput chieftains. While Bahawalpur and Dera Ghazi Khan were under the possession of Bahawal Khan, a Daudputra chief, Dera Ismail Khan was in the hands of Abdul Samand Khan. The province of Multan was under Nawab Muzaffar Khan Sadozai. Different Muslim rulers ruled over Mankera, Bannu, Kohat and Tonk, where as Wazir Khel chief, Jahandad Khan held the fort of Attock. The province of Kashmir administered by Azim Khan; and his brother Fateh Khan Barakzai ruled over the valley of Peshawar.[5]

In the northern India, apart from the political powers mentioned above, the English East India Company had established its influence over Awadh and had been able to establish their power against the Marathas. On the other hand, the Marathas had recovered their position to a certain extent after the third battle of Panipat, under the leadership of Mahadaji Sindhia. By 1785, Sindhia had succeeded in occupying Agra and persuading the Mughal Emperor, Shah 'Alam, to declare him the viceregent of the Mughal Empire. The third power was that of the Sikhs. Since the death of Ahmed Shah Abdali, the Sikhs had over-run the Eastern Punjab as far as the river Jamuna.[6]

At the time of Maharaja Ranjit Singh's accession to the throne, the English East Company felt no direct interest in extending their influence beyond the river Jamuna and was content with the defence of Awadh. This position remained unchanged till the beginning of the 19th century and the English remained aloof while the Sikhs and the Marathas came in to conflict.[7]

Ranjit Singh's rise to prominence synchronized with the arrival in India of the Marquess Wellesley. It was not without its bearing upon the fortunes of the British. Ranjit Singh got engaged in carving out a dominion for himself in that State that was contiguous to the passes from which numerous invaders had come into India from the north-west. "Thenceforth the Sikhs were not only able to hold the line of the Indus river against fresh invaders, they also cut off the channels of supply between Central Asia and the Muhammadan powers to the south of the Sutlej, who were, moreover, kept in constant alarm by this actively aggressive community on their northern frontier. The effect was to maintain among the fighting powers in northern India an equilibrium that was of signal advantage to the English by preserving their north-west frontier unmolested during the last quarter of the eighteenth century, a critical period when they were fully occupied with Mysore and the western Mahrattas."[8] Had not Ranjit Singh succeeded in creating a strong Sikh kingdom in the Punjab, which formed a barrier against incursions from the Central Asia, the task that the Marquess Wellesley had set himself to, of consolidating the British possessions, might have been rendered far harder than it actually was. While the Sikh monarch was consolidating his power, the British were also consolidating theirs, and their consolidation had one effect, which could not have been altogether palatable to him. By the time it was completed the thin red line had reached and absorbed Delhi and formed an impenetrable barrier against his own further advance southwards.

It is quite possible that the English might have heard of the Sikhs as early as 1715, when the agents of the East India Company had gone to the Court of the Mughal Emperor in quest of trading privileges. However, it was only in 1785 when they officially took note of the Sikhs. The latters' temporary alliance with Scindhia attracted the attention of Warren Hastings, the then Governor General of the East India Company.

The English East India Company came into contact with the Maharaja when Lord Wellesley came to India as Governor-General. At that time there was every possibility of an attack of Zaman Shah, the ruler of Afghanistan. Zaman Shah had been invited by Tipu Sultan, the ruler of Mysore and perhaps the greatest enemy of the English in India. The Afghan ruler had been encamping at Lahore and was seriously thinking of repeating the exploits of his predecessors.[8] It was to save India from the aggression of the Afghans that the English government sent a mission, headed by Yusuf Ali to the court of Ranjit Singh. Though one may not attach so much importance to this mission as Ranjit Singh was not a very important ruler during those days. However, the mission had for the first time brought the East India Company into contact with Ranjit Singh and his promise to be a friend of the former in case of an aggression of the Afghans.[9] It clearly indicated that Ranjit Singh had no ill feeling towards the English.

In 1803, some of the *cis*-Satluj chiefs joined Sindhia against the English army under the command of Lord Lake in the battle of Delhi. The Marathas under Sindhia were defeated, and Sikhs tendered their allegiance to the English commander. Henceforward, general friendship and cordiality existed between the English and the Sikh chieftains of Kaithal and Jind.[10]

In October 1804, Jaswant Rao Holkar attacked Delhi but was repulsed by Colonel Ochterlony and Colonel Burn and was, thus, forced to drive back to Rajputana. In 1805, Holker again advanced North, closely followed by Lord Lake. Holkar was compelled to escape into Punjab and sought help from the Sikh chieftains. He first entered Patiala, remain their for some months, "..but its Maharaja would not risk much to aid him, and other *cis*-Sutlaj Chiefs seeing that his cause was hopeless, were equally discreet."[11] In October 1805, being threatened by the approach of Lord Lake, Holkar continued his march towards the Satlej. On realising that none of the *cis*-Satluj chiefs would listen to his requests for help, he crossed the river and passed through the territories of Fateh Singh Ahluwalia, and entered Amritsar. Ranjit Singh, who at that time was carrying on raids in the direction of Jhang and Multan, hastened back to Amritsar. Ranjit Singh treated Holkar with due courtesy and in a befitting manner. He showed him the city, took him to the Golden Temple, held military parades in his honour and paid him every attention. He even took counsel with him in matters of military and financial organization.[12] Holkar endeavoured to obtain the alliance of Ranjit Singh, who, it seems, was much inclined to assist him.

The conversations that took place between Maharaja Ranjit Singh and Captain Wade in 1827 and 1831 reveal the considerations that influenced his judgement and ultimately dissuaded him from this step. Ranjit Singh dreaded the discipline of the English army, which he had just observed in disguise on the banks of the river Bias. He told Captain Wade in 1827 how impressed he had been with the spectacle of Holkar's hundred thousand soldiers flying before a few trained battalions under Lord Lake. He drew the conclusion that the addition of a small Sikh force to the vast horde of the Maratha chief would not change the situation. He was also advised against joining Holkar by his maternal uncle, Bhag Singh, Raja of Jind and one of his own counsellors, Fateh Singh Ahluwalia. Moreover, the presence of English forces on the borders of his own territory offered little temptation to Ranjit Singh to plunge into an armed intervention. Even a slight reverse in the situation would have brought the enemy to Amritsar, i.e., the very heart of his small kingdom. It appears from the conversations in 1831 that Ranjit Singh long wavered between acceptable and refusal of Maratha Chief's proposal. He got so much distracted between the two alternatives that he decided his course by lot.[13] Ranjit Singh sent Fateh Singh Ahluwalia to the English camp, to draw up the terms of an agreement which would pledge "friendship and amity between the Honourable East India Company and the Sardars Ranjit Singh and Fateh Singh."

Lord Lake and Ranjit Singh came to a settlement entitled the Treaty of Lahore on 1st January 1806. According to this Treaty, Ranjit Singh was to compel Holkar to go away at a distance of 30 *kos* south of Amritsar. He was to have no connection with the Maratha Chief and he was not at all to help him even in case if Maratha chief asked for his friendship. Some of the soldiers of Holkar were discouraged after their defeats at Dig and Ferrukhabad. They had a mind to desert Holkar. Thus, it was declared that Ranjit Singh should not try to molest any soldier of Holkar who wanted to go back to Deccan. Ranjit Singh even was to help the Maratha forces in case they wanted to go back to their country. Ranjit Singh and Fateh Singh "agreed to cause Jaswant Rao Holkar to at once leave Amritsar and never again to hold connection with him, or aid him with troops, or assist him in any matter whatever. The British Government . . . promised that as long as those chiefs abstained from holding friendly connection with its enemies, or from committing any act of hostility on their part against it, the British armies would never enter their territories nor would the government form any plans for the seizure or sequestration of their possessions or property."[14]

These agreements, which excluded Holkar from the Punjab, practically secured Ranjit Singh from English interference in his plans of conquest north of the Satluj. Regarding Ranjit Singh's attitude towards the English in future and through out his life, Griffin has very aptly remarked, "To one friendship the Maharaja remained ever constant, from one alliance he never sought to shake himself free. This was friendly alliance with the British government, then represented in Hindustan by the East India Company."[15]

In 1806, Ranjit Singh turned his attention towards the rich lands of Malwa and crossed the river Satluj on the invitation of his uncle Raja Bhag Singh of Jind. The Maharaja had been invited with the object of settling serious disputes between that chief and that of Patiala. Having crossed the river Satluj at the head of a large force, Ranjit Singh captured Ludhiana and made it over to Bhag Singh. The following year he conquered Qasur. In the beginning of 1808 A.D. various places in the upper Punjab were taken from the independent Sikh rulers and brought under the direct management of the new kingdom of Lahore, and Mohkam Chand, the *Diwan*, was at the same time employed in effecting a settlement of the territories which had been seized on the left bank of the Satluj.[16]

At this stage to the British in India designs or desires of Napoleon appeared to render a defensive alliance with the Afghans and with the Sikhs imperative. Elphinstone was deputed to the court of Shah Shuja, and in September 1808 A.D. Metcalfe was sent on a mission to Ranjit Singh for the purpose of bringing about the desired confederation. Metcalfe was received by Mian Aziz-ud Din, on behalf of Ranjit Singh on the bank of the Satluj, and had conference with Ranjit Singh. During these conferencs Sikh chief affected to consider himself as the head of the whole of the Sikh people, and to regard the possession of Lahore as giving him an additional claim to the supremacy over Sirhind. He suddenly broke off negotiations, and made his inroad to the south fo the Satluj. He seized Faridkot and Ambala, levied exactions in Malerkotla and Thanesar, and entered into an alliance with the *Raja* of Patiala. The British remonstrated against these virtual acts of hostility and Metcalfe remained on the banks of the Satluj until Ranjit Singh crossed that river. Metcalfe was then brought to Lahore where he stayed for seven or eight days in a house on the bank of the river Ravi.[17]

In the meantime Ranjit Singh received a letter from Nand Singh, through Diwan Mohkam Chand, that the Sikh chiefs from the eastern bank of the Satluj have written to Shahjahanabad that Ranjit Singh, having become very powerful, had a design in a view to seize from them the land that they had inherited from their ancestors. It was also reported that he was planning to move towards Shahjahanbad after annexing that territory. A request was made to stop him in return for which loyalty and submission to the British rule was promised. All this correspondence from Shahjahanabad was re-directed to Calcutta. This correspondence determined the Governor-General, if doubtful before, to advance a detachment of troops to the Satluj. Four platoons were accordingly moved across the river Jamuna in January 1809 A.D. under the command of David Ochterlony.[18]

Here it becomes quite imperative to understand the reasons behind the change in the attitude of the Company's Government towards Ranjit Singh. It is on the record that the Company had raised no objections to Ranjit Singh's expeditions of 1806 and 1807 into the *cis*-Satluj region and the political changes effected by him during the campaigns. Rather, when some of the chiefs of the region had felt alarmed and approached the British resident at Delhi for protection against Ranjit Singh, they had been put off with an equivocal and non-committal reply.[19] Even when, at the beginning of Lord Minto's period (1807-1813), it was decided, in view of the deteriorating situation in the Near Middle East and in Europe[20] and to build up some counter bulwarks of defence against the possible threat of a French, later a Fraco-Russian, invasion of India, to send a diplomatic mission to Ranjit Singh, no change was effected in the approved policy of indifference towards the chiefs of the *cis*-Satluj region. While on the way to Ranjit Singh's camp at Kasur, Metcalfe was offered by the Raja of Patiala, Sahib Singh, the keys of his fort with the request that they might be returned to him as a gift from the British. The offer was politely declined[21] giving the reason that the Company had no intention to enter into any commitment on the issue. The same is clear from the instructions given to Metcalfe on the eve of his departure for Punjab that, in case Ranjit Singh made a demand for British recognition of his suzerainty over the states of the *cis*-Satluj chiefs, the matter was to be referred to the Governor-General.[22]

Metcalfe had asked Ranjit Singh simply a mutual defensive alliance for "the protection of the Punjab and the British possessions in India against the apprehended invasion of Napoleon Bonaparte."[23] Ranjit Singh was sceptical about the *bona fides* of the British[24] but did not reject the proposal. He made some counter-demands in which the pride of place was assigned to the British recognition of his sovereignty over the *cis*-Satluj Sikh chiefs.[25] In response to this Metcalfe wrote to the Governor-General and expressed emphatically, "I take the liberty of expressing my opinion, founded upon the observations made in my present situation, that if it is viewed to attach Ranjit Singh to the British Government and to make him a friend by conciliation, the concession which he requires is essentially for that purpose. As long as the British Government appears to be the bar, and the only bar, to his subjugation of the Sikhs and consequent aggrandisement, he will not, I conceive, be cordially attached to it; and if this attachment is to be gained by any means, none other are so likely to secure it as this concession, without which all other attempts to obtain his cooperation by conciliation would probably be fruitless.[26]

On December 10, 1808, presented the Maharaja a letter from the Governor-General saying, "His Lordship has learned with great surprise and concern that the *Maharaja* aims at the subjugation of chiefs who have long been considered under the protection of the power ruling in north of Hindustan. It is hereby declared that the British government cannot consent that these chiefs, according to the established custom, are and will remain under the protection of the British government. . .The British government cannot acknowledge any right of the *Maharaja* to any territories that he may have taken possession of, situated between the Sutlej and Jamuna, since the first reference of this question to the British government."[27]

It was a complete diplomatic somersault or reversal of policy. A reference made to their (*cis*-Satluj rulers) being successors of the Marathas in regard to their rights in that area, while the previous indifference to it was explained in terms of non-exercise of rights, which, it was emphasized, was not the same thing as relinquishment.[28]

N.K. Sinha[29] and many other historians are of the view that this sudden and complete change was due to a marked improvement in the international situation. However, it appears to be completely unfounded. In this regard following points may be taken into consideration:

- The decision to drive Ranjit Singh beyond the river Satluj was taken in the second week of November, 1808, when Metcalfe was still encamped at Gongrara and the Maharaja was exchanging turbans at Patiala with the local chief.

- The appointment of Lt. Col. Ochterlony to the command of the military detachment was made on November 14, 1808.[30]
- The improvement in the international situation came much later.
- The Treaty of Dardeanells between England and Turkey was not concluded till January, 1809.[31]
- The treaty between England and Persia was signed still later in March, 1809.
- The rising in Spain had, no doubt, begun earlier but the favourable turn in the situation of the British appeared much later.
- There is recorded evidence showing that first intelligence of "the favourable change in the aspect of affairs on the continent of Europe," was not received earlier than the third week of January, 1809.[32]

In the light of the above remarks, the real cause of the somersault has to be sought elsewhere. The Governor-General, in his letter of November 14, 1808 to Ochterlony, wrote the undermentioned two reasons for sending armed forces against Ranjit Singh:

1. The course of events and transactions at the court of the Raja of Lahore;
2. Necessity to provide eventually for military arrangements of a more extensive nature in the north-western quarter of Hindustan.[33]

Charles Metcalfe, in one of the communications to be Governor-General, made some significant observations about Ranjit Singh. He wrote, "No part of personal character presents any satisfactory assurance of cordiality, good faith, consistency or hearty co-operation. For want of consistency and good faith he is justly notorious; my despatches will have described repeated instances of deceit and evasion; he has no regard for truth and can descend even to the violation of solemn promises; and the whole tenor of his behaviour impress me most strongly with the conviction of his total want of principal. In the crisis when his exertions may be required, he will, doubtless, without regard to previous engagements, act according to his view of his interests at the moment. If ever the agents of French intrigue should find a way to his ear, he is a character well suited for them. He will probably soon fall under the guidance of French negotiations who would flatter his pride and vanity, raise ambitious hopes by unbounded promises and work on upon his credibility by any falsehoods.[34] Metcalfe also wrote about the uncomfortable position of the *cis*-Satluj chiefs and their jealousy of Ranjit Singh's increasing power. He was of the view that these positions could always be exploited by the Company to its advantage.[35]

The opinions expressed by Metcalfe made a deep impact upon the Governor-General and his colleagues. "The expectation of making a friend of him (Ranjit Singh) was abandoned as vain and it was determined to restrain him in that quarter in which he might be considered most dangerous as an enemy."[36] Writing about the advantages of forcing Ranjit Singh to give up all the conquests he had made in the *cis*-Satluj region, Metcalfe commented, "The advantages of having the Sutlej instead of Jamuna for our boundary in that direction were: first, as acquiring an addition of power and influence for ourselves; secondly, as abstracting in a still greater degree, power and influence from a political enemy; thirdly, as preventing the union of the Sikh nation under an aspiring ruler of extraordinary character; fourthly, as interposing between our frontier and that of a powerful rival the territories of our dependent states, by which war, defensive or offensive, would be kept at a distance from our country; fifthly, for the greatest security afforded to the capital city, and an important political post of Dihlee, to which otherwise the power of Ranjit Singh would have approximated within a few miles, affording him the opportunity of attacking it suddenly in the event of our being involved in war with other powers; lastly, perhaps the assumption of our proper station as the protectors of the weak and the oppressors of the oppressor was not the least of the advantages of the arrangement, with reference to its impression on all parties.[37]

Despite the above points being clearly indicative of Company's ultimate decision, the provision of measures for external security against the political ambitions of Ranjit Singh was not the only consideration. The English also wanted to have a dependable system of defence in the region of the Punjab against the threatened French or Franco-Russian invasion of India. It was feared that the presence of Ranjit Singh so close to the Company's frontiers, if he was really as easily amenable to French intrigues as Metcalfe had portrayed him, would serve to enhance rather than reduce the dangers apprehended from the north-west. The matter being so urgent, the English government was not prepared to tolerate any obstacle or impediment coming in the way. Ranjit Singh was to be driven out by force, if he showed any resistance. In case the *cis*-Satluj chiefs objected to the advance of the English troops they were to be told that "no consideration will induce the British Government to abandon the policy which it was now resolved to adopt."[38]

The English government, in the first instance, wanted to destroy Ranjit Singh's influence southward of the Satluj. This was to be followed by negotiations with the Maharaja for the conclusion of a defensive alliance against France and, in the case of intransigence, by subversion of his power even in the trans-Satluj area.[39]

As a result, a strong military force headed by Lt. Col. Ochterlony crossed the Jamuna and entered the *cis*-Satluj region on January 16, 1809, followed by another force under the command of St. Leger. About a month earlier, order had been passed concerning the withdrawal of the British embassy from the court of Ranjit Singh.[40] The stage seemed to have been set for an open rupture with the Maharaja. But before things had gone very far, the arrival of favourable intelligence from Europe rendered extreme measures, unnecessary. On January 23, 1809, fresh instructions were issued to Metcalfe enjoining upon him a policy of pacification towards Ranjit Singh.[41] A week later, similar instructions were sent to Ochterlony.[42] The General advanced towards Ludhiana, where he was welcomed by Sirhind chiefs. Ranjit Singh on receiving this intelligence started collected his troops and although outwardly looked very much unconcerned yet on account of the fear of the near presence of British force felt like a wall of sand, which was constantly disintegrating. At this stage it was made known to Ranjit Singh that the object of the British was to keep under their control the country lying on the left bank of the Satluj and free from the encroachment of Ranjit Singh. He was told to withdraw his troops to the right bank. Not being in a position to fight the British, the Sikh chief agreed to their proposals and the British commander, to remove all cause of suspicion, returned to Ludhiana with the troops. On the 23rd Zulhijja, 1223 A.H., (February 9, 1809 A.D.), Sir David Ochterlony issued a proclamation declaring the *cis*-Satluj states to be under British protection, and that any aggression of the Chief of Lahore would be resisted with arms.[43]

It was in these changed circumstances that the question of signing a treaty between the two parties was favoured and brought to a conclusion. Ranjit Singh had suffered a great humiliation and was anxious to save himself and his little state from its evil consequences by securing a treaty of friendship from the British. Besides, Ranjit Singh's authority over the Punjab was not yet well established. Most of his Sardars, having been recently dispossessed, were jealous of his ascendancy, and were awaiting an opportunity to shake it off; and, perhaps in the event of a military reverse, they might have revolted from Ranjit Singh and transferred their allegiance to the English. He then perceived that the British were in earnest, and the fear struck him that the still independent leaders of the Punjab might likewise tender their allegiance and have it accepted. All chances of empire would thus be lost, and prudently made up his mind without further delay. After withdrawing his troops as required, he relinquished his last acquisition, and at Amritsar, on the 25th April, 1809 A.D., Ranjit Singh signed a treaty which left him the master of the tracts he had originally occupied to the south of the Satluj, but confined his ambition for the future to the north and westward of that river.[44]

The Treaty of Amritsar prevented the extension of Ranjit Singh's authority over the whole of the Sikh population and, for the first time, created a political cleavage between the Manjah and the Malwa sections of the Sikhs. Apart from the political and territorial loss to Ranjit Singh, this situation would also mean a great economic loss, too. However, it secured his borders of the south and was no more to keep an army on that side. It was not at all possible for Ranjit Singh to estrange his relations with the Britishers when he had already quite a big number of enemies around him and to add an enemy of the calibre of the Britishers was not at all good for him.

After having occupied Lahore in 1799 A.D., Ranjit Singh realized that he could never consolidate his rule unless the Afghans were expunged from the Indian territories. This could, however, be possible after he had secured his eastern frontier by signing the above treaty by which he had accepted Satluj as the eastern boundary of his kingdom. All criticism against Maharaja Ranjit Singh that by signing this Treaty, he inhibited weakness against the English is rather unrealistic, for he would not have been able to face challenge on the two fronts, i.e. east and west. Rather this enabled him to build a strong kingdom at Lahore, with all potentialities for expansion even towards north in the Himalayas.[45] By the Treaty of Amritsar, the English East India Company recognized Ranjit Singh as the sole sovereign ruler of the Punjab. In the first article of Treaty, it was stipulated that 'the British Government will have no concern with the territories and subjects of the Raja to the northward of the river Sutlej'. For more than two decades then, the English did not interfere with the affairs of the chiefs in the north of the Satluj. The English indirectly allowed him to go for the conquests in the erstwhile Mughal *subah* of Lahore, and to oust from Multan and Kashmir and finally, to turn the tables against the successors of Ahmad Shah Abdali in the former Mughal province of Kabul. Before his death in 1839, Ranjit Singh's authority over all the conquered and subordinated territories between the river Satluj and the mountain ranges of Ladakh, Karkoram and Sulaiman was recognized by the ruler of Kabul as well as by the British rulers of India.[46]

Since a military demonstration was involved in the above Treaty, a large amount of suspicion and distrust continued for several years. Ranjit Singh even kept a large army within the fort of Philour under the leadership of Mokham Chand for an emergency. He would also, at times, patronise those soldiers who had deserted the British army and always kept a hostile attitude towards the Britishers. Slowly the mutual distrust was partly removed. In 1812, Ranjit Singh invited Ochterlony, the English agent at Ludhiana, to Lahore, to attend the marriage of his son, Prince Kharak Singh. The invitation was accepted and the English agent was received in a cordial manner. The conversation that took place during the visit soon resulted into the consent by the Governor-General for the supply of a large number of muskets and flints asked by the Maharaja. The English East India Company maintained strict neutrality towards the transactions of Ranjit Singh with all chieftains as the former was not at all at that time interested. Meanwhile the English also utilized the time in bringing down the Marathas, the Napalese and the Rajputs and thus were in a position to establish their ascendancy over the whole of northern India.[47]

Until February, 1823, British attitude towards Ranjit Singh as a *cis*-Satluj neighbour was very much influenced by Murray, who was Political Assistant at Ludhiana. The relations between Ranjit Singh and the English government were not relations of intimate and cordial friendship and one must not be misled by the rhetorical language of diplomatic intercourse. In 1823, with the appointment of Wade as Political Assistant at Ludhiana and the transfer of Murray to Ambala there was a noticeable change in the tone and temper of British dealings with the Lahore Durbar.[48] However, the Company's government saw to it that Ranjit Singh's *cis*-Satluj territories remained scattered and slightest attempt at territorial exchange was not encouraged. Over Wadhni[49] the English government accepted Maharaja's claim of sovereignty as also over *cis*-Satluj Ahluwalia possessions[50] granted by Ranjit Singh. These territories were declared amenable to Lahore *Darbar* supremacy. Similarly Sardar Hari Singh was declared to be Ranjit Singh's vassal. The *Sodhis* of Machiwara, Makhwal and Anandpur were recognized as subject to the jurisdiction of the Lahore Darbar.[51] In case of Ferozepur, however, there was no departure in the stand taken earlier. The English disallowed Ranjit Singh's claim to Ferozepur.[52] The post of Ferozepur "for every point of view seems of the highest importance to the British Government whether as a check on the growing ambition of Lahore or as post of consequence." Ultimately, Ferozepur was occupied by the British in 1835 and in 1838 was made a military cantonment.

Some historians are of the view that while the British government had a mind to come into conflict with Ranjit Singh, the latter hesitated and avoided a conflict. In 1815, Prithi Bilas, the *vakil* of the Gurkhas, and Shiv Dat Rai, a reliable person of the Raja of Bilaspur, approached him. He was requested to help the Gurkhas in their war with the British, to speak to the bankers to lend them five lakhs of rupees and to help the Gurkhas cross the rivers Ganges and Jamuna. The Maharaja declared his inability to help the Gurkhas against the British.[53] In 1820, Ranjit Singh would not go the rescue of the ex-ruler of Nagpur nor would he respond to the appeal of Baji Rao II. In 1825-26 he refused to respond to the repeated requests of the people of Bharatpur.[54]

On social front the Maharaja enjoyed a very cordial relations with the English. Some such instances were:

- When Ranjit Singh fell sick (1826) he sought the services Dr. Murray, an English army surgeon at Ludhiana. During his stay of nearly eight months with Ranjit Singh the former thoroughly studied political and military situation in the Punjab and regularly supplied the information to the authorities at Ludhiana and Delhi.
- Ranjit Singh sent a complimentary mission, composed of Dewan Moti Ram and Faqir Imam-ud-din, to Shimla to wait upon Lord Amherst, the Governor-General, who returned the compliment by sending Captains Wade and Pearson and Surgeon Gerard to Punjab. They were accorded a hearty welcome by the Maharaja.
- In 1831 Lord William Bentinck arrived in Shimla and received a complimentary mission from Ranjit Singh. Captain Wade was in turn deputed to the Sikh ruler with letter of thanks, and secret instructions to ascertain if the Maharaja wished and was prepared to propose a meeting with the Governor-General. Several accounts of the pomp and pageantry which attended the two rulers at Ropar have survived.
- Soon after this, Lieut. (afterwards Sir) Alexander Burnes arrived with horses from England, which were presented to Ranjit Singh on behalf of King William IV.

Meanwhile The English were becoming increasingly conscious of Ranjit Singh's growing power. In 1827-28, a new dispute arose about the Maharaja's claims over Chamkaur, Anandpur, Makhowal and Ferozepur. Ranjit Singh's claim to the possession of the places other than Ferozpur were recognized by the English. The insurrection at Peshawar led by Syed Ahmed kept Ranjit Singh's energies confined to that quarter. But the final defeat of Syed Ahmed in 1831 added still greater prestige to the Maharaja's name.

Ranjit Singh turned his attention towards Sindh. It also became a bone of contention between the English and Sikhs. The English government could not tolerate Ranjit Singh in Sindh as he would have got an outlet to the sea, formed relations with different parts of Europe and thus overawe the British government. While William Bentinck and Ranjit Singh were making friends at Ropar, Colonel Pottinger was on his way to Sindh with a navigation treaty in his pocket. Soon after the meeting the Governor-General deputed Captain Wade to the court of Lahore, to explain the object of Pottinger's mission of Sindh. He explained that the intention was to propose a free navigation of the Sutlej in continuation of that of the Indus, and that the objects of the Company's government were merely commercial. Moreover, one object of sending King William's presents to the Maharaja by water was to ascertain quietly the commercial value of the Indus. As such, "Ranjit Singh was checked in the guise of material utilitarianism. But Ranjit Singh had seen the beginning of those trading aspirations which bestowing a power to interfere had led to the absorption of Bengal."[55] The chief obstacle on the way of English plans arose from the plans already laid by the Maharaja against Sindh. Bentinck resolved to remove these by persuation, or to counteract them by diplomacy. Ranjit Singh suspected the English after 1832 of entertaining deeper designs against Sindh than the establishment of commercial relations only. But Ranjit Singh recurred to his claim on Shikarpur and his designs on Sindh during the years 1834-1836. He was already feeling his way towards Sindh; and had expelled Bahawal Khan from his territories on the right bank of Satluj. He was now maturing plans to seize Shikarpur. Finally, due to the determined attitude of the British government, Ranjit Singh, with greatest hesitation and reluctance, yielded to the suggestions of Captain Wade. Ranjit Singh agreed to the common use of the Satluj and the Indus, and to the residence of a British officer at Mithenkot to superintend the navigation. He also temporarily gave up his intentions against Shikarpur, but not without telling Captain Wade plainly that the commercial measures of the English hindered the attainment of his military ambitions. The British extorted from the Amirs a very reluctant consent of the admission of a British Resident at Hyderabad in 1838.[56]

Meanwhile Ranjit Singh had been negotiating with Shah Shuja about the latter's restoration on his throne. He was also occupied with the annexation of Peshwar and hostilities with Dost Mohammed. The English attitude towards the plans of Shah Shuja remained studiously indifferent. In 1836, certain new developments modified the English government's views and caused an alteration in its policy. This was the danger of Russian invasion on India. The new Governor-General, Lord Auckland was preparing for a threefold alliance against possible Russian attack. Alexander Burnes, who was already at Kabul on a commercial mission, was now invested with diplomatic authority. Captain Wade was at Lahore, and was instructed to sound the Sikh ruler. It became apparent that Peshawar was the real bone of contention, which forbade the reconciliation of the Sikh and the Afghan just as later on it proved an insuperable obstacle in the way of an Anglo-Afghan alliance.[57]

Lord Auckland decided to help Shah Shuja to recover the throne of Afghanistan and Ranjit Singh was also to be a party to the enterprise. The Maharaja did not show any liking for the scheme, and seemed to distrust the active co-operation of the English. He wanted to avoid furthering a measure which threatened to surround him with English influence. It was not till he had been expressly informed that the expedition would be undertaken whether he joined it or not that he consented to the conclusion of the *Tri-partite Treaty* in 26th June, 1838[58]

In the later part of 1838, Ranjit Singh's health began to decline and died on 27th June, 1839, in the fifty-ninth year of his life.

The policy of conciliation that Maharaja Ranjit Singh maintained towards the English, it seems, was inspired by the dread of their power and his own limitations. It was not the result of any genuine feeling of trust or good-will, as has been supposed by several writers. He repeatedly professed friendship and regard, and often sought similar assurances from the Company's representatives. The specific attitude adopted by Marquis of Hastings and Lord Amherst did help in partly dispelling his earlier fears. But they were once again revived when Lord William Bentinck informed him of his commercial projects. It seems he saw the likelihood of the absorption of regions which were the object of his military ambition, and felt grave apprehensions even about the safety of his own kingdom. It was during this period that, glancing at an English map of India and noticing the division of the area in red and yellow lines, he gave vent to his innermost feelings by exclaiming "*Sab Lal Ho Jaiga*" ("all will become red"). However, Ranjit Singh differed from many other great eastern potentates in his statesmanlike recognition of the strength of the East India Company, the reliance he placed on British promises and his loyalty to his plighted word. Ranjit Singh is said to have remarked, "I might perhaps drive the British (*Ungrez Bahadur*) as far as Allyghur but I should be driven back across the Sutlej and out of my kingdom."[59] The Maharaja, no doubt, told Mackeson, Wade and other gentlemen that he consulted the Guru Granth Sahib on the policy of entering into friendship with the British and received a favourable answer. He certainly profited by British friendship during the period 1809-1824. After that he had to yield on vital matters on every conceivable occasion.[60] Although he adopted for a time a very defiant attitude, he did not push matters to the extreme, but fell back on his old policy of conciliation and forbearance.

After British occupation of Ferozepur, admission of British Resident at Hyderabad and the *Tri-partite Treaty*, it was natural for Ranjit Singh to cease to be pacific and conciliatory.[61] "Had Ranjit survived to witness the English disaster in Kabul, he would readily have discerned that they arose entirely from local circumstances and in no way deteriorated from English provess."[62] No doubt, in the last three years of his reign he showed a marked disposition towards pursuing an independent line of action, irrespective of English interests, and good-will. In this he was supported by several of his ministers, notably Raja Dhyan Singh.[63] A clear proof may be found in the reluctance of the Sikh rank and file to perform their part of the *Tri-partite Treaty*, and in their subsequent satisfaction at the disastrous retreat of the British troops from Afghanistan.[64]

The documents like, *Calendar of Persian Correspondence* also reveal that the Sikh chiefs in the *cis*-Satluj areas had been persuaded by the English India Company to side with the English, especially against the Rohillas, on the payment of some money.[65] This shows that the Sikhs and the Sikh Sardars were in no way different from their contemporary Indian political chiefs, e.g. the Nawabs of Carnatic, Awadh and Bengal etc. They (Sikhs) had also failed to understand the aggressive and expansionist nature of the British , who wanted to check the growth of the Sikhs as well.[66] On the contrary, there is nothing on records to show that Maharaja Ranjit Singh ever helped the English against any other contemporary Indian power. Moreover, he was quite aware of the type of expansion and the alliances that the English had made in India, and, as such, would also have to fight in an hostile field. If the Punjab did not remain independent after the death of the Maharaja, it was no way because of any of his faulty policies or misjudging of the situations but was mainly due to the lack of farsightedness and internal strife on the part of his successors.

References

1. The boundaries of *subah* Punjab or *subah* Lahore or *Wilayat-i-Punjab* or Darul Saltanat Lahore extended from the river Sutlej in the east to the river Indus (Sind) in the north-west. The whole *subah* comprised of five *doabs* or *sarkars viz.*, Bet Jalandhar, Bari, Rechna, Chenhat and Sind Sagar. Moreover, some hilly regions to the north of Bet Jalandhar not covered in the *doabs* entitled as *Berun-i-Panjnand* also formed part of the *Subah.* The mountainous regions (*parganas*) to the north of the *doabs* formed the respective *doabs* or *sarkars.* However, the core of the Punjab was the Bari *doab* with headquarters at Lahore. By the end of 17th century, five *parganas* of *subah* Multan were also transferred to *subah* Punjab. At the same time, Bari, Rechna and Sind Sagar *doabs* with *mahals* beyond the five rivers of Multan territories continued to form the part of *subah* Multan.
2. Maharaja Ranjit Singh also possessed forty-five *t'aaluqas* in the *cis*-Satluj territory. These territories broadly included Ludhiana and Ferozepur as well as areas lying between river Satluj and Beas inclusive of the hilly regions. The Lahore Darbar, as per the treaty of 9th March, 1846, perpetually ceded these territories to the English East India Company, Aitchison, C., *Collection of*

Treaties Engagements and Sunnuds Relating to India and Neighbouring Countries, Calcutta, 1892, Vol. VIII, p. 160.

3. No doubt, Ranjit Singh was a great organizer, but the kingdom of Punjab of which he became the ruler, had been inspired by Guru Gobind Singh. However, a critical assessment of the history would reveal that the dream of the Guru was far from fulfilled, as he wanted a united government of the Sikhs. As per Guru Gobind Singh's popular saying, "Waho Waho Gobind Singh, Ape Guru Chela", all the Sikhs including himself were equal. Guru Gobind singh had ordained a democratic setup but Ranjit Singh was not a true believer of democracy. He had abolished *Gurumatta* and had himself become the central authority. There is a well-known saying in the Sikh literature that if the powers of the Guru were 20 points, the power of the assembly of the Sikhs was 21. Guru Arjan Dev had refused to marry his son Har Gobind to the daughter of Chandu Shah due to the opposition of the Sikhs. (See for example, Gian Singh, Giani, *Tawarikh Guru Khalsa,* Part 2 (reprint—first published 1878). Languages Department Punjab, Patiala, 1970). Moreover, Guru Gobind Singh had fought for the depressed humanity of the Punjab; Ranjit singh's fight was political. Ranjit Singh's words "Sab Lal Ho Jaiga" were not the words of a true Sikh of Guru Gobind Singh but those of a demoralized and degenerated man. Guru Gobind Singh would never give up hopes. Despite having a grand army at his disposal, Ranjit Singh was afraid of the consequences of a war with the English East India Company. Therefore, it would not be easy to justify saying that Guru Gobind Singh dreamt of an empire and Ranjit Singh fulfilled that dream.
4. Chopra, G.L., *Chiefs and Families of Note in the Punjab,* vol. 2, Lahore, 1940, p. 242.
5. Chopra, Gulashan Lall, *The Panjab as a Sovereign State (1799-1839),* 2nd edition, Hoshiarpur, 1960, pp. 5-6.
6. Dua, J.C., *British Historiography Eighteenth Century Punjab : Their understanding of the Sikh struggle for power and role of Jassa Singh Ahluwalia,* Delhi, 1992, pp. 5-8.
7. Gordon, Stewart, *The New Cambridge History of India II. 4 The Marathas 1600-1818,* Cambridge University Press, 1993, p. 139.
8. Lyall, Sir Alfred C., *The Rise and Expansion of the British Dominion in* India, London, 1914, p. 154.
8. Letter from the Right Honourable the Governor General to the Court of Directors, dated Fort St. George 3rd August 1799, *Mysore State Papers: Selection,* vol. II, Mysore, 1922, pp. 113-149. Wilks, Lieut. Colonel Mark, *Historical Sketches of the South of India in an attempt to trace the History of Mysore...* 1810, Mysore 1932, pp. 633, 656, 699.
9. Singh, Khushwant, *A History of the Sikhs,* Oxford, 1963, vol. I, pp. 187-91. Malik, Ikram Ali, *The History of the Punjab 1799-1947,* reprint, Delhi, p. 4.
10. Chopra, Gulshan Lall, *The Punjab as a Sovereign State (1799-1839),* Hoshiarpur, 1960, 2nd edition, p. 31.
11. Griffin, Sir Lepel, *Ranjit Singh (Rulers of India* Series), Oxford, 1892, p. 171.
12. Sohan Lal, *Umdat-ut-Tawarikh* (in Persian), Lahore, 1885, *Daftar* II, p. 60. It is a large and important history of the Sikhs, divided (in its final form) into five *daftars* and extending from the time of Guru Nanak to the author's own time (to 1831) extending upto 1849 in the published edition.

13. *Ibid.;* Captain Wade to the Resident at Delhi 1st August 1827; and Captain Wade to the Governor General 31st May, 1831 National Archives of India, New Delhi, *Foreign/Political Consultation Files* 125/33 and 126/22.

14. Aitchison, C., *Collection of Treaties Engagements and Sunnuds Relating to India and Neighbouring Countries,* Calcutta, 1892, Vol. VIII, p. 160. Griffin, Lepel H., *op. cit.,* p. 170.

15. Griffin, Lepel H., *op. cit.,* p. 167.

16. Mufti Ali-ud-Din, *Ebratnamah (Ebtatnamah wa Umadut-ul-Tawarikh),* 1854, Ed. By Muhammad Baqir, Lahore, 2 vols. 1961, pp. 224-227. Cunningham, J D, *History of the Sikhs from the Origin of the Nation to the Battles of Sutlej,* London, 1853, pp. 130-37.

17. Mufti Ali-ud-Din, *Ebratnamah,* pp. 227-28. Baqir, Muhammad, *Lahore Past and Present (Being an account of Lahore compiled from original sources),* Indian Reprint, Delhi, 1993, p. 203.

18. Mufti Ali-ud-Din, *Ebratnamah,* pp. 228-29. Baqir, Muhammad, *Lahore Past and Present (Being an account of Lahore compiled from original sources),* Indian Reprint, Delhi, 1993, p. 203-4.

19. Banerjee, A.C., *Anglo-Singh Relations,* Calcutta, 1949, p. 19.

20. Sinha, Narendra Krishna, *Ranjit Singh*, Calcutta, 1960, pp. 24-25. French replaced the British influence in Persia and Turkey. In May 1807, the Treaty of Finkenstein was signed between France and Persia. Turkey did not conclude any anti-British alliance, but there, too, France replaced England as the most favoured power. The Treaty of Tilsit was signed in July 1807, whereby Napoleon and the Czar of Russia agreed to make a joint invasion of India.

21. *Ibid.,* p. 26.

22. Kaye, J.W., *The Life and Correspondence of Charles, Lord Metcalfe, Governor-General of India, Governor of Jamaica, and Governor-General of Canada; from Unpublished Letters and Journals Preserved by Himself, His Family and His Friends,* 2 Vol., London, 1854, I, p. 251.

23. Kaye, J.W., *Selections from the Papers of Lord Metcalfe; Late Governor-General of India, Governor of Jamaica, and Governor-General of Candana,* London, 1855, p. 12.

24. *Ibid.,* p. 13.

25. National Archives of India, New Delhi, *Foreign Secret Consultations,* November 28, 1808, No. 4.

26. *Ibid.*

27. National Archives of India, New Delhi, *Foreign Secret Consultations,* January 2, 1809, No. 2, 94.

28. *Punjab Government Records, Ludhiana Agency, 1808-15*, vol. II, p. 37, A: Seton to Ochterlony, January 23, 1809. "The mere non-exercise of a power, while unaccompanied by any declaration, can never be considered as tantamount to the relinquishment of the right of exercise."

29. Sinha, Narendra Krishna, *op. cit.,* p. 28.

30. *Punjab Government Records, Ludhiana Agency, 1808-15,* vol. II, p. 1. Edmonstone to Ochterlony, November 14, 1808.

31. Sinha, Narendra Krishna, *op. cit.,* p. 25.

32. *Punjab Government Records, Ludhiana Agency, 1808-15,* vol. II, p. 45, Edmonstone to Ochterlony, January 30, 1809.

33. *Punjab Government Records, Ludhiana Agency, 1808-15,* vol. II, p. 1.

34. Kaye, J.W., *Selections from the Papers of Lord Metcalfe; Late Governor-General of India, Governor of Jamaica, and Governor-General of Canada,* London, 1855, p. 20.

35. *Ibid.*

36. *Ibid.*, p. 13.

37. *Ibid.*, p. 15. Written by Metcalfe for Lord Hastings in 1814.

38. *Punjab Government Records, Ludhiana Agency, 1808-15,* vol. II, p. 8, Edmonstone to Seton, Resident at Delhi, December 27, 1808.

39. *Ibid.*, p. 79.

40. *Ibid.*, vol. II, Edmonstone to Ochterlony, December 29, 1808.

41. *Foreign Secret Consultations,* January 23, 1809, No. 2.

42. *Punjab Government Records, Ludhiana Agency,* vol. II, p. 46.

43. Mufti Ali-ud-Din, *Ebratnamah,* pp. 228-29. Baqir, Muhammad, *Lahore Past and Present (Being an account of Lahore compiled from original sources),* Indian Reprint, Delhi, 1993, p. 203-4.

44. Chopra, Gulshan Lall, *The Panjab as a Sovereign State (1799-1839),* Hoshiarpur, 1960, 2nd edition, p. 40. The Treaty of Amritsar 25th April, 1809 runs as follows:—

1. The two governments will maintain friendly relations each other and while the British Government will have no concern with the territories to the North east of Sutlej. Ranjit Singh will never again think of crossing river Sutlej and to capture the *cis*-Sutlej States.

2. All the *cis*-Sutlej States will be under the protection of the British Government. The Maharaja was called an independent ruler of the Punjab and was within the list of the favourite friends of the British East India Company.

3. The Maharaja was not to maintain more than the required number of soldiers and he was never again to think of attacking the territories beyond river Sutlej which was declared the boundary line between the two empires.

4. Neither of the two States was to keep a large army on the borders of river Sutlej.

If the Maharaja violated any of the clauses the British Government was no more to consider the treaty in practice and the British Government had every right to march upon the territories of the Punjab.

Ranjit Singh signed it on the 25th day of April 1809 and the British Government represented by C.T. Metcalfe. Aitchison, C., *Collection of Treaties Engagements and Sunnuds Relating to India and Neighbouring Countries,* Calcutta, 1892, Vol. VIII, p. 164.

The Treaty left Ranjit Singh in possession of the tracts he had occupied to the south of the Satluj before the arrival of Metcalfe's mission. The friendly clauses were added according to the Governor-General's final instruction, and in conformity with the Maharaja's special desire and request. See, [22] Kaye, J.W., *The Life and Correspondence of Charles, Lord Metcalfe Governor-General of India, Governor of Jamaica, and Governor-General of Canada; from Unpublished Letters and Journals Preserved by Himself, His Family and His Friends,* 2 Vol., London, 1854, I, p. 308.

45. Grover, B.R., 'Political and Social Situation of Punjab after Ranjit Singh Era', Punjabi Academy, Delhi, *Maharaja Ranjit Singh Memorial Lecture*, 9th October, 1992.

46. Grewal, J.S., *The New Cambridge History of India II.3 The Sikhs of the Punjab*, Cambridge University Press, 1990, pp. 101, 103.

47. Chopra, Gulashan Lall, *The Punjab as a Sovereign State (1799-1839)*, 2nd edition, Hoshiarpur, 1960, pp. 41-42. Malik, Ikram Ali, *The History of Punjab 1799-1947*, Indian Low Price Publication, Delhi, 1993, p. 16.

48. Sinha, Narendra Krishna, *op. cit.*, pp. 77-8.

49. Wadhni, to the south of river of Satluj, had been transferred by Ranjit Singh to his mother-in-law, Sada Kaur, in 1808. The English Agents at Ludhiana and Ambala treated her as an independent head of the Kanhiya Misl, and they now wanted to protect her possessions on the left bank of the river. The occasion for this arose from a quarrel with her son-in-law. The Prince, whose troops occupied the fort of Wadhni, imprisoned her. On this, the Agent at Ludhiana ordered English detachment to eject the Sikhs. This was done. Ranjit Singh prudently avoided a collision; but, growing apprehensive of his neighbour's policy, he began defensive preparations within his own territory, as well as presenting matters to the Governor General. The latter recognized the Agent's mistake and receded from the position, which had been taken up.

50. In 1825-26 certain complications threatened to arise between Ranjit Singh and the Company, owing to the flight of Fateh Singh Ahluwalia and Kutub-ud-Din Khan of Kasur across the Satluj; but they soon afterwards returned to the Punjab and the excitement subsided. The attitude of the English in this affair was entirely reasonable.

51. Sethi, R.R., *The Lahore Darbar: In the Light of the Correspondence of Sir C.M. Wade (1823-1840)*, The Punjab Government Record Office Publication, Monograph No. 10, Simla, 1950, Chapter IV and p. 18 fn.

52. *Ibid.*, p. 21.

53. Ranjit Singh later expressed his disappointment when the Gurkhas were driven out of the neighbouring region as per the Treaty of Sagauli (1816) after the Anglo-Napalese War. See Garrett, H.L.O. & Chopra, GL (tr. & ed.), *Events at the Courts of Ranjit Singh (1810-1817)*, (reprint), The Punjab Government Record Office Publication, Monograph No. 17, Language Department, Punjab, Patiala, 1970, p. 191.

54. Ranjit Singh told Osborne some year later that at the time the British army was marching against Bharatpur he had an army in arms preparing for an expedition to Kashmir. The Bharatpur chief offered him 1,00,000 rupees for every day's march and 50,000 rupees for every day he remained with him, if he would bring 20,000 troops to his assistance. Osborne, W.G., *The Court and Camp of Runjeet Singh, with an Introductory Sketch of the Origin and Rise of the Sikh State, London*, 1840, p. 45.

55. Cunningham, J.D., *History of the Sikhs from the Origin of the Nation to the Battles of Sutlej*, London, 1853, p. 193.

56. Wade, C.M.Lt.Col, *A Narrative of the Services: Military and Political*, London, 1847, pp. 17-18. Chopra, Gulshan Lall, *The Panjab as a Sovereign State (1799-1839)*, 2nd edition, Hoshiarpur, 1960, pp. 44-46.

57. Bisheshwar Prasad, *The Foundations of India's Foreign policy: 1860-1882*, Delhi, 1967, pp. 7-8.

58. The terms of the treaty were:

Ranjit Singh was to help Shah Shuja in restoration to the throne of Kabul. The three parties *i.e.*, the Britishers, Shah Shuja and Ranjit Singh agreed to the following terms:—

(1) Shah Shuja and his successors were never again to claim territories on either bank of river Indus. He was also to disclaim his rights on the regions of Peshawar. Ranjit Singh was thus confirmed by the Afghan ruler in his possessions of Peshawar.

(2) Both the sides agreed not to disturb the border regions, to discourage the unruly element, which might create a trouble in the neighbouring State. Neither of the two sides was to give shelter to the absconders and the robbers of the other country. Ranjit Singh was to have the waters of the streams of Khaiber for his fort of Fateh Garh.

(3) The Maharaja was to have a full control over river Sutlej as far as it stretched his territories and no body was to be allowed to travel through the regions without a passport of the Punjab Government.

(4) Shah Shuja was to agree to all those decisions, which had been arrived at between the British Government and Ranjit Singh over the question of Sind, and he was to no more claim his supremacy over the said regions.

(5) After his accession to the throne of Afghanistan Shah Shuja was to supply horses, mules and other articles as required by Ranjit Singh.

(6) All the three powers were to address one another on the principle of equality and none of the three was to consider the other as subordinate to it.

(7) The merchants from Afghanistan were to be allowed to come to the regions of Lahore and Amritsar to exchange trade with them. The Maharaja was to assure them their safety and none of them was to be molested within the territories of the Maharaja. The Maharaja was to send several articles like Shawls, Comkhab, Dopatas, Turbans and Bara-rice in exchange for the articles he imported from Afghanistan.

(8) When the soldiers of the two countries or the men of the two countries had a meeting they were to abstain from the slaughter of the kine.

(9) Both the countries were to have frequent exchange of mission, (may those be like that of the days of Jahangir).

(10) There was to be a mutual help to one another in case any of the country was facing an internal rising or an external attack.

(11) Enemies of the one country were to be considered enemies by the other. They were never to join in an engagement which directly or indirectly were organized against the other.

(12) The Maharaja was to have an amount of Rs. 2 lakhs from the ruler of Afghanistan for the help of 5000 soldiers, which he was to give to the latter.

(13) None of three powers was to have any ascendancy or right over the Amirs of Sind.

(14) Shah Shuja was not to attack the regions of Herat.

(15) Shah Shuja was not to have any relations with other powers of the world without permission of Ranjit Singh and the British Government.

All the three powers agreed to the terms and none of them was to go against the writ.

Aitchison, C., *Collection of Treaties Engagements and Sunnuds Relating to India and Neighbouring Countries*, Calcutta, 1892, Vol. VIII, pp. 252-53.

59. M'Gregor, W.L., *The History of the Sikhs; containing The Lives of the Gooroos; The History of the Independent Sirdars, or Missuls, and the Life of the Great Founder of the Sikh Monarchy, Maharajah Runjeet Singh*, 2 vols., London, 1847, reprint, Patiala, 1970, II, p. 35.

60. Sinha, Narendra Krishna, *op. cit.*, pp. 88-89.

61. *Ibid.*, p. 90.

62. M'Gregor, W.L., *The History of the Sikhs;. . . op. cit.*, p. 33.

63. *Tawarikh-e-Panjab*, by Bute Shah *alias* Ghulam Muhiy-ul-din Aman, written in July 1848, Khalsa College, Amritsar, f. 403.

64. Gulshan Lall, *The Punjab as a Sovereign State (1799-1839)*, 2nd edition, Hoshiarpur, 1960, p. 49.

65. 279. An account of the Vazir's (Nawab Asafu'd-Daulah's) overtures to the *Khalsa* Sikh Chiefs for an alliance against the Rohillas, dated September 20, 1776; and 280. From Nahar Singh, Chief of the Gujars, dated September 20, 1776, National Archives of India, New Delhi, *Calendar of Persian Correspondence*, vol. V, 1778-88, pp. 41-42, and 42-43.

66. Dua, J.C., *British Historiography Eighteenth Century Punjab: Their understanding of the Sikh Struggle and Role of Jassa Singh Ahluwalia*, New Delhi, 1992, p. 117.

I am grateful to late B.R. Grover, my teacher & mentor, for having provided me some of the original sources, translation and interpretations of the Persian sources.

9

Socio-Economic And Cultural Life of The People Under the Rule of Maharaja Ranjit Singh

Maharaja Ranjit Singh rose from a petty *Sardar/Chief* of Gujranwala to a mighty ruler of extensive kingdom. The kingdom established by Maharaja Ranjit Singh (1799-1839 AD) covered all the territories of the erstwhile Mughal *subah* of Punjab[1], Kashmir, Multan, some of trans-Indus *ilaqas* of *subah* Kabul viz., Peshawar, Kohat, Bannu and few tribal Kingdoms. On the eastern side, the Chiefs of *cis*-Sutlej territories viz, the chiefs of Malwa and Sirhind being under the British protection remained outside the territorial boundaries of Ranjit Singh[2].

The capture of the territories beyond the river Indus was all the more significant, as Ranjit Singh was the first after Anangpal to do so. There was recurring stream of invasions from the northwestern covers of India around eight hundred years ago. Maharaja Ranjit Singh like Anangpal had also subdued and governed a fairly good amount of territories in that region. As such, Ranjit Singh, to a large extent, fulfilled the cherished dream of Guru Gobind Singh, *viz.,* the unity of all the Sikhs under the "commonwealth of Gobind"[3]. He was able to bring the scattered people of the Punjab under a consistent and uniform system of administration, and was instrumental in evolving a young and vigorous nation. The character of Maharaja Ranjit Singh can be summed up as a valiant soldier and a simple peasant who excelled both at the sword and the plough, a gentle king with a sensitive heart, had deep concerns for his people who had suffered for hundreds of years, and would consider sovereignty as people's preserve with him as its trustee. His social, economic and cultural measures had a human face.

Paper presented at the *Seminar on the Life and Achievements of Sher-e-Punjab Maharaja Ranjit Singh* at Mata Sundari College for Women, (University of Delhi), New Delhi, 26th September, 2001 and published in Dr. Mohinder Kaur Gill (ed.), *Secular Sovereign: Maharaja Ranjit Singh,* Delhi, 2002, pp. 72-85.

As far as history of Punjab is concerned, the period of Maharaja Ranjit Singh (1799-1839) and until its annexation in 1849 have, perhaps, attracted the largest attention of the British and the Indian historians. Several historical accounts in Persian, written both by the Hindu and Muslim historians, had been produced even during the lifetime of Ranjit Singh. Since the Sikh rule was the immediate predecessor to the English rule, it produced a likely temptation for the British writers to produce works on the past history of the Sikh community. In fact, a large number of Indian writers have produced a fairly good number of works both in Persian and vernacular languages. Apart from the above works, we the students of Punjab history, are fortunate enough to have inherited original archival source material in the form of *Khalsa Darbar Records* as well as the Persian correspondence of various categories entitled *Bhandari Collection* preserved at State Archives, Patiala. Moreover, the English reports of various categories are immensely valuable. There are some very good works on Maharaja Ranjit Singh, his successors and on the circumstances that led to the annexation of Punjab by the East India Company. Leaving aside some rare exceptions, very little analytical work has been attempted to cover various aspects of socio-economic and cultural life of the people of the Punjab under Maharaja Ranjit Singh.

In order to have a dependable and accurate picture of socio-economic and cultural life of people especially of the pre-colonial period one has to have a disciplined and objective approach to the subject. Since the gullible mind is always prone to misconceived past historical analysis, more especially on the socio-religious matters, it is imperative that such work should not be influenced by vested political interests. It is also necessary to understand the social and political scenario of the historical phase under analysis. This understanding should be essentially based upon the contemporary source-material and connotations. Extreme caution is required to be adopted against the indiscriminate use of the European terminology in the Indian context. There are supposed to be regional variations in the socio-economic analysis of the Indian society. The problem is, despite having ample of source material in English, Persian and regional languages (Punjabi and Urdu) at our disposal, most of us have carried on the tradition from the British times to bank mainly on the Persian chronicles and English sources. It is extremely inadequate methodology. Unless the full range of source-material available is fully exploited, it would never be possible for us to reconstruct a proper perspective of the social development of the people during Ranjit Singh's period.

In medieval polity hallmark of a liberal state broadly constituted the religious tolerance, equity in taxation and coexistence of different religious communities. Despite a partial deviation in one respect or another, a state could still consider itself to be broad minded and tolerant. Within the limitations imposed by the contemporary social atmosphere as a result of socio-political background of the Durrani rule in the Punjab, Ranjit Singh had been able to establish a liberal and just state. However, he would act according to the demands of the time and keeping in view safety and welfare of the people and the empire. Maharaja Ranjit Singh was far above the caste, creed and religious considerations as far as the matter of appointments of the state was concerned.

Ranjit Singh was of the firm opinion that the Sikhs were most suitable for fighting, the Hindus for the financial matters, and the Muslims for the foreign and diplomatic affairs. If Hari Singh Nalwa was the Marshal of the *Khalsa*, Faqir Aziz-ud-Din was similarly enjoying a position of the foreign minister. Similarly, Misr Dewan Chand, Dewan Moti Ram, Dewan Bhawani Dass were the chief administrators of the revenue affairs of the state[4].

Hugel wrote, "Punjab was safer than India"[5]. These remarks don't seem to be exaggerated ones. Because there was a time when a Sikh was considered synonymous to a "robber"[6], whereas during Ranjit Singh's period very few thefts were heard. It was very seldom that one would hear about those wholesale forays to which the Sikh Sardars were earlier so much addicted[7]. Historians may be tempted to equate Ranjit Singh's period with 'despotism', but if it was so, it was without cruelty[8]. Rather the special interest that the Maharaja took in the affairs of the people, we can call him an enlightened despot.

Not doubt, being a leader of the Sikhs, many expected of Ranjit Singh to take revenge from the Muslims for their past atrocities. He believed in the principles of extinguishing the fire of hatred by broad-minded policy than to follow the policy of persecution. He would rather threaten those people with severe punishments if they talked of a distinction between a man and a man simply over the religious beliefs[9]. If Ranjit Singh had to rule Punjab, he had to evolve a kind of strategy wherein, despite being member of the smallest community in the state, he could take the majority along with him. To do this after a history of more than a century of confrontation with the majority community was almost an impossible task, but Ranjit Singh performed with exemplary success. The question before him was—How to deal with the Muslims? Should he settle old scores? He ruled it out both on ideological and political grounds. While ideologically this would have been inconsistent with the Sikh tradition, politically such a course of action would have been self destructive.

Ranjit Singh did not interfere within the Muslim social practices in any way. Both the police system and the judicial system which had evolved over the preceding centuries were kept intact. Fakir Waheed-ud-din, great grand son of Fakir Aziz-ud-din, Maharaja's Foreign Minister, in his book '*Real Ranjit Singh*' has given a vivid picture about Maharaja's secular commitments and policies. He has described that among the top ranking Muslim officers there were two Ministers, one Governor and several district officers. There were 41 high ranking Muslim officers in the army, two of them Generals, several of them Colonels and the rest holding important ranks. The revenue administration was mostly in the hands of Hindus and traders were from all communities. The Muslim population of the Maharaja was governed by the Muslim Personal Law while the other communities were covered by their respective codes. It is because of his social vision, his economic measures coupled with his secular outlook that not a single communal riot took place in his reign of 40 years, no conversion, no second-class citizenship, no minority problem.[10]

It is on the record that he stopped the practice of cow slaughter (*gau kushi*), and as a symbol of ascendancy of the *Khalsa*, he put one great restriction on Muslims in regard to the liberty of worship and forbade public calls for prayers (*azan*) at certain significant mosques in some cities. However, it may be pointed out that this prohibition did not begin with Ranjit Singh's reign. The Muslims had been deprived of this right for more than eighty years. As a matter of fact, the Shia Muslim community had been the target of repression and intermittent persecution during the Afghan rule and even earlier during the later Mughal time[11]. "Ranjit indeed kept it in force, but it was more to maintain his popularity among the Sikhs, and his prestige among the Muslims, than from any special love of the measure"[12]. The period of Ranjit Singh witnessed only one unfortunate communal Shia-Shunni riot (1830-31) which was crushed with an iron hand by the administration.

Even though it is conceded that because of certain social inhibitions of the age, the period of Maharaja Ranjit Singh was not completely secular in the modern sense of the word, it was liberal enough to foster peaceful co-existence amongst different religious communities. With all his limitations, he gave a stable government, which Punjab had not known since the times of the Great Mughals[13]. Ranjit Singh was neither a bigot nor a vain religious dreamer. Although he utilized to the fullest extent the fervour of the *Khalsa* against Muslims in general and Afghans in particular, he was diplomat enough to recognize that the inauguration or encouragement of an avowed policy of persecution would ultimately prove detrimental to his own best interests. He would refrain from interfering with the religious right of the different sections of his subjects, nor did he approve of such actions on the part of the governing classes among the Sikhs. He tried to keep in check the fanatical tendencies of the *Akalis,* and entrusted some of the most responsible positions in his government to Muslims[14].

Though in line with the Mughal practice and continued by the Sikh Sardars, Ranjit Singh's charities are also fairly well recorded by his contemporaries[15]. He was rather typical Sikh ruler in this respect. The practice of granting revenue free lands or making cash payments to individuals or institutions of various religious communities covered under various nomenclature i.e. *madad-i-maash, aimma, muafi* and *waqf* for philanthropic, charitable and educational purposes. Ranjit Singh, as a matter of fact, had set up the department of *Dharamarth,* which maintained regular records under different heads of *dharmarth.* The assignment of revenues of the villages in kind or cash were made to religious persons viz., *Imams, Khadims* (attendants), *muzawars* (holy persons), *faqirs,* Pandits as well as institutional establishments of mosques, *khankas,* temples, *tiraths,* and *dharamasalas.* The grantees included all the religious communities and their sects. The beneficiaries were the Sunni adn Shia (Muslims) as well as the Hindus, more especially the *Udasis* of the *Nanak Panth.* The administration of Ranjit Singh was quite liberal in the *dharmarth* grants. Even the grants prevalent in the Afghan period, with rare exception, were renewed by the *Khalsa Darbar*[16].

Under Ranjit Singh's rule "every land holder was treated as equal, being regarded as a revenue producing machine"[17]. Even the tenants were treated essentially like proprietors. So long as the tenants paid the revenue to the state and charges due to the village or the proprietor, they were not ejected from their lands. Ranjit Singh's land revenue system and his agricultural policy revolved around the cultivator and the peasant. The cultivator during his period was the most important man and citizen whereas the tiller was most favoured individual.

"The Maharaja knew by heart the names of thousand of villages of his empire together with their cash crop, flora and fauna, population and produce."[18] Maharaja Ranjit Singh made all round attempts to promote agriculture and its production which resulted into the reduction of prices of food grains throughout Punjab.[19] The Lahore *Darbar* was keenly interested in the extension of the irrigation facilities to the cultivators for the development of agricultural economy. "Large productive lands are watered by never failing springs of the Himalayas which swell into the Punjab streams capable of bearing their largest vessels and favoured with delightful climate. People are happy and there is plenty to eat." Ranjit Singh would induce the people to dig new and restore old canals, and bring in cultivators from neighbouring areas. A *chakdar* would acquire his rights in the land by having sunk the well. A *chakdar* was generally a trader who built a well with his own capital. He also had the right to get his land cultivated by tenants[20]. He commenced the system of revenue remissions for the introduction of improvements by the peasantry. During the days of draught, Ranjit Singh did not collect any land revenue. He not only remitted the land revenue but even opened relief centres in temples and mosques of respective regions and distributed two times meals to the people free of charge. Whereas for flooded lands, a moderate share of produce was taken in kind. He would also make advances to the cultivators for carrying on their programmes[21]. Moreover, there were three distinct types of land tenures—*zamindari, pattidari* and *bhaichara.*

The members of the village community especially the professionals like the priests, cobbler, cotton-stuffer, tailor, water-carrier, barber, washermen, potter, carpenter and blacksmith etc. who were indispensable persons for the agricultural families, were paid allowance of grain per plough for their professional assistance[22]. The *Punjab Government Records* have recorded, "On the average, the blacksmith, the carpenter, the barber and the water carrier received one maund per plough; the potter, the washermen, the bearer, the sweeper, the guide, the police informer and musician received 20 seers per plough; the tailor received 15 seers per plough, the cotton suffer, the cloth stamper, the dyer and the messenger received 10 seers per plough, and the Brahmin received 3/4 seer per plough"[23].

The Punjab under Maharaja Ranjit Singh had a well established integrated pattern of commercial life. Though the concept of village self sufficiency could no longer be maintained in the developed regions, the group of adjacent villages were dependent on the local *mandis* for commercial crops and non-agricultural products. *A qasba* was also the main commercial centre of the rural areas. The organizations of the *banjara* communities, as in many other parts of India, though sometimes with different nomenclature, played an important role in the statewide trading. The *Hundi* system was an integral part of the commercial life of the Punjab[24]. The stable government in the Punjab overcame the havoc caused by the turbulent conditions of the 18th century to the commercial set up and the trade routes. The period of Ranjit Singh witnessed the resumption of discarded trade routes. While the Maharaja had dreams of exporting goods to foreign countries (though that dream could not be realised because of his inability to have access to Sind), trade within Punjab and the neighbouring areas was consistently promoted. The Punjab during his period came to be recognized by its trade and industry. The small towns like Amritsar, Gujranwala, Gujarat, Wazirabad and Phillaur were, during his period converted into centres of trade, commerce and industry.

While the already big trade centres like Lahore, Multan and Peshawar acquired international status in industry.[25]

Ranjit Singh's period was marked by the tone of cultural life being set by thinkers, poets and *Kissa* writers. This was the period when Waris Shah's *Hir* was written. No literary work of the earlier period had projected the concept of the Punjab so pointedly, and so compellingly as this particular long poem had done. This also signifies the fact that even when fighting was going on all around, things were happening on the literary and cultural plane at the same time. There was the slow emergence and some degree of definition of a Punjabi identity. There was a certain amount of flowering of that new culture which was beginning to unfold at that time. Its strong characteristic was that its leadership lay with those Muslim writers who had been able to work out a synthesis of a mode of thinking and expression which was a blend of the indigenous elements as also the Islamic elements. The *Kissa* poetry represented by Waris Shah and several others as well as the distinct mystic elements represented by the poetic tradition of Sheikh Farid and Buleh Shah emerged into a broad and vigorous stream of literary creation.

A very authentic and important picture about the socio-cultural life of the people of Punjab during the period of Maharaja Ranjit Singh can be drawn with the help of Mufti Ali-ud-Din's *Ibrat Nama* (1854)[26], Rae Kali Rai and Lala Tulsi Ram's work, *Kitab-i-Sair-i-Punjab*[27], Ganesh Dass Badhera's *Chahar Bagh-i-Punjab*[28], the *Vars* and the *Kissas.* Contrary to the general nature of the medieval chronicles, which mostly deal with the political history, the *Ibrat Nama* has extensively dealt with the social life of the common people during the period under study. The importance of this work can be gauged by the fact that the later English works like Ibbetson's *A Glossary of Tribes and Castes of Punjab, Griffin and Massey's Chiefs and Families of Note* and Richard Temple's *Legends of the Punjab* and various other works are mostly based upon it. This work written in Persian and published in Pakistan, has so far, not been translated into English or any other regional languages in India or Pakistan.

For the consumption of this Paper only a gist of the detailed information about the socio-cultural aspects of Punjab during Ranjit Singh's period is being mentioned here The society, according to Mufti Ali-ud-Din comprised of three major groups of people viz. The Muslims, the Hindus and the Sikhs. According to him Muslims formed nearly two-third of the entire population. They were soft spoken, courteous and brave, were mostly fond of sports, like horse riding and fighting, and keeping guns, swords, spears, daggers and *nachakhs.* They were economically backward, and had social segregation and stagnation. The main reasons given by *Mufti* were their laziness and lack of initiatives for accumulation of wealth. Despite being literate, they showed fanatic attachment to Laws of *Shariat*, and despite lack of financial resources never gave up their claims for the plurality of wives. The author further wrote that the *Akalis* and the *Nihangs* among the Sikhs equally matched their fanaticism. They would never eat food cooked by a Sikh. These traits would certainly account for their economic backwardness and aloofness from the general social life[29].

Ibrat Nama is equally critical about the Hindus and their watertight compartments due to caste system. Not only this , there were distinct subdivisions even amongst the Brahmins. They were not free from ordinary social vices of sex and greed. They had strong aversion to army service. The *khatris,* the business class, though prosperous, lacked sense of morality in business and hospitality. Accumulation of wealth was their main priority. They would marry their children at a very tender age of 6 to 10 years. They were equally averse to military service. The *vaishyas* and the *shudras* mostly continued their normal traditional ways of life[30].

The Sikhs, according to Ali-ud-Din, generally divorced themselves from the rituals that the Brahmins had thrust upon the Hindu society. Professionally they mostly took to agriculture and invariably joined army. Many of them belonged to the *zamindari* clans. Though meat was their staple diet, they would never eat meat of any animal slaughtered by a Muslim. On meeting somebody, they would utter *Wahe Guruji Ki Fateh.* In the morning hours, they would recite only the Guru's *Bani,* i.e., *Japji* and the *Sukhmani.* A large number of those who embraced Sikhism called themselves *Singh Guruji Ka* and were engaged in the trade. They were fond of wearing arms and, if could afford, riding horses and elephants. They made an extensive use of *Gurumukhi* and wrote in that script. The section of the Sikhs known as the *Akalis* and *Nihangs* were extremely fanatics[31].

The information given in the *Ibrat Nama* can be, to a fairly large extent corroborated by *Kitab-o-Sair-i-Punjab, Vars and kissas.* These sources also provide comprehensive account of the religious beliefs and practices, food habits, dress, amusements and recreation, fairs and festivals and customs and traditions of the common people of Punjab during the period under discussion.

No doubt Persian was the court language of the Lahore *Darbar*, the common people, irrespective of their religious beliefs, (Muslims, Hindus and Sikhs), spoke Punjabi and wrote it both in Arabic and *Gurumukhi* script. It was in 1882 that the British government, as an official vernacular language, introduced Urdu. It was, by and large against the wishes of a large section of the Punjab society.

In the end it may be emphatically reiterated that right from the 16th century down to at least the mid 19th century, the *Nanak Panth* was regarded as an integral part of the Hindu society. Despite being distinct from other Hindu faiths[32], it remained within the Hindu socio-religious structure. After the annexation of Punjab. British administrators, while writing their memoranda and reports in English language, started giving connotations to the existing technical aspects of socio-religious orders, made Sikhism as distinct from Hinduism.

It seems that Ranjit Singh, because of his social, cultural and populistic ideas and policies, still continues to be a popular figure amongst the village folks. To quote Waheed-ud-din, "Ranjit Singh still lives, large as life, in the imagination of his people. He does so not where the Sikhs live now but also where they lived before, for the Muslim village-folks shared with him as a legendary figure with the Sikhs and they have not let him depart with them latter. The image that persists of him is that of a popular king well known to his people through his frequent appearances in their midst, ready to listen to him and to redress their grievances at all times, and looking upon all his subjects, irrespective of caste and creed, with one eye. That the one eye in his case was literally so seems to have been the subject of innumerable good-natured jokes, which it is said, he would not only ask people to repeat in his hearing, but to which he himself contributed. There are even stories of this physical defect of his having been hurled at him with impunity by common people to drive home to him some grievances which they had but had he had not redressed personally. It is immaterial whether these stories are true or false. They can only have gained currency because they fit in with Ranjit Singh's reputation."[33]

References

1. The boundaries of *subah* Punjab or *subah Lahore or Wilayat-i-Punjab* or *Darul Saltanat* Lahore extended from the river Sutlej in the east to the river Indus (Sind) in the north-west. The whole *subah* comprised of five *doabs* or *sarkars viz.* Bet Jalandhar, Bari, Rechna, Chenhat and Sind Sagar. Moreover, some hilly regions to the north of Bet Jalandhar not covered in the *doabs* entitled as *Berun-i-Panjnand* also formed part of the *subah.* The mountainous regions (*parganas*) to the north of the *doabs* formed the respective *doabs* or *sarkars.* However, the core of the Punjab was the Bari *Doab* with headquarters at Lahore. By the end of 17th century, five *parganas* of *subah* Multan were also transferred to *subah* Punjab. At the same time, Bari, Rechna and Sind Sagar *doabs* with *mahals* beyond the five rivers of Multan territories continued to form the part of *subah* Multan.

2. Maharaja Ranjit Singh also possessed forty-five *t'aaluqas* in the cis-Satluj territory. These territories broadly included Ludhiana and Ferozepur as well as areas lying between river Satluj and Beas inclusive of the hilly regions. The Lahore Darbar, as per the treaty of 9th March 1846, perpetually ceded these

territories to the English East India Company. Aitchison, C., *Collection of Treaties Engagements and Sunnuds Relating to India and Neighbouring Countries*, Calcutta, 1892, Vol. VIII, p. 160.

3. No doubt, Ranjit Singh was a great organizer, but the kingdom of Punjab of which he became the ruler, had been inspired by Guru Gobind Singh. However, a critical assessment of the history would reveal that the dream of the Guru was far from fulfilled, as he wanted a united government of the Sikhs, As per Guru Gobind Singh's popular saying, "*Waho Waho Gobind Singh, Ape Guru Chela*", all the Sikhs including himself were equal.

   Guru Gobind Singh had ordained a democratic setup but Ranjit Singh was not a true believer of democracy. He had abolished *Gurumatta* and had himself become the central authority. There is well-known saying in the Sikh literature that if the powers of the Guru were 20 points, the power of assembly of the Sikhs was 21. Guru Arjan Dev had refused to marry his son Har Gobind to the daughter of Chandu Shah due to the opposition of the Sikhs. (see for example, Gian Singh Giani, *Tawarikh Guru Khalsa,* Part 2 (reprint-first published 1878). Languages Department Punjab, Patiala, 1970). Moreover, Guru Gobind Singh had fought for the depressed humanity of the Punjab, Ranjit Singh's fight was political. Ranjit Singh's word "Sab Lal Ho Jaiga" were not the words of a true Sikh of Guru Gobind Singh but those of a demoralized and degenerated man. Guru Gobind Singh would never give up hopes. Despite having a grand army at his disposal, Ranjit Singh was afraid of the consequences of the war with the English East India Company. There, it would not be easy to justify saying that Guru Gobind Singh dreamt of an empire and Ranjit Singh fulfilled that dream.

4. Chopra, Gulshan Lall, *The Punjab As a Sovereign State (1799-1839),* Hoshiarpur, 1966, pp. 95-118.

5. Hugel, C.A. Von, *Travels in Kashmir and the Punjab,* London, 1844, p. 45.

6. It may here be pointed out that this is a concept usually used from the imperialist view point. Whenever, the revolting *zamindars* or *Sardars* realized the revenue of a particular area after occupation, from the imperialist angle it was described as plunder, loot, pillage, robbery etc. Same is true about the Mughal description about the Marathas and the Sikhs and the British description about the palegars in the south India and the Sikhs in Punjab, etc. See for details—Dua, J.C. *British Historiography Eighteenth Century Punjab: Their understanding of the Sikh Struggle for power and role of Jassa Singh Ahluwalia,* Delhi 1992, p. 114 and 115; and *Palegars of South India: Forms and Contents of their Resistance in Ceded Districts.* Delhi, 1998, p. 50.

7. Masson, Charles, *Narrative of Various Journeys in Baluchistan, Afghanistan, and the Punjab,* 3 vols, London 1842, I, 54.

8. Burners, Alexander, *Travels into Bokhara containing the Narrative of a Voyage on the Indus from the Sea to Lahore,* 3 vols. John Murray, London MDCCCXXXIX, ii, 72.

9. There are several instances to prove this contention. For example, the *Khatris* of Gujarat approached Ranjit Singh and asked him to appoint some Hindu in place of an already appointed Mussalman in the City. He reprimanded them and told them that it was talents and not on religion that an appointment was made in particular territory. He was also very considerate in his attitude towards his officers, when Fakir Aziz-ud-Din opposed the candidature of Hari Singh Nalwa in Kashmir, Ranjit Singh listened to him patiently. Aziz-ud-Din explained that Nalwa was a fanatic and Kashmir would never prosper under his government.

Ranjit Singh cancelled his appointment and instead, sent Moti Ram to take up the charge of Kashmir (1819-1826). Most of the contemporary writers are unanimous that later on when Nalwa was appointed the governor of Kashmir in 1830, his *regime* was generally characterized as oppressive and, as such, did not prove to be successful one. In another important incident, when the Muslims of Lahore approached Ranjit Singh and represented him that they should be allowed to bring out their *tazias* in procession on the day of *Moharram,* Ranjit Singh did not agree and told them that they could observe the same within their houses. They could not be allowed to bring them out in the bazar. The Muslims felt it and when conveyed their grievance through Kharak Singh, he agreed and allowed them to do to their satisfaction. He, thus, yielded when so ever he found the people as justified. See, Hugel, C.A. Von, *Travels in Kashmir and the Punjab,* etc. London, 1854, pp. 254-255; *Tawarikh-e-Mulk-e-Hazara,* by Mehtab Singh copied from the original in 1854, f. 42; *Amir-ul-Imla,* by Dalpat Rai (written about 1800), ff. 70-71.

10. Waheed-ud-din, Fakir Syed, *The Real Ranjit Singh* (4th ed.), Lion Art Press, Karachi, 1965, pp. 53-54.

11. Amir-ul-Imla, *op. cit., Punjab Government Records,* Vol. I (*Delhi Residency and Agency, 1807-1857*), Lahore, 1911, 1847-48, p. 372.

12. Chopra, Gulshan Lall, *The Punjab As a Sovereign State,* Hoshiarpur, 1960, p. 128.

13. B.R. Grover, "Presidential Address", *Punjab History Conference Proceedings,* Patiala, 1986.

14. Chopra, *op. cit.,* p. 128.

15. Shohan Lal Suri, *Umdat-ut-Tawarikh,* Daftars I-IV, New Imperial Press, Lahore, 1887-89, II, 215, 261, 267, 314, 322 etc.

16. For details, see, *Khalsa Darbar Records, Punjab State Archives, Patiala, Bundles B-4 and B-5* (These records contain numerous references to *madad-i-maash* and other *dharamarth* grants); *Foreign/political Proceedings,* esp. 15 October 1852, No. 116, 14 January 1853, Nos. 212-23; 10 June 1853, No. 217, National Archives of India, New Delhi; B.R. Grover, 'Elements of Continuity and Change in Land Ownership and Rights from the Mughal Age to the Early British administration in India', Presidential Address, 37th session, 1976, *Indian History Congress,* Calicut, 1976; B.R. Grover, 'Political and Social situations of Punjab after Ranjit Singh Era', *Maharaja Ranjit Singh Memorial Lecture, Punjabi Academy, Delhi,* 9th October 1992; Irfan Habib, *The Agrarian System of Mughal India (1556-1707),* Bombay, 1963, pp. 298-316; Indu Banga, *Agrarian System of Sikhs; Late Eighteenth to Early Nineteenth Century,* Delhi, 1978, pp. 148-167; and Dua, J.C., *Glossary of Revenue and Allied terms of South India,* Delhi, 1998.

17. Baden Powell, B.H., *The Land Systems of British India: Being A Manual of the Land-tenures and of the Systems of Land Revenue Administration Prevalent in the Several Provinces,* 3 vols., Oxford, At the Clarendon Press, London, MDCCXCII, (1892), 3 vols. (Reprint) ii, p. 635.

18. Jacquemont, Victor, *Letters from India: Describing a Journey in the British Dominions of India, Tibet, Lahore and Cashmere during the years 1828, 1829, 1830, 1831, undertaken by the orders of the French Government* (2nd Ed.), 2 Vols. Edward Churton, London, 1835, I, p. 27.

19. Wheat and rice sold at rupee a maund, barley two maunds and two seers for one Nanakshahi. Barley was sold at 90 seers for one Kashmiri rupee, rice at 48

seers for the same amount. (157 Kashmiri rupees were equal to one hundred Nanakshahi. 20 Seers tin of ghee was available for one Nanakshahi. Superior commodities such as cotton, indigo, silk, sugarcane, poopy, oil seeds were available cheap in abundance. The rates could be very favourably compared with those prevailing even during Akbar's reign. *Punjab Administration Report, 1865-66*, pp. 91-92; *The Ain-i-Akbari* by Abul Fazl, Tr. Blochman and Jarret, II, p. 62; also Brij Narain, *Indian Economic Life, Past and Present*, reprint, Delhi, 1990, pp. 15, 108-110.

20. The terms *chakdar* was derived from *chak,* a circular wooden frame on which the masonry cylinder of a well was built. *Chakdar* was the owner of the *Chak* or well, as opposed to the land attached to well, acquiring certain rights over the produce of the land irrigated from his well. *General Report upon the Administration of the Punjab of the years 1849-50 and 1850-51,* Lahore, 1854, pp. 103-04.

21. Douie, Sir James Mc C., *Punjab Land Administration Manual,* Lahore, 1931, pp. 65-66; *Punjab Famine Commission Enquires Report (1878-1879),* 2 vols., Lahore 1878 and 1879, ii. p. 552; *Papers Connected with the Questions of Tenants Right in the Punjab, Selection from Records of the Government of the Punjab*, Lahore, 1869, p. 67.

22. B.R. Grover, 'The Concept of Village Community in North India during the Mughal Age and The Pre-British Era', *Paper presented at the Institute of Advanced Studies*, Simla in 1966 (seen through the copy given by the author); Satish Chandra, "Some Aspects of Indian Village Community in Northern India during the 18th century', *Indian Historical Review*, Vol. I, No. 1, p. 51.

23. *Punjab Government Records,* Vol. I, Lahore 1911-1915, p. 81.

24. B.R. Grover, 'An Integrated Pattern of Commercial Life in the Rural Society of North India during 17th and 18th centuries', *Indian Historical Records Commission Proceedings,* 34th Session, Vol. XXXVII, Delhi, 1966, pp. 121-153; Bayly, C.A. *Rulers, Townsmen and Bazaars: North Indian Society in the Age of British Expansion, 1770-1870,* OUP, Delhi, 1992, pp. 57-73.

25. Hugel, Baron Charles, *Travels in Kashmir and the Punjab* (tr. & ed. by T.B. Jervis), John Petheram, London, 1845, p. 72.

26. Mufti Ali-ud-Din, *Ibrat Nama,* Ms. SHR 1277, Khalsa College, Amritsar.

27. Rae Kali Rai and Lala Tulsi Ram, *Kitab-i-Sair-i-Punjab,* tr. Punjabi and ed. Giani Lal Singh and Fauja Singh, *Punjab di Sair,* Punjabi University, Patiala,1971.

28. Grewal, J.S. and Indu Banga (tr. and ed.), *Early Nineteenth Century Punjab (Ganesh Dass Char Bagh-I-Punjab),* Guru Nanak Dev University, Amritsar, 1975.

29. *Ibrat Nama, op. cit.,* 152-171.

30. *Ibid.*

31. *Ibid.*

32. The Brahmanical order, Vaishnavism, Shaivism, other *bhakti* cults and the socio-religious orders like the Jains, *Jogis (faqirs, i.e. Kanphattas* and *Augars,* etc.).

33. Waheed-ud-din, Fakir Syed, *The Real Ranjit Singh* (4th ed.), Lion Art Press, Karachi, 1965, pp. 80-81.

10

Comparative Position of the Village Headman During the Early British Rule in The Punjab and the Madras Presidency

In this paper the author traces in detail the evolution of the institution of the village headman and his role in the economic and political sphere at the village level.

R.K.G.

The institution of the village headman has served as a link or intermediary between the higher officer and the agriculturists making it convenient for the state to deal with the village affairs through him. This office has been a very ancient, indispensible and more or less hereditary one, originally bestowed on the founder of a village in return for the benefits the state derived from his exertions. This village headman played a very significant role in the economic and at times political matters at the local level. With the establishment of the English rule, notwithstanding certain significant changes in his position, except in the Permanent Settlement areas, where the headman was no longer considered a necessary institution and had thus, been reduced purely to an honorary one, he continued to remain an integral part of the local revenue administration. In this paper a tentative attempt has been made to underline the characteristic difference in the policy and ultimate shape given to this institution by the early English rulers in the Madras Presidency (excluding Northern Circars), one of the first to be brought under a regular settlement and the Punjab, the last.

By the time of the annexation of Punjab, because of vast administrative experience, political authority and military power, the English had attained better position to suppress the armed and recalcitrant elements, if present, rather more easily and effectively. Besides they would not hesitate in

---

Paper presented at *Punjab History Conference*, Patiala, 23rd Session, 1987.

deviating from the position and policy adopted by earlier rulers in a bigger way. Moreover, there is no denying the fact there was great difference in the political conditions and the composition of villages inherited by the English in the Madras Presidency *vis a vis* Punjab.

In the Madras Presidency due to the political disturbance and rapid change of the governments during past many years before the English took over, the village headman, the *patels* (or by whatever name they were known in different parts of the Madras Presidency),[1] taking full liberty of the prevailing situations, had, thereby, assumed the role of political chiefs or *palegars*[2] having the capacity to muster a party of armed personnels at a very short notice.[3] The recalcitrant attitude of the village headmen during the period of political instability had not only helped them in attaining a unique political position, they had also managed to improve considerably their economic condition as well. As a rule, a village headman was remunerated with hereditary land and the previous governments would not allow more then 10% of the revenue as the total *in'am* to both the *patel* and *karnum* (village accountant) in a village.[4] It is also evident from the *Hukamnama-i-Tipu Sultan* that the *in'ams* of the village headmen were fixed according to the customary practices of the region. In fact, all the *in'am* lands pertaining to the headman, *karnums,* other *riaya* as well as relating to the religious assignees like the *devasthans* and Brahmins etc., were regularly measured, assessed and recorded in the *jamabandi* documents.[5] But despite the fact that the *in'am* of the headman even during the Mughal Period "depended on the customary practice and would vary from region to region and at times from village to village,"[6] the variations during the period immediately preceding the English rule had increased in a very disproportionate manner. Thomas Munro, the first principal collector of the 'Ceded Districts'[7] (1800-1807) and later the Governor of Madras Presidency (1820-1827), thought that the variations in the *in'am* lands of the *patels* were mainly because of the frequent changes of the government and lack of proper attention on the part of the previous rulers.[8] The attraction of the *in'am* land was so much that the *patels* would not hesitate to attack their counterpart in the neighbouring villages or even their own relations if they happened to possess any *in'am* land.[9] At times, even the *karnums* would be compelled to allot tracts of the state land and enter that in their accounts as waste.[10] Despite all this, there seems to be a great amount of exaggeration in the views expressed by Thomas Munro that the actual position enjoyed by the *patels* was far more superior to that of the higher classes of zamindars the *deshmukhs* and *deshpandyas* etc.[11] Though, theoretically wrong, due to the lack of a detailed information available for all the regions of the Madras Presidency, it could be surmised that the chaotic conditions during the period immediately preceding the English rule might have temporarily resulted into this type of development in certain areas.

In the Punjab, the English inherited comparatively settled and stable local administrative machinery. As a matter of fact, Maharaja Ranjit Singh, who succeeded the Sikh Sardars and the Afghans had to witness almost similar type of political instability that English witnessed in the Madras Presidency. There is hardly any instance on record regarding the revolt of a village headman against the English rule. On the other hand Maharaja Ranjit Singh had to face such type of resistance in certain areas like Hasan Abdal,[12] Pindi Gheb[13] etc.

The village headman in the Punjab, known as *muqaddam,* was also an important functionary in the machinery of revenue collection who was generally appointed for each sub-division known as *taraf* and/or *patti* of a village.[14] But Ganesh Das writes that the office of the headman was not necessarily an exclusive one and the *chaudhari* of a *tappa* could also be the *muqaddam* of his own village.[15] Maharaja Ranjit Singh and even the earlier Sikh and Muslim rulers used to remunerate the *muqaddams* with the *in'am* or revenue-free lands[16] and/ or in majority of the cases the *pachotra* or 5% of the revenues collected.[17] However, in some cases they used to receive much more indeed. Moreover, Ranjit Singh confirmed several such *in'am* lands given by the earlier rulers.

The early English administrators in the Madras Presidency found that it was an established practice to entrust a village headman with the management of the village and the inhabitants were also used to that. As such, despite certain flaws in the character and working of the *patels,* it was rather impossible to ignore or do without them.[18] Moreover, for the extension of cultivation the influence enjoyed by the *patels* over the *rayats* could be used in a more profitable manner. At the same time English, inspite of accepting them as more capable for making the settlement correctly, never wanted to entrust the *patels* with the power of fixing the revenue lest there should be any room for favouritism until and unless certain checks were imposed upon them.[19] Despite conceding that the revenue settlement of the villages was not possible if full cooperation was not forthcoming from them, they thought it as an administrative and agrarian necessity to at least reduce all those *patels* who had acquired political power to the normal position. Realizing that it was beyond their capacity to convert the *patels* into the most honest village officials, their recently acquired political power was definitely curbed, even by resorting, if necessary, to military action against them. In short, the English retained the institution of *patels* keeping their position and functions precisely on the same footing as in theory they were meant for.[20]

As regards the Punjab, the early English administrators applied the policy of suppression and coercion right from the top down to the most common man. It is very interesting to observe that almost everyone bowed to the dictates of the English without offering any serious opposition. Maharaja Duleep Singh was pensioned off;[21] all the property and other valuables of Maharaja Ranjit Singh were confiscated[22] and the members of aristocracy, especially those who had fought against the English, were deprived of their ranks and estates.[23] Despite strong dissent and ultimate resignation by Henry Lawrence, the *jagirdars* and revenue free grantees were also subjected to unfavourable treatment by the early English administrators. They were out to prevent "any but a small part of it (land tax) going to the coffers of the aristrocracy (and) stood for their destruction."[24] The holdings of these individuals were sealed, records were inspected, oral evidence was taken, their limits were surveyed and the application of the proceeds was tested. The grants, if at all given, were bestowed under the seal of the Board of Administration and Secretary's signature declaring that the grant was a free gift of the British Government.[25] In short, the men of talent and of social or religious influence lost their high positions.[26] In the local administration, corresponding roughly with or in place of earlier *muqaddams,* the early English administrators appointed the *lambardars.* As many villages had several sections, it necessitated the existence of several *lambardars* in a village, thereby losing, to some extent, the advantage of the original representation of many co-shares by one man. In order to cover up this *lacuna* and to lessen the inconvenience caused by the excessive number of *lambardars* as well as to make communication easier, the institution of the office of chief headman or *ala lambardar* in estates with several headmen was created. However, considering that this office had not served any useful purpose, the *ala lambardari* posts were first reduced and in 1909 it was ordered to gradually abolish this system altogether.[27]

As compared to the regions under study, the village headman, for example in the Central Provinces, had also received the name of *lambardar* in place of the *muqaddam* and was either the sole proprietor i.e. the *malguzar* or one of the proprietors whereas in the villages which had two grades of proprietary rights—superior and inferior—there used to be sub-*lambardars* for the inferior body. At the same time the *muqaddams* also continued to exist who were responsible for the executive functions mainly to control and superintend the *patwari* and watchman, their remuneration, to look-after the paths, roadways, survey marks and to report about the state of the village, violation of rules as well as births and deaths.[28] In the North-Western Provinces like the Punjab, the village headman had been renamed as *lambardar.*[29] It is interesting to observe that in the hill districts of the 'Assam Range', the early English administrators, by and large, maintained the *status quo* in respect of the nature and functions of the village headman.[30]

As regards the power, position and the functions of the village headman, in the Madras Presidency, barring the curtailment of his political and military power, he, to a great extent, continued to enjoy the influential position in the village administration. In the eyes of the early English administrators, he was the "natural and permanent authority of the country," and "whoever rules the province they (headmen) rule the village."[31] In the beginning, due to the absence of a detailed survey, when the *mauzawar* or Village Settlement was introduced, the settlement was made with the *patels* of the respective villages and were made severally answerable for the revenue of their own villages and jointly for the whole district. Later, with the introduction of *kulwar* or *rayatwari* system, a *patel* was supposed to manage the whole village but was answerable for the revenue of the land which he occupied and every *rayat* was answerable for his own revenue, though jointly they were made answerable for the revenue of the village concerned.[32] Unlike the Punjab, the village headman in the Madras Presidency did not represent any one in a revenue engagement rather the powers of the *patel* and *muqaddam* were combined in him. He was perhaps better educated, wealthier and more important person than the *lambardar* of Punjab. Apart from aiding in the collection of the revenue, which was ultimately paid through his hands, he was a petty magistrate and civil judge. He was empowered to deal with petty crime, assaults, affrays, etc. and as a village *munsif,* decide suits for money and personal property upto Rs. 20/- in value (without appeal) (whereas with the consent of the parties) (given in writing) could adjudicate, as arbitrator, any claim upto Rs. 200/- in value.[33] Moreover, the early English administrators, reverting back to the old village police system, made the village watchmen who were mostly hereditary, work under the direction of the village headmen. The *patels* were, thus, at the bottom of the police hierarchy and themselves employed the establishment of *taliyaris* or *totis* (village constables) for revenue and police purposes.[34] As such, the village headman in the Madras Presidency was an indispensable and important functionary and an essential part of the village constitution.

The institution of *lambardar* in the Punjab, which was the latest addition in the village administration, existed chiefly for revenue and administrative purposes. The burden of the distribution of land revenue, which was assessed on the village as a whole, was distributed by the co-proprietors themselves. The co-sharers were jointly and severally liable for the payment of the whole revenue. The *lambardar,* on his own account, or jointly with others, or as representative of the whole or part of the proprietary community, engaged with the government for the payment of the land revenue. But as a *lambardar* he was not held responsible for any revenue in arrear due from an actual defaulter as such in this case the former was not treated as defaulter. However, in the North-Western Provinces, both the *lambardar* and the actual holder of the land would become defaulters. In the Punjab, it was the duty of the *lambardars* to acknowledge every payment received from the land-owners and tenants in their *parcha* books. They were also to collect and manage the common village fund and to give an account to the share-holders for all receipts and expenditure. They were supposed to inform the *tahsildar* regarding the deaths of assignees and pensioners and their absence from the village if for over a year, as well as the cases of encroachments on, or injury to the government property, if any. They would also help in carrying out harvest inspections, surveys, the record of mutations and the other revenue business. Above all, they were to assist in providing, of course, on payment, supplies or means of transport for troops and officers of government.[35] Contrary to the *patels* in the Madras Presidency, the *lambardars* in the Punjab were not vested with the magisterial or *munsif* powers. Commenting upon this particular aspect and the difficulties faced by the people of the Punjab under the circumstances, some contemporary English writers on Indian land systems remarked that of late, there had been some movement in the Punjab for the adoption of that kind of agency as a means of settling disputes locally and without kindling ill-feeling and wasting money over pleaders and law suits at head-quarters remote from the village.[36] As regards the system of the police, the *lambardars* once again, did not have much say in this department, as well. The early English administrators had organised the Police force on lines comparable to those in Sind. It consisted of a Military Preventive Police and a Civil Detective Police. The village police was to remain an official apparatus, being brought into direct relationship with the general constabulary.[37] As such, the union of the revenue, judicial and police functions in the *patels* in the Madras Presidency and their absence in the position of the *lambardars* in the Punjab had made the former's position much more distinct and influential as compared to the latter.

As regards the remuneration for the services rendered by the village headmen, prior to the establishment of the English rule in different parts of India, the general practice, by and large, was to grant them a hereditary *in'am* land or *watan*. This is equally borne by the revenue documents and the village records of the 18th century which clearly brings out the proportion of the *in'am* land vested with the *muqaddam* in a village as against the total revenue (*mal-o-jahat, sair* and *jama*).[38] Whereas in the

Madras Presidency, the early English rulers continued, to a great extent, the established practice, a glaring deviation could be found in the Punjab. In the Punjab, the rules provided for the levy of a cess at a rate not exceeding 12½% on the land revenue and canal owner's rate for the remuneration of village officials, i.e., *lambardars, ala lambardars* and *patwaris.* Out of this, the *lambardar* was remunerated by a *pachotra,* or fee of 5%. The *ala lambardars,* if any, got an extra 1%. On account of collections of canal occupier's rate, the headmen usually received an allowance of 3%. In case of all estates, in the Kulu and Saraj *tehsils* of the Kangra district (except Lahul and Spiti) the surcharge amounted to 7% on the land revenue and the *lambardar's* share was Rs. 1% annually. The only saving feature for the headmen was that since they themselves collected their own *pachotra,* it might be doubted whether the rules were always carried out.[39]

In the Madras presidency the remunerations fixed for the *patels* were in the shape of certain percentage of *in'am* lands calculated according to the survey rent fixed by the early English administrators. It has also been computed that more the survey rent of a village less would be the percentage of *in'am* allowed to a *patel* and *vice versa.* For instance, if the survey rent of a village was 50 C. Pagodas the *patel* was allowed a maximum of 8% as *in'am* land and similarly on 500 C. Pagodas 3.60%;on 1000 C. Pagodas 2.80%; on 2000 C. Pagodas 1.90%; on 3000 C. Pagodas 1.43%; on 4000 C. Pagodas 1.20%; on 5000 C. Pagodas 1.06%; and on 6000 C. Pagodas 0.97%. Moreover, the *in'am* allowed was to be inclusive of *marah wartanah* or *mera* i.e., the perquisites from the crops or fees from the revenue or share of the grain. In the case the *in'am* together with *marah wartanah* was less than the approved percentage, the difference was made up but in case the *in'am* exceeded the required sum, a *patel* was permitted to enjoy the whole. However, in the latter case, the excess land was charged according to the official survey rent. At the same time the law did not prohibit a *patel* from taking any amount of land on the usual revenue fixed by the government. The *patel* usually had the best land and often a large central site for the residence, fortified by mud walls.[40]

Like Punjab in other areas, especially, Central Provinces, North Western Provinces and the non-*taluqdari* estates of Awadh the headmen also received *haq-ul-tahsil* @ 5% on the *jama* or the revenue assessment of the village. Where as in Sambalpur they received upto 10% of the *bhogra* land and in the Central India, like the Madras Presidency, the *in'am* lands or *watans* were given to them as remunerations.[41]

Regarding the nature of the appointment of the village headmen, lot of similarities can be found in both, Madras Presidency and the Punjab. In the former areas the headmen enjoyed hereditary position and the early English administrators feared that the change or his removal might put the government in great inconvenience as well as even loss of revenue. Except in the case of misconduct and incapacity, the collector of the area had no authority to remove him from the office, nor could he interfere in the appointment of his successor.[42]

In the Punjab, where the introduction of the *lambardari* arrangement, by and large, coincided with the regular revenue settlement initiated by the early English rulers. There is no doubt that the position of a *lambardar* was hereditary who invariably held the office for life and was often succeeded by his son. Despite the above position, a Deputy Commissioner in the Punjab had enormous and final authority in the initial appointment, succession and dismissal of a *lambardar.* A *lambardar* could be dismissed due to the loss of the status of landowner in the estate, poverty, persistent neglect of duty, and crime. It was at the discretion of the Deputy Commissioner to temporarily allow the mortgagee of the *lambardar's* holding to act as a headman or allow a substitute or *sarbarah* in case of temporary inability of a *lambardar.*[43]

After the early period of English ruler, an attempt was made not only to further curtail the power but even to abolish the post of the village headmen in certain parts of the Madras Presidency. The available records reveal that there was lot of controversy in regard to usefulness of the institution of the *patels* and recommendations were made to abolish all the offices connected with the revenue collection and judicature except that of the *karnums* or *patwaris.* Moreover, the ideas of Lord Cornwallis regarding the separation of the judicial and magisterial powers from that of revenue functions of the collector downwards were also making impact on the minds of the administrators and the Court of Directors. But major portion of the Madras Presidency having different land revenue system i.e., *rayatwari,* the officials from collector downwards had altogether different functions and responsibilities hardly known to their counterparts in Bengal. The Madras Regulations of 1816 not only decided in favour of the continuation of the institution of the *patels* but also put at rest the controversy regarding the powers and functions they were to be vested with, thereby uniting revenue, judicial and police functions at village, taluk and district levels.[44]

The *lambardar* in the Punjab also faced somewhat similar problem and the existence of many of them was thwarted after the early period of English Administration. The administrators there found in inconvenient due to the multiplication of headmen's posts and attempts were made to reduce their number. However, considering the necessity of this institution and inability to lay down universal rules for the reduction of their number, it was insisted upon to look into the history of the past appointments, the constitution of the each estate and the composition of the village proprietary body wherever recommendations for reductions were made. Keeping in view the above pre-conditions, such proposals could generally be made if the *pachotra* of a *lambardar* was less than Rs. 20/- per annum or if the estates were homogeneous as regards caste and tribes. At the same time reduction was not advisable if it was likely to place a considerable number of proprietors of one religion, tribe or caste under a *lambardar* of another *patti* or sub-division of a different religion etc. In short, the estates having several headmen and also the institution of *ala lambardar* were adversely affected resulting into considerable reduction in the number of the *lambardars* and ultimate abolition of *ala lambardari* system.[45]

References

* Dyal Singh College (evening), New Delhi.

1. Some of the other names were: *nattamkar, maniakkaren, monigar, naidu, reddi, poddacapu,* etc.
2. For more details about palegars, J.C. Dua, 'Poligars: Their Rise in the Ceded Districts,' *I.H.C.*, XXXIII (1972), pp. 467-474; also J.C. Dua, 'Nature of the Poligar Revolts in the 'Ceded Districts' during the first half of the 19th century,' *I.H.C.*, Jadavpur, 1974.
3. Tamil Nadu State Archives (TNSA) *William Thackeray's Report on Malabar, Canara and the Ceded Districts, 8 September, 1807,* ASO (D) 66; *Madras Board of Revenue Consultations,* 31st August, 1801, *Col. Munro's Report regarding Poligars in the Ceded Districts with a Memorandum on Poligars 1801-1802,* RSO (D) 66 21), Letter from Thomas Munro to the President and Members of the Board of Revenue, 12 August 1801.
4. *Bellary Records,* 382/4, letter from the Collector of Bellary District to the Board of Revenue, 22nd August, 1817, 384/54, Thomas Munro to the Collector of Adoni, 14 April, 1807, TNSA; also J.C. Dua, 'Position of the Patels and Karnums in the Ceded Districts during the first quarter of the 19th century,' *I.H.C.*, Chandigarh, 1973; also in Sabyasachi Bhattacharya (ed.), *Essays in Modern Indian Economic History*, New Delhi, 1987, pp. 25-40.
5. *Hukamnama-i-Tipu Sultan,* dated, Fasli 1216 (Persian), clause No. 33, folio 4b; clause No. 63, folio 7b, Andhra Pradesh State Archives, Hyderabad.
6. B.R. Grover, 'Nature of *Dehat-i-Talluqa* (Zamindari Villages) and the Evolution of the Taaluqdari System during the Mughal Age; *I.E.S. H.R.*, II, July 1965, p. 259.
7. 'Ceded Districts' constitute the present districts of Cuddapah, Kurnool, Anantapur and the taluks of Madanpali and Vyalpad in Chittor District in Andhra Pradesh and the district of Bellary in Karnatka.
8. *Madras Board of Revenue Consultations,* 24 August 1807; *Col. Munro's Correspondence regarding the survey and rayatwari settlement of the Ceded Districts, 1802-1807,* ASO (D) 79, Thomas Munro to the Board of Revenue, 26 July, 1807, TNSA.

9. *Op. Cit.*, f.n., 3.

10. *Col. Munro's Report regarding the Poligars etc.* RSO (D) 62 (21), Munro to the Board of Revenue, 20 March, 1802, TNSA.

11. *Madras Board of Revenue Consultation,* 26 Sep., 1805; *Selections from the Old Records,* ASO (D) 72, Munro to the Board of Revenue, 25 August, 1805, TNSA.

12. *Foreign/Political Consultations,* 9th January, 1857, No. 229-30, 'Report on the *In'am* Zamindaries in the Rawalpindi District,' N.A.I. The above report indicates that on the conquest of Hasan Abdal, Maharaja Ranjit Singh found that due to the weakness of the Afghan rule each headman had become virtually the master of his village and in many cases he had to give *Chaharam* or one-fourth of the government share of the proceeds in order to get remainder.

13. *Foreign/Political Proceeding,* 7 January, 1853, No. 228. NAI, The headman of Pindi Gheb, because of his local influence for a long time enjoyed ¼th of the revenues.

14. See, for example, Ibbetson, D.C.J., *Final Report of the Revised Settlement of the Karnal District (1872-1880),* Lahore, 1885, pp. 93-94; L.S. Saunders, *Report on the Revised Settlement of the Lahore District (1865-1869),* Lahore, 1873, p. 66.

15. Wadhera, Ganesh Das, *Char Bagh-i-Panjab* (*ed.*, Kirpal Singh), (Amritsar, 1965), pp. 163, 205 and 208.

16. *Foreign/Political Consultations,* 5 September 1856 Nos. 109-15, NAI, 'Statement of *In'am zamindaris* in Purgannah Gurdaspur.

17. *Khalsa Darbar Records,* Bundle 3, Vol. I, 317; Bundle 4, Vol. V, 201-202; Bundle 5, Vol. III, 63-64. (Punjab State Archives, Patiala).

18. *Madras Board of Revenue Consultants,* 5 January, 1807; *Selections from the Records of the Bellary District, Political, Revenue and Agricultural Matters, 1800-1856, ASO* (D) 72, letter from Thomas Munro to the President and Members of the Board of Revenue, 30 November 1806 (TNSA).

19. *Ibid.*

20. *Op. cit.*, f.n. 11.

21. *Foreign Secret Consultation,* No. 21, April 28, 1849, NAI.

22. *Ibid.*, No. 20, April 1849, 'Governor-General's Secret Despatch to the Court of Director's, Para 139.

23. *Ibid.*, Nos. 68-71, May 26, 1849, Nos. 41-42, October 25, 1850.

24. Dutt, Romesh C., *Economic History of India in the Victorian Age* (London, 1903), p. 86.

25. *Calcutta Review,* 1853, Vol. XXI, pp. 269-270, 272.

26. *Foreign Political Consultations,* No. 124, 4, February 1853, NAI.

27. Baden-Powell, B.H., *The Land-Systems of British India, 3 vols.* Vol. II (Oxford, 1892), p. 740; James McC., Douie, *Punjab Administration Manual* (Lahore, 1931), pp. 129, 140.

28. Baden-Powell, *op. cit.,* Vol. I, pp. 152-153; Vol. II, pp. 504-506.

29. *Ibid.*, Vol. II, p. 285.

30. *Ibid.*, Vol. III, p. 453.

31. *The Fifth Report from the Select Committee on the Affairs of the East India Company,* Madras Presidency, Vol II London, 1812 (Madras, 1883), pp. 646-663, Report of Principal Collector of the Ceded Districts, 15 August, 1807.

32. *Bellary Records,* 1806, 301/30, Thomas Munro to William Bentinck, Governor, F.S.G., 8 May 1806 (TNSA).

33. *The Regulations of the Government of Fort St. George in Madras, 1801-34,* Regulation IV of 1816; Bedan-Powell, *op. cit.* (iii), pp. 88-89.

34. *Ibid.*

35. Douie, James, *op. cit.,* pp. 129-30; Baden—Powell, *op. cit.,* Vol. I, pp. 154-55, II, pp. 285-86, 505, 506.

36. Baden-Powell, *op. cit.,* Vol. III, p. 88, f.n. 4.

37. Misra, B.B., *The Administrative History of India, 1834-1947* (Oxford University Press, 1970), pp. 537-38; *District Administration and Rural Development in India,* (1983), p. 36.

38. Dua, J.C., 'The Position and the Role of the Village Headman in the Village Administration of the 'Ceded Districts' during the first half of the 19th century,' Seminar on *Studies in the Socio-Economic History of Deccan—15th to 19th centuries,* Osmania University, Hyderabad, Sep. 7-9, 1977.

39. Douie James, *op. cit.,* pp. 122, 130; Beden-Powell, *op. cit.,* ii, p. 740.

40. Bellary Records 384-85; *Selection from the Records...* ASO(D) 72, Circular issued by Thomas Munro, 14th April, 1807.

41. Baden-Powell, *op. cit.,* Vol. I, pp. 152-154; II, pp. 286-87, 505.

42. *Op. cit.,* f.n. 11 and 18.

43. Douie James, *op. cit.,* pp. 130-136.

44. Dua, J.C. 'The Position and Role of the village Headman...'; B.B. Misra, *District Administration and Rural Development in India,* pp. 38-41.

45. Douie, James, *op. cit.,* pp. 130, 137-140.

11

Comparative Position of the Village *Patwari/Karnum* during the Early British Rule in the Punjab (upto 1885) and the Madras Presidency (upto 1855)

In this paper the author has discussed in detail the position of the village *Patwari/Karnum* in the Punjab and the Madras Presidency upto 1855 and 1885 respectively. The British government made the position of *Karnum* secure regarding appointment, dismissal and remuneration. In *Patwari's* case his position was given a boost in respect of his working conditions and promotions.

P.B.S.

With the growing interest in the regional studies, we have, in the recent years, been presented with a number of valuable studies on the social and economic history of specific regions. But despite significant advancement in the research methodology, comparative village level study and the British policy in the two different regions has not received due attention from historians. The purpose of this paper is to make an attempt to underline the characteristic difference in the position of the village *patwari/karnum*[1] before the establishment of the British control and difference in the policy and ultimate shape given to this institution by the early English rulers in the Madras Presidency, one of the first to be brought under a regular settlement and the Punjab, the last. The paper is based upon the relevant records preserved in the Andhra Pradesh State Archives, Hyderabad, Tamil Nadu State Archives, Madras, Punjab State Archives, Patiala and National Archives of India, New Delhi.

The institution of the village *patwari/karnum* has been of the utmost importance and an essential feature of the land revenue settlement and administration. He has also served as an official chain connecting the village

Paper presented at *Punjab History Conference*, 24th Session, Patiala, 1988.

with the *tehsil/ta'aluqa.* In Punjab the office of *patwari* seems to have been inherited from the medieval administration.[2] The office of the village accountant in the South India, as is evident from the epigraphical sources, seems to have been regularly established during the Chola period.[3]

The main functions of a *patwari/karnum* mainly included the maintenance of the village maps, records of the crops grown; land revenue due and paid by the individual peasants; its payment to the authorities; changes in ownership due to succession and transfer and also recorder of statistics of the village.[4] Notwithstanding certain variations, during the English rule the position of the village accountant as a state official in the non-landlord villages and the servant of the proprietary body in others changed into a government servant, pure and simple, paid, controlled and appointed by the state. Despite the significant changes introduced in the position of a village *patwari/karnum,* except in the permanent settlement areas where he either disappeared or became merely a servant of the landlord, continued to remain an integral part of the local revenue administration.[5]

By the time the English government got the responsibility of introducing regular settlement in the Punjab (1849 onwards), they had attained vast administrative experience, political authority and military power which accounts for their unhesitating deviation from the position enjoyed by the village officials and the policy towards them adopted by the earlier rulers in a bigger way. Besides, there was great difference in the political conditions and the composition of villages inherited by the English in the Madras Presidency *vis a vis* the Punjab.

In the Madras Presidency, generally every village had *karnum* (known as *shenbogue* in Canara, *menon* in Malabar and *kulkarni* in the Deccan). There were cases when some villages had more than one *karnum,* while at times more than one villages shared one *karnum.* The office of the *karnum* though initially not hereditary, had become so in due course of time subject, of course, to the condition that the duties assigned to him were properly performed.[6]

The office of the *karnum* in the Madras Presidency was invariably bestowed on the Brahmins. No doubt the earliest known *karnums* were Goldsmiths, Buddhists and Jains but during the period of successive Hindu kingdoms various categories of Brahmins were introduced in that position and ultimately it was the Niyogi group of Brahmins which became the strongest. The Niyogi influence had increased to such an extent that some of the Golkonda villages witnessed the post named '*Patel-Pattavarie'* which combined the office of headman and accountant in one person.[7]

The *karnum* in Madras Presidency was remunerated by hereditary *manyams* (revenue-free grants) or by lands on very favourable terms or occasionally by *me'ra* (share from the revenue) either in cash or in kind notwithstanding, of course, other privileges and gratuitous services from the village.[8] However, political disturbances and rapid change of governments for many years preceding the English rule had helped the *karnums* in improving their economic status by acquiring considerable amount of land illegally as well and had also developed recalcitrant attitude. During the period of Tipu Sultan, as is evident from the *Hukamnama-i-Tipu Sultan* that all *in'am* lands pertaining to the village officials, other *riaya* and relating to the religious assignees like *Devasthanams* and Brahmins etc., were regularly measured, assessed and recorded in the *jamabandi* document.[9] Moreover, the English reports point out that no previous government would allow more than 10% of the revenue as the total *in'am* to both the *patel* and *karnum* in a village. But variations in the *manyams* enjoyed by the *karnums* as also the *patels* during the period immediately preceding the English rule had increased in a very disproportionate manner. The survey conducted by Thomas Munro shows that their *manyam* was seldom in any uniform proportion to the rent of their respective villages.[10]

The English government in the Punjab inherited comparatively a more settled and stable local administrative machinery than in the Madras Presidency. As a matter of fact, Maharaja Ranjit Singh, who succeeded the Sikh Sardars and Afghans, had already put the administrative structure on a sound footing. The English, in the initial stage, continued with the then existing system of local administration and introduced reforms at a later stage whereas in the Madras Presidency they worked for more than two decades in trying to reduce the local officials to a position for which, in theory, they were meant for.

Contrary to the Madras Presidency, where the Mughal administration was not generally established, in Punjab the framework of the revenue administration units and the administrators in vogue during the Mughal period had, without any substantial change, continued to exist during the Sikh rule. The Mughal administration provided every village with a *patwari* and there was the possibility of one *patwari* maintaining records of more than one village. He was the representative of the peasants, compiler and keeper of the village records and accountant for recording income and expenditure of village. He had also to assist the *pargana* revenue officials in the measurement and assessment work.[10a] During the Sikh period there was, perhaps, hardly a village which had a *patwari* entirely for itself. He usually looked after a *tappa/tope* i.e., a cluster of villages, the number of which varied from region to region. For example, in the Majha, *tappa* consisted of three to eight villages and in Gujranwala, a *patwari* on an average, covered nearly five villages.[11]

As regards the remuneration paid to the *patwari,* as during the Mughal period, it depended upon customary practice and would vary from region to region and at times from village to village. It was paid in the form of a share in the revenue collection made from a village either in cash or kind. Though according to the customary practice the *patwari's* remuneration ranged between 1% to 2%, actually it ranged from .625% to 3.125% of the collection made from the villages under his jurisdiction.[12] Despite the fact that generally the remuneration to be paid to the *patwari* was deducted from the share of the government but there were instances when additional levies were made and the cultivators paid from their own share.[13] Moreover, barring a few exceptions of the *patwaris* being paid in the form of land grants,[14] there is, contrary to the Madras Presidency, hardly any reference of their being paid in the form of hereditary land grants, nor did they enjoy hereditary status, nor was this post confined to a particular section of the society.

One of the common features of the village accountants in the Punjab and the Madras Presidency was that they were notoriously unreliable. In this respect the *karnums* were even better example than the *patwari.* In the Madras Presidency the books on statecraft,[15] folklores etc., in the local languages and number of English reports testify untrustworthy character of the *karnums.* One of the English reports of 1846 revealed that the *karnums* would often prepare three sets of records: one for the *zamindar,* one for the state and the third, the true one[16] This shows that for nearly fifty years the English administrators had been groping in the dark in their efforts to dig out the exact working of the village accountants. In Punjab, because of their experience elsewhere, the English had well guarded themselves. They believed in the maxim, 'Organize your *patwaris,* and your records will organize themselves'. They found that no efficient revenue administration was possible unless the *patwari* staff was strictly and carefully supervised.[17]

The English administrators in the Madras Presidency simply attempted to regulate the office of *karnum* but could not make drastic changes in his position and power. The office of *karnum* in every large village or group of two or three small villages was officially recognised and established according to the Regulation XXIX of 1802. Despite certain objections and reservations on the part of the administrators, the office remained hereditary for pretty long time. The collector was obliged to appoint a son or descendant of a late *karnum,* irrespective of his fitness for employment. The Regulation II of 1802 (Section I & II) prohibited a collector from dismissing a *karnum* without the authority of Board of Revenue. A *karnum* could be suspended or dismissed only due to gross misappropriation in the accounts.[18] In this respect also the government had to compromise with the situations. Inspite of frequent explanations from the *karnums* by the collectors, the maximum that the latter could hope to get was only tolerably accurate accounts, that too, on account of fear of removal or suspension.[19] Even this was not true about all the parts of the Madras Presidency.[20] At the same time government was firm on the point that any land holder would not be allowed to hold the appointment of a *karnum* nor should he be assigned the duties of a headman. In case of emergency it could be possible only after the office of *karnum* had been taken away from him and conferred on some other person.[21]

In the Punjab the English government found that despite sound principles of revenue policy and effective measures been taken to secure the proper performance by the *patwari,* the official machinery was too weak to secure effective compliance and the result was that the revenue statistics remained incomplete and unreliable until the late nineteenth century.[22] It was only after the suggestions and recommendations of the *Indian Famine Commission Report 1880)*[23] that the British Government paid serious attention in this regard and new code of *patwari* and *kanungo* rules was framed.

Continuing with the practice of the Sikh rule, a *patwari,* instead of being appointed to each village, during the English period, was appointed to a uniform and regular circle. It was for the Commissioner to decide the limit of the circle. Due consideration like, the distance to be covered, the nature of area and land tenures etc., was given before limiting the circle. Usually a *patwari's* circle contained 4,000 to 5,000 *Khasra* (i.e. number given to each field in the village map) and 1,200 to 1,600 *Khatauni* numbers (i.e., the number allotted to each cultivator's holding). A circle generally consisted of several adjoining estates. But some large estates had one *patwari* each whereas some had even more than one *patwari* or had an assistant *patwari.*[24]

In Punjab, there was no question of treating the post of a *patwari* as hereditary, though, of course, in some exceptional cases some weightage was given to a relation of the late incumbent provided he was qualified and fit and fulfilled other conditions. A candidate for the post of *patwari* would stand disqualified if he or any of his near relations lent money to the agriculturists in the circle or was engaged in trade or was a tout for any legal practitioner or had borrowed money from agriculturists. Like the Madras Presidency, he could not acquire land in circle except by inheritance and if he possessed the land anywhere during the service he was to report the fact to the *tehsildar.* However, the sons of agriculturists were encouraged to come forward as candidates. A candidate was supposed to have good handwriting, ability to solve simple arithmetic sums quickly and correctly and should have good physique, health and eyesight. In due course of time, with the establishment of better educational facilities, in most of the districts, middle school and *patwari* examination passed had become compulsory qualification and the age limit was fixed between 15 and 25 years. Lot of stress was also given to the teaching of practical character. A *patwari* could be dismissed if he was deeply in debt, as well as, for misconduct, neglect of duty or incompetence. However, an officer not below the rank of a collector had the authority to appoint, punish or dismiss a *patwari.* This aspect is, of course, different from the Madras Presidency where a collector could not dismiss a *karnum* without its reference to the Board of revenue.[25]

After AD 1885, provision for having three different grades of *patwaris* and also of an assistant *patwari* were made.[26] Provision was also made for the promotion of first two categories of *patwaris* to the post of *kanungos* provided they had three years of experience and were below thirty five years of age. Two third of the posts of *kanungos* were to be filled by promoting the *patwaris.*[27]

In both Punjab and Madras Presidency, because of the importance of and clerical work demanded from the *patwari/karnum* it was obligatory not to keep/remain away from the circle/village for more than a minimum period possible. Moreover, one important difference in their functions was that whereas in the Punjab the *patwari* had to correct the maps as boundaries changed, in the Madras Presidency the boundaries had to be kept correct according to the maps.[28]

During the Mughal period the *patwari* usually maintained his records, known as *bahi* or *kaqhaz-i-kham,* in 'Hindwi' or the local language.[29] During the Sikh rule, more or less, same practice seems to have continued. There were instances when the *patwari* simply stood by, while a *munsarim* wrote the returns and forms for him. It was only in 1885 that the books entitled *Rules for Patwaris* and *Mensuration and Survey Manual* were prepared which provided details regarding the rules for his appointment, his duties, instructions for the preparation of the land records and statistical return, and the method of making inspections of the harvest and other local matters. It was only from that year that the old type of *patwaris* were got rid off. In their place decently paid, well-taught, Urdu-writing men were appointed who could also survey, map neatly and accurately, and prepare their records.[30]

In the Madras Presidency, though Marathi was not the mother tongue of the majority of the people living there, the land revenue accounts were maintained in this language. At the same time, despite the script being Marathi, there was extensive use of number of vernacular revenue terms dating back to Chola or Pallava times and also those popularised and used by the Maratha and Muslim rulers. No doubt, the *karnums* were free to use local dialects but their accounts, before submitting in the *taluk* office, were translated into Marathi.[31] Even when Tipu Sultan in 1792, ordered that the accounts be submitted in Persian, three sets of copies of accounts were maintained. The accounts were first written in Kannada and then translated into Marathi and Persian.[32] Marathi was so widely used in the government records that the English rulers created a special *Maratha Daftar* in the Madras Presidency in the year 1822. Moreover, the *karnums* wrote their accounts on *cadjans* i.e. strips of flatterned palm-leaves and there was complete absence of standard stationery to be used by the above officials. The same practice had continued for more than half century of the English rule. It was only in 1855 and after that a thorough revision of the system of maintaining accounts under the supervision of Jayaram Chetty, the Head *Sherishtadar* of the Board of Revenue was undertaken.[33] Not only the use of Marathi was discontinued but proper account-forms in the language of the respective regions were introduced which have, of course, been revised from time to time.[34]

One of the most difficult problems that the English administration faced in the Madras Presidency was the fixation of the remunerations to be paid to the *karnums.* Taking advantage of the disturbed political conditions that prevailed throughout the eighteenth century village officials, including the *karnums* had managed to acquire, apart from the *manyams* legally assigned to them, a considerable amount of illegally acquired *manyam* land as well. A sample study of few districts reveals that of the total land capable of cultivation amounting to acres 1,20,66,923 as much as acres 4,02,011-21-33 was with the *patels* and *karnums* alone as *manyam* land.[35] In 1807 the English government, continuing with past practice, planned to remunerate the *karnums* with hereditary *manyams* and fixed the maximum percentage as well. The percentage of the *manyams* was based upon the survey rent fixed upon the respective villages. The table below, in which the survey rent of the villages taken into account is between C. Pagodas 50 to 6000, shows the percentage of the *manyam* allowed to a *karnum.*[36]

Survey Rent in C. Pagodas	% of manyam allowed to a *karnum*
50	12
100	9
150	7.33
200	6.75
250	6.40
300	6
400	5.63
500	4.80
600	4.42
700	4.14
800	4
900	3.89
1000	3.70
1500	2.93
2000	2.55
2500	2.16
3000	1.90
3500	1.71
4000	1.57
4500	1.47
5000	1.38
5500	1.31
6000	1.25

The important feature of the fixation of the *karnums'* remunerations were that the *manyams* that they got were higher than allowed to the *patels* which was contrary to the position enjoyed by the *lambardars* in the Punjab. Secondly, the *karnums* did not get identical remunerations in all the villages and thirdly, as the survey rent increased the percentage of their *manyams* decressed.[37] However, the total amount of remunerations to be paid comprised the *manyam* and the *marah wurtana,* i.e., perquisites from the crop.[38] Whenever the value of the *manyam* together with the *marah wurtana* was less than the amount allowed, the difference was made up. In case it exceeded the approved amount, the excess land was charged according to the survey rent.[39] A *karnum* could also take any amount of waste land in his own name from the government on the fixed *cowle.* He was permitted to rent out the whole or part of that land at higher rate to cultivators, granting them *patta* specifying the quantity of the land and the revenue to be charged.[40] This will not only bring a *karnum* an extra source of income but also a great boost to his position. However, shortly after this order, a slightly modified and simplified formula was also suggested which did not make significant change in the total remuneration of a *karnum.* Same position, by and large, continued till the enactment of Act IV of 1864, when certain modifications in regard to the nature of appointment and mode of payment were made.[41]

During early English rule in the Punjab a separate *patwari* cess was levied in the villages of the circle concerned for the payment of the remuneration to the *patwari.* The government had not fixed any amount but the percentage of the cess to be levied was fixed. This had resulted into more remuneration to the *patwari* in a highly, though small in size, cultivated area and less remuneration to the *patwari* was the liability of the land-owners of circle concerned.[42] After 1885, however, some drastic changes were introduced and not only the *patwaris* were divided into three different grades, their monthly salaries were also fixed.[43] A cess (not exceeding 12.50%) continued to be levied on the land revenue and canal owner's rate of which around 6.50% was made available for the payment of salaries to the *patwari* staff. Apart from the salary a *patwari* was also entitled to get .40% share of the fees levied for the entry of mutations in the record of rights and small charges for allowing the inspection of their records and giving certified extracts. A provision of small rewards, payable on retirement to well conducted *patwaris* having served for long time, was also made. In 1906 the liability of the land-owners for the pay of the *patwari* staff was abolished.[44]

The above study shows that the English government, during the period under study, aimed at regulating one of the old but necessary institutions connected with the agrarian life of India. It wanted to make *patwari/ karnum* a responsible public official with a clearly defined set of duties. At the same time in introducing changes or reforms due consideration was given to the traditions and past practices. However, during the first fifty to sixty years of its rule, whereas in the Madras Presidency the English government was occupied in curbing the illegally acquired power and position of the *karnums,* in Punjab it tried to improve the lot of the *patwari's.* In both the regions it would not compromise with the quality of work expected from them. Comparatively speaking the position of *karnum* remained somewhat secured in regard to his appointment, dismissal and remuneration, and *patwari's* position was given a great boost in respect of his working conditions and promotions etc.

References

* Dyal Singh (E) College, University of Delhi, New Delhi.

1. Also known as *Shenbogue, Kulkarni, Menon etc.*
2. In ancient India he was probably known as *gopa* during the Mauryan period, *Lekhaka* during the Kushan period and *divirapati* in Gupta period (Dwijendra Narayan Jha, *Revenue System in Post-Maurya and Gupta Times,* Calcutta, 1967, pp. 165-6). The term *patwari,* though the office being an old one, appears for the first time in Barni's *Tarikh-i-Firuzshahi* corresponding with the period of Alauddin Khalji (Also see, Irfan Habib *The Agrarian System of Mughal India (1556-1707),* 1963, p. 134).
3. Inscriptions of South India indicate that the administration during the Chola period was highly organised and also give minuteness of organisation for revenue administration. They not only give the working and responsibilities of the village accountant but one of these inscriptions points out his dismissal and still another mentions the term *'karnum'*. (See especially *South Indian Inscriptions,* Archaeological Survey of India, New Imperial Series, Vol. III, part iii, No. 128. Gordon Mackenzie, *A Manual of Kistna District,* Madras, 1883, p. 342, says that this office "was regularly established about the year 1144. . ." But it does not seem to be technically correct.
4. Tamil Nadu State Archives, Madras (TNSA), *Board's Consultations,* 5 Jan. 1807; *Selections from the Records of the Bellary District, Political and Agricultural matters, 1800-1856,* ASO (D) 73; Letter from Thomas Munro to the President and Members of the Board of Revenue, 30 Nov. 1806. Also Douie, Sir James McC, *Punjab Land Administration Manual,* 1931 (*PLAM*), p. 118; Baden Powell, B.H., *The Land Systems of British India,* I (Oxford, 1892), p. 326.
5. Baden Powell, I pp. 154, 674, 677.
6. *Epigraphia Indica,* VII, Cl. 62, Inscription of A.D. 1565; Also TNSA, *Bellary Records,* 382/14, Letter from the Collector of Bellary to the Board of Revenue, 22 August 1817.
7. Khan, Yusuf Husain, ed., *Farmans and Sanads of the Deccan Sultans* (Hyderabad, 1963), Document 15, pp. 42-3, *Farman* of Abul Hasan, dated 1 April 1686; Elliot Mss., *Local History* ((India Office Library, Mss Eur. F. 46, pp. 93-97, 106; III, F. 48, pp. 91-104; also TNSA, *The Proceedings of the Board of Revenue on Introduction of the Village Lease in the Ceded District, 1811,* ASO (D) 31 and 32, Minutes of the Board of Revenue, 9 May 1811.
8. TNSA, *Bellary Records, op. cit.,* f. 6; T.V. Mahalingam, *Administration and Social Life under Vijayanagar,* second edition (Madras, 1969), p. 227; Baden Powell, iii, pp. 89-120.
9. APSA, *Hukumnama-i-Tipu Sultan,* A.H. 1216 (Persian) clause No. 33, f. 4b; clause No. 63, f. 7b.
10. TNSA, *Bellary Records,* 384/54, Thomas Munro to the Collector of Adoni Division, 14 April 1807; *Board's Consultations,* 24 August 1807 and *Col. Munro's Correspondence Regarding the Survey and Rayatwari Settlement of the Ceded Districts, 1802-1807,* ASO (D) 79, Thomas Munro to Board of Revenue, 26 July 1807.

10a. For the position of *patwari* during the Mughal period, see Irfan Habib, *Agrarian System,* pp. 134-135.

11. Saunders, L.S., *Report on the Revised Settlement of the Lahore District (1865-1869),* Lahore 1873 (*RRS Lahore*), p. 69; See also William Murray, *Punjab Government Records (1807-1857),* I, p. 235.

12. For more details see, Ghulam Muhammd, *Dastur-al-Amal,* f. 14b, quoted by Indu Banga, *Agrarian System of the Sikh : Late Eighteenth and Early Nineteenth Century,* Delhi, 1978, p. 87.

13. *Punjab Government Records, Vol. V, Lahore Political Diaries, 1847-49,* Allahabad, 1909, Diary of P.S. Melvill, pp. 204-07, 213, 215-217; Also *RRS Lahore,* p. 61.

14. NAI, *Foreign/Political Proceedings,* 14 January 1853, Nos. 222-23; 10 June 1853, No. 217.

15. See for example, *Sumati Satokamu* (in Telugu) verses 30, 81 and 85.

16. TNSA, *Madras Revenue Proceedings and Consultations,* December 6, 1847, Walter Elliot to Government of Madras, April 17, para 27.

17. Douie, *PLAM,* p. 118.

18. TNSA, *Bellary Records* (1805), 403/154; 410/27, Circular—Collectors—Ceded Districts, 16 August 1806; (1806), 408/215, Thomas Munro to Fredrick Gahagan, Collector of Adoni Division, 16 August 1806; *Punlic Sundries,* 123A, *MBRC,* 19 May 1803; *Col. Munro's Correspondence regarding the Survey. . .,* ASO (D) 79, Thomas Munro to Collectors, 30 September 1802; *MBRC,* 26 September 1805; *Selections from the Old Records,* ASO (D) 72, Munro to the Board of Revenue, 25 August 1805. *MBRC* 5 January 1807: *Selections from the Records of the Bellary Districts. . .*ASO (D) 73, Thomas Munro to the President and Members of the Board of Revenue, 30 November 1806. Also Baden Powell, iii, pp. 88. 101.

19. *Op. cit.,* fn. 4.

20. *Op. cit.,* fn. 16.

21. TNSA, *MBRC,* 26 September 1805; *Selections from the Records. . .,* ASO (D) 72, Munro to the Board of Revenue, 26 August 1805.

22. Douie, *PLAM,* p. 118.

23. *Report of the Indian Famine Commission (1880),* Chap. II, pp. 101-104.

24. *Financial Commissioner's Standing Order* No. 15, para 1; Douie, *PLAM,* pp. 121-22 and Baden Powell, ii. p. 734.

25. *Financial Commissioners' Standing Order* No. 15, paras 9, 11, 15 and 25; No. 19, paras 2 and 3; Douie, *PLAM,* pp. 123-125. Beden Powell, ii, p. 735.

26. According to the new provisions 20% posts were to be of first grade, 40% posts of second grade and another 40% of the third grade. Their salaries were also fixed as Rs. 26/-, Rs. 23/- and Rs. 20/- p.m. respectively. The assistant *patwari's* salary was fixed at Rs. 15/- p.m; Douie, *PLAM,* p. 122.

27. *Ibid.,* pp. 123, 127.

28. *Ibid.,* pp. 124, 157; Also Baden Powell, ii, p. 735, iii, p. 96.

29. Irfan Habib, *Agrarian System,* p. 135.

30. Baden Powell, ii, p. 733.

31. TNSA, Jayaram Chetty, *Memorandum of the Revision of the Village Accounts,* 21 March 1855.

32. TNSA, Colin Mackenzie, *Report on the Mysore Survey,* Appendix III, pp. 58-59. Memoir on the Civil Administration, Police, Commercial and Revenue Management of the Ballaghat Karnatic.

33. *Op. cit.,* fn. 31.

34. Baden Powell, iii, p. 90.

35. TNSA, *Board Consultations,* 24 August 1807, *Col. Munro's Correspondence regarding the Survey...* ASO (D) 79, Thomas Munro to the Board of Revenue, 26 July 1807, APSA, *Cuddapah Records* (1809), 626/245, W. Wayte, Secretary Board of Revenue to the Collector of Cuddapah, 14 Dec. 1809.

36. TNSA, *Bellary Records,* 384/54 and *Selections from the records of the Bellary Disrict, 1800-1807,* ASO (D) 72, Circular issued by Thomas Munro, 14 April 1807.

37. Dua, J.C. 'Position of Patels and Karnums in the 'Ceded Districts' During the first quarter of the Nineteenth Century', Sabyasachi Bhattacharya, (ed.) *Essays in Modern Indian Economic History,* New Delhi, 1987, pp. 25-40; J.C. Dua, 'Comparative Position of the Village Headman during the Early British Rule in the Punjab and the Madras Presidency,' *Proceedings of Punjab History Conference,* Twenty First Session, 1987, pp. 242-252.

38. *Marah Wurtana* was not collected in all the villages. The rate also differed from place to place and item to item. For example on sugarcane and betel plantations, it was much higher than even the government rent.

39. *Op. cit.,* f.n. 36.

40. TNSA, *Selections from the Records of Bellary,* ASO (D) 73, Circular issued by Thomas Munro (Undated) but issued sometime in 1801-02 (Fusly 1211).

41. Maclean, C.D., *Manual of the Administration of the Madras Presidency,* Madras 1885, i, pp. 187-191.

42. Douie, *PLAM,* p. 122.

43. *Op. cit.,* f.n. 26.

44. *Punjab Land Revenue Act,* XVII, 1887, section 29, *Punjab Government, Department of Revenue and Agriculture,* Revenue Notifications Nos. 268 and 269, dated 22nd November, 1906; *Punjab Land Administration Acts,* ii, Rules, p. 7, Punjab Government Notification No. 273 dated 20th November 1909, *Financial Commissioner's Standing Order* No. 15, paras 36, 49 and 56, Douie, *PLAM,* pp. 122, 123 and 125.

12

Dr. Ganda Singh and Sikh *Itihas*

I am grateful to the respected Principal and Divinity Society of S.G.T.B. Khalsa College for inviting me to contribute my views on the contributions made by one of the most respectable historians on Sikh *Ithias,* Dr. Ganda Singh *Sahib*. It is by no means an easy task and to my view is an onerous and gigantic piece of work. It involves sitting on a judgement of the work of a historian who is a giant in the field and has contributed maximum on the history of Punjab by a dwarf in the field. These comments are in no way formal but real ones. There is no other historian on Sikh *Itihas* who has contributed so much in the form of books and articles and that too in several languages. As far as my knowledge goes Dr. Ganda Singh *Sahib* has written a large number of books. The most important of them number (as shown in the *Appendix*) more than 30 books in English, around 26 books in Punjabi, 10 books in Urdu/Persian, and as many as 60 articles based upon original Persian, Urdu, Punjabi, Marathi and English sources. There is hardly any aspect of Punjab *Itihas* from the years 1469 A.D., when Baba Nanak Dev Ji was born, to 1849 A.D., when the Punjab was annexed by the British on which Dr. Ganda Singh did not write either in the form of a book or an article. Also, there is hardly any source in any language on Punjab History, which missed the attention of this all time great historian.

Dr. Ganda Singh had been associated with several historical bodies as their life member and even as their President. To name some of his associations:—

(i) He was life member of the Indian History Congress since 1938.

(ii) Life member of the Asiatic Society, formerly Asiatic Society of Bengal.

(iii) Life member of Royal Asiatic Society of Great Britain and Ireland since 1949.

Paper presented at the Seminar held by Divinity Society, SGTB Khalsa Post Graduate Evening College, University of Delhi, New Delhi, 2001

(iv) Corresponding Member of Bharat *Itihas* Samshodan Mandal, Poona since 1964.

(v) Corresponding Member of Indian Historical Records Commission, Government of India from 1938 to 1949, and Member of the Commission from 1950 to 1956.

(vi) He was Secretary of the Sikh Historical Society, Lahore in 1931.

(vii) Secretary of the Sikh Tract Society, Lahore.

(viii) Founder Member of Punjab History Conference.

(ix) He was President of the Medieval Indian History Section of Indian History Congress, Ranchi, 1964.

(x) President of Medieval Indian History Section of Punjab History Conference, Patiala, 1968.

(xi) President of Institute of Historical Studies, Calcutta for its 12th Session, Shillong, 1974.

(xii) In 1963, the Punjab Government honoured him with the State Award for Literature for his services to the cause of Punjabi Letters.

(xiv) In 1964, Aligarh Muslim University awarded him Hon. Degree of D. Lit.

(xv) On March 28th, 1964 Shiromani Gurdwara Prabandhak Committee honoured him for his monumental work on Sikh *Itihas*.

(xvi) Acclaimed for his work by the Sikh Educational Conference at Kanpur, October 25-27, 1974.

(xvii) General President, Indian History Congress, 35th Session, Jadavpur University, Calcutta, December 22-24, 1974.

Moment one thinks of Sikh *Itihas,* one inevitably thinks of Dr. Ganda Singh. These two things have become synonymous and are inseparable. There are other eminent names in this area of history, but none commands greater respect and affection than Dr. Ganda Singh.

Long back in 1966, when I started doing research, the first lesson that I got from my teacher was to try to know about the background of the historian before trying to assess his/her commitment to the subject or ideology and contribution to the cause of the subject. It also helps in pinpointing a turning point in ones life that led one to write on a particular theme or subject. That is the precise reason why I intend to study the subject, 'Ganda Singh and Sikh *Itihas*' by dividing it into three subdivisions viz. (a) a brief background and life of Dr. Ganda Singh, (b) assessment of his contributions to the cause of Sikh *Itihas,* and (c) with due respect to the great historian of Sikh *Itihas* and with due apology from the learned audience present, some critical remarks about his writings.

Dr. Ganda Singh had a very humble background. Born on 15th November 1900 at Hariana, an ancient town in Hoshiarpur district, Dr. Ganda Singh had his early schooling in the village *madarsa,* and eventually took his matriculation from Government High School, Hoshiarpur. His college education at Forman Christian College, Lahore got interrupted when he joined the Indian Army in the Third Afghan War. In Army he first served in the Supply and Transport Corps Base Depot at Rawalpindi in 1919 and then at the Divisional Supplies at Peshawar. Thereafter he was first posted at Makina, Basra and then at Margil, Basra (1920-21). In 1921, Dr. Ganda Singh joined the Royal Army Pay Corps, British Army, Basra. Thereafter he spent a period of nine years (1921-30) with the Anglo-Persian Oil Company in Iran. This posting proved to be *first turning point* in Dr. Ganda Singh's life as it was here that he got an opportunity of showing his inclination towards academic activities and showed the signs of the type of life that he was going to lead. In Iran he came in touch with Sir. Arnold T. Wilson, who was then engaged with his work *Bibliography of Persia.* Wilson could gauge Dr. Ganda Singh's interest in oriental studies and thus introduced him to English journals and societies devoted to such studies. It was a turning point because after this Dr. Ganda Singh started building up his private library which during his life time turned into the largest collection of material on Sikh *Itihas.* While he was in Iran, his first book—*My First Thirty Days in Mesopotamia*—was published, which followed two books—*Inkishaf-i-Haqiqat* (in Urdu) and *Sikhi Parchar* (in Punjabi). Meanwhile Dr. Ganda Singh had been deeply impressed by valuable work on Sikh history done by Sardar Karam Singh. His desire to take up historical works in a, more systematic manner brought him back to India. In 1930, he settled down in Lahore and initially joined the well-known journal devoted to Punjabi letters and history namely, *Phulwari.* But a deep urge and interest in the study and investigation of Sikh history brought him to Khalsa College, Amritsar. While at Khalsa College, Dr. Ganda Singh not only did his Master's Degree in History in the first grade from Aligarh Muslim University, Aligarh (1944), but was also made the anchorage of the department of research in Sikh *Itihas.* Appointment in Khalsa College, Amritsar was another landmark in Dr. Ganda Singh's career. During his tenure in Khalsa College, he equipped it with rarest books and manuscripts on Sikh *Itihas* and turned the College into a leading institution of its kind in the country. In his efforts to enrich the Research library of the Khalsa College, Dr. Ganda Singh got a very sincere assistance from Maulavi Faiz-ul-Haq, who in very elegant calligraphy transcribed many rare and valuable Persian manuscripts from different collections in India. *Another landmark* in Dr. Ganda Singh's life of historical research brought him right into the ocean of the records pertaining to the Sikh *Itihas.* This was so when he acted as Director of Archives and Curator Museum at Patiala from Feb. 14, 1950 to March 2, 1956. From 1950 to 1953 he simultaneously held charge as Director of the Punjabi Department of Patiala and East Punjab States University. Meanwhile he also received his Ph. D. at Punjab University, Chandigarh in 1954. While as Director of Archives he would not allow his official responsibilities to interfere with his scholarly pursuits. Moreover, in an effort to enrich the Archives, Dr. Ganda Singh prevailed upon Punjab Princely states to donate a vast amount of historical material so that it could be well preserved in the Archives and used by the scholars working on Punjab *Itihas.* The large collection of records, manuscripts and books thus brought to the Archives were properly organized. The permanent landmarks that Dr. Ganda Singh left at Patiala was Central Public Library, and Khalsa College of which he became the founder Principal from June 1, 1960 to Sep. 15, 1963. Thereafter he was invited to organize the Department of Punjab Historical Studies at the newly established Punjabi University. This proved to be *another landmark* in Dr. Ganda Singh's illustrious career of academic pursuits as the period spent here was also one of sustained and creative work on Sikh *Itihas.* He headed the Department from Sep. 16, 1963 to Sep. 15, 1966. His retirement from the Punjabi University by no means meant the end of his work for Punjab History as Punjabi University conferred upon him fellowship for life. Till he took his last breath (27th November 1987), we could find Dr. Ganda Singh surrounded by his books and continued to carry out his historian's errand with a deep sense of personal commitment to the cause of Punjab *Itihas.* The numerous books, which carried his name not only, represented his learning and judgement of the highest order but has also helped us in enhancing our understanding of the Punjab *Itihas.*

The historian in Dr. Ganda Singh has left a vital pervasive influence in historical scholarship in the Punjab. Exploring material pertaining to Punjab *Itihas* was the one single passion that this great historian cherished through out his life. More than half a century of productive research of high quality produced by Dr. Ganda Singh played a major role in the evolution of studies related to Punjab *Itihas* in India and abroad. Dr. Ganda Singh has dozens of books in English, Punjabi, and Urdu/Persian to his credit. His first major work *Life of Banda Singh Bahadur,* a biography in English came out in 1935. It was based on contemporary and original source material and was an example of a meticulous historical composition. This book was an instant successful introduction of Dr. Ganda Singh to the scholarly world. It was immediately followed by another well compiled from original sources, judicial records and contemporary materials, and books *History of Gurdwara Shahidganj,* from its origin to November

1935. There are a few more biographies to Dr. Ganda Singh's credit, which are equally well documented. While *Maharaja Kaura Mall Bahadur* (1942), *Sardar Sham Singh Attariwala* (1942), and *Sardar Jassa Singh Ahluwalia* (1969) were in Punjabi; *Maharaja Ranjit Singh: A Life Sketch* (1939) and *Ahmad Shah Durrani* (1959), his doctoral theories were in English.

In his edited and annotated work, *Early European Accounts of the Sikhs* (1962), Dr. Ganda Singh a master of Persian language pointed out and commented shortcomings and several serious errors of omission and commission pertaining to the development of Sikh Community in the work of James Browne. He pointed out that many of these defects were due to the faulty English translation and that the European scholars were guilty of committing blunders in translating Persian texts. He further opined that English writers' tendency to paraphrase complicated linguistic constructions would very often lead to gross errors. It had become very essential for a scholar on Punjab *Itihas* of Dr. Ganda Singh's repute to point out the errors because the writers on Punjab history were extensively using Browne's work as a historical source.

During his tenure as Director of Archives, Dr. Ganda Singh did a yeoman service to the cause of the Punjab *Itihas* by making available enormous amount of original source material to the prospective scholars working in Punjab history. He edited volumes of government records and published numerous learned books and papers. A notable example in this regard was *Private Correspondence Relating to the Anglo-Sikh Wars* (1955). This work contained voluminous amount of letters written by English army and political officers involved in the events which were in a way precursors to the annexation of Sikh dominions. In the light of the evidence thus provided in the above work, the story of the occupation of Punjab stood stripped of the muddle which had till then surrounded it and of the glib simplifications of the writers of history textbooks. More especially by the long introduction added to this *Correspondence,* Dr. Ganda Singh revealed the range of his historical erudition and his power of the cogent reasoning.

As anchorage of the Department of Historical Studies at the Punjabi University, Patiala, the services rendered by Dr. Ganda Singh to the cause of Sikh *Itihas* were *par excellence.* The set up initiated by him helped in transforming the Department a dynamic centre for research in Punjab *Itihas.* His tireless energies and love and commitment to Punjab history resulted in — (i) beginning of the quest for bibliography and manuscript material; (ii) sponsoring the publication of primary sources on the history of the Punjab; (iii) started the work on a comprehensive eight volume history of the Punjab modeled on the Cambridge History; (iv) a four volume series of documents on the role of Punjab in the national struggle for independence; (v) published, by now a prestigious work, *A Bibliography of the Punjab* (1966); (vi) founded the Punjab History Conference (1965); and (vii) the journal *Punjab, Past and Present.* The Punjab History Conference was called first in 1965 by Dr. Ganda Singh himself. The Conference has by now become a substantive medium of research on Punjab/Sikh *Itihas.* It religiously meets annually under the auspices of the Department of Punjab Historical Studies, Punjabi University, Patiala. It helps in bringing together scholars interested in the region from all over India. They give Papers on Punjab/Sikh History, which are debated upon. It has maintained the healthy, and rather exceptional, tradition of objective writing and publishing its annual proceedings. The latter publication is an achievement that has started providing the avènues, which encourage a combination of fresh scholarly articles and carefully edited primary material in articles inaccessible to students working on Punjab history. It also provides facilities for easy communication among those interested in Punjab *Itihas.* As such, the semi-annual journal, *Punjab, Past and Present,* include not only scholarly articles (both original and reprints) but also a number of original sources not readily available but nonetheless deemed useful to future students of the subject in order to make the journal, as written by Dr. Ganda Singh in his 'Editorial', *Punjab Past and Present,* I (April 1967), "a series of reference books on the history and culture of the Punjab."

The contributions of Dr. Ganda Singh to Punjab *Itihas* have no ism, no bias, and are non-controversial. He set high standards in terms of academic honesty and discriminate use of source materials. Normally the profession of history writing is often susceptible to factions and preconceived trends of interpretations. In contrast the writings of Dr. Ganda Singh reveal a stubborn proclamation that only honest pursuit of historical truth, of true scholarship, ultimately reveals the character and worth of a scholar.

Throughout his writings, Dr. Ganda Singh maintained an intellectual discipline of having a characteristic of critical discrimination. He would invariably combine an extraordinary capacity for marshalling historical facts and a conscientious regard for truth. He had an immaculate archival sense. A majority of the books and articles published by him have been acknowledged as the most authoritative on the subjects they deal with. It would not be an exaggeration if I say that on certain periods of Punjab *Itihas,* especially the eighteenth and part of the nineteenth centuries, he had been the most knowledgeable of scholars. The works on these periods have been documented with minute, painstaking care.

Dr. Ganda Singh's contribution to Punjab *Itihas* may also be judged in a different criterion as well. The spadework that he did, the amount of new material that he unearthed and brought to light, and the biographies that he compiled are beyond the capacity of any historian. Moreover, it was largely due to Dr. Ganda Singh's efforts that the history of the years from 1469 to 1849 started receiving by far the largest amount of scholarly and the framers of University syllabus' attention, as that was considered (and quite rightly so) to be the definitive period in the Sikh *Itihas.*

Under the able stewardship of Dr. Ganda Singh, Punjab *Itihas* now is by no means a barren field. He gave a lead to meet the demands of a vision of the whole framework within which the Sikh *Itihas* could be told. He showed the path and prepared the grounds for evaluating the fruitfulness of the various approaches, which come to mind, and scholarly considerations, including a concern for sound methodology. Dr. Ganda Singh, in short, did a lot of spadework and prepared the ground for further research, gathered and published source materials, started holding the *Conference* and publication of journals.

The works of Dr. Ganda Singh are so well documented and researched that, if not impossible, it is very difficult to pinpoint shortcomings in them. However, it has been observed that majority of Dr. Ganda Singh's works relate to the history of the period 1469 to 1849 (leaving aside the works e.g. *Some Confidential Papers of Akali Movement* (1965); 'Bhai Vir Singh as Scholar of History' (1954); 'A Diary of the Partition Days 1947' etc.) and that post-annexation period is largely ignored. It is generally believed to be due to the tendency to equate Punjab history with the history of the Sikh people and to neglect modern Punjab history. No doubt in this age of specialization it is foolish on our part to expect from every scholar to write about all the phases of Punjab history. But Dr. Ganda Singh *Sahib* was not amongst those 'every scholar', and we would have got benefited if he had attempted a work on post annexation period as well.

While going through the different works of Dr. Ganda Singh, whether biographies or history, we find that while all of them have been written by consulting all the available sources, printed and manuscripts, quite a few of them are without *foot-notes.* It makes little difficult for we students of Punjab history to pinpoint exactly the source of information about a particular event or viewpoint.

The books on 18th century Punjab viz. *Ahmed Shah Durrani, Father of Modern Afghanistan,* Bombay, 1959; *Sardar Jassa Singh Ahluwalia* (Punjabi), Patiala, 1969, etc. have been written by making extensive use of many Persian, Marathi, English and Punjabi sources. While writing about

Ahmed Shah Abdali, the books have mostly highlighted his campaigns against the Mughals and Marathas as well as Afghan-Sikh struggle for supremacy in the Punjab and in *cis*-Sutlej area (of *subah* Delhi) during the second half of the 18th century. They have given an excellent narration of political and narrative aspects. There is no significant mention of the fact that with the annexation of the *subahs* of Lahore, Multan, Kashmir in 1752 and *chakla* Sirhind (*subah* Delhi) in 1757, not only the Afghan empire had extended from Afghanistan to Karnal (*chakla* Sirhind), a new administrative set up, both for the purposes of governance and realization of the revenue, had also been established. The *chakla* Sirhind was detached from the Mughal *subah* of Delhi and put under the direct Durrani administration.

Dr. Ganda Singh's works on the 18th century also do not mention about the revelation made by the contemporary documents that the incursions of Sikhs (*Sikhan*) or Singhs (*Singhan*) in his territories, Raja Ala Singh, used the above terms with utter contempt. It suggests that in the 18th century, the term Sikh or group of Sikhs did not essentially connote persons belonging to a particular religious faith. It seems that the Sikhs and *Singha* denoted those militant followers of the *Nanak Panth* and Guru Gobind Singh who had taken to arms against the Mughals or Durranis for the vindication of their religious rights and temporal power. Moreover, the adversaries were usually mentioned with contempt and adjectives used for them were derogatory in Character. Actually they were fighting for a cause.

Another point worth mentioning, which does not find reference in Dr. Ganda Singh's writings is, that the Durranis after their victory continued to appoint their own *subadar*/administrators/*vakeel* in different parts of Punjab and *cis*-Sutlej territories for general political control and for the realization of the revenues. Raja Ala Singh or even Maharaja Amar Singh were not sovereign or independent chiefs but only *vakeel* and *zamindar*-cum-*jagirdar.* Despite the capture of Lahore by Sardar Jassa Singh Ahluwalia/Sikhs (1758) and their incessant campaigns and incursions in the *cis*-Sutlej and Haryana territories (*subah* Delhi), regular *subedars* (of *subahs* Lahore, Multan and Kashimir), *faujdars* and *vakeels* were appointed by the Durranis.

Despite the above insignificant shortcomings to the Punjab history Dr. Ganda Singh's contributions are of permanent value. In some areas they broke new grounds and are recognized as most authoritative on the subjects they deal with. I would like all of us present here register gratitude to the Ganda Singh and acknowledge his contribution to historical research and Sikh *Itihas.*

Appendix

Some of the Most Important Works of Dr. Ganda Singh

English

Books

Life of Banda Singh Bahadur, based on contemporary and original sources. Khalsa College, Amritsar, 1935.

History of the Gurudwara Shahidganj, from its origin to November 1935, compiled from original sources, judicial records and contemporary materials. Amritsar, 1935.

Maharaja Ranjit Singh: First Death Centenary Memorial Volume, edited in collaboration with Professor Teja Singh. Khalsa College, Amritsar, 1939.

Maharaja Ranjit Singh: A Life-Sketch, Amritsar, 1939.

Qazi Nur Mohammed's *Jang Nama,* giving an account of the seventh invasion of Ahmad Shah Durrani (1764-65), edited. Khalsa College, Amritsar, 1939.

Louis Bourquin (in French), Pondicherry, 1940.

Guru Nanak: His Life and Teachings. Singapore Sikh Missionary Tract Society, Singapore, 1940.

Nanak-Panths: The Sikhs and Sikhism of the Seventeenth Century, translated from the original Persian (*Dabistan-i-Mazahib*) and edited with notes. *The Journal of Indian History,* vol. XIX, part II, August 1940.

A History of the Khalsa College, Amritsar, Khalsa College, Amritsar, 1949.

A Short History of the Sikhs, vol. I (1469-1765), in collaboration with Professor Teja Singh. Orient Longmans, Ltd., Bombay, 1950.

The Patiala and the East Panjab States Union: Historical Background. Archives Department, Government of Patiala and East Punjab States Union, Patiala, 1951.

The Panjab in 1839-40: Selection from the Panjab Akhbars, Panjab Intelligence, etc., *preserved in the National Archives of India,* New Delhi, edited with an introduction. Sikh History Society. Patiala, 1952.

The first Anglo-Sikh War (1845-46): Colonel Mouton's Rapport sur les derniers evenements du Punjab, translated and edited.

A Bibliography of the Patiala and East Panjab States Union. Archives Department, Government of Patiala and East Punjab States Union, Patiala, 1954.

Private Correspondence Relating to the Anglo-Sikh Wars, being private letters of Lords Ellenborough, Hardinge, Dalhousie and Gough and of Political Assistants addressed to Sir Frederick Currie as British Resident at Lahore, etc., edited with an Introduction. Sikh Society, Amritsar/Patiala, 1955.

The British Occupation of the Panjab. Sikh History Society, Amritsar/ Patiala, 1955.

A Brief Account of the Sikh People (revised edition of *A Brief Account of the Sikhs,* February 1956). Sikh History Society, Amritsar/Patiala, 1956; Sikh Cultural Centra, Calcutta, 1959; Delhi Gurdwara Parbandhak Committee, Delhi, 1971. (Also translated into Marathi by Ishwar Singh Thakur, pub. Kesar Singh Dang, Poona, 1963).

Ahmed Shah Durrani. Asia Publishing House, Bombay, 1959.

The Sikhs, and Sikhism. Sikh History Society, Amritsar/Patiala, 1959.

History of the Origin and Progress of the Sicks by James Browne (1788) edited. Indian Studies Past and Present, Calcutta, 1961.

Early European Accounts of the Sikhs edited and annotated. Indian Studies Past and present, Calcutta, 1962.

Some Confidential Papers of the Akali Movement. Shiromani Gurdwara-Parbandhak Committee, Amritsar, 1965.

Bhagat Lakshman Singh: Autobiography, edited. Sikh Cultural Centre, Calcutta, 1965.

A Select Bibliography of the Sikhs and Sikhism. Shiromani Gurdwara Parbandhak Committee, Amritsar, 1965.

A Bibliography of the Punjab. Punjabi University, Patiala, 1966.

Guru Arjan's Martyrdom Reinterpreted. Guru Nanak Mission, Patiala, 1969 (also *The Sikh Review,* June 1974).

National Bibliography of Indian Literature, 1901-1953, (Punjabi Section), vol. III, Sahitya Akademi, New Delhi, 1970.

Guru Gobind Singh's Death at Nanded: An Examination of the Succession Theories. Guru Nanak Foundation, Faridkot, 1972.

Maharaja Duleep Singh Correspondence (History of the Freedom Movement in the Punjab) edited. Punjabi University, Patiala, 1972.

The Sikhs and Their Religion. The Sikh Foundation, U.S.A., Redwood City, California, 1974.

Papers

"Bhai Gurdas: His Life and Work," *The Khalsa,* Lahore, March 23 to August 10, 1930.

"Maharaja Ranjit Singh as Seen by Historians," *The Khalsa,* Lahore, June 25, 1931.

"The Pledge of the Sikh Army taken on the Eve of Their Departure to the Sutlej in 1845 for the First Anglo-Sikh War," translated from the original Persian. *The Khalsa Review,* August II, 1932.

"Sikh Historical Monuments and Need for Their Preservation," a paper read at the first conference of the Sikh Youth League at Lahore, *The Khalsa Review,* January 22, 1933.

"Contemporary Sources of Sikh History," a paper read at the second session of the *Indian History Congress,* Allahabad, 1938.

"The Persian Akhbars in the Alienation Office, Poona," *Proceedings Indian Historical Records Commission,* 1939.

"The Maratha-Sikh Treaty of 1785," *Proceedings Indian History Congress,* 1939.

"Sir Charles Wilkins' Observations on the Sikhs and Their College at Patna," *The Darbar,* Amritsar, February 1940; *The Panjab Past and Present,* vol. 1, part I, April 1967.

"The Arrest and Release of Sardar Lehna Singh Majithia," *Proceedings Indian History Congress,* 1940.

"Some New Light on the Treaty of Bhairowal (December 16, 1846) Thrown by the Private Letters by Sir Henry Hardinge," *Proceedings Indian Historical Records Commission, 1948; The Journal of 'Indian History'* Vol. XXVII, part I, April 1949.

Early Maratha-Sikh Relations," *Mahamahopadhyaya Professor Datto V. Potdar Commemoration Volume,* Poona. 1950.

"Three Letters of Maharani Jind Kaur," *The Tribune, Ambala,* April. 12, 19, 1953; *The Journal of Indian History,* Vol. XLII, part I, April 1964.

"Bhai Vir Singh as Scholar of History," *Bhai Vir Singh Abhinandan Granth,* New Delhi, 1954.

"Diary of the Partition Days 1947," *The Journal of the Asiatic Society,* Vol. XXXVIII, parts II, and I, April and August 1960.

"Colonel Polier's Account of the Sikhs," *The Journal of the Asiatic Society,* Calcutta, Vol. 1, No, 1, May 1961.

"The Sikhs: A Historical Background," a paper read at the conference on Sikhism and Christianity at the Baring Union Christian College, Batala, on October 1, 1963.

"Development of Sikh Thought up to the end of the 18th Century," a paper read at the seminar on ideas motivating Social and Religious Movements and Politics and Economic Policy during the 18th and 19th Centuries in India, organized by the Department of History, University of Delhi, November 9-15, 1964, *The Sikh Review,* Calcutta, July 1967.

"Christianity in the Punjab: A Bibliographical Survey," a paper read at the conference on Church History held at the Christian Retreat and Study Centre, Rajpur, March 14-18, 1966. *The Panjab Past and Present* vol. I, part II, October 1967.

"Some non-Muslim Sources of the History of the Punjab during the Medieval Period," *The Journal of the Research Society of Pakistan,* vol. III, part IV, October 1966; *Historians of Medieval India, Ed.* Mohibbul Hasan, Meenakshi Prakashan, Meerut, 1968.

"The Maratha-Sikh Relations," *Studies in Indian History-Dr. A.G. Pawar Felicitation Volume,* Ed. Dr. V.D. Rao, Kolhapur, 1968; *The Panjab Past and Present,* vol. II, part 1, April 1968.

Presidential Address, Third Session (Medieval Section), Punjab History Conference, Patiala, March 9-10. 1969.

"The Birthplace of Maharaja Ranjit Singh," *The Tribune,* October 6, 1968; *The Panjab Past and Present,* vol. II, part II, October, 1968; *The Statesman,* New Delhi, November 18, 1968.

"Bibliography on Guru-Nanak," Sahitya Akademi, New Delhi, 1969; *The Panjab Past and Present,* vol. III, parts II, and I 1969.

"Invocation by Guru Gobind Singh," *The Panjab Past and Present,* vol. III, parts II, and I 1969.

"Guru Nanak as Guru Gobind Singh sees Him," *The Panjab Past and Present,* vol. III, parts II, and I 1969.

"Guru Nanak's Visit to Uch," *The Panjab Past and Present,* vol. III, part II, and I 1969.

"Guru Nanak at Puri with Chaitanya and His Followers," *The Panjab , Past and Present,* vol. III, parts II, and I 1969.

"Descendants of Guru Nanak," *The Panjab Past and Present,* vol. III, parts II and I, 1969.

"Contemporaries of Guru Nanak," *The Panjab Past and Present,* vol. III, parts II and I, 1969.

Translations from Persian works regarding Guru Nanak in *The Panjab Past and Present,* Vol. III, parts II, and I, 1969—

Jot Bigas by Nand Lal Goya,

Khulasat-ut-Tawarikh by Sujan Rai Bhandari,

Chahar Gulshan by Rai Chatarman,

Imad-us-Saadat by Sayyid Ghulam Ali Khan,

Khalsa Nama by Bakht Mall,

Tarikh-i-Sikkhan by Khushwant Rai, and

Chahar Bagh-i-Punjab by Ganesh Das Badehra.

"Guru Nanak's Visit to Central Asian Countries," *Proceedings Punjab History Conference,* Punjabi University Patiala, 1970.

"The Sikhs in Canada and California: A Bibliography," *The Panjab Past and Present,* vol. IV, part II, October 1970.

"History in Punjabi," *The Panjab Past and Present, 1971; Historiography in Indian Languages, Dr. G. M. Moraes Felicitation Volume,* Oriental Publications, Delhi, 1972; *History of Modern, Indian Literature,* edited by S.P. Sen, Institute of Historical Studies, Calcutta, 1975.

"Bhai Vir Singh and His Times," *Bhai Vir Singh: Life, Times and Works,* Punjab University, Chandigarh, 1973.

"Raj Karega Khalsa Couplet," *The Panjab Past and Present,* vol. VII, part I, April 1973.

"A Few Observations on Mr. Z. Faruki's Chapter on the Sikhs in his *Aurangzeb and His Times,*" *The Panjab Past and Present, Vol.* VII part 1, April 1973.

Presidential Address, 35 the session of the Indian History Congress held at Jadavpur University Calcutta, December 22-24, 1974.

The impact of Guru Nanak's Teachings on the Lives of the People of the Punjab," Guru Nanak Memorial Lectures delivered at Punjabi University, Patiala, on March 30 and April 6, 1975.

"Guru Tegh Bahadur," *The Panjab Past and Present,* Vol. IX, part I, April 1975.

"The Place of Baba Banda Singh's Martyrdom," *The Journal of Sikh Studies,* Guru Nanak Dev University, Amritsar, Vol. II, part II, August 1975.

"Presidential Address, 13th annual session of the Institute of Historical Studies held at Panaji, Goa, November 7-10, 1975.

"The Martyrdom, of Guru Tegh Bahadur," a paper read at the Punjabi University, Patiala, on March 8, 1976.

Punjabi

Books

Sikkhi Parchar. Published by the author, Abadan, Persian Gulf, 1928.

Sikh Itihas. Khalsa Tract Society, Amritsar, April-May, 1932 (Tracts 857-59).

Kujh Ku Puratan Sikh Itihasik Patre, Amritsar, 1937. Contains translations of portions dealing with the Sikhs from the original Persian of-

Dabistan-i-Mazahib,

Tuzk-i-Jahangiri,

Siyar-ul-Mutakhirin by Ghulam Husain Khan,

Jameh-ut-Tawarikh by Qazi Faqir Muhammad,

Khulsat-ut-Tawarikh by Sujan Rai Bhandari, and

Early Records of British India by J.T. Wheeler (English).

Baintan Sher Singh Kian by Nihal Singh edited and annotated. Amritsar, 1938.

Maharaja Kaura Mall Bahadur. Khalsa College, Amritsar, 1942.

Sardar Sham Singh Attariwala. Amritsar, 1942.

Kukian Di Vithia (A History of the Kukas or Namdharis), 1944, 1946.

Sikh Itihas Bare. Amritsar, 1942, 1946. Contains historical essays on Guru

Arjan's Martyrdom,

A *Hukamnama* of Guru Gobind Singh,

The Last Days of Guru Gobind Singh,

The Real Name of Baba Banda,

Nadir Shah's Invasion of India,

The First Holocaust (*Ghallughara*) of 1746,

An Act of Bravery by Ranjit Singh,

The Meeting at Ropar between Maharaja Ranjit Singh and Lord William Bentinck,

The Deaths of Maharaja Kharak Singh and Kanwar Nau Nihal Singh,

Some New Light on the Treaty of Bharowal,

Maharani Jind Kaur,

Three Letters of Maharaja Duleep Singh, and

Letters of Guru Gobind Singh and Chhatrapati Shivaji.

Sikh Itihas Vall. The Panj Darya, Lahore, 1946. Contains historical essays on-

The Land of the Five Rivers,

History of the Sikhs,

The Martyrs' Week.

Ten so-called Successors of Guru Gobind Singh,

Banda Singh Bahadur,

The Maratha-Sikh Treaty of 1785,

Maharaja Ranjit Singh as Seen by Others,

The Sons of Maharaja Ranjit Singh,

Steel Helmet and the Sikhs,

A Pledge of the Sikh Army, 1845, and

A Bibliography of Sikh History.

Panjab Dian Varan (Ballads of the Punjab), Amritsar, 1946. Contains the following Punjabi ballads—

Aggra's *Var Haqiqat Rai,*

Daya Singh's *Fateh Nama*

Ram Dayal's *Jang Nama Sardar Hari Singh,*

Qadir Yar's *Var Sardar Hari Singh,*

Nihal Singh, *Baintan Sher Singh Kian,*

Shah Muhammad, *Angrezan Te Singhan Di Larai,*

Kahn Singh, *Jang Nama Lahaur,*

Matak, *Jang Singhan Te Farangian Da,* and

Siddh Jin and Mir Lagam's *Jattan Dian Varan.*

Jang Nama Lahaur (Kahn Singh of Banga), edited and annoted, Amritsar, 1946.

Angrezan Te Singhan Di Larai (Shah Muhammad), edited and annotated, Amritsar, 1946.

Sikh Itihasik Yadagaran. Sikh History Society, Amritsar, 1950.

Var Amritsar Ki by Darshan edited and annotated. Sikh History Society. Amritsar, 1951.

Nath Mall's *Amar Nama,* translated into Punjabi. Sikh History Society, Amritsar/Patiala, 1953.

Afghanistan Vich Ikk Mahina. Sikh History Society, Amritsar/Patiala, 1954.

Panjab Utte Angrezan Da Qabza. Punjabi Sahit Akadami, Ludhiana, 1955, 1957.

Afghanistan Da Safar. Prakash and Company, New Delhi, 1958.

Bhai Jodh Singh (Bhai Jodh Singh Abhinandan Granth), Panjabi Sahit Akademi, Ludhiana, 1962.

Panjab 1849-1960 (Bhai Jodh Singh Abhindnadan Granth), Panjabi Sahit Akademi, Ludhiana, 1962.

Banda Singh Bahadur. Shiromani Gurdwara Parbandhak Committee, Amritsar, 1965.

Siharfian Hari Singh Nalwa by Qadir Yar, edited, Punjabi University, Patiala, 1965.

Sri Gur Sobha by Kavi Sainapat, edited, Panjabi University, Patiala, 1967.

Hukamname Guru Sahiban, Mata Sahiban, Banda Singh Ate Khalsaji De Panjabi University, Patiala, 1967.

Bhai Nand Lal Granthawali, Sant Sohan Singh, Malacca, Malaya, 1968.

Sardar Jassa Singh Ahluwalia, Punjabi University, Patiala, 1969.

Urdu and Persian

Books

Inkishaf-i-Haqiqat. Sikh Tract Society, Lahore, Tract No. 67, May-July, 1926.

Tazkirah-i- Baba Banda Singh Shahid translated from the English by Professor Mohan Singh. Sikh Youth League, Amritsar, 1934.

Mirat-u-Tawarikh-i-Sikkhan, Fahrist-i-Nusakh-i-Khatti-o Matbuat Farsi-o-Urdui Mutalliqa Tawarikh-i-Sikkhan. Khalsa College, Amritsar, 1934.

Dtwan-i-Nanak Shah: Persian translation of the Sukhmani of Guru Arjan (Transcribed from the copy in the Bibliotheque Nationale Paris, by Sardar Umrao Singh Shergil Majithia), edited and published. Amritsar, 1935.

Makhiz-i-Tawarikh-i-Sikkhan, vol. I (Guru period). Sikh History Society, Amritsar, 1949. Contains excerpts, dealing with the Sikhs, from-

Akbar-nama by Abul Fazl,

Tuzk-i-Jahingiri,

Dabistan-i-Mazahib,

A pata of land at Kartarpur,

Khulasat-ut-Tawarikh by Sujan Rai Bhandari,

Namah-i-Guru Gobind Singh,

Zafarnama-i-Guru Gobind Singh,

Ahkam-i-Alamgiri, Inayatullah Ismi,

Tarikh-i-Muazzam Shah by Maulavi Abdul Rasul,

Akhbarat-i-Darbar-i-Mulla

Chahar Gulshan by Chatarman, and

Sarb Loh Granth.

Mukhtisar Nanak Shahi Jantri, a book of comparative chronological tables of Nanak Shahi, the *Khalsa*, the Bikrami, the Christian, the Hijri, the Shaka and the Fasli eras from A.D. 1469 to A.D. 1949. Sikh History Society, Amritsar, 1949.

Awraq-i-Parishan-i-Tawarikh-i-Panjab, edited and annotated. Sikh History Society, Amritsar, 1949.

Kuliyat-I-Bhai Nand Lal Goya, containing all the known Persian and Punjabi works of Bhai Nand Lal, edited with an Introduction. Sikh Sangat, Malacca (Malaya), 1963.

[illegible] Law of [illegible] Women [illegible]

[illegible] [illegible]

[illegible]

[illegible]

[illegible]

[illegible] Tables of [illegible] the [illegible] and the [illegible] [illegible]

[illegible]

[illegible] [illegible]